FROMMER'S DOLLARWISE GUIDE TO SKIING USA—WEST

by Lois Friedland

1988–89 Edition

Copyright © 1986, 1988
by Prentice Hall Press

All rights reserved
including the right of reproduction
in whole or in part in any form

Published by Prentice Hall Press
A Division of Simon & Schuster, Inc.
Gulf + Western Building
One Gulf + Western Plaza
New York, NY 10023

ISBN 0-13-217662-9

Manufactured in the United States of America

CONTENTS

Introduction	**DOLLARWISE GUIDE TO SKIING USA—WEST**	1
	1. What's in the Book and How to Use It	2
	2. The $25-A-Day Travel Club—How to Save Money on All Your Travels	5
Chapter I	**BEFORE YOU GO**	9
	1. Overview of Where to Ski	9
	2. Choosing a Resort	11
	3. Getting There	15
	4. Winter Driving	16
	5. Skiing Programs for the Handicapped	18
Chapter II	**THE ESSENTIALS FOR SKIERS**	19
	1. Equipment	19
	2. Health Tips	21
	3. Safety on the Slopes	22
	4. How to Dress	22
Chapter III	**WINTER VACATIONS FOR NON-SKIERS**	24
Chapter IV	**COLORADO'S MOST FAMOUS RESORTS**	27
	1. Aspen	30
	2. Snowmass	42
	3. Vail	48
	4. Beaver Creek	58
Chapter V	**COLORADO: THE CENTRAL ROCKIES AND FRONT RANGE**	64
	1. Winter Park/Mary Jane	65

	2. SilverCreek	72
	3. Steamboat	74
	4. Copper Mountain	81
	5. Keystone Resort	87
	6. Breckenridge	93
	7. Ski the Summit	97
Chapter VI	**SOUTHERN COLORADO**	**100**
	1. Telluride	101
	2. Purgatory	105
	3. Crested Butte	110
	4. Monarch	115
	5. Cuchara	117
	6. Other Colorado Ski Areas	118
Chapter VII	**UTAH**	**121**
	1. Park City	122
	2. Deer Valley	132
	3. Snowbird	136
	4. Alta	140
	5. Salt Lake City Area	143
	6. Interconnect Tour	147
	7. Golden Spike Empire	147
	8. Southern Utah: Brianhead	148
	9. Other Utah Ski Areas	151
	10. Utah Liquor Laws	151
Chapter VIII	**THE LAKE TAHOE AREA**	**153**
	1. Mount Rose	156
	2. Slide Mountain	157
	3. Ski Incline	158
	4. Homewood	159
	5. Tahoe Ski Bowl	160
	6. Alpine Meadows	160
	7. Sugar Bowl	162
	8. Sierra Ski Ranch	163
	9. Squaw Valley	164
	10. Kirkwood	166
	11. Northstar-at-Tahoe	169
	12. Heavenly Valley	170

	13. Smaller Ski Areas Around Lake Tahoe	172
	14. Cross-Country and Other Facilities	173
	15. Lodging and Dining	174
	16. Practical Matters	182
Chapter IX	**CENTRAL CALIFORNIA**	184
	1. Mammoth Mountain	184
	2. June Mountain	191
	3. Mount Reba/Bear Valley	193
	4. Other California Ski Areas	195
Chapter X	**SOUTHERN CALIFORNIA**	196
	1. Mtn. High	197
	2. Snow Summit	198
	3. Snow Valley	200
	4. Goldmine	201
	5. Other Ski Areas	202
	6. Lodging, Dining, and Other Practical Matters	202
Chapter XI	**IDAHO**	205
	1. Sun Valley	205
	2. Ski Schweitzer	216
	3. Bogus Basin	220
	4. More Idaho Ski Areas	222
Chapter XII	**WYOMING**	224
	1. Jackson Hole Ski Area	225
	2. Grand Targhee	227
	3. Snow King Ski Area	229
	4. Lodging and Dining	229
	5. Daytime and Evening Entertainment	233
	6. Non-Skier Activities	233
	7. Practical Matters	234
	8. Other Wyoming Ski Areas	235
Chapter XIII	**NEW MEXICO AND ARIZONA**	236
	1. Taos	236

	2. Ski Apache	243
	3. Red River	244
	4. Angel Fire	246
	5. Sandia Peak	248
	6. Other New Mexico Ski Areas	248
	7. Fairfield Snowbowl	250
	8. Apache Sunrise	250
	9. Other Arizona Ski Areas	251
	10. Arizona Cross-Country Skiing	251
Chapter XIV	**MONTANA**	**252**
	1. Big Mountain	252
	2. Big Sky	256
	3. Bridger Bowl	261
	4. Red Lodge	262
	5. Other Montana Ski Areas	265
	6. Montana Cross-Country Skiing	266
Chapter XV	**OREGON**	**268**
	1. Mount Bachelor	269
	2. Mount Hood Area: Mount Hood Meadows, Mirror Mountain, and Timberline	276
	3. Other Oregon Ski Areas	281
Chapter XVI	**WASHINGTON**	**282**
	1. Crystal Mountain Resort	282
	2. Mission Ridge	286
	3. Ski "The Big 3"	288
	4. Other Washington Ski Areas	290
Chapter XVII	**SKIING IN WESTERN CANADA**	**291**
	1. Whistler and Blackcomb	291
	2. Banff National Park: Lake Louise, Sunshine Village, and Mount Norquay	292
	3. Nakiska at Mount Allan	297
	4. Heli-Skiing and Snowcat Skiing	299
	5. Information Sources	300

Chapter XVIII	**BEYOND LIFTS**	301
	1. Heli-Skiing	301
	2. Snowcat Skiing	304
	3. Cross-Country Skiing	305
	4. Snowboarding	307
	5. A Ski Cruise	308
Appendix	**RATING THE SKI AREAS**	309

MAPS

Colorado	28–29
Utah	123
Salt Lake City Ski Areas	124
California	155
Lake Tahoe Ski Areas	157
South Lake Tahoe	168
North of Los Angeles	184
Idaho, Montana, and Wyoming	206–207
Sun Valley	211
New Mexico	237
Oregon	270
Washington	284

INFLATION ALERT: We don't have to tell you that inflation has hit the United States as it has everywhere else. In researching this book, we have made every effort to obtain up-to-the-minute prices, but even the most conscientious researcher cannot keep up with the current pace of inflation. As we go to press, we believe we have obtained the most reliable data possible. Nonetheless, in the lifetime of this edition—particularly its second year (1989)—the wise traveler will add 10% to 15% to the prices quoted throughout these pages.

A DISCLAIMER: Although every effort was made to ensure the accuracy of the prices and travel information appearing in this book, it should be kept in mind that prices can and do fluctuate in the course of time, and that information does change under the impact of the varied and volatile factors that affect the travel industry.

Introduction

DOLLARWISE GUIDE TO SKIING USA—WEST

1. What's in the Book and How to Use It
2. The $25-A-Day Travel Club

YES, I SKI! As bizarre as it sounds, "Do you ski?" was the question I was asked most while touring ski areas the first winter I gathered information for this book.

This body has skied for more years than need be specified here. During those years on the slopes, it has slid downhill (admittedly not always on skis) as a recreational skier, a professional ski instructor, and a ski writer gathering information for various national publications.

For those of you who wonder "How did she get all this information? Did she pick up a telephone and talk to some public relations person? Did she actually try the runs? Did she look at lodges and eat at all those restaurants? Did she talk to the locals?" The answer is yes to all of the above. (Although a qualified yes comes to eating at the restaurants. I relied heavily on local and well-traveled skiers' opinions, because turning into a blimp was not included in my book contract.)

When I visited a ski area (and I went to more than 40, some long familiar and some new ones, during that winter two years ago when I first wrote this book), days were spent on the ski slopes. The nights were occupied looking at lodging, dining, and gathering opinions from other skiers. When I updated the book last winter, I again wandered through ski country using the same approach.

Those ski slopes I've come to know well in recent years (a benefit of living in the Rockies) were easy to outline on paper and update during ski trips. When going to an area I'd never visited, I skied at least a sampling of the green, blue, and black runs. Although I didn't ski every single run (remember, there are more than 150 trails, slopes, and bowls at Mammoth Mountain alone), I had discussions about the runs not tried but mentioned in this book with skiers who challenge them regularly.

These days I'm rarely asked "Do you ski?" The question is usually: "Tell us how well you ski so we know which runs to take you down and which runs to let you look up at!"

2 DOLLARWISE GUIDE TO SKIING USA—WEST

During my wanderings to "update" this book and handle my job as western editor of *Ski* magazine, my skiing skills have been finely tuned from hours on the slopes. (My bar-hopping and dining skills also improved.) However, everyone has limits as to where they'll ski, and for those of you who insist on knowing where the line between my real experiences and the "as told to by others" descriptions stands. . . .

As the char woman said to the society matron who was interviewing her for employment: "I dust, I vacuum, I change sheets, *but I don't clean windows!*"

As this skier/writer responded to numerous ski patrol/ski instructors/locals pushing me to take the "complete" grand tours: "I ski green and blue runs, single and double diamond black runs. *But I don't ski tight, ultra-steep chutes.*"

Those of you who do will have to grab locals about to jump in—and ask them for the safest way down!

1. What's in the Book and How to Use It

Skiing, of course, is the main focus of this book. Where to ski, from the southernmost Rockies in New Mexico up to the Cascades in Washington, is covered through descriptions of the terrain and general ambience. Megaresorts such as Aspen and Vail, regions like Lake Tahoe, and major destination resorts such as Sun Valley, Mammoth Mountain, and Steamboat Springs are all described. Those far western–style resorts, including Mount Bachelor, where lodging is driving distance from the mountain; the smaller ski experiences like Ski Schweitzer and Red Lodge with primarily a regional draw; and those fledgling resorts that have local followers are all listed. For an overview, see the next chapter.

A good ski vacation involves much more than one's choice of slopes. Comfortable accommodations, good food, ease of travel to the resort (and how to move around when you are there), and the style of après-ski life are all vital parts that make up the difference between a memorable trip and a disaster. They're all discussed in this book.

MORE ABOUT SKIING: When you're deciding whether to go to Mount Mild or Terror Mountain, treat the sections on skiing in each resort description as an introduction to the ski slopes. Of course each section outlines the number of lifts, trails, or skiable acreage, and other basic facts. But it also includes descriptions of specific trails and slopes for each skill level with the breakdown including blue runs for low versus high intermediates, and black runs for barely advanced versus experts. If you're big on green and easy blue turf, the copy will give you a sense of whether you can spend a week on the green and blue trails without becoming bored. If you're an intermediate skier and want to edge into advanced terrain, the listing of blacks (which in many cases are shaded from light to deep black, à la one to ten), should help tell if this resort is the place for you.

When you are at the area, the skiing section can be read as a quick primer to the slopes. It is not a complete summary; it is a jumping-off point! Think of it as a way to cheat on those three days (of a six-day vacation) too often spent exploring a mountain to find those runs "just right for me." You should be able to ski straight to specific slopes geared for your skill level, then go exploring on your own. The Insider's Tips sections include well-proven ways to move around the massive mountain complexes (those with 15 lifts or more) easily or beat lift lines, as well as a few hidden sections of snow passed on by garrulous locals. Other parts in the skiing sections discuss cross-country, ski school for adults and children, childcare, and more.

APRÈS-SKI AND MORE: As with any Frommer book, this one is also designed to provide the information needed to find a comfortable place to stay within your price range (the book covers budget to expensive), a variety of good restaurants to satisfy both hungry skiers and discerning diners, and lots of general information covering everything from nightlife to means of transportation, both to and when in resorts.

Words about Prices Quoted

Inflation is a fact of life! Every effort has been made to ensure that the prices listed here are an accurate guide, but there are no price guarantees, especially in ski resorts. Ski areas have been known to publicize next winter's daily lift ticket rate the spring before, then change it in August. Furthermore, in ski towns lodging prices vary widely according to season. (Holidays are premium rates; beginning and end of season are bargain times.) Most of the prices listed in this book are approximate and good for the regular season. They are simply guideline figures, and you can expect the actual cost of lodging to vary according to the time of year you want to vacation. See the following sections on lodging and restaurants for a detailed explanation of how to read prices for accommodations and food.

Accommodations and restaurants were placed in categories ranging from More Expensive to Less Expensive. They were graded against other lodges and restaurants in that resort! For instance, the restaurants in Crystal Mountain listed as more expensive would be in the Moderate or Less Expensive category in Deer Valley. Even if there is a variation in price of lodging, a medium price-range lodge will probably still be medium priced as compared to other accommodations in the resort. The chart near the end of the book compares the prices of lodging and restaurants between resorts so you can find a resort in your price range.

Lodging

The lodging sections include a range of accommodations stretching from More Expensive through Moderate to Less Expensive. When categorizing accommodations, lodges and condominiums were rated against others within the resort. Value for the money spent was an important consideration in placing a lodge in a specific category. Be wary when reading lodging prices. In most cases, the prices in this book are a guide to the approximate per-night costs for lodging during *regular* season. A survey of ski resort brochures will quickly show that the dates of regular season vary from resort to resort, although most of February and March are considered regular season at most resorts. A complete breakdown of prices during the many seasons (which include high, low, regular, and special value at some resorts) would have taken up a full book. So be aware that the price of the same room can vary widely depending on the season. *Tack on 30% to 50% for that room during the Christmas holiday or school spring-break weeks. Drop the price 10% to 30% for that room during low season, usually those weeks before the Christmas holidays and the last weeks of the season.* When comparing prices, remember that a single room usually holds two skiers (more for additional cost). Condominium prices will be higher but a condominium can hold two or more in a bedroom, and almost every unit in a ski town has bedding for two in the living room. When you get a lodging quote from a reservationist, ask if tax is included. In many states it is against the law or the accepted practice to quote a room rate that includes the tax.

When totaling the cost for a vacation, compare the cost of purchasing lodging and lift tickets separately against lodging/lift packages. If you're going to a destination resort such as Telluride for a weekend, ask about three-night lift/

lodging packages. It might be cheaper to buy the package and not use the third night!

Restaurants

The restaurants are priced in similar categories with the addition of moderate to expensive—the final bill being, of course, directly dependent on the discretion used in ordering. Many of the restaurants were chosen because they have proved to be consistently good through the years. Others are new but are receiving rave reviews and look to be around for a while.

Every effort has been made to give a broad range of entree prices. However many restaurants in ski towns change their menus from year to year and add items that change the price range. In cases where there were one or two items (such as lobster) significantly higher than all the other higher-priced items, that high-priced item was not included as the upper end of a range. Unless otherwise specified, most items include a salad or soup and/or vegetable. Of course, adding on hors d'oeuvres, desserts, or drinks will up the bill. Hours are listed, but be aware that when business is slow, particularly very early and very late in the ski seasons, many restauranteurs close their doors early or open late.

Après-Ski and Other Activities

Each resort has sections outlining daytime activities for non-skiers and skiers who want a day off the slopes. (Those resorts most popular with non-skiers are listed in Chapter III, "Winter Vacations for Non-Skiers.") The après-ski hour as skiers head off the slopes and nightlife scene are described.

WHAT DO THOSE STRANGE WORDS MEAN?:
Throughout the book new skiers may find unfamiliar words that are used primarily by skiers. Some of those same words, I've discovered, have varying shades of meaning to longtime skiers. This glossary includes the working definitions for this book.

Black: Because every ski area must split its terrain between beginner, intermediate, and advanced, a black trail at a tiny day area may not be rated black at a major ski complex. In the Skiing sections, especially those with a lot of advanced terrain, readers may find reference to gray, murky, and deep black. Gray or light black is for skiers venturing onto advanced terrain for the first time. Deep black is experts-only turf.

Bumps: See moguls.

Cruising: "Let it all hang out" on well-groomed, moderate terrain with no bumps.

Falsie flakes: Man-made snow.

Moguls: Big mounds of snow formed when many skiers turn in the same place. (For extreme examples, think front cover of ski magazines where hot skiers bash through Volkswagen-size bumps.)

Mountain architecture: A popular building style with the heavy use of natural woods inside and out, vaulted ceilings, lofts, rock or brick fireplaces, and big windows for views.

Skier visits: You can tell the popularity of an area by looking at its number of skier visits. Vail, one of the busiest ski areas, has more than a million skier visits a year. Some of the smallest ski areas number skier visits in the few thousands.

Skier rustic: Lodging so basic and worn that even ski boots can't destroy it.

Skier spawning grounds (also called skier factories): The breeding areas for entry-level skiers who move on to the mid-size or larger ski areas. The ski industry depends heavily on these small day resorts that feed skiers who have learned the basics on to mid-size areas. Eventually many of these skiers wind up spending weeks at the biggest resorts.

Trail ratings: Every ski area must split its terrain into three categories: easiest, more difficult, and most difficult (or beginner, intermediate, and expert). These trails are colored green (for easiest), blue (for more difficult), and black (for most difficult) on most trail maps. Some larger areas add red, between blue and black, for advanced intermediate trails. Certain larger ski areas add single or double diamonds on the black-rated trails to indicate the degree of difficulty, while other ski areas add yellow for extremely difficult slopes and triangles to indicate chutes. Keeping in mind the basic premise—that all trails have to be rated—good skiers know that the greens at Keystone are for beginning skiers but a green at Aspen is just a way for intermediates to ski around the most difficult terrain.

The Skiing sections for many of the resorts break out the trails comfortable for low intermediates and the runs more enjoyable to better intermediates. All blacks are not equal! Anyone who skies the black terrain on a 550-vertical-foot midwestern ski area and charges down an Aspen black trail is in for a startling—possibly damaging—surprise. That is why the black terrain in many of the Skiing sections is split into light, murky, and deeper black. (Just think of the one through ten rating scale.)

Vertical drop/vertical rise: Draw a line from the highest elevation at the ski area to the lowest elevation, usually the base lodge, to figure the number of vertical feet. Most of the ski areas in this book range between 900 and 4,139, the highest in the U.S. This is not to be confused with the length of the ski runs, which range up to four or more miles at some ski areas.

2. The $25-A-Day Travel Club—How to Save Money on All Your Travels

In this book we'll be looking at how to get full value for your money on your western ski trips, but there is a "device" for saving money and determining value on *all* your trips. It's the popular, international $25-A-Day Travel Club, now in its 25th successful year of operation. The Club was formed at the urging of numerous readers of the $$$-A-Day and Dollarwise Guides, who felt that such an organization could provide continuing travel information and a sense of community to value-minded travelers in all parts of the world. And so it does!

In keeping with the budget concept, the annual membership fee is low and is immediately exceeded by the value of your benefits. Upon receipt of $18 (U.S. residents), or $20 U.S. by check drawn on a U.S. bank or via international postal money order in U.S. funds (Canadian, Mexican, and other foreign residents) to cover one year's membership, we will send all new members the following items.

(1) Any *two* of the following books

Please designate in your letter which two you wish to receive:

Frommer's $-A-Day Guides
    Europe on $30 a Day
    Australia on $25 a Day
    Eastern Europe on $25 a Day
    England on $40 a Day
    Greece including Istanbul and Turkey's Aegean Coast on $30 a Day
    Hawaii on $50 a Day
    India on $15 & $25 a Day

Ireland on $30 a Day
Israel on $30 & $35 a Day
Mexico on $20 a Day (plus Belize and Guatemala)
New York on $50 a Day
New Zealand on $40 a Day
Scandinavia on $50 a Day
Scotland and Wales on $40 a Day
South America on $30 a Day
Spain and Morocco (plus the Canary Is.) on $40 a Day
Turkey on $25 a Day
Washington, D.C., on $40 a Day

Frommer's Dollarwise Guides
Dollarwise Guide to Austria and Hungary
Dollarwise Guide to Belgium, Holland, & Luxembourg
Dollarwise Guide to Bermuda and The Bahamas
Dollarwise Guide to Canada
Dollarwise Guide to the Caribbean
Dollarwise Guide to Egypt
Dollarwise Guide to England and Scotland
Dollarwise Guide to France
Dollarwise Guide to Germany
Dollarwise Guide to Italy
Dollarwise Guide to Japan and Hong Kong
Dollarwise Guide to Portugal, Madeira, and the Azores
Dollarwise Guide to the South Pacific
Dollarwise Guide to Switzerland and Liechtenstein
Dollarwise Guide to Alaska
Dollarwise Guide to California and Las Vegas
Dollarwise Guide to Florida
Dollarwise Guide to the Mid-Atlantic States
Dollarwise Guide to New England
Dollarwise Guide to New York State
Dollarwise Guide to the Northwest
Dollarwise Guide to Skiing USA—East
Dollarwise Guide to Skiing USA—West
Dollarwise Guide to the Southeast and New Orleans
Dollarwise Guide to the Southwest
Dollarwise Guide to Texas

(Dollarwise Guides discuss accommodations and facilities in all price ranges, with emphasis on the medium-priced.)

Frommer's Touring Guides
Egypt
Florence
London
Paris
Venice

(These new, color illustrated guides include walking tours, cultural and historic sites, and other vital travel information.)

A Shopper's Guide to Best Buys in England, Scotland, and Wales
(Describes in detail hundreds of places to shop—department stores, factory outlets, street markets, and craft centers—for great quality British bargains.)

THE $25-A-DAY TRAVEL CLUB   7

A Shopper's Guide to the Caribbean
(Two experienced Caribbean hands guide you through this shopper's paradise, offering witty insights and helpful tips on the wares and emporia of more than 25 islands.)

Bed & Breakfast—North America
(This guide contains a directory of over 150 organizations that offer bed & breakfast referrals and reservations throughout North America. The scenic attractions, and major schools and universities near the homes of each are also listed.)

Dollarwise Guide to Cruises
(This complete guide covers all the basics of cruising—ports of call, costs, fly-cruise package bargains, cabin selection booking, embarkation and debarkation and describes in detail over 60 or so ships cruising the waters of Alaska, the Caribbean, Mexico, Hawaii, Panama, Canada, and the United States.)

Dollarwise Guide to Skiing Europe
(Describes top ski resorts in Austria, France, Italy, and Switzerland. Illustrated with maps of each resort area plus full-color trail maps.)

Fast 'n' Easy Phrase Book
(French, German, Spanish, and Italian—all in one convenient, easy-to-use phrase guide.)

Guide to Honeymoons
(A special guide for that most romantic trip of your life, with full details on planning and choosing the destination that will be just right in the U.S. [California, New England, Hawaii, Florida, New York, South Carolina, etc.], Canada, Mexico, and the Caribbean.)

How to Beat the High Cost of Travel
(This practical guide details how to save money on absolutely all travel items—accommodations, transportation, dining, sightseeing, shopping, taxes, and more. Includes special budget information for seniors, students, singles, and families.)

Marilyn Wood's Wonderful Weekends
(This very selective guide covers the best mini-vacation destinations within a 175-mile radius of New York City. It describes special country inns and other accommodations, restaurants, picnic spots, sights, and activities—all the information needed for a two- or three-day stay.)

Motorist's Phrase Book
(A practical phrase book in French, German, and Spanish designed specifically for the English-speaking motorist touring abroad.)

Swap and Go—Home Exchanging Made Easy
(Two veteran home exchangers explain in detail all the money-saving benefits of a home exchange, and then describe precisely how to do it. Also includes information on home rentals and many tips on low-cost travel.)

The Candy Apple: New York for Kids
(A spirited guide to the wonders of the Big Apple by a savvy New York grand-

mother with a kid's-eye view to fun. Indispensable for visitors and residents alike.)

Travel Diary and Record Book
(A 96-page diary for personal travel notes plus a section for such vital data as passport and traveler's check numbers, itinerary, postcard list, special people and places to visit, and a reference section with temperature and conversion charts, and world maps with distance zones.)

Where to Stay USA
(By the Council on International Educational Exchange, this extraordinary guide is the first to list accommodations in all 50 states that cost anywhere from $3 to $30 per night.)

(2) A one-year subscription to *The Wonderful World of Budget Travel*

This quarterly eight-page tabloid newspaper keeps you up to date on fast-breaking developments in low-cost travel in all parts of the world bringing you the latest money-saving information—the kind of information you'd have to pay $25 a year to obtain elsewhere. This consumer-conscious publication also features columns of special interest to readers: **Hospitality Exchange** (members all over the world who are willing to provide hospitality to other members as they pass through their home cities—); **Share-a-Trip** (offers and requests from members for travel companions who can share costs and help avoid the burdensome single supplement); and **Readers Ask . . . Readers Reply** (travel questions from members to which other members reply with authentic firsthand information).

(3) A copy of *Arthur Frommer's Guide to New York*

This is a pocket-size guide to hotels, restaurants, nightspots, and sightseeing attractions in all price ranges throughout the New York area.

(4) Your personal membership card

Membership entitles you to purchase through the Club all Arthur Frommer publications for a third to a half off their regular retail prices during the term of your membership.

So why not join this hardy band of international budgeteers and participate in its exchange of travel information and hospitality? Simply send your name and address, together with your annual membership fee of $18 (U.S. residents) or $20 U.S. (Canadian, Mexican, and other foreign residents), by check drawn on a U.S. bank or via international postal money order in U.S. funds to: $25-A-Day Travel Club, Inc., Frommer Books, Gulf + Western Building, One Gulf + Western Plaza, New York, NY 10023. And please remember to specify which *two* of the books in section (1) above you wish to receive in your initial package of members' benefits. Or, if you prefer, use the last page of this book, simply checking off the two books you select and enclosing $18 or $20 in U.S. currency.

Once you are a member, there is no obligation to buy additional books. No books will be mailed to you without your specific order.

Chapter I

BEFORE YOU GO

1. Overview of Where to Ski
2. Choosing a Resort
3. Getting There
4. Winter Driving
5. Skiing Programs for the Handicapped

KNOWING YOUR OPTIONS makes all the difference in deciding where you want to go, choosing accommodations most suitable for your style and budget, and getting there easily and safely. This chapter aims to provide you with just that kind of information.

1. Overview of Where to Ski

"They're different!" Every skier who's been around agrees. But the "Why?" and the "How Come?" skiing near Salt Lake is different from skiing in Colorado, which is different from skiing around Lake Tahoe, create endless lift-line discussions, conversational gambits during après-ski, and never-fail lift-line openers.

"What about the restaurants and the discos at Steamboat?" asked the guy on the left.

"Tell me about the slopes at Squaw," said the woman on the right to the skier crammed between them on the triple-chair lift.

First the snow job: après-ski follows as usual.

To explain it most simply: The snow in the most western states makes better snowballs than the snow in the Rockies because it's wetter! Weatherpersons say that the majority of storms hitting the ski slopes come from storm systems starting offshore in the Pacific. First they pass over the Pacific coastal mountain ranges, which leaches out much of the moisture. So the snow dumping on those ski areas in the Cascades of Washington, the volcanic mountains of Oregon, and the day areas in southern California is often heavy and wet. (Skiers may also get rain/snow if the temperatures are too high.) However, state-of-the-art snowmaking equipment and slope grooming can turn even impossible conditions into good skiing. Drier snow falls on Idaho, and even drier snow falls on Wyoming. What's left in the storms moving along at high altitudes, which retain little moisture, falls on the Rockies as powder—the powder captured in photographs of skiers floating hip-high in snow and trailing white smoke.

"But I don't like to ski all the time. What are the towns like?" asked the third chair-lift rider while readying to unload.

There is a place for you, whatever is on that personal wish list of après-ski amenities, among the ski resorts listed in this book. Want a megaresort? Try

Vail or Aspen, which each have more than 100 boutiques and shops, plus activities ranging from rides on sleighs pulled by huskies to racquetball. For tame wilderness experiences such as a sleigh ride through the Elk Refuge or a snowcoach trip to Old Faithful at Yellowstone National Park; or tougher backcountry trekking, try Jackson Hole. Families and other skiers who are self-sufficient during the après-ski hours might try one of the mid-size ski areas with lodging on the slopes, such as Bogus Basin or Ski Schweitzer. Skiers who want to sample several ski areas during a vacation might try the Salt Lake or Lake Tahoe. The following paragraphs highlight many of the resorts and ski areas described in this book.

UTAH: Utah has some 15 ski areas and seven of them are etched onto mountainsides near Salt Lake City. Snowbird and Alta in Little Cottonwood Canyon, just a ridge away from each other, are the original odd couple. Snowbird is a 20th-century resort from its linear concrete buildings to its tram, while Alta conscientiously remains one of the nation's best skiing experiences offered for one of the country's lowest-priced lift tickets. The resort town of Park City in a neighboring canyon anchors Park City Ski Area, a sprawling ski complex with good terrain for all ski levels, the posh Deer Valley Resort, and ParkWest, a local's area with good cruising terrain. Skiers (especially those vacationing with non-skiing friends or spouses) lodging in Salt Lake City have easy access to all these ski areas, as well as to Brighton and Solitude, day areas in yet another canyon, as well as city amenities at night. Brainhead, a small, primarily intermediate mountain with good lodging at the base, is tucked away in southern Utah roughly three driving hours from Las Vegas.

WYOMING: Scenic Jackson Hole offers Jackson Ski Area with its outstanding terrain for advanced intermediates to experts, and Grand Targhee, with its mainly intermediate terrain so popular on powder days. Side trips to nearby Yellowstone for cross-country skiing, snowmobiling, or snowcoach rides to Old Faithful are popular with guests in this town, which has a distinct western flavor.

MONTANA: The same light powder falls on Montana's Rockies where the ski areas are smaller and family oriented. Big Sky is a relaxed resort; Big Mountain, close to the Canadian border, has lots of skiers from that country on the slopes; and Red Lodge is low-key.

PACIFIC NORTHWEST: The areas in the Pacific Northwest range from small day areas to medium-size resorts with big mountains. The day ski areas in the Pacific Northwest draw skiers from the main cities in Oregon and Washington. The destination spots, especially Mount Bachelor and Crystal Mountain (also considered a day area for Seattle and Tacoma residents), draw from as far away as northern California and Canada.

IDAHO: Idaho houses Sun Valley, a longtime popular resort with celebrities and sophisticates but equally entertaining to all other skiers. This state also contains a few little-known mid-size areas geared for families or skiers who don't want a lot of nightlife.

CALIFORNIA: California's 35-plus ski areas promise and deliver just about any kind of skiing experience imaginable. At one end of the spectrum, skiers will find tiny day areas that have changed little since the 1960s where rope tows and double chairs rise from primitive basic lodges. At the opposite end are the fashionable ski areas with dozens of lifts and runs whose names are tossed out by fashionably dressed skiers who collect resorts like kids collect bottlecaps. Most of these areas ring Lake Tahoe, a winter/summer playground. Skiers here can mix their ski runs at Squaw, Heavenly, or Alpine Meadows and several other areas with frenetic nightlife, fine dining, and gambling in Nevada, which butts against California here. The San Francisco Bay area skiers take the four-hour drive here in stride. Los Angeles skiers board buses and cram into cars for the seven-hour ride up to Mammoth because it's the closest major ski resort. Several mid-size ski resorts with limited lodging dot mountainsides stretching down the length of the state. California's other cluster of ski hills are the skier spawning grounds within a two-hour drive of Los Angeles.

NEW MEXICO: Skiers who vacation in New Mexico can combine a cold-weather vacation with some warm-weather sightseeing in historic and culturally rich towns such as Taos and Santa Fe. Many of the ski areas reach above 9,000 feet; these southwestern towns are less than a half hour away, but several thousand feet lower and usually many degrees warmer.

COLORADO: Colorado boasts more major ski resorts than any other state. Over 30 ski areas are operating in Colorado's Rockies and many resorts are set in the middle of two or three ski mountains. Skiers from all over the world visit the fabled Aspen/Snowmass region, with four ski areas. Lodging in the Vail valley opens a major resort town full of amenities as well as the ski slopes at Vail and Beaver Creek. Staying in Steamboat or Breckenridge opens up a mountain with many peaks, as well as thriving resort towns. Copper, Keystone, and Winter Park are for skiers who demand good mountains but don't need unlimited choices of après-ski activities. As air flights increase to the resorts in southern Colorado—Purgatory, Telluride, and Crested Butte—these resorts so familiar to southwestern and Texas skiers are being "discovered" by skiers from all over the country.

2. Choosing a Resort

Remember the day you rolled into Sleek Slide Resort expecting a Walt Disney–style scene and discovered you were in something closer to a rock video set. You got a stiff neck from looking up at the front slopes, recalling how the brochure promised "lots of beginner terrain." You wore a conservative outfit to the resort's hottest nightspot, and the dancers were in leather. You cursed the brochure that swore this ski resort had slopes and après-ski for "everyone."

Most vacationers have a "wish list" detailing those pleasures they intend to pursue while on a winter vacation, but few people verbalize it. Cruising terrain or terrifying steeps, fast food or candlelight meals—outline it all in mind, or on paper. Then browse through the resorts listed in this book to see which qualify. Today ski resorts have to compete against each other and against warm-weather resorts, so most have made it easier for you to book vacations by adding central reservation services. Write or call (many have toll free "800" numbers) for brochures listing the current packages. Work through your travel agent or write if the number is a toll call.

FAMILY VACATION TIME? There are ski resorts that cater to every size ski boot wearer's needs, and even to the non-skier dragged along. Many popular resorts have become so because they offer a smörgåsbord of options guaranteed to fill every pleasure-bent vacationer's needs. During the lift-riding hours there's day care with or without ski school for the young ones, ski school for the older children, and even special ski weeks, such as recreational racing or women's ski seminars. Après-ski the family can relax tired muscles in a heated whirlpool, then dine at a pizza parlor or split up for the evening—kids to a fast-food spot, then a movie, while the adults indulge in a fine meal. Among the resorts competing for G ratings are: Steamboat, Vail, Snowmass, and Keystone in Colorado; Park City in Utah; Alpine Meadows in California; and Taos in New Mexico.

Taking Children

Accepting the reality that the mass of skiers is aging, and younger ones are needed to fill the slopes in upcoming years, many ski resorts offer terrific savings for children coming with their parents. Steamboat's Kid's Ski/Stay-Free program is one outstanding example, but many other resorts let youngsters stay free in their parents' rooms, and a few offer free skiing at certain times of the year.

Opinions differ as to when youngsters should start skiing. It depends on the children's personalities (Do they want to ski? Are they aggressive and independent?) and how much energy the parents want to expend (Are they willing to spend the hours in a wedge to stay close to tiny youngsters? Are they willing to cart equipment around for a 4-year-old?) If parents and their youngsters 3 to 6 years of age are determined, many ski areas have snow play programs that introduce youngsters to the basics of skiing in a play setting. Other schools will teach youngsters 4 to 6 years old how to ski and take them on lifts during regular children's classes. Some ski areas demand that any child younger than 5 be in a private lesson.

Rent or buy equipment that fits and is the appropriate length. (Children with boots fitted with too much "room to grow" have been seen coming out of ski and boot during falls.) The cash outlay to buy that first set of skis, poles, and boots may be high, but the equipment can be cycled through other youngsters in the family, then sold at a used-ski-equipment sale. (Many parents who take their children skiing frequently have learned that doing it this way balanced well against the cost of renting equipment every time the child skis.) If you buy new equipment, work with a salesperson who understands how to fit children. If you buy skis and boots at a used-equipment sale, take the equipment to a ski shop for a safety-binding check before your child uses the equipment. (Have the shop check the equipment with your child in the bindings rather than letting them do it by taking down the weight and ability level.) Some parents rent children's ski equipment for a full year through a local ski shop. It's easier than taking the youngster through the rental shop every time the family skis—and parents know the equipment will fit properly.

Make sure the children are warmly dressed in waterproof or water-resistant clothing. A freezing youngster won't like skiing! Consider dressing them in bib-tops (which go chest-high, so children won't get snow up their shirts) and a ski jacket with a high collar. (This outfit is good for any outdoor play so you aren't shelling out money "just for skiing.") Long underwear is essential and it comes in very small sizes. Turtlenecks and a heavy sweater are the next layer. A warm hat and proper (waterproof) gloves are essential.

NEED A SKI GROUP?

Ski clubs are so popular because they make it easier and cheaper for skiers to reach the slopes. The combined clout of all those skiers (the Texas Ski Council, which claims to represent 15,000 skiers, may bring 1,000 skiers to the slopes during the annual Texas Ski Week) represents tremendous buying power and ski club councils have learned to use it. Many ski councils (umbrella organizations for several ski clubs) ask the ski areas for bids! The resort chosen is, of course, the one promising the best deals on a lifts/lodging package complete with wine and cheese parties, races, and more. Most good ski shops should know if there is a local ski council, and probably will have a contact source for some of the local ski clubs. Many major cities have ski councils that represent clubs. For instance, there is a Detroit Metropolitan Ski Council and a Chicago Metropolitan Ski Council. The Crescent Ski Council represents 27 clubs in southern states. The National Brotherhood of Skiers is the umbrella organization for black skiers. Many large companies also have ski clubs, as do YMCAs and even some health clubs. The **United States Ski Association,** U.S. Olympic Complex, 1750 E. Boulder St., Colorado Springs, CO 80909 (tel. 303/578-4600), the **American Ski Association,** P.O. Box 18749, Denver, CO 80218 (tel. 303/861-7669), and the **United States Recreational Ski Association,** 221 W. Dyer Rd., Santa Ana, CA 92707 (tel. 714/641-0724), have benefits for recreational skiers and should be able to provide some information about regional ski clubs.

SEASONAL SAVING: Unless you're determined to ski when the children are out of school at Christmas or during their spring break, ask about the "value" seasons (usually early and late season and sometimes January) when lodging prices plummet. Many skiing packages aren't finalized until fall and new ones crop up through the ski season, especially during the spring, so ask about the latest deals.

LODGING: Think carefully about where you want to bed down. The choice will affect the cost of the vacation. Obviously, staying in a dormitory will be considerably less expensive than staying in a four-star hotel. But know also that the price of condominiums and hotel rooms varies considerably according to amenities such as their closeness to the slopes, and whether or not there is a pool, Jacuzzis, and restaurants on site. Furthermore, a deluxe room at an "in" resort such as Aspen will probably cost much more than the equivalent at a less famous playground.

Lodging in most ski resorts is split between lodges, inns, hotels, motels, condominiums, and houses. In the older ski towns there tends to be a broader cross section; the newer ski resorts tend to have more condominiums.

What are the advantages of each?

Condominiums offer space to move around in, the opportunity for groups to stay together, and a kitchen. For larger groups the basic per-person price of staying in a deluxe condominium may be much cheaper than staying in a string of lodge or hotel rooms. (Then add on the money saved by eating in.) If the condo is slopeside, skiers can meet there for lunch, and the living room, especially if there is a fireplace, becomes a popular après-ski spot. Most condominium complexes offer a variety of accommodations ranging from one-room units (where guests sleep on a murphy bed or the sofa bed) to three-bedroom/three-bath units with a loft. (These can sleep eight comfortably; more if the management allows.) Even the efficiency condominiums, one large room with a refrigerator and sometimes a stove, tend to be larger than the normal hotel room. A family of four staying in a one-bedroom condo can put parents in a private bedroom and youngsters in the living room on the sofa bed—standard in most condos. In most condo complexes rented on a weekly basis, the units are cleaned midweek and after the guests leave. Daily service may be available for a fee.

Many rental condominiums are owned by individuals who use them infrequently. (If the owners bought for investment purposes, they are only allowed to use the unit personally a few weeks of the year.) The owners hire management companies to rent the properties to the public and keep the condos in good condition. Other condos are time-share units (which are rented during the unsold weeks), and yet others, having been designed for rental rather than sale, belong to the building owners. Unless it is a time-share complex or the units in a particular building were decorated before being sold, the decor will vary according to the owner's tastes. Many of the newer complexes are designed to attract winter vacationers who enjoy luxuries such as whirlpools, saunas, outdoor heated pools, game rooms, and even restaurants and lounges with nightly entertainment. The condos themselves are often "mountain style" with high beamed ceilings, lofts (light sleepers should beware of open lofts because sound floats up from the living room), natural woods framing each room, and a fireplace. The price per unit in these complexes is usually higher. The older condominium complexes (unless recently refurbished) usually have a more basic four-square-walls styling and few amenities, so they are priced lower—a good buy for budget-conscious families.

Hotels may be the best buy for skiers who only want a bedroom and prefer to have restaurants and lounges in-house, as well as amenities like daily maid service and room service. Generally, the atmosphere in these hotels (and many of the major chains now run hotels in ski towns) is more formal than in the inns or lodges. Some resorts have condo-hotels in which each room (or suite with kitchen) is owned individually but rented to the public part of the year.

Skiers who like to lace their vacation with atmosphere stay in **inns or lodges** where the hosts may treat guests as friends. A good inn will have one or more "living rooms" where guests can relax after skiing and mingle with friends or meet other guests. (They may not have a bar, although bringing your own is permissible and there is often an après-ski spread. Coffee and hot chocolate are usually on tap throughout the day.) Generally, the dining rooms will be comfortable and set with long tables for family-style dining or with smaller tables for groups who don't want to mingle. In many inns and lodges breakfast comes with the room price. In a few, especially in European-influenced ski towns, dinner may be part of the package. Some of the inns are located in historic buildings, which may have been a way station for travelers for many years, and have individually decorated rooms with antiques. The lodges tend to be larger with uniformly decorated rooms. Many have dorm-style rooms. Most will have ski-storage rooms where skiers can wax or file skis. Many lodges will offer card or recreation rooms with Ping-Pong, pool, or even a few video games.

Motels often line the road leading up to ski towns or resorts. Because guests must drive to the slopes, the motels may be less expensive than lodges and hotels within walking or shuttlebus distance of the runs.

Skiers on a minuscule budget might investigate **dormitories** (but be sure to compare the price against piling a large group into a condo). Most major ski towns have at least one or two places where strangers are matched four to a room and the bath is down the hall.

Bed-and-breakfast housing is an increasingly popular alternative in ski towns. There are locals who—for a reasonable fee—will give skiers a room (often with bath down the hall) and make them a hearty breakfast in the morning. Even skiers with looser pockets sometimes opt for bed-and-breakfast spots because they have a chance to visit with the locals and learn about the latest "in" spots. For more information about B&B in the Rockies contact Bed & Breakfast Rocky Mountains, P.O. Box 804, Colorado Springs, CO 80901 (tel. 303/630-3433).

Some of those **houses** slopeside or on the way to the ski resort can be rented. Generally, the tariff is higher than renting a condo or a room in a hotel or lodge. However this option provides the ultimate in privacy and often extreme luxury.

Once you've determined the type of lodging you want, contact central reservations in the resort of choice to see what is available. Many of the employees at **central reservations services** have actually seen the accommodations so they should be able to give you accurate, honest information about the individual lodges, condominiums, or hotels.

COLORADO SNOBANK: The Colorado SnoBank is a free-access computer bulletin board for skiers. The different sections include descriptions and updated information about conditions at Colorado ski areas, a Nordic skiing section, a price-fighter's board listing consumer deals, and information about consumer-oriented ski associations and ski clubs. Skiers who want to communicate with others involved in the sport can chat via the message board. Call 303/671-SNOW to sign on. Baud rates are 300/1200/2400. The board is open 24 hours a day and users are limited to 30 minutes. Parameters are 8, N, 1.

3. Getting There

Skiers flying to most major resorts must go through gateway cities, such as Denver, Salt Lake, and Reno, then take either commuter flights to tiny mountain airports or ground transportation for the final leg of the trip. Several ski resorts are close to Amtrak stops. Driving is the only way to reach many resorts.

AIR TRANSPORTATION: Most of the major airlines fly to the gateway cities that service most ski resorts. Denver is the primary gateway to most of Colorado's resorts. Grand Junction and Crested Butte are gateways for some resorts and stopping points for the many ski charters (open to any skier) from major cities. Continental Express and United Express are the two major commuter operations that move skiers on into the high country, stopping at airports in Aspen, Avon (near Vail), and Steamboat. Salt Lake City is the gateway for most of Utah's resorts. Reno is the major gateway for the Lake Tahoe resorts. There are smaller fields for commuters from major California cities. Albuquerque is the gateway for most of New Mexico's resorts. The details on reaching specific resorts are listed in the Getting There sections in each chapter.

Currently, Delta, Continental, United, Northwest, and America West fly to many of the important gateways. Continental and United (and their commuter lines, Continental Express and United Express) also fly to many of the cities close to ski areas, including those in more remote locals such as Jackson Hole, Boise, and Kalispell. Skiers using Continental flights to Denver for the Summit County resorts can also book (when making flight reservations) the Continental Connection. After Landing at Denver's Stapleton International Airport, skiers head for waiting buses, do a visual check on their luggage gathered nearby, then board buses which drop them and their luggage at their lodging in Summit County. Several smaller companies, including Mesa Airlines, Horzon, and Skywest, offer feeder flights such as Boise to Sun Valley or Denver to Telluride.

With the way tickets fluctuate in price, either sign up for a package deal arranged through the resort or an airline desk, or have your travel agent price-shop. Many airlines have fly/ski packages. Check with your travel agent for details.

RAIL: Amtrak runs both eastward and westward daily. Trains stop at or near several resorts including Winter Park, the Salt Lake City ski areas, the Lake Tahoe ski areas, and Sun Valley. The trips through the mountains are scenic and some skiers take sleeping berths for the night and step off ready to ski in the morning. Contact your travel agent or Amtrak at the Amtrak Distribution Center, 1549 W. Glenlake Ave. (P.O. Box 7717), Itasca, IL 60143 (tel. toll free 800/USA-RAIL), about ski/rail packages.

4. Winter Driving

Even when the sun is shining at the airport, don't count on good weather in the mountains. Most mountain ranges—especially those in Colorado and Utah—create their own weather patterns. So always enter the high country well prepared. When you have a choice, rent a front-wheel-drive car because the traction can be superior on ice and snow. A car with a manual shift can provide additional control and eliminate the need for braking when going downhill. If you are willing to spend the extra money, rent a four-wheel-drive vehicle.

In the Rockies (and many other mountainous areas) snow tires are a must! When reserving a rental car, make sure it will have snow tires. When you pick up the car—*check!* Never assume that the request was filled. (Radial tires are not considered adequate in mountain snowstorms unless they have a snow tread configuration and are marked "M&S" for mud and snow.) If cars with snow tires aren't available (a distinct possibility in the Lake Tahoe region), make sure chains are included.

Anyone heading into the high country should carry chains. Many states, including Colorado, Utah, and California, have laws requiring cars to have adequate snow tires or have chained tires while in the mountains during heavy snowstorms. In some states, vehicles heading over major mountain passes (even on heavily traveled Interstate highways) must go through checkpoints, and cars with poor snow tires, or radials, or regular tires that aren't chained can't go on. In California there are often "chain installers" who will put on your chains for a fee.

Before heading into the mountains, check the local forecast and road conditions. Rental-car companies should have current information and the local phone number for road conditions so you can call for updates as needed. If the storm is really bad, the local radio and television stations will be monitoring and reporting the conditions regularly.

Other points—which may be so obvious that many forget—include having a good scraper and brush so the windows can be cleared constantly if needed. In Colorado, for example, drivers are required to have "full vision" through the windshields; a tiny space the size of the driver's eyes isn't acceptable. Always carry a flashlight, flares, jumper cables, and a warm blanket when heading into ski country. Always head into a potential snowstorm area with a full gas tank. If you are stuck in a six-hour-long traffic jam because the road ahead is closed (not uncommon in the mountains), you'll need that full tank. Traction mats and a bag of abrasive material such as salt or kitty litter can help get the car out of icy parking lots.

TIPS FOR DRIVING ON ICE AND SNOW: At the **Ford Ice Driving School** (sponsored with Michelin), P.O. Box 774167, Steamboat Springs, CO 80477 (tel. 303/879-6104), recreational skiers taking a few hours off the slopes careen around the slick course learning how to control vehicles when they start to slide. A study shows that 80% of the drivers don't know how to control their car in a slide. (The school offers half-, full-, and 1½-day courses to teach the everyday driver the theory and practice of driving safely and confidently on slippery roads.) The "absolute rule" hammered into every driver's head is: "Adjust your speed to the driving conditions." Never overestimate your driving skills or the capabilities of the car. The goal is to give the students the knowledge and the ability to control their vehicles in any situations they might encounter in everyday driving, and not only in bad weather conditions. Students attending this school are told that smoothness is a key to safe winter driving. Try to avoid the rough use of the brakes and accelerator.

Hand Position

One of the first topics of discussion, rarely thought about by most drivers, is hand position. If you only have one hand on the wheel when starting to skid, the time needed to take corrective action may be gone by the time you put the other hand where it can help steer. According to the Ford school's director (Jean-Paul Luc, who has driven in world-championship rally events for years), on straight roads the hands should hold the wheel firmly at the 9:15 position as on the face of a clock (because that's the best position to turn the wheel any way necessary to respond to an emergency). To turn, slide the hand on the side of the turn up to pull the steering wheel in the direction of the turn. The other hand slides loosely on the wheel so that in the middle of the turn the hands should still be in that 9:15 position. At the end of the turn, do the opposite maneuver rather than letting the steering wheel come back by itself.

Braking

Every primer on winter driving stresses "Never slam on the brakes when driving over ice." Braking transfers the weight of the car forward, loading the front wheels and unloading the rear wheels. Hard braking can cause the front wheels to lock up, resulting in loss of steering control and a possible skid.

To avoid or correct the problem, tap the brakes hard for an instant then ease off slightly when you want to slow down. This squeezing motion offers the best combination of braking power and directional control. If the car has disc brakes, apply a gentle pressure to the pedal, but if you are unable to sense if the wheels are locking up while braking, return to the gentle pumping technique. If you go at an appropriate speed through a curve, braking probably won't be necessary.

Skidding

During rear-wheel skids, do not accelerate or brake. Steer in the same direction the back wheels are sliding. As traction resumes, gradually turn the steering wheel in the right direction and apply slow, steady pressure to the accelerator.

During front-wheel skids, follow the same directions as with rear-wheel skids, *except* don't move the steering wheel. The front tires will grip the road on their own.

Steering

Smooth, careful movements are the way to control a steering wheel when driving over ice. Jerking the wheel can start a skid, so anticipate lane changes, turns, and curves so you can steer through them smoothly.

Driving Uphill

To maintain traction, accelerate (watch how the trucks do it) within reason when approaching an uphill portion of the road. Once on a slippery uphill portion, keep a steady pace. A heavy foot on the accelerator could start the wheels spinning—once traction is gone you might not get it back. Stay far enough from the car in front of you so it's not necessary to slow down or stop. This allows you to maneuver around stuck vehicles.

Heading Down a Mountainside

Use gears—that's what they're for. Putting the car in a lower gear (or "L" on an automatic transmission), lets the engine slow the drive wheels of the car. Braking is the last maneuver to attempt on an icy downhill stretch.

Stuck?

Start moving very slowly so the wheels don't spin. Traction is greatest just before the wheels start to spin. If the wheels begin spinning, ease up on the accelerator until traction returns. Once the wheels start spinning, the car just settles deeper into the rut. Try putting some dirt, kitty litter, or sand beneath the wheels—but make sure no one is behind the car because they could get hit by the debris churned up by the wheels. Keep the wheels straight and don't turn them until after the car has regained traction. (When wheels spin, they get hot and provide even less traction, so wait a moment for them to cool down before trying it again.) If all else fails, try rocking the car out of the rut by carefully shifting from drive to reverse. (But check the car's instruction booklet first to see if there are any special instructions for rocking the car. If it's done improperly, you can damage the car.)

Stranded?

Stay in the car. It's safer to stay in the car and wait for others to find you than to wander outside in a storm. Pile on all those ski clothes in the luggage. Only run the engine for a few minutes every hour and always keep a window slightly open when the engine is running so there is no carbon monoxide buildup. If the car is buried in the snow, don't run the engine since the toxic vapors may come through the car instead of being scattered by the wind.

5. Skiing Programs for the Handicapped

Each year, more ski areas develop or refine learn-to-ski programs for athletes with sensory and/or physical disabilities. Some are taught by ski instructors who have had special training; others are taught by trained volunteers. There are 54 organizations and clubs in 39 states which are associated with the National Handicapped Sports and Recreation Association (NHSRA), and most have programs. Contact the **National Handicapped Sports and Recreation Association**, P.O. Box 33141, Farragut Station, Washington, DC 20033 (tel. 303/652-7505), for more information about the programs and a list of the chapters.

The number keeps increasing, but as of spring 1987 there were 39 ski areas with established handicapped ski schools. (These are schools which provide instruction from formally trained teachers, and have the appropriate equipment to teach skiers with a range of disabilities. **Winter Park Handicapped Program**, P.O. Box 36, Winter Park, CO 80482 (tel. 303/726-0961, or 892-0961 in Denver), is generally acknowledged as having the best program in the country. (Winter Park did 15,000 lesson hours last season.) Other top schools include the **Lake Tahoe Handicapped Ski School**, based at Alpine Meadows; the **Seattle Handicapped Sports and Recreation Association**; the **Flying Outrigger Ski Club**, based in Portland; and the **Breckenridge Outdoor Education Center**. The cost varies widely from less than $10 at Winter Park to $30 for equipment and a private instructor at Purgatory. The NHSRA has a staff which travels around the country helping ski areas open programs for the handicapped and train local ski instructors. Many regular ski schools have instructors trained to teach skiers with certain disabilities.

Many disabled skiers participate in recreational racing programs, including NASTAR. There is a U.S. Disabled Ski Team which competes yearly against 29 other national teams in the World Winter Games for the Disabled. Contact the NHSRA for more information about competition.

Chapter II

THE ESSENTIALS FOR SKIERS

1. Equipment
2. Health Tips
3. Safety on the Slopes
4. How to Dress

PICKING THE RIGHT EQUIPMENT, health and safety tips, and dressing for warmth—and fashion—are the skier-basics covered in this chapter.

1. Equipment

Rent or buy? An increasingly valid question. Traditionally, novices were (and still are) told to rent. Make sure you like the sport before investing a lot of money in equipment! Beginners were and still are urged to buy shorter, more forgiving skis. Intermediates routinely bought equipment and choices were based on input from sources as varied as ski instructors and magazine articles to best friend's opinions. Experts, of course, "knew" what they wanted. But a new trend placing high-performance or demo models in rental shops is blunting some skiers' urges to buy. Even advanced skiers who now only see the slopes for a week or two each year are opting to rent top-of-the-line equipment, which is priced higher (but not unreasonably so) than standard rentals. As one commented, "It allows me to always have the latest equipment at far less than I would spend if I bought my own." You can call from your home to reserve regular or high-performance rental equipment at several major ski resorts (and ski clothing at some) from Pro Select (tel. toll free 800/262-6319).

With the incredible variety of ski equipment on the market today, there is no way a recreational skier who wants to buy equipment can analyze all the equipment available. The key to success is finding a salesperson you feel comfortable with, who appears to know what he/she is talking about. The best way to do that is, of course, to shop! Not spend money—just browse so you'll know where to spend it when the time comes. If the salesperson in Ski Pros Ltd. assures you that Brand J is best for you, without bothering to ask more than "are you a beginner, intermediate, or advanced skier? How much do you want to shell out?"—move on. On to the shop where the help eases into the conversation with a "Hi. Where do you like to ski? Do you find the runs under the gondola at Vail tough or are the back bowls more your speed? Do you like to ski cautiously or does fresh powder snow start your adrenalin flowing?"

The salesperson who asks all those questions has a much more accurate reading of your skiing style. And skiing style has just about everything to do with the equipment you ultimately choose!

BOOTS: Booting up properly before buying skis is promoted by many pros who believe that skis and bindings come in second to boot fit. So use the boot search to tap into accommodating, knowledgeable sales help. (It's also nice to know who to gripe to if there's a future problem with the equipment.)

Years ago, the logic ran "if my boots hurt—they must be right!" Today, if your boots hurt—the fit is wrong! Size-6 boots from three different manufacturers will fit three different sets of feet—perfectly. Because the manufacturers each have their own last, the shape and the construction of boots varies. So trying on boots—lots of boots—is the only sound way to find what you're willing to wear eight hours a day. In recent years a number of sophisticated fitting systems, and all sorts of pads to fill in loose areas or raise arches, have surfaced to allow for one's crooked little toe and bony feet. Today there are conventional boots (translate that to read front-buckle footwear) and rear-entry boots, which have gone from the status of "fad" to matching conventional boot sales in just a few years. The use of orthodics, various types of custom insoles, is another way some skiers get the best boot fit.

Whereas years ago only the highest-priced boot models had the fancy trappings, today most name brands offer goodies such as the use of closure systems, forward lean, and better linings on lower- and medium-priced models too. If the salesperson suggests moving up a grade for extra options because you're getting back into skiing, that's okay. But if the shill knows you are a low intermediate and suggests a $300 pair of boots to get those "extras"—watch out!

When buying boots, by the way, it's not out of line to ask if the salesperson has been to a training session to learn how to fit that boot properly. (Most boot and binding manufacturers run clinics to teach sales staffs to fit and maintain the equipment properly.)

Now that you're clunking around in those new boots, it's time to head to the ski rack.

SKIS: Quite simply, skis have got to suit the skier.

Most of the skiing professionals questioned for insights made cracks to the tune of "pick your skis to match your parka color." And at many levels, that's what choosing skis has come to. In different words, they each commented that it's hard for the average skier to notice the difference between similarly constructed models made by three different reputable companies with good quality control.

Contrast the fight for sales between ski companies to the fight for sales between each of General Motors's car divisions. Each ski company offers models for beginners, racers, and even powderhounds; each of General Motors's divisions produces economy, middle-priced and luxury models to compete against those built by the other divisions, explains one ski shop buyer.

So what really matters?

Length—for starters (although some pros say you should find your "construction preference" first). The current trend is back to longer skis, but the word for beginners is still "stay short" and buy "forgiving" models. More timid skiers might prefer chest-high skis, which are easier to control through the bumps. More aggressive skiers who like to cruise and snake through bumps need longer skis. Even most of the shorter skis today are stable enough to hold heavier skiers.

Now what's this thing called "construction preference"?

The way a ski performs stems from the way it is constructed. Most skis are a core of material—wood or foam—and layers of glass, and the variable is a layer of metal, which makes a ski a bit more durable and tortionally stiffer, according to one pro. (Of course each ski company has its own refinements.) Skis constructed one way will perform beautifully on hard pack but torpedo in deep powder. Other skis won't hold an edge on an icy surface but will be perfect in deep snow. (With the myriad ways skis are constructed currently, pin down a salesperson for an explanation of how the different skis you're interested in are constructed. This will really tell you how much he/she knows.) State the type of snow you like to ski on, because it will have a bearing on the type of skis you should buy. Once you decide which type of construction you prefer, then look at models with that construction in your price range, regardless of the brand name.

But just looking at skis lined against a store wall won't tell you how they feel under your feet on the slope, so now it's time to demo! Testing is the best way to stack the odds in favor of having the ski you buy be one you'll enjoy skiing on. Demo several models before charging your choice. (In fact, many skiers who are on the slopes less than ten days a year are now renting high-performance demo equipment rather than owning their own skis and boots.) Many shops will take the price of demo rentals off the pair you actually purchase. Check how well the skis are tuned before leaving the shop, because tuning can make or break your ski day.

BINDINGS AND A POLE: Now that you've picked boots and skis, how are you going to keep them together? In spite of manufacturers' claims, it's hard for many skiers to distinguish between many of the well-known, proven bindings. Boot sole shapes have been standardized in recent years so they will be compatible with all bindings. (But those older boots—and new-old boots at garage sales—may not be compatible, hindering the binding's release mechanism.) Binding preferences nowadays are often dictated by innovations or how to get in or out of the bindings.

A pole—is a pole—is just a pole—was the general consensus. Just make sure the length is right. Although breakaway grips have been popular in recent years, the ski-school directors report that many pros are going back to straps.

Charge back into that ski shop forewarned. The equipment you choose will effect your enjoyment of this sport. So buy equipment to suit your skiing style.

2. Health Tips

Remember that most western ski slopes are at elevations thousands of feet above city office buildings. Many in Colorado, for instance, stretch from 8,000 feet up to more than 10,000 feet above sea level. Even the fittest athletes may notice breathlessness, fatigue, and possibly headaches when moving around. Sometimes visitors wake up at night a little short of breath or are very, very thirsty. (Of course anyone with heart, lung, or other medical problems should check with a doctor before coming.)

Include time in the trip to acclimate your body to the higher altitude. Consider planning the trip so there's an evening on the town and a good night's sleep before heading out on the ski slopes. (But be aware that alcohol—and medicines—will probably affect you more quickly or differently at higher altitudes.) Let your body be the guide, but consider limiting your skiing for the first day or two. Most important, heed any early warning signs of altitude sickness such as shortness of breath, fatigue, or headache, and cope with them by resting or even returning to a lower altitude. Drink more liquids than you would normally do at lower altitudes. The body dries out faster in the rarified air and needs replenishing.

The sun is strong, and when the snow also bounces it back at you, beware!

Bring good sunglasses, goggles, and lots of sunscreen. Skin (and eyes) can get sunburned even when the sun is behind clouds at the higher altitudes.

3. Safety on the Slopes

There's a nationally accepted safety code, on the back of most trail maps, which reads:

"Code: There are elements of risk in skiing that common sense and personal awareness can help reduce.

"1. Ski under control and in such a manner that you can stop or avoid other skiers or objects.

"2. When skiing downhill or overtaking another skier, you must avoid the skier below you.

"3. You must not stop where you obstruct a trail or are not visible from above.

"4. When entering a trail or starting downhill, yield to other skiers.

"5. All skiers shall use devices to help prevent runaway skis.

"6. You shall keep off closed trails and posted areas and observe all posted signs."

This is a partial list. Be safety conscious!

The key rule is to *use common sense.* Pick up a trail map and stay on trails appropriate for your skiing ability. Squelch your herd instincts and refuse to follow your friends down a slope if that slope is obviously too difficult for you. If another skier comes barreling toward you, don't assume the other person can stop. Move! The superb grooming at many areas creates baby-bottom-smooth slopes, so some skiers cruising downward believe their skills are better than they actually are. Reality comes when they try to stop. If a tree, post, or you are in the way. . . . Statistics indicate that male skiers between the ages of 18 and 24 are the most apt to get themselves killed. Several of the skier deaths in recent years have resulted from skiers moving fast along the edge of the trail, losing it, and crashing into a tree.

When passing someone, call out "On the left" or "On the right" so they don't turn right into you as you flash past. Always stop below other skiers. I once saw the domino effect in action: a whole line of advanced skiers fell, one by one, because someone stopped at the top and toppled over on the next skier.

Closed trails are posted for a reason—not because the ski patrol wants first tracks. For instance, the snow may be in frozen ruts or there may be too many rocks and bare spots. Closed steep runs may be potential slide areas. A skier cutting under the rope could create a slide that could cover unsuspecting skiers on the slopes below.

4. How to Dress

Warmth and fashion can be synonymous in today's ski world! Years ago skiers had to pile on heavy clothes and top them with a down jacket to ensure warmth. Today, layering outer garments made of durable, water-resistant fabrics that have thin insulation; turtlenecks and/or sweaters; and the new types of long underwear provide a very warm and chic look.

Start with underwear! Look for fabrics that keep you warm and also wick moisture away from your body. Long underwear comes in cotton, wool, and silk (for those willing to pay more). Polypropylene, which wicks moisture away from the body, is the latest buzzword (but don't put it in the dryer because it can shrink) for alpine skiers. Most long underwear comes in separate tops and bottoms so skiers can mix sizes and weights. (If you get cold legs, buy a lightweight top and a heavier bottom.) Union suits are grabbed by skiers who want a smooth line under a tight one-piece suit.

Turtlenecks, available in a smörgåsbord of colors, come next. That basic cotton/polyester-blend turtleneck now comes both with the conventional tight neck and in a zip-front model. Top that with a sweater that should be tried on with your jacket to make sure you can still move comfortably. Styles range from the hand-knit Scandinavian designs to the wool/acrylic high-fashion and racing sweaters with padded elbows.

Some skiers prefer pants and parkas, while others would rather wear one-piece suits. Try both on in the store and decide which is more comfortable. Pants range from stretch pants, which are tight and figure-hugging, to insulated bibtops that cover you from ski boot to mid-chest. Some skiers add warmup pants, which zip up the sides, over stretch pants on colder days.

Make sure the parka you pick is functional as well as fashionable. Look for the following touches: stretch panels allow extra movement (but make sure there is a lining underneath to block the wind); powder cuffs to keep out the snow; heavy-duty zippers that go all the way to the top of the collar so you can pull the collar over the lower face on windy, cold days; lots of outer pockets closed by heavy-duty zippers. An inside pocket closed with Velcro is a nice touch. Gor-Tex or one of the other laminates that makes a jacket waterproof is worth considering, especially in the Northwest. One-piece suits are very fashionable, and extremely comfortable because they don't bind at the waist. However, in the lodge skiers can only take off the top part and let it hang, unless they zip apart at the waist (which few do). (When picking one, do deep knee bends in the store to make sure there is enough stretch.) Some have a layer of insulation and are good in heavier weather (with appropriate layering underneath) while others are just a thin shell. The thin shells are wonderful for spring skiing, and with two layers of underwear underneath they can be worn in much colder weather.

Après-ski wear depends on your personality. In the smaller and more rustic resorts, jeans or casual slacks and comfortable shirts topped by ski jackets are accepted wear. In the more fashionable towns, such as Sun Valley, Deer Valley, and Vail, there will always be casually clad skiers intermixed with the "dressed-to-the-hilt topped with fur jackets" groups.

Chapter III

WINTER VACATIONS FOR NON-SKIERS

SO WHAT IF YOU DON'T SKI but those you vacation with do? There's a long list of ski resorts with amenities to entice the "non-skier" dragged along. Steer your family/friends toward the right resort and you could end up having the best time of all!

Tennis? Massages! Hot-air ballooning! Gourmet dining! Do these pique your interest?

Skating! Gambling! Browsing through art galleries! Boogying till dawn then picking yourself up with a late brunch! More along your line?

Fishing! Touring the backcountry tucked into a husky-drawn sleigh! Swimming in a heated outdoor pool? Snowmobiling to Old Faithful?

All of the above—and more—are options for the non-skier, and/or the skier who wants to take a break, at the right resorts. Today the larger ski resorts, from Aspen to Park City to Lake Tahoe, are designed for vacationers who demand amenities—be they skating rinks and outdoor hot tubs or health clubs and branches of boutiques also found on Rodeo Drive—as well as ski slopes.

Let's take it leisure hour by hour. . . .

If your favorite view of the slopes is through a large glass window, settle into a chair at one of the restaurants offering a front-row look at the skiers. At some resorts you'll find the best view from the base lodge. At others the best seat is in a cafeteria or one of the sit-down restaurants located on the ski slopes. On a snowy, cold day, Ragnar's, in a midmountain lodge at **Steamboat,** is filled with skiers taking two-hour lunches.

Browsing through boutiques, shops, and galleries is always a pleasant way to fritter away time. In either **Aspen** or **Vail** visitors can match the price of their plane tickets against a purchase in many of the boutiques. Shopkeepers strive to display the novel and unusual, as well as the more common high-end merchandise for the well-heeled clientele walking through the door. But if the wallet is thin this week, just looking at a piece of western leatherwork in **Big Sky** or trying on a new ski sweater in **Sun Valley** can occupy an hour or two.

One of the greatest villages for non-skiers is **Salt Lake City,** less than an hour's drive from many of Utah's ski areas. Exploring the local bits of history in **Crested Butte, Telluride,** or many of the older mining-towns-turned-ski-resorts is another way to take a few hours out of a day.

WINTER VACATIONS FOR NON-SKIERS

If you want to stretch those muscles during the day, there are many options. Skating rinks are a meeting place at many resorts. At **Sun Valley,** you are apt to be gliding near a professional skater out practicing for the day. Cross-country skiing sets you in the wilderness, and with today's packed trails even never-evers can enjoy the first day out. At **Jackson Hole,** cross-country skiers can take guided tours in the Tetons. The **Royal Gorge** near **Lake Tahoe** may be the country's biggest cross-country ski operation. Snowshoeing is another way to set yourself in the wilderness and away from the ski-slope crowds. Ice fishing is also popular. (Remember you may need a license. Check with the local chamber of commerce for the details and names of outfitters for fishing gear and tips about local spots.) With luck and patience, you can have the fish you caught in the Roaring Fork River on your plate in an **Aspen** restaurant that night.

If you'd rather opt for warmer sports, swim in one of the outdoor heated pools, a "basic" amenity at many ski lodges. **Park City, Snowmass, Vail,** and **Snowbird** all have lodges with private health clubs on the premises. Some of these clubs actually have "spa" weeks during the winter seasons. Of course there are health clubs in many ski towns where you can spend the day playing racquetball or tennis, exercising in the weight room, and finish up with a massage and a sauna before dressing for après-ski!

There are ways to explore the outdoors without exerting any effort. Sleigh rides are a favorite at most resorts. In **Jackson Hole,** visitors can take a sleigh ride through the National Elk Refuge, the winter home for thousands of elk. In many ski towns, sleigh rides include dinner in rustic cabins and a quiet ride home under a starry sky. Old Faithful in Yellowstone National Park is just a snowmobile or heated snowcoach ride away from the south or western entrances. (Visitors in **Jackson Hole** start at the southern gateway; visitors from **Big Sky** enter through the western entrance.) The snowmobiles provide colder, wilder rides. The snowcoaches offer a heated haven for viewing.

In **Snowmass,** visitors are tucked into a sled pulled by 13 huskies for a half-day trip through the Snowmass Wilderness area. In **Jackson Hole,** visitors can take a snowmobiling ride to Granite Hot Springs for a swim. Glenwood Springs, where the water gushes out at 104° but cools slightly by the time it reaches the massive outdoor pool, is just an hour away from **Aspen** and **Snowmass.** Overlooking the crowded slopes from the quiet of a hot-air balloon is a special way to spend a few hours. There are ballooning operations out of several resorts, including **Steamboat** and **Snowmass.**

If you're a watcher by nature, plot the vacation around a winter carnival. These are days packed with parades, special races, and parties designed to keep vacationers entertained and let locals bust loose. **Big Sky** runs a Western Winter Carnival. The Whitefish Winter Carnival is an old-fashioned party with a parade, ice sculptures, and friendly crowds in the street, located just eight miles from **Big Mountain,** one of Montana's most popular destination ski resorts. One of the wildest events in the Rockies is the Cowboy Downhill at **Steamboat** in mid-January. Pegged to Denver's annual stock show, cowboys spend their off-day in Steamboat participating in a dual slalom race where they (including cowboys on skis for the first time) must race through a course, then rope a ski hostess and saddle a horse before crossing the finish line. **Aspen's** Winternational and **Vail's** American Ski Classic are both multiday parties wrapped around World Cup Races.

Non-skiers and skiers who want to make their trips tax-deductible can wrap their vacation around a seminar. Such trips have long been enjoyed by vacationing medicine men, but now those morning and evening meetings cover everything from dealing with stress to computer applications. One company runs alternating seminars. One is a medical, dental, legal seminar on medical malpractice; the other covers investments, tax shelters, and financial planning. There are several companies running seminars, including the American Educational Institute which offers seminars for medical, dental, and legal professionals weekly at 12 western areas. The 20-hour program is presented from 7:30 to 9:30 a.m. and from 4 to 6 p.m. so the day is open for skiing. For a list of areas and more information about the current programs, contact the **American Educational Institute,** 24700 Northwestern Hwy., Suite 400, Southfield, MI 48075 (tel. 313/354-3506, or toll free 800/354-3507). Several other companies offer a variety of seminars designed to interest business owners, operations executives, and in fact any intelligent person who wants a chance to mix business with pleasure and possibly legitimately deduct part of the trip's expenses.

Ski towns for non-skiers dot the mountainsides in the Rockies. However, here is a starter list of spots for vacationers who believe wedges are chunks of cheese.

Salt Lake City is, perhaps, the greatest ski resort of all for groups with vacationers who don't even want to feel snow. The skiers can roll out of bed early and hop a local bus to **Snowbird, Alta, Park City, Deer Valley,** or one of the other resorts within a 1½-hour drive. The non-skier can have breakfast in bed, then spend the day exploring Temple Square, home of the Mormon Tabernacle Choir; or browse through the shops in Trolley Square, a complex of fashionable shops set in restored trolley barns. Nighttime opens up all the entertainment available in a big city from discos to the symphony.

Aspen and **Snowmass** are perfect towns for non-skiers. Combined, these two ski resorts, just a 20-minute bus ride apart, offer every amenity a pleasure-bent non-skier could want. Late-night partying and gourmet brunches, seminars, sleigh rides, shopping, health clubs, hot-air ballooning, fishing, and more are all available.

Park City is another sure bet for non-skiers. Main Street in Park City looks like "main street" in many western flicks, but the shops offer contemporary goods. Up by the ski area, there's another set of shops and restaurants and health club facilities where vacationers can lose a few hours. Everything in Salt Lake City is just a 45-minute ride away.

Jackson Hole is a spectacular spot in the wintertime. Non-skier amenities include sleigh rides in the National Elk Refuge, snowmobiling in Yellowstone National Park, and utilizing health club facilities. Non-skiers staying in Teton Village at the base of the slopes have some shops and restaurants, but vacationers staying in Jackson, 12 miles away, just walk out of their lodges to explore shops, restaurants, and nightlife.

The **Lake Tahoe region** is for gamblers and frenetic nightlife lovers. Visitors staying on the south shore or in the **Reno** area can wave good-bye to skiers and spend the day at the tables. They can meet their friends again in the evening for a leisurely meal, watch a "big name" show, then win/lose a few more bucks.

Ski towns are designed for non-skiers too. But why not drag your skiing friends along for the ride?

Chapter IV

COLORADO'S MOST FAMOUS RESORTS

1. Aspen
2. Snowmass
3. Vail
4. Beaver Creek

IN SPITE OF VAIL'S AND ASPEN'S longtime reputations as havens for sophisticated skiers and jet-setters, these two megaresorts come closest to offering something for everyone. In either the Vail valley or in the Aspen/Snowmass area, there are more shops, galleries, and restaurants than one would find in most small cities. Between the two regions, skiers have a choice of more than 37,000 pillows. So how do you choose between them?

Vail valley has more than 20,000 pillows for skiers intent on using the ten square miles of skiable terrain at Vail and the 40-plus runs at Beaver Creek. Vail's slopes have been nirvana for flatlanders from all over the world. The addition of Beaver Creek's terrain just added to the lure. In the Vail valley (which stretches from East Vail to Beaver Creek), the blend of sophisticated vacation clientele and Colorado's day skiers has created a town where sit-down dining is available at mid-mountain restaurants, but the shop selling just-baked cookies is the busiest place in town as the lifts close. In Vail $5,000 furs are on the rack— and $5 trinkets are on sale down the block. Luxury accommodations book up fast, but four-in-a-room lodges also fill up. The pace is much slower in Beaver Creek, a pedestrian-oriented village 20 minutes down the road.

Aspen has some 10,000 pillows and Snowmass has more than 7,000 pillows for skiers tired from a day at one of four ski areas: Aspen Mountain, Aspen Highlands, Buttermilk, and Snowmass. In Aspen bed-and-breakfast homes aren't too far from posh condominiums and lodges. Famous fast-food chains vie for customers with restaurants whose names are bandied around in other countries. Game arcades are housed near galleries and jewelry shops where the price of the ski trip won't cover the cost of the work of art. There's a variety of restaurants and nightlife centered in the mall anchoring the pedestrian village at Snowmass. However, this village surrounded by ski slopes is set up so families can have a good time and parents can keep their children on looser strings.

28   DOLLARWISE GUIDE TO SKIING USA—WEST

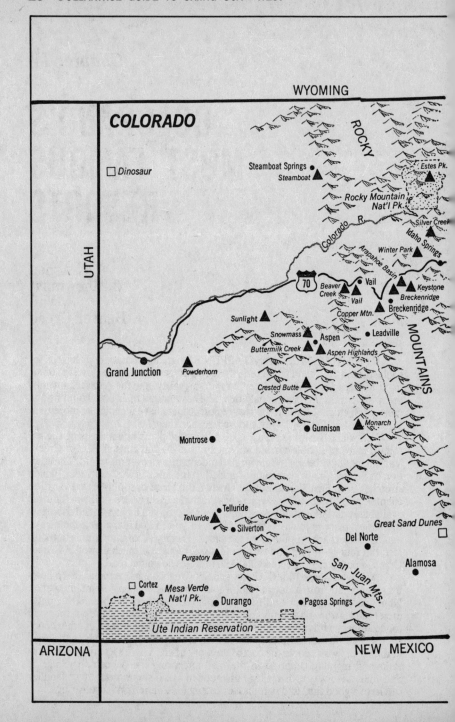

COLORADO RESORTS: INTRODUCTION

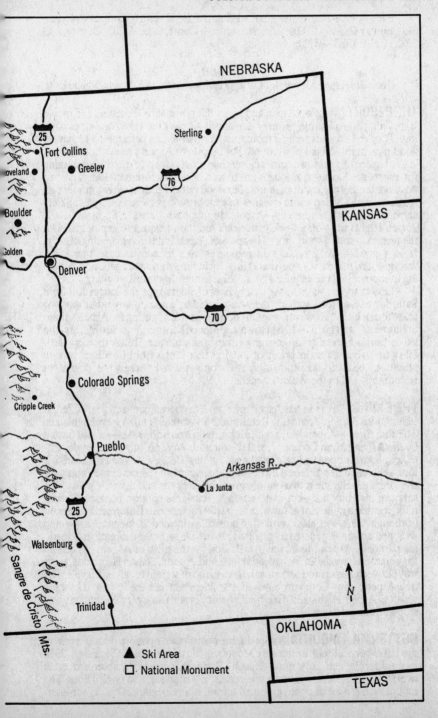

For a detailed consumer guide to Colorado's ski resorts, contact **Colorado Ski Country USA**, 1410 Grant St., Brownleigh Court, Suite A-201, Denver, CO 80203 (tel. 303/837-0793).

1. Aspen
(Includes Aspen Mountain, Buttermilk Mountain, and Aspen Highlands)

THE RESORT: Mention Aspen and many skiers visualize jet-setters and movie stars skiing down Ruthie's Run or dancing at Andre's until the band stops playing. They're here—as well as thousands of other skiers determined to have a good time in this fabled playground. For in spite of Aspen's reputation as a jet-setter haven, this ski town comes closer than most resorts to offering something for everyone. Dorm-style lodges are tucked in old Victorian buildings next to posh contemporary condominiums, fast-food outlets coexist with gourmet restaurants, and a video game house is next door to expensive boutiques. Skiers can challenge four mountains—Aspen Mountain, Buttermilk, Snowmass, and Aspen Highlands—on a weekly lift ticket, but don't expect to explore fully all the terrain in such a short time. The town of Aspen is steeped in mining history. It is a good town for non-skiing spouses and friends because there is a smörgåsbord of activities beyond skiing, including touring art galleries, browsing in shops, sleigh rides pulled by huskies, fishing, and snowmobiling.

Less than ten years ago a steady flow of skiers kept the lodges full from Saturday to Saturday and anyone who wanted to come on any other day was told "tough luck." However, as more ski areas started fighting for Aspen's share of business—and got it—this ski town's approach became more flexible, and the ski corporation even began courting group business again. Today there's a flexibility in arrival days, in prices of lodging that range from luxurious private homes to bed-and-breakfast, and stiff competition between the dozens of restaurants—all to the visitor's benefit.

THE SKIING: Skiers in the Aspen area have to choose between four different mountains: Aspen Mountain, Buttermilk, Snowmass, and Aspen Highlands. The first three—Aspen Mountain, Buttermilk, and Snowmass—are all owned by the Aspen Skiing Company, and the three-day and six-out-of-seven-day lift-ticket packages open up lifts at all the mountains. Because Aspen Highlands is a lone ski area under different ownership, management has developed competitive pricing including a two-out-of-seven-day package and a family plan. Visitors can also buy a six-out-of-seven-days, four-area coupon booklet. Buttermilk, located a mile west of town, is primarily beginner and intermediate terrain (although there are black slopes). Snowmass, located 20 minutes away and wrapped around a pedestrian-oriented resort village, is the ultimate intermediate paradise. Aspen Mountain, overshadowing the town of Aspen, has terrain for better intermediates, advanced skiers, and experts. Aspen Highlands, partway between Aspen and Snowmass, has a blend of terrain for all skill levels. The free Aspen Skiing Company buses shuttle skiers between the town and its three resorts. Aspen Highlands' free "jelly bean" buses run every 15 minutes and stop at three locations in Aspen.

BUTTERMILK MOUNTAIN: Six double chairs open up more than 20 runs on the 2,030-vertical-foot Buttermilk Mountain. Terrain is rated 35% easiest, 29% more difficult, and 26% most difficult. Buttermilk has been described as an overlooked mountain with wide open trails, lots of space, and few lift lines. The mountain has a lot of open, groomed terrain where beginners and lower intermediates can practice their turns. The terrain is similar to that at Snowmass, but the runs are shorter and there's not as much variety.

Beginners might explore the West Buttermilk area first, then try the longer runs off chairs 1 and 2 in the Tiehack area. Buckskin and the Ridge trail (the blue section is easy blue) are particularly popular. Intermediates explore the blues on the Tiehack area. Advanced intermediates can challenge many black runs here, including Javelin and Tiehack, which compare to blue runs like Ruthie's Run on Aspen Mountain.

Insider's Tips

Skiers can get a half-day morning ticket here.

Mountain Facilities

The main Buttermilk restaurant is at the base of the mountain. The Cliffhouse restaurant is located at the top of chairs 2 and 5, Romeo's Tiehack restaurant is at the bottom of chair 4, and Café Suzanne is at the bottom of chair 3.

Snow Coverage

The annual snowfall is 200 inches at this area, which is normally open from mid-December through early April. Snowmaking equipment covers 80 acres on the face of the mountain. There is extensive trail grooming.

Ski School

The Aspen Skiing Company Ski School handles the ski instruction at all three mountains. In spite of the impression that Buttermilk's ski school is just for novices, the instructors here teach all skill levels. There are first-timers classes, all-day adult classes, and children's classes for ages 5 through 12 which include a supervised lunch hour. Private lessons, NASTAR clinics, and telemarking lessons are available. Friends can form their own class (up to nine people of equal skiing ability) and hire an instructor for four hours.

The **Vic Braden Ski College** at Buttermilk (tel. 303/925-1220) emphasizes "targeted laughter" to reduce fear, mechanical analysis of body movements to provide direction, and other novel methods of instruction. Call for details. The Fit for Life program is geared for skiers 55 years of age and older. Programs can be geared for individual groups and also taught on Aspen Mountain or at Snowmass.

Childcare

There is no childcare facility at the mountain. The **Aspen Resort Association** (tel. 925-1940) maintains a list of babysitters. Children between the ages of 3 and 5 can join the Powder Pandas, a supervised day of ski lessons and play. Ask for an "Activity and Children's Guide."

Rental Equipment

Aspen Skiing Company's rental shop is based at the bottom of Buttermilk Mountain. Regular, deluxe/high-performance, and demo/competition rentals are available.

Cross-Country Skiing

See the separate section on cross-country skiing.

ASPEN MOUNTAIN: The trail map stresses that the "symbols and color codes indicate the skiing difficulty of trails and runs on this mountain and are relevant *only for this mountain."* Aspen Mountain is a wonderful place for experts, advanced skiers, and better intermediates. It's not a mountain for beginners or low intermediates. The Silver Queen gondola zips skiers up to the top in six passenger cars opening up the 3,267-vertical-foot mountain. A high-speed quad, two regular quad chairs, and three double chairs open up the terrain rated 35% more difficult, 35% most difficult, and 30% expert. It's easy to move around the mountain quickly now, thanks to the new gondola and the overhaul and addition of other chairs during the last few years.

Ski school runs a free tour of the mountain every Monday morning, a good way to learn where the runs for you are located. Newcomers to Aspen Mountain might want to start skiing off chair 3. Dipsy Doodle, Silver Dip, and the other are blue trails with good pitches, and the steeper sections tend to be wide open. Try Spar Gulch before it becomes too crowded, often a problem in the late afternoon; then move over to chair 8 and cruise the always-popular Ruthie's Run, a broad nicely pitched swath that is groomed often enough so that the moguls don't really build. Copper Bowl, a gully ripe for banking turns, provides good entertainment for advanced intermediates or better.

If you're still challenged by the black runs at Snowmass, explore the lighter black runs here first. Sunset is one place to start because, although there are moguls, it's open enough for wide traverses. Another tester black trail, according to one ski-school supervisor, is the relatively short black run called FIS, with one short, steep pitch. The usually moguled Red's Run, next to FIS, is steeper than Sunset but not as steep as the runs off Ruthie's Run heading into Spar Gulch. Once past that point most of the mountain opens up. The runs off International have big moguls, are very steep, and are never groomed. The steepest is the Elevator Shaft of Silver Queen.

Bell Mountain is the prime piece of turf on this mountain. Experts explore it for seasons without getting bored. The never-groomed terrain varies from steep to steepest, and skiers must negotiate trees and/or bumps depending on their lines. From the top of chair 5, head for Back of Bell #1 and Back of Bell #2, possibly the least difficult terrain because they are formal trails. The face of Bell is tree skiing at its best. (It's also skiing between the trees and over or around moguls.) Generally, the trees are even tighter and the terrain is steeper on the ridge of Bell.

The longest and possibly the most challenging black on the mountain is Jackpot, off Gentleman's Ridge. A blend of trail and tree skiing, it's for very skilled skiers only.

Another quad chair climbs from Gentleman's Ridge to the Sundeck Restaurant at the summit. It opens up 65 acres of expert terrain as well as providing faster access to runs on the back side of Bell.

Insider's Tips

After everyone's on the mountain, the 1A chair is often less used than others on busy days. Chair 7 is rarely crowded.

Mountain Facilities

Lift tickets are available at the base of the Silver Queen gondola and the 1A lifts. Ski school is at the base of the gondola. Silver Queen Sports, at the base of the gondola, has regular and high-performance rentals. Restaurants include the Sundeck, at the top of the mountain; Bonnie's, at Tourtelotte Park; and Ruthie's, next to the top of chair 1A. There is a lovely sit-down dining area at Ruthie's Café with an imaginative menu and spectacular views. There are dozens of restaurants in Aspen within a five-minute walk from the slopes.

Snow Coverage

An average of 300 inches falls most years on this mountain, which is normally open from just before Thanksgiving to mid-April. Snowmaking equipment covers 210 acres. The blue runs and cat walks are groomed.

Ski School

Lessons here are for intermediate, advanced, and expert skiers. Adult intermediate and advanced classes leave from the ski school meeting place outside the Sundeck Restaurant late in the morning. Private lessons are very popular at Aspen. Skiers can form their own class with a group of seven friends of equal skiing ability.

The Aiki Ski program is a special week-long class and weekend class incorporating the martial art of aikido to help students master skiing techniques. It's also taught on Buttermilk.

Childcare

There is no childcare facility on the mountain. Currently there isn't a childcare facility close to the mountain for drop-ins. The **Aspen Resort Association** (tel. 925-1940) maintains a list of babysitters. Ask for an "Activity and Children's Guide." **Aspen Sprouts** (tel. 920-1055) takes drop-ins between the ages of 1 and 5, but it is located near the airport, approximately two miles from town.

Cross-Country Skiing

See the separate section on cross-country skiing.

ASPEN HIGHLANDS: Eight double chairs and four poma lifts open up 64 runs at this ski area with a vertical of 3,800 feet, the longest in Colorado. Terrain is rated 25% beginner, 50% intermediate, and 25% advanced. There's a good variety of intermediate and advanced terrain, and the runs are designed so skiers of different skill levels can head up together, take different trails, and meet again for the lift ride.

The beginners' area is at the bottom, but low intermediates have four good green runs from midway up the mountain: Prospector, Norway, Exhibition, and Red Onion. Scarlett's Run, a wide trail with some light bumps, is the most popular blue run at the area. Wine Ridge, Heatherbedlam, Gunbarrel, and Deane's are other well-frequented intermediate runs. Advanced intermediates head toward Robinson's Run, Upper Stein, and Olympic—light black runs that have a steeper pitch and aren't always groomed. Experts head toward the Steeplechase section, a huge sort of bowl with 1,800 vertical feet of bumps and tree skiing. All or parts of the Steeplechase section are roped off-limits at various times, so check the board at the top of the Loges Peak lift or talk to the ski patrol. There's no lift here and skiers must take the Grand Traverse out.

Insider's Tips

Aspen Highlands offers "flexible pricing" to attract skiers. One of the most intriguing is the family plan with a preset rate whether the family has three or ten members. It can make skiing much more attractive to large families. Contact **Aspen Highlands**, P.O. Box T, Aspen, CO 81612 (tel. 303/925-5300), for details.

Eat at the Merry Go Round on Friday, then watch the Freestyle Exhibition at Midway in front of the restaurant. Gretel's strudel is a hit.

Ski patrol members grab their toboggans and jump over the deck at Cloud Nine, weather permitting, every day at 1:30 p.m. It's quite a show and watchers can sample crêpes and/or strudel, which are on the menu here.

Skiers using the first day of a multiday four-ski-area lift ticket at Aspen Highlands will get a free ski lesson.

Aspen Highlands' lifts climb up a ridge, and the runs head off both sides, so skiers can follow the sun all day by switching sides or skiing the face.

Locals claim that Powder Bowl is the place to ski first on a powder day. Take two or three runs, then head up to the Steeplechase area, which opens late after control work is finished.

The four chairs that tend to have the lightest lines include Smuggler, Thunderbowl, Nugget, and Loges Peak. (Anyone with a fear of heights should be wary about heading up the Loges Peak chair.)

Mountain Facilities

In the base area there is a cafeteria, two bars, ski school, a ski photo concession, and the Highlands Rental Center. The Aspen Highlands Ski Shop is in the parking lot. The Merry Go Round restaurant is located midway up the mountain, and Cloud Nine is at the top of the Cloud 9 lift.

Snow Coverage

There is snowmaking on the lower slopes at this area, which receives an average of 300 inches of snow each year. The area is normally open from the third week in November through mid-April. The green and blue slopes are groomed regularly.

Ski School

Aspen Highlands boasts of having the largest Graduated Length Method school in the country. Never-evers need at least three days, and preferably five, to reach the intermediate level. The three- and five-day packages include rentals for GLM.

The ski school also has half- and full-day classes and private lessons, and the conventional American Teaching Method. Instructors lunch with students during all-day classes. Ballet and racing classes are available. There are children's classes, and youngsters from 3½ to 6 years of age can join the Snowpuppies.

Childcare

There are no childcare facilities on the premises, but youngsters between the ages of 3½ and 6 can enter the all-day Snowpuppies program.

Rental Equipment

Rentals are available at the Highlands Rental Center in the base lodge and at the Aspen Highlands Ski Shop in the parking lot. Many shops in Aspen and Snowmass have equipment rentals.

Cross-Country Skiing

See the separate section on cross-country skiing.

SNOWMASS: See the Skiing section in the following discussion of Snowmass Resort in Section 2.

CROSS-COUNTRY SKIING: More than 80 km (48 miles) of continuous, linked cross-country trails are set in the scenic countryside around Snowmass and Aspen. The trails are free, groomed and maintained by the Aspen/Snowmass Nordic Council, a nonprofit organization.

There is easy touring on the Aspen and Snowmass golf courses and there are touring centers at both courses. The two centers are linked by the Owl Creek Trail, a corridor of easy/intermediate trails. Other trails include the Snowmass Club upper trails and the High School trails, for both intermediate and more advanced skiers. The Aspen Club trails are east of Aspen. By 1988 the entire trail system will be linked from east of Aspen to Snowmass Village.

Lessons, rentals, and guided tours are available at either the Snowmass Club Touring Center in Snowmass or the Ute Nordic Center in Aspen. There are regular clinics where you can improve your skiing skills, and there are numerous races throughout the winter for all ability levels.

The **Ashcroft Ski Touring Center,** 12 miles up Castle Creek from Aspen by car, has 30 km (18 miles) of trails with some of the most beautiful views in the region. There is a $7 trail fee. Skiing into Pine Creek Cookhouse for lunch or dinner is a special experience.

The trek to **Gracie's** (tel. 923-3649) rustic log cabin is easy, and it's a great place for private parties. Picnic lunches and dinners need a week's notice. Moonlight and miner's lights let skiers head in during the evening.

Summer hiking routes enable the more adventurous to explore the backcountry. These trails are not groomed or maintained, and should only be tried if you are experienced in backcountry skiing.

Skiers who want to spend several days in the wilderness can utilize the huts already set in the mountains near Aspen. There are four huts in the Tenth Mountain Trail (tel. 925-5775) system, northwest of town, and four more will be built by late 1988 linking Aspen to Vail. The Fred Braun system (tel. 925-7162), to the south, has six huts with a seventh, the Friends Hut, effectively connecting Aspen to Crested Butte. Reservations for the huts must be made well in advance after October 1 for the following winter.

For more information, call or write the **Aspen/Snowmass Nordic Council,** P.O. Box 10815, Aspen, CO 81612 (tel. 303/925-4790).

WHERE TO STAY: Skiers can find everything from posh private homes and luxurious condominiums to basic motel rooms and dorm-style lodges in this town. Information about all of the locations listed below and more is available from the central reservations service (below). Query the reservations clerk closely about the age and condition of the property suggested. Because skiers have clamored to come to this town for so many years, it's possible (more so than at many other resorts) to "pay more for less." There are many good properties priced at the going rate in this town. And in recent years many of the older properties have been renovated and most are quite comfortable—a few are luxurious. However, there are still some charging more than they should, especially when compared against similarly priced accommodations of sounder construction (so you don't hear the people next door) and with more amenities. Contact the **central reservations division of the Aspen Resort Association,** 700 S. Aspen St., Aspen, CO 81611 (tel. toll free 800/262-7736, or toll free 800/421-7145 in Colorado), for reservations. According to central reservations, during high season the average hotel room goes for $125 a night and the average one-bedroom condominium goes for $175 a night. Ask for the visitor's guide, which rates lodging properties according to maintenance and cleanliness as well as staff attitude and ambience. Also see the Where to Stay section on Snowmass Resort in Section 2 for more lodging in the region.

More Expensive

The **Hotel Jerome,** 330 E. Main St., Aspen, CO 81611 (tel. 303/920-1000, or toll free 800/331-7213), was a class coach stop many years ago, and the recent multi-million-dollar restoration has again turned it into a special place to stay. The rooms are decorated as they were in its Victorian heyday, but the amenities are all modern. Room rates go from approximately $200.

The renovated **Aspen Club Lodge** (tel. toll free 800/882-2582, 800/443-2582 in Colorado), formerly the Woodstone Inn, next to the Silver Queen gondola at the base of Aspen Mountain, has 91 rooms and suites. Amenities include an outdoor heated pool, outdoor Jacuzzi, restaurant and bar, concierge service, and continental breakfast. Rates range from approximately $85 to $250.

Formerly a private residence, the historic Victorian **Sardy House**, 128 E. Main St., Aspen, CO 81611 (tel. 303/920-2525), has five luxurious suites and 15 guest rooms. There's a full breakfast, room service, heated pool, spa, and sauna. Room rates run from approximately $160 and suites go for $255 and up.

The **Aspen Ski Lodge**, 101 W. Main St., Aspen, CO 81611 (tel. 303/925-3434), is a facility that caters to your every need. The basic rooms are very small, but quiet. Amenities include a heated pool, Jacuzzi, a gourmet continental breakfast, limousine service, and health-club privileges at the Aspen Club. Room rates go from approximately $110 for a standard to $262 for an ultra-deluxe room.

The **Hotel Lenado**, 200 S. Aspen St., Aspen, CO 81611 (tel. 303/925-6246), is an attractive small lodge, from the high-ceilinged lobby with twig furniture piled with down-filled plaid cushions to the individually decorated guest rooms and suites with four-poster or carved applewood beds. Good service is the standard and extras include a full complimentary breakfast, a sundeck hot tub, wood-burning stoves in some rooms, and rooftop whirlpool baths in others, a stocked library, and piano bar. Rooms run approximately $150 and up.

The small, intimate **Molly Gibson Lodge** (tel. 303/925-2580) is very luxurious. It has a heated pool, whirlpool, a fireside lounge and bar, a conference room, and a continental breakfast. Rooms range from approximately $125.

The **Gant**, P.O. Box K-3, Aspen, CO 81612 (tel. 303/925-5000, 595-4022 in Denver, or toll free 800/345-1471, 800/824-8730 in Colorado), is a deluxe condominium complex with comfortable, mountain rustic one- to four-bedroom units. Located a few blocks from the ski lifts, the Gant runs a morning and afternoon shuttle to the lifts for guests. There are a heated swimming pool, Jacuzzis, and saunas. Prices range from $149 for a one-bedroom to $469 for a four-bedroom during regular season.

The **Hotel Aspen**, 110 W. Main St., Aspen, CO 81611 (tel. 303/925-3441), has spacious, beautifully decorated rooms, many with Jacuzzi tubs, wet bars, and separate sitting areas with solarium or enclosed porches. Breakfast is served in a communal living room which has a mountain view (a favorite spot during World Cup Races). Prices range from $90 to $155.

The **Aspen Club Management Company**, 709 E. Durant Ave., Aspen, CO 81611 (tel. 303/925-6760, or toll free 800/882-2582, 800/443-2582 in Colorado), handles a wide selection of vacation condominiums and private homes in the Aspen area. Amenities include concierge service, airport shuttle, maid service, and privileges at the Aspen Club.

Aspen/Snowmass Vacations, 730 E. Durant Ave., Aspen, CO 81611 (tel. 303/920-3000, or toll free 800/824-6280), manage more than 100 rental properties varying in size, location, and amenities. The company offers discount lift tickets, rental cars, and American Express services.

Moderate

Murphy beds and rocking chairs are set in many of the 28 attractive rooms decorated in country French style at the **Independence Square Hotel**, 404 S. Galena St., Aspen, CO 81611 (tel. 303/920-2313), in the center of town. There is concierge service, continental breakfast, and a rooftop whirlpool at this renovated historic hotel. Room rates range up from $90.

The **St. Moritz**, 334 W. Hyman Ave., Aspen, CO 81611 (tel. 303/925-3220), is a European-style lodge, five blocks from the center of town. There are dorms, standard rooms, and luxury apartments in this well-cared-for property. Amenities include a heated pool, Jacuzzi, and sauna. Private rooms cost around $95.

The **Tipple Lodge**, 747 S. Galena St., Aspen, CO 81611 (tel. 303/925-1116), is a well-kept, cozy place with ten rooms and a studio unit located just 50 yards from the Little Nell lift. Room rates range from $74 to $114.

The **Limelite Lodge**, 228 E. Cooper Ave., Aspen, CO 81611 (tel. 303/925-3025), is a relatively large place set in a good location, between the lifts and the most active part of town. The price includes clean, basic rooms and a continental breakfast. There is a heated pool, Jacuzzi, and sauna. Room rates run approximately $78 to $122.

The one-, two-, and three-bedroom units at the **Durant Condominiums**, 747 S. Galena St., Aspen, CO 81611 (tel. 303/925-2260), have a contemporary feel and ski-in/ski-out access to Little Nell's lift. Many have fireplaces. There's a heated pool and Jacuzzi. Room rates range from approximately $130 to $340 depending on the size of the unit and the number of people.

The **Lift One Condominiums**, 131 E. Durant Ave., Aspen, CO 81611 (tel. 303/925-6760), about a block and a half from the lifts, has comfortable units with fireplaces. Amenities include a whirlpool, heated pool, sauna, and use of the Aspen Club facilities. Prices range from approximately $135 for a one-bedroom to $305 for a three-bedroom.

There are brass beds topped with comforters in the rooms at the **Brass Bed Inn**, 926 E. Durant Ave., Aspen, CO 81611 (tel. 303/925-3622). Guests can relax in the communal home-like living room après-ski and enjoy the breakfast buffet in the dining room every morning. Amenities include a Jacuzzi and a sauna at this inn at the east end of town but on the shuttlebus line. Prices range from approximately $94 for a room to $265 for a three-bedroom apartment.

The **Boomerang Lodge**, 500 W. Hopkins, Aspen, CO 81611 (tel. 303/925-3416), is located in a quieter section of town just a block from the shuttlebus route. There are elegantly furnished rooms and apartments, a heated pool, a whirlpool, a sauna, and complimentary continental breakfast. Rates range from approximately $102 to $132 for rooms or a studio up to $337 for a deluxe three-bedroom apartment.

Less Expensive

The alpine-style **Crestahaus Lodge**, 1301 E. Colo. 82, Aspen, CO 81611 (tel. 303/925-7081), is at the eastern end of town but on the shuttlebus line. Breakfast is included in the room rate, which goes from approximately $68 to $74.

The **Little Red Ski Haus**, 118 E. Cooper St. (tel. 303/925-3333), is located in a historic Victorian building just two blocks from a ski lift and close to the center of town. Rooms hold one to four persons. Rates run $24 to $28 per person in a shared room with a shared bath, to $34 to $38 for double occupancy with a private bath.

Another homey bed-and-breakfast place, the **Snow Queen Lodge**, 124 E. Cooper, Aspen, CO 81611 (tel. 303/925-8455), has private rooms, kitchenettes, and dorms. Rates range from approximately $22 for a space in the dorm to $72 for a studio with a kitchenette and a shared bath.

The **Midnight Inn**, P.O. Box 3053, Aspen, CO 81612 (tel. 303/925-2349), offers bed-and-breakfast in a delightfully rustic mountain house set high on the mountainside with lots of glass overlooking the Steeplechase section of Aspen Highlands. There are two rooms sharing a bath on one level, and a third bedroom with a private bath in a loft area. (Plans were under way to glass in this section for privacy yet retain the views.) Nighttime includes a turned-down bed and a tiny bottle of Bailey's Irish Cream on the night stand. Rooms are approximately $50 per person per night. The house is on a dirt road a few miles from town so skiers need a four-wheel- or front-wheel-drive car.

WHERE TO EAT: The word on some of Aspen's restaurants has spread worldwide, thanks to this ski resort's international clientele. The more than 75 restaurants in this resort provide a variety of tastes designed to appeal to even the most finicky and to fit every wallet. Skiers spending the day in Snowmass might want to try one of the restaurants at that resort. See the Where to Eat section on Snowmass Resort in Section 2.

More Expensive

Dinner at **Gordon's,** 205 S. Mill (tel. 925-7474), is an elegant, delicious—and pricey—experience. Many ingredients are flown in fresh almost daily so the chef can prepare his "contemporary cuisine." The menu changes daily, but the Heath Bar cake is a steady item. Reservations are recommended. Entrées range from $23 to $30. Dinner is from 6 p.m.

Charlemagne, 400 W. Main St. (tel. 925-5200), is considered one of Aspen's most elegant restaurants by locals who enjoy fine French cuisine and good service. Reservations are recommended. Dinner is from 5:30 p.m. Entrees range from $16.50 to $24.50.

Classic French cuisine is prepared at **Maurice's** in the Aspen Alps at 700 Ute Ave. (tel. 925-7822), by the former personal chef to the Rothschilds. Guests relax in the countrified dining room and enjoy a gourmet meal. Reservations are requested at least three days in advance. Dinner is served from 6:30 to 9:30 p.m. Monday through Friday.

The Sea Grill and Oyster Bar at the **Copper Kettle,** 535 E. Dean (tel. 925-3151), has long been known for its excellent food and good service. Set in the lower section of one of Aspen's most popular bars, the decor is wrapped around copper fixtures and wall adornments which provide for a casually elegant atmosphere. The main attraction is seafood, but there are other items as well, such as lamb, fowl, steaks, and pasta. Prices range from $10, and hours are 6 to 10:30 p.m. daily. Reservations are recommended.

The **Crystal Palace,** 300 E. Hyman Ave. (tel. 925-1455), is Aspen's Victorian dinner theater, which has two seatings nightly, at 6 and 9:15 p.m. This strictness of hour is because your waiter or waitress will be appearing in the two shows provided nightly. Headed by Mead Metcalf, the cabaret revue features original songs with satiric barbs. Six specialties are offered, including prime rib and duckling. Dinner and show run $28, plus tax and tip. Reservations are required.

The owners of the Crystal Palace created their own competition when they opened **The Grand Finale** (tel. 920-1488) next door. Guests dine on continental cuisine at this dinner theater. The price for dinner and show also averages $28, plus tax and tip. There's one seating nightly, at 6 p.m.

The **Chart House,** 219 E. Durant Ave. (tel. 925-3525), is the oldest in the chain, started in 1961. One of the most popular restaurants in Aspen, it features steaks, prime rib, and fish, and a salad bar. Prices range from $10 to $20. It's open daily from 5:30 p.m. No reservations are accepted.

The **Parlor Car,** 615 W. Hopkins (tel. 925-3810), features seven private dining alcoves in a restored railway car. The cuisine is French and the menu varies daily. Dinner is served from 6 to 9 p.m. at a fixed price in the $30s. Reservations are suggested.

Guido's, 403 S. Galena St. (tel. 925-7222), is a well-established restaurant featuring continental fare, fondue, and scampi in the price range of $10 to $20. It's open daily for lunch at 11:30 a.m. and for dinner at 6 p.m. Reservations are suggested.

The **Golden Horn,** located in the lower level of 320 S. Mill, at Cooper (tel. 925-3373), has an alpine atmosphere and a continental menu. Featured are fresh fish, venison, and steaks. Dinner is served daily from 6 to 10:30 p.m. Prices range from approximately $11 to $26, and reservations are suggested.

Expensive to Moderate

Andre's, at 312 S. Galena St. (tel. 925-6200), is well known as a disco, but also serves breakfast (7 a.m. to noon), lunch (noon to 5 p.m.), and dinner (7 to 11 p.m.). Marvelous weekend brunches are served until 2 p.m. Dinner is new continental cuisine, and prices range from $10 to $16. Reservations are suggested for dinner.

The **Ute City Banque** is set in a remodeled 1880s bank at 501 E. Hyman Ave. (tel. 925-4373). It's open daily from 11:30 a.m. to 2:30 p.m. for lunch, and dinner is served from 6 to 10 p.m., with the bar remaining open until 2 a.m. The Ute offers continental, American regional, and nouvelle cuisines, specializing in rack of lamb. Prices range from $10 to $21. Reservations are suggested for dinner.

Sushi Masa, at 409 E. Hyman Ave. (tel. 925-5263), has outstanding Japanese food, featuring sushi, tempura, steak, and teriyaki. They also provide take-out food. Sushi prices depend on your appetite. Dinners run from $10 up. They are open for lunch from noon until 3 p.m., and for dinner at 5 p.m. Reservations are recommended for dinner.

The food is good at the downstairs **J.J.'s Grille,** 220 S. Galena St. (tel. 925-4576). Entrees, stretching from southwestern specialties (and a strong California wine list) to prime rib and roast chicken basted with fresh herbs, run $11.75 to $16.25. Dinner hours are 5:30 to 10:30 p.m. daily. There's a late-night menu after 10:30 p.m. to 12:30 a.m.

The food is reasonably priced and very tasty at **The Grill on the Park,** 307 S. Mill (tel. 920-3700). Dinner features fresh fish and meat cooked on a mesquite grill. Lunch is from 11:30 a.m. and dinner is from 5:30 p.m. nightly.

A family restaurant, the **Steak Pit** (tel. 925-3459), in the City Market Building, promises good, aged beef at fair prices. Prices range from $9 to $15 for steak to prime rib. Dinner is served daily from 5:30 p.m. No reservations.

Moderate

Billed as Aspen's oldest continually running restaurant, the **Skier's Chalet Steak House,** 710 Aspen St. (tel. 925-3381), located at the bottom of lift 1A, still offers the best beef in town at the lowest prices, according to locals. Prices run from $6 to $17, but most of the steaks are in the $8.50 to $12 range. Dinner is served from 5:30 p.m. daily.

Eastern Winds, at 520 E. Cooper Ave. (tel. 925-5160), features Szechuan and Mandarin food in a Polynesian setting. Among their specialties are Peking duck, Hunan beef, fresh seafood, and tropical drinks. They are open daily at 11:30 a.m. Prices vary from $4.50 to $17.

The **Hickory House,** at 730 W. Main St. (tel. 925-2313), is another popular spot because the food is good and reasonably priced. Almost everything comes doused in hickory sauce, from ham and chicken to, of course, ribs. Prices for regular dinners run $6 to $12 and light dinners average $5. Reservations are not accepted. Dinner is served from 5 to 9:45 p.m.

The **Cooper Street Downstairs,** 508 E. Cooper Ave. (tel. 925-8866), a casual restaurant, features family-style American meals with barbecued ribs, T-bone steaks, and seafood. Entrées go from $5.95 to $11.95. Dinner is served daily from 5:30 to 10:30 p.m.

Less Expensive

Pour La France, 411 E. Main St. (tel. 920-1151), has sandwiches, soups, fabulous baked goods, and excellent coffee. Sandwiches average $5. Open from 7 a.m. to midnight.

Pinocchio's, 424 E. Cooper Ave. (tel. 925-7601), is an Aspen institution. Italian food, pizzas, burgers, and sandwiches are all on the menu. Prices range from $5 to $10. Lunch is from 11:30 a.m. to 3 p.m. and dinner is from 5 to 10 p.m.

Little Annie's, 517 E. Hyman Ave. (tel. 925-1098), which looks like an old western saloon, is one of the most reasonably priced restaurants in town. The menu lists hefty sandwiches, good soups, ribs, and chicken with a side of Annie's potato pancakes. Prices go from $3.50 to $10. Hours are from 11:30 a.m. to 11:30 p.m.

The Charcuterie and Cheese Market, in the Ajax Mountain Building at 520 E. Durant Ave. (tel. 925-8010), has an excellent selection of gourmet deli offerings, "from caviar to corned beef and pâté to pastrami." Pick up après-ski snacks or dinner—or have them prepare sandwiches or party trays. Hours are 10 a.m. to 6 p.m. Monday to Saturday and 11 a.m. to 5 p.m. on Sunday.

Locals frequent **Dudley's Diner,** 40 Atlantic Ave. (tel. 925-6262), at the airport business center, which has American and Mexican food, including just-made waffles. It's open for breakfast from 7:30 to 11:30 a.m. and lunch is served from then until 2 p.m.

La Cocina, 308 E. Hopkins (tel. 925-9714), features Mexican and American food, including pasole, chili, and blue corn tortillas. It's open for dinner daily from 5 to 10 p.m., and prices range from $4.25 to $9. Reservations aren't accepted.

The **Red Onion,** at 420 E. Cooper Ave. (tel. 925-9043), has long been headquarters for the locals. It is Aspen's oldest bar, and serves American and Mexican food. Prices range from $3.25 to $5. Reservations aren't accepted.

Schlomo's Deli, at the base of Little Nell, 611 E. Durant Ave. (tel. 925-3354), has the real stuff. Sit down (or order to take out) matzoh-ball soup, corned beef and other deli sandwiches, lox and bagels, blintzes, falafel, and homemade desserts. It's open daily at 7 a.m. for breakfast, lunch, and dinner. Prices vary from $3.50 to $8.

Toro's, 430 E. Hyman Ave. (tel. 925-2134), has served Aspen since 1966. The Mexican food includes chile rellenos, nachos, and gaucamole, washed down with pitchers of margaritas. They also have a limited American menu and are open daily from 11:30 a.m. to 10 p.m. Prices vary from $4 to $8.

ENTERTAINMENT: The type of music varies, but nightclubs with live entertainment include **Bentley's,** Hyman and Mill (tel. 920-2240), which often has music après-ski and again in the evening. At **Andre's,** 312 S. Galena (tel. 925-6200), forever trendy, the upstairs dance floor is usually crowded. The **Tippler,** 535 E. Dean (tel. 925-7627) often has local rock musicians performing. There's live music après-ski and again later in the evening. There's rock and roll at **Little Nell's,** 611 E. Durant (tel. 925-3636), and there's often jazz or country music at the **Red Onion,** 420 E. Cooper (tel. 925-2416).

The historic **Wheeler House** is the scene for classical concerts. Check locally for the schedule.

The oyster bar at the **Paragon** (tel. 925-7499) is usually crowded après-ski. Be sure to examine the stained glass as you walk through the building.

SHOPPING: About the only thing to be said is: explore! The goods on display in this resort town range from highly humorous to incredibly, expensively outrageous. It would be an easy task to drop the price of one's ski trip on a bauble—although those with a more limited pocket can still find some interesting items. Jewels, trendy clothing, leather, ski fashions and equipment, and much more are on display in the windows of the many shops lining the streets in the main section of town. A very incomplete list includes: **Footloose and Fancy Things,** at 400 E. Hyman Ave. offers custom-fitted and designed ankle- to knee-high moccasins. **Stefan Kaelin,** 424 E. Cooper St., features unusual designs in clothing. **Bright and Shiny Things,** 424 E. Hyman Ave., is the place for toys to take home to the kids. **Smith,** in the 601 E. Hopkins Building, is a place for cowboy boots. **Waterfall Hope,** at 307 S. Mill, has American crafts.

There are more than two dozen art galleries and studios in town. Just wander through the main part of town and/or pick up a visitor's guide which lists the galleries. A scattering includes: the **Heather Gallery,** at 555 E. Durant Ave., specializes in contemporary American crafts. The **Upper Gallery,** at 406 E. Hyman Ave. Mall, has original southwestern art and poster reproduction. The **Squash Blossom** is at the corner of Durant Avenue and Galena Street.

NON-SKIER ACTIVITIES: There are several health clubs in town for visitors who prefer indoor sports including tennis and racquetball. **Aspen Club** (tel. 925-8900), **Grand Champions** (tel. 920-1533), and the **Aspen Athletic Club** (tel. 925-2531) offer limited memberships to visitors. There's ice skating at the **Aspen Ice Garden** (tel. 925-7485). Balloon flights over the mountaintops are offered by **Unicorn Balloon Company** (tel. 925-5752). **Snowmobiling tours** through the ghost town of Independence are offered by the T Lazy 7 Ranch (tel. 925-4614). **Sleigh rides** are available at the T Lazy 7 Ranch and at Snowmass Stables (tel. 923-2000). Snuggle into the blankets on a **dog sled** and let a team of huskies take you into the wilderness. For information, contact Krabloonik Kennels (923-3953). **Trout fishing** on the Roaring Fork River is popular in the winter. (Check with the local shops for gear and licenses.)

Drive down to **Glenwood Springs** and jump into the large outdoor pool fed by hot mineral springs. For information, call 945-6571.

GETTING THERE: Aspen is located 200 miles west of Denver, via I-70 and Colo. 82, and 130 miles east of Grand Junction, the major gateways. **United Express** (tel. toll free 800/525-0256) and **Continental Express** (tel. toll free 800/525-0175) have frequent flights during the peak ski season from Denver's Stapleton Airport to Aspen, four miles from Aspen and eight from Snowmass Village. Limousine and taxi service is available at the airport.

Trailways has daily transportation to and from the Denver airport to Aspen and also from Grand Junction. Call **Trailways Tour and Travel Department** (tel. 303/292-2291) for schedules and information.

By car, Aspen is a four- to five-hour drive from Denver, and 2½ from Grand Junction. Major car-rental companies are available in the Denver and Grand Junction airports. **Amtrak** (tel. toll free 800/USA-RAIL) service is available from Chicago through Denver, and from San Francisco through Grand Junction to Glenwood Springs.

MOVING AROUND: There is a free shuttlebus service in Aspen, and taxis, limousines, and horse-drawn sleighs are available upon request. There is also shuttlebus service between the ski areas owned by Aspen Ski Company: Aspen Mountain, Buttermilk, and Snowmass. Aspen Highlands runs its own shuttlebuses through town. The **Roaring Ford Transit Agency** (tel. 303/925-8484) will take you to Snowmass during the day and evening. Schedules are located at the Snowmass bus stop and the information booth. Taxi services include **Aspen Limousine** (tel. 925-2400), **High Mountain** (tel. 925-TAXI) and **Mellow Yellow Taxi** (tel. 925-2282).

TOURIST INFORMATION: Information about Aspen can be obtained by calling **Aspen Central Reservations**, 700 S. Aspen St., Aspen, CO 81711 (tel. 303/925-9000, or toll free 800/421-7145 in Colorado). For visitor information, you can call 303/925-1940.

Call 911 for **emergencies.** The **Aspen Valley Hospital** (tel. 925-1120 or 963-1467 down valley) is located at 200 Castle Rd.

2. Snowmass

THE RESORT: Snowmass is jokingly called slowmass by some locals, but that nickname simply underlines its advantages. The livelier après-ski hours are limited, but then most families (some 60% bring children) aren't into raucous nightlife. (Night-scene aficionados tend to stay in Aspen 20 minutes away.) Snowmass is a pedestrian village with most of the restaurants and shops located in a central mall, from which the lodges and condominiums stretch both up and down the slope. Skiers, including ski-carrying parents, walk a level path to the sides of the slope where everyone puts on skis and slides down to the nearest chair lift. The slopes here have been billed by many skiers as the greatest intermediate playground on earth.

THE SKIING: Three high-speed quads, including the new Big Burn lift installed last summer which triples lift capacity; nine double-chair lifts; and two triple-chair lifts open up the 3,596-vertical-foot mountain.

The best way to tackle this mountain is to explore it section by section because the terrain is so vast it takes time to traverse from one edge of the area to the far peak. Fanny Hill and Assay Hill are the two open beginner slopes. Low intermediates will find lots of terrain off the Burlingame and Funnel chairs. Better intermediates will enjoy the terrain around the Elk Camp chair because it's easy but it dips and rolls a bit, creating some variety. Located high up at one end of the ski area, this Elk Camp area is rarely crowded and provides some of the most spectacular views. The blue runs of the Alpine Springs and Naked Lady chairs are wide, have rolling terrain, and are well groomed. Naked Lady and Green Cabin are popular ones. More than one local's favorite is the informally named Skateboard Alley (start down Green Cabin and stay to the left), a trench where skiers can wander up and down the sides. The Big Burn area is the wide, open patch of mountain that put Snowmass on many skiers' maps. Many of the trails down the Big Burn blend into the next one, and in some areas the trees are far enough apart so better intermediates will enjoy the terrain.

The advanced terrain around the Campground lift (chair 5) is light black, ego runs for good but not expert skiers. The runs are long and the best place in Snowmass to be on a powder day. Because these runs are rated black and are off at one end of the ski area, they are rarely crowded. The terrain around the High Alpine chair is steeper and often moguled, but the runs are shorter. The expert terrain at Snowmass is loudly marked on the map with double diamonds and yellow lines. The Hanging Valley section (which is sometimes closed, depending on weather conditions) rates on a par with some of Aspen Mountain's blacks and is an expert powderhound's dream after a fresh snow. Hanging Valley Glades offers powder glades and tight tree skiing while Hanging Valley Wall is open and steep.

Insider's Tips

Aspen Skiing Company offers guided snowcat powder tours in the bowls and glades on the back of Aspen mountain. For information and reservations, call 303-925-1220.

On powder days, head to Wildcat trail in the Campground area.

If the Big Burn area is crowded, continue to the Alpine Springs lift, and if that chair is crowded, keep heading over to the Naked Lady lift. The Elk Camp and Campground areas, at opposite ends of the mountain, are usually the least crowded.

If arriving by car on a busy day, park by the Krabloonik Restaurant and ski down to the ticket window at the base of the Campground lift.

Stay away from the Alpine Springs chair at lunchtime unless you're eating there. Everybody who spends time at Snowmass knows to head to the High Alpine at the top of the Alpine Springs chair for the best food on the mountain. For leisurely dining go to Gwyn's, the sit-down gourmet restaurant. For faster meals, line up in the cafeteria where the food is made by the same folks.

Ski to Krabloonik Restaurant, in the Campground area, for lunch in this rustic cabin at the site of the kennels where they train huskies to pull dog sleds.

Mountain Facilities

Everything a skier needs can be found in the core village, from lift tickets to lunch spots. The on-mountain restaurants are at Elk Camp at the bottom of the Elk Camp chair, at High Alpine at the top of the Alpine Springs chair, at Ullrhof at the bottom of the Big Burn chair, and at Sam's Knob at the top of the Sam's Knob and the Campground lifts. There is sit-down dining at Gwyn's, the Top of the Knob, and Krabloonik, a rustic cabin where you can dine on wild game.

Snow Coverage

Approximately 300 inches of snow falls most years on Snowmass, which is usually open from before Thanksgiving to mid-April. There is extensive grooming of trails.

Ski School

There are all-day adult classes and children's classes that include supervised lunch. Teens have their own classes complete with supervised after-ski social functions. Any group of up to nine friends of equal skill level can form their own class. Mountain Masters is a special four-day class, starting on Monday, for skiers who want to explore the mountain while improving skills. The handicapped program here is run by experienced instructors. Private lessons, NASTAR, and race training are available. Women's Ski Seminars are offered in two-, three-, and four-day sessions.

Childcare

Youngsters from the ages of 4 to 12 can go into the children's ski school, which meets at the Ski School Youth Center. There are two childcare facilities in the core village: **Snowbunnies** (tel. 923-4620) is for children between the ages of 1½ and 5. **Kinderheim** (tel. 923-2692, or toll free 800/525-9408 outside Colorado) also takes youngsters between the ages of 1 and 5. Both offer skiing programs combined with childcare for youngsters 3 to 5 years old. Call the Aspen Resort Association (tel. 925-1490) for a copy of the "Activity and Children's Guide."

Rental Equipment
Rental equipment is available at several ski shops in the core village.

Cross-Country Skiing
See the separate section on cross-country skiing in Section 1 on Aspen.

WHERE TO STAY: There's a wide range of lodges and condo complexes stretched along the edges of the ski slopes. All the accommodations in the core village are within a two- to four-minute walk of the slopes. There are condo complexes not in the core village but close to other lifts. Skiers can also stay in Aspen, 20 minutes away, and take the shuttlebus to and from Snowmass daily.

Lodging in Snowmass can be booked through the **Snowmass Resort Association's Central Reservations,** P.O. Box 5566, Snowmass Village, CO 81615 (tel. 303/923-2000 for information, 303/923-2010 for reservations, or toll free 800/332-3245, 800/237-3146 in Colorado). Discuss your lodging needs with the reservations office. There are 45 swimming pools and spas located throughout the village and open to all guests. Most are within easy access of the lodges.

Snowmass prices are based on week-long packages that include lodging and six days of lifts. Call for per-night prices. Lodges range from approximately $393 to $425, depending on the luxuriousness of the accommodations and the amenities. One-bedroom condominiums range from approximately $550 to $960, depending on the same factors as lodge rates. Three-bedroom condos, six guests in a unit, range from approximately $490 to $700.

More Expensive
Luxury in decor and service is the approach at the **Snowmass Club,** located a few miles down the road but a free shuttlebus ride to the slopes. The rooms are very attractive and have refrigerators and coffee makers. There's a complete health club on the premises with indoor tennis courts, a gourmet restaurant, and a lounge. The one- to three-bedroom units in the mountain contemporary **Country Club Villas,** next to the Snowmass Club, are equally luxurious, and guests have access to the health club, 24-hour desk service, and more.

The well-appointed units in **Woodrun Place** are spacious, have varying floor plans, and many have high ceilings with lots of windows opening up the views. There are whirlpool tubs or steam showers in each unit at **Woodrun Place,** which has ski-in/ski-out access.

The deluxe studios to three-bedroom units at the **Crestwood** are individually owned and decorated, but the standard is high. Most have stone fireplaces and balconies. The Crestwood specializes in service to guests, such as buying groceries. There is a swimming pool, sauna, and hot tub in the complex.

Moderate
The **Stonebridge Inn** is three levels below the mall, close to the slopes. The rooms are comfortable, fairly spacious, and each has a refrigerator and coffee maker. The striking Tiffany Green restaurant and lounge are in this lodge, and there is a swimming pool and hot tub at the complex. **Stonebridge Condominiums** also has one- to four-bedroom condominiums, some with lofts and dens in nearby buildings. Saturday arrivals for the condominiums.

The **Timberline,** with its studio to three-bedroom units, has ski-in/ski-out access. Amenities include a restaurant, a lounge, a sauna, and a Jacuzzi the size of a swimming pool.

The **Mountain Chalet,** at the edge of the slopes, has comfortable rooms with refrigerators. There's an indoor hot tub and a swimming pool close by. A complimentary full breakfast is served every morning.

The **Silver Hotel** is located one level above the mall next to the slope. Amenities include two swimming pools, outdoor hot tubs, a restaurant, and a lounge. Continental breakfast is served. The Kinderheim Child Care is located here.

Less Expensive

The **Pokolodi** is one of the most reasonably priced properties on the mountain. The rooms are small but have refrigerators and coffee makers. A complimentary continental breakfast is served every morning.

The **Aspenwood,** located two levels above the mall, has studio to two-bedroom units with fireplaces. There is a swimming pool and hot tub.

WHERE TO EAT: The sound of huskies barking rarely is heard inside the truly rustic log cabin housing the **Krabloonik Restaurant** (tel. 923-3953), on the site of the kennels housing huskies that run dog slegs taking visitors into the wilderness during the winter. Dinner guests enjoy specialties such as wild mushroom soup, smoked meats, buffalo, caribou, pheasant, and trout. Skiers can stop by for lunch. (Take the Dawdler Catwalk through the Campground parking lot from chair 2, 3, or 5.) Dinner reservations are a must for this restaurant which only seats 60. Dinner entrees range from $15 to $36. Lunches run much less. Reservations recommended. Lunch from 11:30 a.m. Dinner from 6 p.m.

Chez Grandmère, in a restored Victorian farmhouse in Snowmass Village (tel. 923-2570), is even smaller. This restaurant has only seven tables, so reserve way ahead for this enjoyable French countryside dining experience during busy times. The menu changes nightly, but it's a fixed-price running approximately $35. Reservations are a must.

Moderate to Expensive

Shavano's, overlooking the mall (tel. 923-4292), named after the Ute Indian chief, features nouvelle American and continental fare. The menus are printed in calligraphy and changed daily. Prices range from $11 to $22 for fresh fish, veal, filet mignon, and other well-prepared dishes. Dinner is served from 5:30 p.m. and reservations are suggested.

Plan on a drink in the bar at the **Tower Restaurant,** on the mall (tel. 923-2650), so you can watch "Doc the Magician" do his tricks while unwinding before dinner. This menu features prime rib, steaks, veal, and vegetarian specialties. J.D.'s barbecued shrimp are good; they're named after John Denver, whose photographs are displayed throughout this casual restaurant. Dinners range from $10 to $17. Lunch is from 11:30 a.m. to 3 p.m.; dinner is from 5:30 to 10:30 p.m.

The **Mountain Dragon** (tel. 923-3576) features Mandarin and Szechuan cuisine. Prices range from $9 to $17. The après-ski hour is from 3 to 5:30 p.m. and dinner is from 5 to 10 p.m. Appetizers are available in the lounge from 3 p.m. to midnight. Take-out and delivery service are offered at this Chinese restaurant located on the mall above Sport Kaelin.

Moderate

Hites, on the mall (tel. 923-2748), features trout, steak, and eggs Benedict for breakfast. Evening entrees include fresh pasta dishes, stuffed chicken, veal, and steaks. Breakfast prices are $3 to $8 and dinner is $9 to $14. Reservations are encouraged. Hours are 7:30 to 11 a.m. and 5:30 to 10 p.m.

The **Timberline Restaurant,** above the mall at Timberline Condos (tel. 923-4000), is billed as affordable family dining. The regular menu includes Italian, European, and American cuisine, and there are nightly specials. Entrees are from $8 to $16. Timberline is open daily from 5 to 10 p.m.

Less Expensive

The line is long outside the door of the **Stew Pot,** on the mall (tel. 923-2263), but it's worth the wait, especially for skiers on a budget or for families. Homemade soups, stews, sandwiches, and salads are available in this small, casual restaurant, which serves the same menu during lunch and dinner hours. There is beer and wine. Hours are 11:30 a.m. to 3 p.m. and 5 to 9 p.m. daily. Prices run $3 to $7.

The portions are big at **La Piñata,** located one level below the mall (tel. 923-2153), which has Mexican fare and an American menu. Prices average $5 to $9. Hours at this restaurant with Mexican decor and a roaring fire in the fireplace are 3 to 5 p.m. for après-ski and 5 to 10 p.m. for dinner.

Breakfast, lunch, and dinner are served at the **Snowmass Beach Café,** on the balcony level of the mall (tel. 923-2597). Lunches and dinners include sandwiches, quiche, raclette, and fondue. The café packs ski lunches and makes trays for entertaining in your condo. Beer and wine is available. Prices range from $4 to $6. Cheese fondue for two runs approximately $12. Hours are 8 a.m. to 9 p.m.

Continental breakfasts to eggs Benedict and vegetarian Benedict are available from 7:30 to 11 a.m. daily at **Pour la France,** on the patio level of Snowmass Center (tel. 923-5990). Soups, salads, and sandwiches are served the rest of the day until 9 p.m., and you can call ahead for take-outs. Sandwiches range from $3.50 to $5.50.

ENTERTAINMENT: In between rustling up drinks, "Doc the Magician" keeps drinkers at the **Tower Bar** spellbound with his magic tricks. Big spenders get the thrill of watching their $100 bills end up plastered to the ceiling in Doc's most popular sleight of hand maneuver. (Shirley Temples and Roy Rogers do a landmark business here because kids accompanied by parents are packed in to watch early in the evening.) His protegé, Uncle Hookey, performs when Doc has a day off. There's a live band at the **Timbermill** (tel. 923-4774), which kicks off the après-ski hour as the slopes close. The **Brother's Grill,** the **Snowmass Club,** and **Hite's** all offer evening entertainment. Of course there's plenty of action in Aspen, 20 minutes down the road. See the Entertainment section of Section 1 on Aspen for details, and when in town look at the local visitor's guide.

NON-SKIER ACTIVITIES: Snowmass is a resort that understands there's often one family member who doesn't ski. There are weekly medical and professional business management seminars throughout the winter season, including two different five-day schooling packages offered weekly that could make the vacation partially tax deductible.

The resort maintains 45 heated swimming pools and hot tubs throughout the village that are open to every guest. Chances are good there's one close to your lodge, but there are also dressing rooms by the large pool one level below the village. Naturalist-guided snowshoe tours are available three days a week. On the tours, which include equipment and basic snowshoe instruction, guests learn about plant and animal adaptations to mountain living, the region's geology, and more. Contact the **Snowmass Resort Association** (tel. 303/923-2000, or toll free 800/332-3245 in Colorado) for more information.

Children are into **sledding and sliding on trays** down Fanny Hill, the beginner's slope which parallels the village, after the lifts close. Après-ski activities at the various restaurants also start around the same time.

Balloon flights over the mountaintops are offered by Unicorn Balloon Company (tel. 925-5752). **Snowmobiling tours** through the ghost town of Independence and the Maroon Bells are offered by the T Lazy 7 Ranch (tel. 925-4614 or 925-7040). **Sleigh rides** are available at the T Lazy 7 Ranch and at Snowmass Stables (tel. 923-2000). Snuggle into the blankets on a **dog sled** and let a team of huskies take you into the wilderness. For information, contact Krabloonik Kennels (tel. 923-3953). Trout fishing on the Roaring Fork River is popular in the winter. (Check with the local shops for gear and licenses.) **Ice skating** at the Aspen Ice Garden (tel. 925-7485) is another option. The **Smuggler Mine**, opened in 1882, is open for tours year round. For information, contact 925-7159 or 925-2049. The **Snowmass Repertory Theater** (tel. 923-2618) runs a six-week season of repertory theater.

Of course the shops and art galleries in Aspen are just a 20-minute shuttlebus ride away. See the section on Shopping in Aspen in Section 1 for more details.

Drive down to **Glenwood Springs** and jump into the large outdoor pool fed by hot mineral springs. For information, call 945-6571.

SHOPPING: The **Village Mall** has everything from ski shops to jewelers and an art gallery. The shops in Aspen are also open for visitors.

GETTING THERE: Snowmass is located 210 miles west of Denver via I-70 and Colo. 82, and 130 miles east of Grand Junction, the major gateways. **United Express** (tel. 303/925-3400, or toll free 800/525-0256) and **Continental Express** (tel. 303/925-2352, or toll free 800/525-0175) have frequent flights during the peak ski season, from Denver's Stapleton Airport to Aspen's airport, eight miles from Snowmass Village. Major airlines fly into Grand Junction and bus skiers into Snowmass. Limousine and taxi service is available at the airport, and some condominium complexes in Snowmass will pick you up.

Trailways has daily transportation to and from the Denver airport to Aspen, and also from Grand Junction. Call **Trailways Tour and Travel Department** (tel. 303/292-2291 or 303/925-1234) for schedules and information.

By car, Snowmass is a four- to five-hour drive from Denver, and 2½ hours from Grand Junction. Major car-rental companies are available in the Aspen, Denver, and Grand Junction airports. **Amtrak** (tel. toll free 800/USA-RAIL) service is available from Chicago through Denver, and from San Francisco through Grand Junction to Glenwood Springs.

MOVING AROUND: Since most lodges at Snowmass are ski-in/ski-out, no transportation is needed. However, there is free shuttle service, which runs around Snowmass Village, and bus service for a minimal fee between Snowmass and the town of Aspen. There is also free shuttlebus service between the ski areas owned by Aspen Ski Company: Aspen Mountain, Buttermilk, and Snowmass. The **Roaring Ford Transit Agency** (tel. 303/925-8484) will take you to Aspen during the day and evening. Schedules are located at the Snowmass bus stop and the information booth. Taxi services include **Aspen Limousine** (tel. 925-2400), **High Mountain** (tel. 925-TAXI), and **Mellow Yellow Taxi** (tel. 925-2282).

TOURIST INFORMATION: Call the **Snowmass Resort Association** (tel. 303/923-2000 for information, 303/923-2010 for reservations, or toll free 800/332-

3245, 800/237-3146 in Colorado) for information and reservations. While in Snowmass, stop at the information booth in the village mall.

Call 911 for **emergencies**. The **Aspen Valley Hospital** (tel. 925-1120 or 963-1467 down valley) is at 200 Castle Rd.

3. Vail

THE RESORT: This megaresort offers a village stocked with more than 80 restaurants and bars, as well as more than 100 shops set in the shadow of the largest, most developed ski complex in North America. The brochures boast ten square miles of groomed terrain on the front and more than 800 acres of ungroomed terrain in the infamous back bowls. The reality is more skiing than most skiers can explore in a week. Vail Associates also owns Beaver Creek, a 20-minute shuttlebus ride away, and the lift tickets are interchangeable.

Vail's streets are people with a polyglot society; every language from Spanish to Japanese can be overheard during an afternoon stroll. The clothing ranges from the highest-priced designer one-piece ski suits and casual après-ski fur jackets to the more average-priced brand-name ski jackets. This town, more than most, is geared for winter vacationers who want to wander through galleries and small museums, take sleigh rides, swim, play tennis, and do anything but ski.

SKIING: With more than ten square miles of terrain to ski on (60 miles of slopes and trails), there is a lot of well-groomed terrain of this 3,100-vertical-foot mountain for every level of skier—and of course, there is the ungroomed terrain in Vail's infamous back bowls. The terrain is rated 32% easiest, 36% more difficult, and 32% most difficult. Eighteen lifts, including a six-passenger gondola, open up the mountain.

The addition a few years ago of the Vista Bahn, a covered high-speed quad, and the other high-speed quad chairs on the mountain, changed skiing styles considerably. Skiers are moved uphill so quickly now that they spend more time heading downhill and tire earlier in the day. (Even though the line at the base of the Vista might look horrendous, it moves so quickly that skiers are usually on the lift within ten minutes, except during major holidays.) In fact, many skiers at Vail (and other areas where high-speed quads have been installed) are coming to the slopes later, taking longer lunch hours, and leaving earlier with tired bodies.

Because it can take days to sort out where to ski, consider taking Vail's free "Meet the Mountain" tours offered several days each week. A ski instructor leads the groups along beginner or easy intermediate slopes, pointing out various runs while giving a little history of the area, as well as some ecology, geography, and tidbits about how a ski area is run. The following suggestions are simply starting points on where you can start to explore.

Beginners can start at Golden Peak's chair 6. (In the morning there will probably be less traffic in the lower gondola area where there are also green runs.) Then take chair 10 and ski on the green rounds surrounding chair 14 (near the top of the mountain) before taking the green trails that meander their way back to the bottom. Later explore the green trails off the gondola.

Intermediates gravitate toward the Lions Head gondola; the group of runs underneath provide good scenery and comfortable cruising for intermediates and beginners. Along the entire front face, between the gondola and Mid-Vail, at the top of the mountain there are several well-graded blue runs and a few more challenging light-black runs. The easy intermediate terrain on Golden Peak can usually support more skiers than are using it.

There are several sections on this mountain where the better skiers in a group can take a black run and the less skilled can take blue or green runs, then meet at an intersection. The Game Creek Bowl, serviced by a high-speed quad, is a good choice. The just-intermediates can ski Lost Boy, while the comfortably intermediate can try Dealer's Choice and the bump skiers can play on Wild Card, but they can all meet at the bottom for the ride back out of the bowl. (On nice days there can be a long wait at the chair. Check the lift status board before going into the bowl.)

When the mountain is crowded, or there is fresh powder, head to the older, slower chairs 2 and 17. There's good intermediate terrain around these chairs, probably shorter lines, and usually untracked powder.

Advanced and expert skiers gravitate toward chair 10. Highline is a showcase run—and testing ground—for bump skiers. The best snow is usually right under the lift. Blue Ox sucks you in, starting gently, then getting relentlessly more difficult. It's a terrific cruiser when groomed, and a heavy-duty bump run when it's not! Roger's Run has some tight, squirrely sections to challenge expert skiers. Prima and the upper portion of Riva Ridge are popular spots. Riva Glade narrows into bump skiing between the trees, for those who like to get away from the crowds.

When word spreads that "the bowls are open," advanced skiers migrate to Sun Up and Sun Down Bowls, 800 acres of never-groomed terrain. Vail's reputation for expert skiing is based on this vast expanse, particularly popular on powder days. You can pick cruising terrain or bumps, just by watching where you are going or traversing. Ricky's Ridge and Forever are entertaining runs. On powder days, locals traverse all the way around to the far side of the bowls to Yonder and Over Yonder (which they call other, less polite names).

Skiers can sample Siberia Bowl, an area slated for a chair within the next two years, via snowcat. Ask at the ticket office or look for a sign at the bottom of the Mountaintop Express saying the snowcats are running. The per-ride charge is reasonable.

Insider's Tips

There are lift-status boards placed around the mountain that indicate the rough time of the current wait at nearby chairs. Green means the maze isn't filled, yellow means there is a 20-minute wait, and red means the lift is closed.

Pick up the pocket-size "Vail/Beaver Mountain and Ski School Guide." It's filled with basic facts covering everything from a time/price/description breakdown of the many ski classes and clinics to dining on the mountain.

Through the years regulars have developed routes to lengthen their skiing days. Heading up the lifts when they open at 8:30 a.m. (especially on powder days) promises several extra runs while other skiers are waiting in lift lines. The lines at the gondola at Lions Head are often long in the morning, especially when the ski-school classes are heading up the lift. (However, around midday the line is often short.) The quickest way up the mountain is the Vista Bahn, early, or via Golden Peak's chair 6 and chairs 1 and 16 in the main village. On rough-weather days the covered Vista Bahn or those are the chairs to ski because they only go halfway up the mountain. After the morning rush hour, the lines at these chairs may be minimal, because skiers are spread out around the mountain. Plan lunchtime around the high-noon rush; the food lines or table service will be faster when you eat and the lift lines will be shorter while everyone else eats. At the end of the skiing day, steer yourself down runs ending near your lodging place so there is no need to fight the crowds waiting for buses. If unsure how to plot the course, ask any Vail host or hostess—recognizable by the green jacket with a host/hostess patch.

There is indoor ski storage at the Golden Peak rental shop. The basket checks at Lions Head Gondola Center and Golden Peak can fill up quickly during busy periods. (Overnight storage of ski equipment is available, but it's at your own risk.)

Theft is admittedly a problem at ski areas. In Vail, skis can be registered with the Vail Police Department (476-2626) or Vail and Beaver Creek Security. The service is free; registration is good for three days.

Leisurely lunches are a bonus on cold days, and Vail has two full-service restaurants on the mountain. The **Cook Shack** at Mid-Vail features a gourmet menu (tel. 476-6050 for reservations); the **Wine Stube** at Eagle's Nest prepares international cuisine. Both are open from 11 a.m. to 3 p.m.

There are grooming information signs at Lions Head, Vail Village, and Golden Peak.

Mountain Facilities

Buy lift tickets the day before at the Vail Village ticket office near chairs 1 and 16, at Golden Peak, and at Lions Head. Some lodges offer a lift-ticket service. Vail also has automatic ticket machines; just insert your credit card.

There are cafeterias at Mid-Vail, Eagle's Nest, Golden Peak, and Trail's End at Lions Head. The full-service restaurants are at Mid-Vail, Eagle's Nest, and Lions Head. There are snack facilities at the Far East Shelter and the Wildwood Shelter.

Snow Coverage

The average snowfall at Vail is between 300 and 350 inches, and the mountain is normally open from Thanksgiving through late April. A computerized snowmaking system covers 279 acres.

Ski School

There are more than 600 ski instructors in the Vail/Beaver Creek Ski School, and there are more applicants than openings, so those who make it are among the best in the business. In addition to the regular full-day (5¼-hour) ski-school classes, Vail offers a variety of interesting programs. Special classes for teens, women, singles, and first-timers are available at selected times and locations. There are super classes (full day) and half-day workshops for skiers who want help with specific areas such as skiing the bumps or powder. Experimental programs for experienced skiers who want to fine-tune their skills may also be offered; contact the ski school for details. Race classes, video workshops and lessons, and even custom videotaping are options. There is a self-timer race course on the Hunky Dory run. Anyone can take the free STEP (Skiing Technique Evaluation Program) program offered daily. In STEP, an instructor will ski with you and give a verbal evaluation of your skiing ability. Private lessons are available for one to five persons. (Some skiers make up a class of friends and spend the day skiing with an instructor who gives them tips.) Book ahead (tel. 303/476-3239) during holidays and other busy periods.

There are special classes for teens during peak weeks. Children's ski schools are based at Golden Peak and Lions Head. Youngsters aged 3 to 6 go into programs that blend skiing and indoor activities. Super Stars is for those who already can stop on skis; Mogul Mice includes two 1½-hour lessons and supervised activities the rest of the day. It is important to register youngsters between 8:30 and 9:15 a.m. for this program. (That lets parents get on the slopes earlier too.) Youngsters will need the appropriate lift ticket and lunch money. All-day classes (with supervised lunches) for children from 6 to 12 years of age start at 9:30 a.m., so parents can enroll the youngsters, then attend lessons themselves. (Lunch money and lift tickets are necessary.)

Childcare

ABC Children's Acres (tel. 476-1420 or 476-2722) takes youngsters between the ages of 2 and 5, and as young as 18 months on weekends. Call for details. See the above ski school section for information about ski school and ski school/day care for youngsters 3 years and older. For non-skier youngsters, there's **Vail Babysitting** (tel. 827-5279).

The **Small World Play School** (located at Golden Peak in Vail and Beaver Creek) is an all-day nursery. There are planned activities, lunch, and snow play for children who can walk independently (approximately ages 1½ to 6). Infant care for children from ages 2 months to 18 months is also available. Enrollment is limited so reserve space (tel. 476-1088 in Vail or 949-5750 in Beaver Creek).

Rental Equipment

There are rental shops at Golden Peak and Lions Head. Many of the ski shops in town also rent equipment on a daily and multiple-day basis. Some have high-performance rental equipment, allowing skiers to test the latest in equipment. There is usually no charge for renting equipment late in the afternoon the day before you ski, and it avoids the morning rush.

Cross-Country Skiing

Cross-country ski trails thread golf courses and lead into the national forest surrounding the town of Vail. Lessons are available through the cross-country ski school headquartered at Golden Peak. One day of a multiple-day lift ticket may be exchanged for a half-day lesson and cross-country equipment rental. The ski school offers daily lessons in track skiing and weekly clinics on telemarking. Stop by the ski school or call (tel. 476-3239) to make arrangements for private lessons. The cross-country ski school also offers combinations of lessons and guided tours into the backcountry. There is a gourmet lunch tour once a week. Track and mountaineering cross-country equipment can be rented at the Golden Peak Ski Rental Shop.

Cross-country instruction is also available at the **Town of Vail Nordic and Nature Center,** located on Sunburst Drive, one block northwest of the golf course clubhouse. Ski rentals, snowshoe rentals, and concessions are available, along with a variety of winter nature programs. Call 476-1000, ext. 197, during the day or on weekends for more information.

Paragon Guides (tel. 476-0553) offers four- to six-day, hut-to-hut trips along the Tenth Mountain trail, which winds through some of Colorado's most beautiful country. The huts have basic essentials and sleep 15.

WHERE TO STAY: Choosing a spot to bed down in Vail can be difficult—there are so many choices. Many of the older buildings with less fancy furnishings or fewer amenities are close to the slopes. Therefore, it's possible to stay in a comparatively inexpensive condo within walking distance of the slopes. In fact, many of the more luxurious accommodations are in the center of town or a shuttlebus ride away. Loding is spread along the entire Vail Valley, but there are two large clusters of accommodations, shops, and restaurants. One is in the Vail's core village; the other is anchored by the LionsHead Mall and the gondola. Guests can also stay in Beaver Creek (see the Where to Stay information in Section 4) and take the shuttlebus to Vail to ski.

Although some lodges require a minimum stay, many accept nonpackage reservations starting any day of the week for any number of days. The **Vail Re-**

sort Association, 241 E. Meadow Dr., Vail, CO 81657 (tel. 303/476-5677, 623-6624 in Denver, or toll free 800/525-3875 outside Colorado), books both nonpackage stays and packages that include lodging and lifts in more than 50 hotels, inns, and homes in the Vail valley. The following accommodations can be booked through this service. Discuss your needs with the reservations agent, and ask for specific details about the property recommended, because there is such a wide range in the quality of the lodging in the Vail valley.

More Expensive

The more posh accommodations in this town come in every style from contemporary home to European-style inn rooms. At the **Vail Athletic Club and Hotel**, 352 E. Meadow Dr. (tel. 303/476-0700), guests stay in comfortably sized rooms or suites with contemporary furnishings. (Many have extra-long beds.) Ask for a room with a mountain view and balcony. The room rates range from $150 a night for a basic hotel room to $750 for the two-story penthouse suite. There are attractive studio apartments with murphy beds and fireplaces, and deluxe suites with two bedrooms and two baths. Outstanding—even in this town —is the two-story Scott Apartment, overlooking the slopes through a greenhouse window, with a master bath that is larger than most hotel rooms (rates on request). Hotel guests can use the athletic club (popular with locals who buy yearly memberships) at no charge, except court fees for racquetball or handball and special services.

The **Mountain Haus**, 292 E. Meadow Dr. (tel. 303/476-2434), next to the covered bridge in the center of town, has owner-decorated condominiums with daily maid service, saunas, and an outdoor heated pool and spa. Limited room service is available, and there is a restaurant on site. Room rates range from $175 to $340 for a two-bedroom condo.

The owner-decorated condos in **Montaneros**, 641 W. LionsHead Mall close to the gondola, are very attractive. Most have natural-wood walls, large living rooms with fireplace, comfortable furnishings, and window walls with mountain views. Many of the fourth-floor condos have high ceilings and loft areas. Some of the lofts are closed and some units have microwave ovens. Condos range from one bedroom with bath to three bedrooms with loft and three baths. Rates range from $130 to $150 depending on the unit and number of persons. Children 12 and under in the same unit with adults are free.

The **Westin Hotel** (tel. toll free 800/228-3000 or 303/476-7111) is one of the more pleasant places in town to stay, although it is located away from the center of the village.

This is a particularly well-run hotel, delivering the quality of guest rooms, service, and hotel amenities expected from this chain. There is a spectacular lobby bar where guests lounge around the two-story fireplace enjoying the mountainside view, two restaurants, an outdoor heated pool, and a whirlpool. Guests can use the Cascade Athletic Club, through a walkway, for a minimal fee. If plans went as expected, a chair lift was installed near the Westin so guests can go out the back door and ride over the ridge to a dropoff point by Simba's Run. At the end of the day guests take the Westin-Ho trail back to the lodge where a bellman takes your skis, hands you hot cider and points you to waiting hors d'oeuvres. Room rates range from $195 for a room, double occupancy, during regular season to $250 for a room, double occupancy, during Christmas.

Marriott's **Mark Resort**, 715 W. LionsHead Circle (tel. 303/476-4444), is a full-service hotel with a range of rooms and attractive suites with fireplaces. Located within walking distance of the gondola, the hotel has an athletic club with indoor and outdoor pools, a rooftop restaurant, a spot for family dining, and one of the liveliest discos in town. Rates run $85 to $650.

The rooms at the **Lodge at Vail** (tel. 303/476-5011) have an old-world charm. When the company that owns the *Orient Express* bought this resort several years ago, they did a first-class renovation of the property. The inn rooms are small but complete and plush. (Request a room not overlooking the parking area.) This is a full-service hotel, with restaurants, a heated outdoor pool, whirlpools, overnight ski check, and more, located at the base of the Vista Bahn lift in the center of the town shops and restaurants. The condominiums at the hotel are individually owned and decorated. Room rates begin at approximately $100 a night, and condominiums at approximately $350. Call for information about lodging and prices.

Moderate

The slopeside lodging in the **Manor Vail** condos is very comfortable. The individually owned condos reflect the owner's taste, but the basic units are nicely sized, and have rock fireplaces and fully equipped kitchens. Manor Vail has the Lord Gore Restaurant and Terrace, a heated outdoor pool, hot tub, and saunas. Some lock-off bedrooms are available during ski season. During regular season, studio suites for two people go for approximately $155 and the Manor House two-bedroom condos for up to six people go for $365. For information, contact Manor Vail Lodge, 595 E. Vail Valley Dr., Vail, CO 81657 (tel. 303/476-5651, 571-5629 in Denver, or toll free 800/525-9165 outside Colorado).

The **Lion Square Lodge and Conference Center**, 660 W. LionsHead Pl., by the gondola (tel. 303/476-2700), which has both hotel rooms and condo units, is popular but the rooms are small. This lodge has hotel amenities, including message wakeup, van and valet service, a pool, saunas and hot tubs, a dining room, and a bar. Prices range from $50 to $550. Children 12 and under are free.

The **Sonnenalp Hotel**, 20 Vail Rd. (tel. 303/476-5081, or toll free 800/654-8312), is actually three buildings: the Austria Haus, the Bavaria Haus, and the Swiss Chalet. A $3.5-million renovation in recent years spruced up the buildings yet retained the design and decor of the respective countries. Management has also kept the charm and personalized service of the small European inn. The buildings are close to one another. Rates range from $130 for the hotel rooms (and breakfast) to $325 for two-bedroom apartments.

Christiania at Vail, 356 E. Hanson Ranch Rd. (tel. 303/476-5641), located at the edge of the ski slopes, offers a variety of lodge rooms, decorated with hand-carved Bavarian-style furnishings and condos. Stacking a few extra beds (at $20 per person charge) could make a stay at this lodge, with its many amenities, a bargain. There's a pleasant communal area; continental breakfast is available (but costs extra) and there is a pool. Some rooms have steam showers or hot tubs. The lodge also has a four-bedroom town house. Rates run from $100 for lodge rooms to $425 for multiperson units.

Less Expensive

The **Best Western Raintree Inn**, 2211 North Frontage Rd. West (tel. 303/476-3890), located in West Vail, away from the main part of town, has comfortable but basic hotel rooms and one- and two-bedroom condos. There's a Japanese restaurant, a pool, a steamroom, a whirlpool and sauna, a lounge, and a game room. There's shuttle service during high season. Room rates range from $90 for a single ro $150 for double occupancy. Children 18 and under are free.

The **Tivoli Lodge**, 386 E. Hanson Ranch Rd. (tel. 303/476-5616), a two-minute walk to the slopes (but you can ski back to the door), has pleasant rooms decorated in heavy, dark woods. The mountain rooms cost a few dollars more but are larger and face the slopes. There's an attractive, large meeting area here where guests gather for breakfast (charge is per item) or for après-ski relaxing in front of the stone fireplace. There are two heated pools, a sauna, and whirlpool. Room rates vary from $80 to $170. Books are Saturday to Saturday during Christmas holidays and February and March. If space is available, shorter bookings can be made close to the date of arrival. Children 12 and under are free in the same room with parents.

The **Sandstone Creek Club,** 1020 Vail View Dr. (tel. 303/476-4405), has a five-star rating with Interval International Resorts. It's located on the far side of the highway (in a quiet area overlooking a stream), so guests take a shuttle to the slopes or the main village. These attractive codos have brick walls, attractive furnishings, and fireplaces. There is an indoor/outdoor pool, a bar, and a recreation room with pool tables and video games. Rates range from $66 to $345 per unit.

WHERE TO EAT: There are more than 80 restaurants in Vail. The offerings range from perfectly prepared gourmet dishes served by attentive waiters to food shoved over the counter at one of the world's most popular fast-food chains. Be aware that in ski towns many restaurants do not take reservations; waiting in line, or at the bar, is common especially during busy weekends. There are good restaurants at Beaver Creek (see Where to Eat in Section 4), including the highly rated Mirabelle.

More Expensive

Alain's, downstairs in the Mountain Haus near the Covered Bridge (tel. 476-0152), serves chicken, rabbit, veal, beef, and fish prepared in the country French or gourmet manner. One of Vail's oldest restaurants, it's housed in a striking modern space with stained glass, artwork by LeRoy Neiman, and lots of plants. Reservations are suggested for dinner, served nightly from 6 to 11 p.m. Lighter fare including soups, sandwiches, and salads is available in the more casual French Quarter Lounge, a piano bar open from 8 p.m. to 2:30 a.m. Tuesday through Sunday. Entrees at Alain's range from $13 to $19.

It's an old-world-style dining in the **Lord Gore restaurant** in Manor Vail (tel. 476-5651). Entrees such as wienerschnitzel, veal forestière, and rack of lamb range from $13 to $20.50. There are inexpensive choices for children under 12. Dinner hours are 6 to 10 p.m. daily, and reservations are suggested. Breakfast hours in the restaurant are 7:30 to 10:30 p.m.

Elegant dining is the trademark of **Ambrosia,** 100 E. Meadow Dr. (tel. 476-1964), where guests relax in highback chairs around beautifully laid tables enjoying continental meals such as roast duck, veal, lamb, and fresh fish. Dinner entrees are from $15 to $23. Call for reservations. Hours are 6 to 10 p.m. nightly.

The place for pastries and good coffee is the **Tea Room Alpenrose and Restaurant,** in the Village Inn Plaza (tel. 476-3194). Lunch is available here, as well as dinners from a continental menu in the pleasant upstairs dining room. Lunch is served from 11 a.m. to 4 p.m. and ranges from $5 to $7.50; dinner, ranging from $15 to $17, is served from 6 to 10 p.m.

Take off your shoes and sit on cushions for a special evening at **Mataam Fez,** 1000 LionsRidge Loop in the Vail Run building (tel. 476-1948). Order Moroccan delicacies from the regular menu or ask the owner for suggestions. A fried piece dinner is in the mid-20's. Then relax and eat with your fingers (forks not allowed here). Belly dancers perform some evenings. This is a terrific place to bring children! Hours are from 6 to 10:30 p.m. daily.

The **Left Bank,** located in the Sitzmark Lodge (tel. 476-3696), is a longtime favorite with big spenders who enjoy French and American cuisine. Entrees range from $13.75 to $22. Call for reservations. Open daily except Wednesday, serving from 6 to 10 p.m. Cash only.

The Antler's room in **Pepi's Restaurant and Bar** (tel. 476-5626), in the Gastof Gramshammer, is well known for its game specialties. The meals are leisurely and the service is good. Entrees range from $13 to $17. Seatings start at 5:45 p.m.

Moderate

Blu's, located creekside under Krismar (tel. 476-3113), is the place for hungry folks who can't make up their minds what they want to eat. Everything from eggs to crêpes, pasta, and a mixed grill is on the menu in this casual, popular dining spot. You can select vintage wines by the glass. Hours are 11:30 a.m. to 10:30 p.m. daily. Entrees range from $ for light meals to $14.

One of the trendiest spots in town, **Cyrano's**, located at the top of Bridge Street (tel. 476-5551), fills up with casually dressed locals after skiing, but fur-draped visitors also move in later in the evening. Drinkers and diners relax in a decor of wood, stained glass, and hanging plants. Dinners stretch from fresh seafood and beef to veal and chicken. Entrees range from approximately $12 to $19. There is an elaborate brunch for non-skiers or those not eager to be first on the slopes. Brunch hours are 9 a.m. to 3 p.m. daily; dinner is 5:30 to 10 p.m. daily. No reservations.

At **Cyrano's Too**, located in the Vail Spa building in Lions Head (tel. 476-1441), the stained glass and plants are backed by Victorian antiques and mahogany. There is a lengthy appetizer menu, entrees from abalone and steak to duckling and veal, and rich desserts. Dinner entrees range from $14 to $28. Reservations accepted. Hours are 5:30 to 10 p.m. nightly.

The **Hong Kong Café**, in Founders Plaza across from the popcorn wagon, is a very popular après-ski spot. The greenhouse bar is usually packed with thirsty folks sampling a variety of exotic drinks. Many stay to sample the Oriental food. Lunch is served from 11:30 a.m. to 2:30 p.m., with appetizers available until closing. The downstairs dining room offers Oriental food prepared from fresh ingredients. Entrees range from $8.25 to $12.75 and dinner is served from 5:30 to 10 p.m.

Well-prepared basic steak or a few unusual chicken dishes, fresh seafood, and the salad bar are popular items at the rustic, casual **Ore House**, located next to the Covered Bridge (tel. 476-5100). Prices average in the low to mid-teens. The bar is open daily from 4 p.m. to 12:30 a.m. and dining is from 5:30 to 10:30 p.m.

The locals (and Vail has a significant year-round population) meet for meals at **Sweet Basil** (tel. 476-0125), a casual, small place with a contemporary decor fronted by a burgundy awning in the Gore Creek Plaza building. Diners choose between aged Colorado beef, fresh fish, lamb, or veal (complimented by California wines). The lunch menu has lighter fare: sandwiches, pizza, and salads. Entrees range from $9 to $16. This restaurant accepts dinner reservations. Lunch hours are 11:30 a.m. to 2:30 p.m.; dinner hours are 5:30 to 10 p.m. daily.

Los Amigos, located in the Golden Peak House at the top of Bridge Street (tel. 476-5847), is the local's Mexican watering hole. Reasonably priced food is available along with margaritas sold by the liter.

Locals and skiers with cars (or those who take cabs) mix at the **Saloon** (tel. 827-5954), in downtown Minturn, a small town about halfway between Vail and Beaver Creek. A classical country saloon (rough wood walls, wood tables, and chairs, and a large bar surrounded by local characters), this place is packed on weekend nights. While waiting for a free table, examine the signed photographs of celebrities who've waited their turn to sample the food, which ranges from

Mexican specialties to quail or duck. Entree prices range from $7 to $16. Hours are 5 to 11 p.m.

The **Minturn Country Club** (tel. 827-4114) isn't as posh as it sounds. In fact, it's a pleasantly decorated restaurant in the old Minturn Post Office Building. Diners choose steak, kebab fish, or chicken teriyaki from the meat case, then cook it themselves on a large charcoal grill. Steaks range from $6 to $9, depending on size. A salad bar is included. Dinner is 5:30 to 10 p.m.

Less Expensive

Bart & Yeti's, located at 553 E. LionsHead Circle, literally 39 feet, 7½ inches from the gondola, offers reasonably priced smoked barbecued ribs and a variety of sandwiches, some offering unexpected bread-mates. Prices range from $4.25 up to $12. Hours are 11 a.m. to 10 p.m. daily.

Burger King doesn't look like Burger Kings elsewhere—but the food is the same. Located on the lower level of the Crossroads Shopping Center, the shopfront blends in with the rest of the center. Hours are 10 a.m. to 10 p.m.

Hungry skiers can sample ice cream or expresso coffees at the **Häagen-Dazs**, located in the Crossroads Shopping Center.

New York Sicilian or Neapolitan pizza by the slice or entire pie are the options at **Pizza Pane & Co.** (tel. 476-7550), located across from the Crossroads Shopping Center. Pizza and pasta are available for take-out.

For mouthwatering cookies—chocolate chip, chocolate chocolate chip, chips with nuts, and more—follow the aroma into one of the **Vail Cookie Company** stores. The cookies are baked daily in both the shops in Lions Head, located between the Gondola building and the bus stop, and in the Vail village store at 520 E. LionsHead Circle.

Vail even has a **Village Inn Pancake House Restaurant,** 100 E. Meadow Dr., offering the breakfast anytime—pancakes, eggs, or crêpes—as well as dinner entrees, including steak, chicken, and salads. There is a children's menu. Prices range from $2.50 to $10. The Village Inn opens daily at 6 a.m.

Le Petit Café is for skiers who want croissants and coffee for breakfast or a snack. There are two shops, one at 1 Vail Pl. in Vail and the other in Lions Head on the mall.

For breakfast any time of the day, **D. J. McCadams,** 616 LionsHead Circle in Concert Hall Plaza, at the west end of Lions Head (tel. 476-2336), offers omelets, crêpes, and other specialties. Beer and wine are served until 2 a.m.

ENTERTAINMENT: This town was built for vacationers, and the amenities include a long list of places to party or to let others entertain you. The **Shadows** (tel. 476-4444) disco at the Mark is a hot spot. **Mickey's at the Lodge** (tel. 476-5011) is a lounge area at the Lodge which was finally named after the resident pianist, Mickey Poage, who has been drawing crowds for years. The **Casablanca** bar at Cyrano's (tel. 476-5551) offers live entertainment frequently. The type of entertainment at **Sheika's** (tel. 476-5626) nightclub varies, and there's usually action for the younger crowd at the **Bridge Street Shuffle** (tel. 476-3858).

SHOPPING: Shops filled with goods from pewter sculpture and decorator decoys to fragrances, cookware, and clothing lines the streets in this town. There are more than 100 shops to explore, so start wandering. A starter list include's **A Place on Earth,** Crossroads Shopping Center, for handcrafted interior accessories and gifts; the **Alaskan Shop,** 184 E. Gore Creek Dr., for arts and crafts from the Arctic Circle; and **Currents,** 520 E. LionsHead Mall, for custom-designed jewelry. Stop by **Parke Gallery,** 174 Gore Creek Dr., which features works by contemporary southwestern and western artists, including hand-painted handmade jackets. The **Golden Bear,** 223 E. Gore Creek Dr., offers custom-designed jewelry and elegant clothing. **This Wicked West,** in the LionsHead Gondola building, has a mix of funky and trendy clothing, and **Gorsuch Ltd.** has top-of-the-line ski clothing and sportswear. **Caroselli's Vail Factory,** in the middle of Bridge Street, has imprinted sportswear including T-shirts and sweaters and will even make a miniature trail sign or golf sign for you. **Pepi Sports,** 231 Bridge St., is another fine clothing shop for men and women, and **Kidsports,** 122 E. Meadow Dr., specializes in children's ski clothing, equipment and accessories.

There are several fur shops in town including **Affinity** (tel. 476-6878), a discount fur outlet.

NON-SKIER ACTIVITIES: Everything from seminars to sleigh rides and museums are options for the non-skier. The **Colorado Ski Museum and Ski Hall of Fame,** across from the First Bank building on the bus route (tel. 476-1876), has a collection of vintage ski equipment and artifacts from the sport's early days. It's open from noon to 5 p.m. Tuesday through Sunday. There is **ice skating** at Dobson Arena and skate rentals are available. For information about **sleigh rides,** some including dinner, call Spraddle Creek Ranch (tel. 476-6491) or the Clubhouse Restaurant (tel. 476-1330 or 476-1154). Call Piney River Ranch (tel. 476-3941) about **snowmobiling.**

The following organizations provide professional seminars that might make your trip partially tax deductible: the **American Educational Institute,** for medical, dental, and legal seminars (tel. toll free 800/354-3507); the **Corporation for Professional Education,** for medical, dental, and legal sessions (tel. toll free 800/525-5810); and **Vail Management Institute / Resort Seminars,** for medical and business meetings (tel. toll free 800/542-5428).

GETTING THERE: Vail is 100 miles from Denver via I-70. Skiers can fly from Denver's Stapleton International Airport to Vail on **Continental Express** (tel. toll free 800/445-0632). The commuter connection lands in Avon's STOLport, ten miles from Vail. There is a general aviation airport at Eagle, 30 miles west of Vail.

The following companies provide ground transportation between Stapleton and Vail: **Airport Transportation Service.** (tel. toll free 800/247-7074); **Colorado Ground Transportation** (tel. toll free 800/824-1104); **Colorado Mountain Express,** for van, limo, and taxi (tel. toll free 800/525-6363); **Colorado Western Stages,** with a charter bus (tel. toll free 800/332-6363); **Louie's Casual Cabs** (tel. 303/476-TAXI); **Summit Taxi-Going Places,** with van, limo, and taxi (tel. 303/476-LIMO), **TCG Limousines** (tel. 303/790-4004); and **Vans to Vail** (tel. toll free 800/222-2112).

Greyhound (tel. toll free 800/445-5287) and **Trailways** (tel. 303/398-5303) serve the Vail Transportation Center from downtown Denver and Stapleton, Trailways also from Grand Junction.

From Denver, Vail lies 100 miles west on I-70. From Grand Junction it's 150 miles east on I-70. **American International** (tel. toll free 800/527-0202), Hertz (tel. toll free 800/654-3131), and **Thrifty** (tel. 303/949-7787) rental cars are located in the Vail area; all major rental companies are at Stapleton Airport.

MOVING AROUND: Cars can be more of a nuisance than a blessing at Vail. Beyond the allotted spot at your accommodations, there are few other places to park. Vail is a walking village, and the extensive transit system will take you anywhere in the village. All buses have ski racks. The free buses run every five to ten minutes from 6:30 a.m. to 1 a.m. The buses to Beaver Crook, 20 minutes away, are $1. Check the current schedule for times and hours. **Louie's Casual Cabs** (tel. 476-TAXI) offers taxi service. Hertz, Budget, and National have car-rental offices in Vail. There is day parking in the Vail Village Parking structure, which usually fills up around 9 a.m. If you are on the bus routes, it's considerably less hassle to use the transit system.

TOURIST INFORMATION: For information or reservations call or write: **Vail Resort Association,** 241 E. Meadow Dr., Vail, CO 81657 (tel. 303/476-1000 for information, 303/476-5677 for reservations, or 623/6624 in Denver, or toll free 800/525-3875 outside Colorado).

Once in Vail, pick up a copy of the latest mountain guide, which highlights everything from the various ski school programs to special restaurants on the mountain. **Vail 800,** 122 E. Meadow Dr., Vail, CO 81657 (tel. toll free 800/445-VAIL), has information on snowmobiling, sightseeing, transportation to the airport, and much more available via a phone call. Brochures are available by mail. Channel 13 on cable TV, available in most lodge rooms, has a continuous update on weather, recently opened trails, and upcoming events.

For **ambulance, fire,** and **police,** dial 911. **The hospital emergency department** is 476-8065. **Vail Valley Medical Center** (tel. 476-2451) is located at 181 W. Meadow Dr.

4. Beaver Creek

THE RESORT: The village of Beaver Creek was designed as a hideaway for the wealthy—and the inn, private homes, and designer-decorated condominiums reflect that bias. However, a vacation at this village, set at the base of many ego-building ski runs, doesn't require a millionaire's checkbook! Cheap it's not (although those on a budget can stay in nearby Avon and ski at Beaver Creek during the day), but it is affordable for those willing to splurge for a little extra posh, and a should-do experience for those skiers not on a budget. The pedestrian-oriented village is a quiet place. The restaurants are good, but limited in number; après-ski activity is also muted. However, Vail with its more frenetic nightlife scene is just 20 minutes down the road.

From the highway, the runs at Beaver Creek are tough to define. They don't look like super freeways blasted into the mountainside. Many runs undulate downward and have islands of trees left in the middle, so skiers feel like they are skiing in glades but don't have to worry about spruce tops. Beginners have terrain at the top of the mountain, intermediates can cruise all over, and advanced skiers have those Birds of Prey. Day skiers from the Front Range, who are bused in from the valley's entrance two miles away, guests staying in the valley, and skiers exploring Beaver Creek but staying at other destination resorts all share the slopes.

THE SKIING: Ten lifts open up the 49 named trails on this 3,340-vertical-foot mountain. the terrain is rated 23% easiest, 43% more difficult, and 34% most difficult, and that includes a good mix of trails for every skill level.

The never-evers' section is at the base, but beginners head all the way to the top of the mountain for the day to enjoy the same panoramic views as the better skiers. The gentle, wide trails off chairs 5 and 8 above the Spruce Saddle mid-mountain lodge provide variable terrain to turn beginners into low intermediates. At the end of the day skiers can head all the way down to the base or just to the top of the high-speed quad and download.

The blue runs off chair 12, Pitchfork and Overshot, are easy, nicely pitched terrain for intermediates. That's enough terrain variation to keep the runs interesting, but they are usually groomed enough for comfortable intermediate skiing. Latigo and the other blue runs below the Spruce Saddle lodge are also entertaining, because they are comfortably wide and nicely pitched but wind through the woods, and the upper portions offer spectacular views of the surrounding mountains. The wide open Larkspur and Rose Bowl have good intermediate terrain.

Centennial, which slashes down the middle of the mountain, is one of the finest advanced intermediate/advanced cruising trails in the country. (Any intermediate can ski the blue portions.) The upper and lower sections are blue (with a touch of green); the middle section is black because it has several steep spots. Between the usually well-groomed surface and the steady downward pitch (which is perhaps deceptive in that it's a shade steeper than one thinks while on it), Centennial provides a marvelous downward ride.

Stacker, the light-black run off chair 12, is a good starter. The black runs off chair 11, Loco, and Lupine are difficult and have good-sized bumps, but are wide enough in most spots for traverse out of tight spots and aren't too long. The experts frequent the longer trails in the Birds of Prey area. A fence is stuck in the middle of Peregrine, which is marked with a double diamond. The heavy-duty, knee-killing bumps are on one side; the more reasonably sized bumps are on the other. The top part of Golden Eagle, which starts off sort of in the woods, is a deeper black and the bottom section is a more open mogul field.

Insider's Tips

When everyone has moved up onto the mountain, ski the lower runs off the high-speed quad.

Take the free "Meet the Mountain" tour for an introduction to the ski area. Guides toss in a little about the history, ecology, and inner workings of a ski area. Ask for days and times.

If in doubt, ask a host or hostess for help.

Skiers can leave their ski equipment in overnight storage in the Ski Basket on the lower level of the Village Hall.

Mountain Facilities

The Village Hall is a complex at the base with restaurants and shops. Beaver Creek runs McCoy's, a large cafeteria area and a bar in the Village Hall, as well as an outdoor barbecue when weather permits. The Spruce Saddle restaurant, with its award-winning architecture, houses a cafeteria and The Rafters, a sit-down restaurant.

Snow Coverage

The average snowfall is between 300 and 350 inches at this ski area, which is normally open from before Thanksgiving to mid-April. Snowmaking covers 170 acres. There is extensive grooming, particularly on the beginners and intermediate trails.

Ski School

The **Vail/Beaver Creek Ski School** offers group and private lessons, as well as a wide range of special programs. The Step I (Skiing Technique Evaluation Program) is a free way to have a ski instructor evaluate your technique. Ask for details at the ski-school desk at Spruce Saddle or at the Village Hall. There are half-day workshops for strong intermediate and expert skiers which include videotaping and race classes. The Children's Skiing Center is based at the Village Hall. Mogul Mice is a combination of ski lessons and supervised play for toilet-trained youngsters from the ages of 3 to 6, while Super Stars is for those in that age group who want to stay out all day. Children between the ages of 6 and 12 go into all-day classes, and teens have their own grouping during peak periods.

Childcare

Infant care is available between the ages of 2 months and 18 months at the **Small World Play School** (tel. 949-5750). Call for details and reservations. Check the above Ski School section for information on programs for children 3 years old and older.

Rental Equipment

Regular, high-performance, and demo rentals are available at shops throughout Vail and Beaver Creek. Nordic rentals are available at the Beaver Creek Cross-Country Ski Center.

Cross-Country

The best cross-country trails are on McCoy Peak. Nordic skiers ride the lift up to the trailhead of 22 km (13½ miles) of groomed tracks. (The ride up is included in the track access fee.) Set tract and telemark lessons and rentals are available at the Beaver Creek Cross-Country Ski Center located at the base. A regular multiple-day lift ticket is exchangeable for a half-day cross-country lesson and equipment rental. Guided backcountry tours, including a special gourmet tour, are also offered.

WHERE TO STAY: Skiers who choose to stay in this tiny village will be in deluxe accommodations—at the minimum. Anyone who wants less luxurious (and correspondingly cheaper) lodging will have to stay in Avon, at the entrance to the valley. Of course many skiers staying in Vail, ten miles down the road, spend time on this mountain. There are regularly scheduled buses between the two resorts. Beaver Creek overnight guests are within a few walking minutes of the slopes or just a few minutes away via the resort's free shuttle system. (Because Beaver Creek is a pedestrian village, skiers must park their cars in provided spaces and use the public transit system.) For information and reservations, call **Beaver Creek/Avon Central Reservations** (303/949-5750, or toll free 800/525-2257).

The **Western Vail Valley Resort Association** (tel. 303/949-5189, or toll free 800/725-AVON, 800/292-AVON in Colorado), featuring properties in Avon and several surrounding communities, has a central reservations service. Call for information.

Most of the properties listed below are all available through central reservations. Arrivals can be any day of the week, and stays of less than seven nights are accepted in most cases, except during holiday weeks.

More Expensive

The **Centennial** (tel. 303/845-7600), just a short walk from the slopes, is centered around a four-story sun-filled atrium. The designer-decorated condominiums range from one- to three-bedroom units. All suites have a fireplace and washer/dryer. Amenities include an indoor Jacuzzi, an outdoor heated pool, and underground parking, but there is no restaurant. Rates range from $132 for a one-bedroom to $380 for a three-bedroom unit.

The **Charter** at Beaver Creek (tel. 303/949-6660) has luxurious one-, two-, and three-bedroom condo units with a European country flavor. Tudor doors with glass windowpanes frame the view, and natural woods are used throughout. Amenities include a health club with a heated pool, Jacuzzis, sauna, steamroom, and an exercise room. There are two restaurants, a casual one and a gourmet dining room, a deli, a cocktail lounge, and underground parking. Prices range from $160 for a lodge room to $490 for a three-bedroom unit.

The condos in the **Park Plaza Lodge** (tel. 303/845-7700), set in the village center just a few steps from the lifts, are very attractive. The two- and three-bedroom suites each have a hot tub in the master bedroom and fireplaces. (Many of the three-bedroom suites have two master bedrooms.) Rates range from $275 for a two-bedroom to $450 for a three-bedroom unit.

Creekside at Beaver Creek (tel. 303-949-7071) is set amid the aspen close to the Village Hall and the lifts. There are spacious two- and three-bedroom condos, with fireplaces, hot tubs, and large balconies or patios. Amenities include a Jacuzzi, indoor sauna and steamroom, and underground parking. Rates run $240 to $380.

The **Fremont House** at the Kiva (tel. 303-949-5470) promises luxury accommodations with a southwestern feel. There is ski-in/ski-out access to the one-, two-, and three-bedroom units with fireplaces and a washer/dryer. Amenities include outdoor hot tubs, a restaurant, and underground parking. Rates start at approximately $130 for a lodge room and go to $700 for a three-bedroom/three-bath unit.

Guests can walk to the lifts from the European-style **Poste Montane** lodge (tel. 303/845-7500) as well as to dining and shopping in the Village Hall. The individually decorated suites are lavish. Lodge rooms and one or two bedrooms are available. The individually decorated suites are luxurious, some have a fireplace, and the communal rooms are particularly attractive. At the base of the ski slopes, the Poste Montane houses a very popular après-ski lounge and restaurant. Amenities include robes in the room, books on the shelves, and refrigerators, and there is a sauna, Jacuzzi, and a steamroom in the lodge. Prices range approximately $160 for a lodge room to $350 for two-bedroom/three-bath suites, depending on the size.

Ridgepoint Townhouses (tel. 303/949-7150) are set on one edge of the valley, a mile and a half from the base of the mountain. In these spacious three-bedroom town homes with lofts all units have fireplaces and a washer/dryer. There is a private clubhouse with a sauna and Jacuzzi. Rates range from $265 for a three-bedroom/two-bath unit to $325 for an extra bath and more space.

There are many luxurious **private homes** and duplexes in Beaver Creek in the rental pool. They are set in the trees and along the golf course and creek. Most have spectacular views. Many have fireplaces, saunas, Jacuzzis, or Jacuzzi bathtubs. Maid service and catering is available for an additional charge. Complimentary van service to the ski slopes is available, but many of these homes are on the bus route. Rates range from $425 to $800, depending on the size of the homes; duplexes go from $350 to $700.

Moderate

The price for one of the 150 guest rooms at the **Wynfield Inn,** 0161 W. Beaver Creek Blvd., Avon, CO 81620 (tel. toll free 800/346-1551, 800/432-0348 in Florida), includes a continental breakfast, a free shuttle to the slopes, and a heated swimming pool and spa. Rooms rates go from $65. For information and reservations, contact the inn.

The **Beaver Creek West Condominiums** in Avon, P.O. Box 5920, Avon, CO 81620 (tel. 303/949-4840, or toll free 800/222-4840, 800/821-7169 in Colorado), designs custom packages for groups. there are one-, two-, and three-bedroom condominiums at this complex; plus a heated pool, sauna, and Jacuzzi. A free shuttle takes guests to the slopes. Winter rates begin at approximately $70.

Avon Center, P.O. Box 964, Avon, CO 81620 (tel. 303/949-6202, or toll free 800/441-4718 in Colorado), in the town of Avon at the entrance to Beaver Creek, offers first-class accommodations and amenities. There is a private guest exercise area and Jacuzzi spa, and several restaurants are nearby. Rates range from approximately $60 for a standard hotel room for two up to $265 for a four-bedroom unit.

Falcon Pointe Lodge, P.O. Box 2021, Avon, CO 81620 (tel. 303/949-0190, or 773-1442 in Denver), with deluxe three-bedroom condos, is also located near the entrance to Beaver Creek. Amenities include an indoor recreational facility with a swimming pool, Jacuzzi, and weight room. Prices run $80 to $300.

The **Christie Lodge,** P.O. Box 1137, Avon, CO 81620 (tel. 303/949-7700, or toll free 800/551-4326, 800/892-7980 in Colorado), is a massive resort facility, with everything from condos, a restaurant, and a swimming pool and whirlpools under one roof. The suites are tiny, but each has a fireplace and a private balcony. Rates run from $110 for a one-bedroom to $185 to a three-bedroom suite for eight.

WHERE TO EAT: The choice of restaurants in Beaver Creek is limited, but those that are available are good. The smörgåsbord of tastes in Vail is just 20 minutes down the road. There are also restaurants in Avon and other towns between the two resorts. See the Where to Eat section in Vail for a list of restaurants in the Vail valley.

More Expensive

Almost every restaurant critic who has reviewed **Mirabelle** (tel. 949-7728) has given it very high marks. Set in a lovely old ranch house once used by the former owners of the land in Beaver Creek at the entrance to the ski resort, the restaurant is decorated with turn-of-the-century furniture. The continental cuisine includes aged beef, duckling, lamb, and fish; there is a good wine list, and the service is excellent. Entrees come with a salad, but the à la carte items are tempting. Entrees range from $13.50 to $21. Reservations are recommended and credit cards aren't accepted. Dinner from 5:30 p.m.

The elegant **First Seasons** (tel. 949-6660, ext. 4506) is located in the Charter at Beaver Creek. The cuisine is continental, elk and quail are often on the menu, and the service is very personable. Entrees range from $15 to $22. It is open for dinner only, from 6 to 10 p.m., and reservations are recommended.

Moderate to Expensive

The **Legends,** in the Poste Montane (tel. 949-5540), is a popular après-ski spot and restaurant serving light American cuisine for dinner. The regular menu features steak and seafood, but the specials are good. The novel decor highlights the legends of skiing. Reservations are recommended for dinner. Lunch is 11 a.m. to 2 p.m.; dinner is from 5 p.m. Dinner entrees range from $7 to $19.

Drinkwater Park (tel. 949-5001), named after a feeding ground for elk and deer, is a popular feed and après-ski watering spot for skiers. Located right in the Village Hall at the base of the mountain, this casual restaurant's fare includes soup and sandwiches. There's a dart board and occasional live entertainment. The fare is primarily sandwiches and Mexican. Meals can run well under $10.

The **Terrace** (tel. 949-6660) in the Charter is a light, airy dining area serving breakfast, and dinner. Open from 6 a.m.

ENTERTAINMENT: The **Legends** and **Drinkwater Park** are lively après-ski spots. Someone's usually working the piano at the **Charter. McCoy's,** the bar

BEAVER CREEK 63

located in Village Hall, is usually filled with skiers snacking and drinking when the slopes close. There is usually entertainment in the evening. There's lots of action just down the highway. See Entertainment in Section 3 on Vail.

SHOPPING: The Village Hall houses several shops, including a **Sport Stalker** ski shop and the **Ski Basket** for overnight ski equipment storage and accessories. For information on the more than 100 shops and galleries in Vail, see the Shopping section on that resort.

NON-SKIER ACTIVITIES: For horse-drawn sleigh rides, call **Beaver Creek Stables** (tel. 845-7770). Explore the history of skiing at the **Colorado Ski Museum** (tel. 476-1876), at Vail Road and West Meadows Drive in Vail. It's open from noon to 5 p.m. Tuesday through Sunday. There is ice skating on Nottingham Lake (tel. 949-5280) in Avon or at Dobson Arena (tel. 476-1560) in Vail. There are several movie theaters in the area. Check the local papers to see what's playing.

GETTING THERE: Beaver Creek is located just off the exit of I-70, 110 miles west of Denver. It's ten miles down the highway from Vail. **Continental Express** (tel. toll free 800/445-0632) provides a 30-minute flight from Stapleton Airport to the Avon STOLport, one mile from the entrance of Beaver Creek. Limos and taxis meet flights on a regular basis (tel. 303/949-1000, 303/393-0653, or toll free 800/762-8548). Eagle Airport is nearby for those who want to fly their own plane.
    Trailways bus service in Denver and Grand Junction (tel. 303/476-5139 or 303/292-2291) makes frequent trips to the transportation center in Vail. From there, free shuttle service is available to Beaver Creek or you can take a taxi or limousine.
    Car-rental service is available in Denver, Avon, and Vail.

MOVING AROUND: There is a sophisticated transportation system in the Vail valley. Overnight guests bring their cars to their lodging places and park them in garages in this pedestrian-oriented village. Shuttlebuses take day skiers from the parking lot at the entrance to Beaver Creek up to the base of the ski area approximately three miles away (parking is very limited to the base area). Buses run between Vail and Beaver Creek, and between Avon and Beaver Creek regularly.

TOURIST INFORMATION: For more information or reservations contact **Beaver Creek/Avon Central Reservations** (tel. 303/949-5750, or toll free 800/525-2257). When in Beaver Creek, pick up one of Vail Associates' pocket guides, which list all sorts of information from the different ski-school class options to where to eat on the mountain.

Chapter V

COLORADO: THE CENTRAL ROCKIES AND FRONT RANGE

1. Winter Park/Mary Jane
2. SilverCreek
3. Steamboat
4. Copper Mountain
5. Keystone Resort
6. Breckenridge
7. Ski the Summit

THOSE SKI RESORTS IN THE ROCKIES within easy driving distance of the Front Range cities are as popular with Colorado skiers as they are with visitors from other states. In fact the other spaces on the lifts at Keystone's ski areas (Keystone Mountain and Arapahoe Basin), at Breckenridge, Copper, and Winter Park's areas (Mary Jane and Winter Park) are as likely to be filled by day skiers as by vacationers. Steamboat, a little too long a ride from the Front Range for day skiing, is likely to have Coloradans up "for a few days."

Steamboat has one of the highest number of skier visits in the state. Visitors are lured to the massive ski area, backed by a ski village and a neighboring town that likes vacationers, by a variety of ski terrain, a good assortment of amenities, and the kids-ski-free program. Winter Park, once considered a day area for Denverites, now has more destination visitors. The lodgings and après-ski life are increasing to reflect this.

Keystone, Breckenridge, and Copper are located at the top of the Rockies in Summit Country. All are well within (weather permitting) a two-hour drive of Denver. Keystone offers superb advanced terrain on Arapahoe Basin and North Peak, part of the Keystone Mountain complex. Of course Keystone Mountain is renowned for its intermediate and beginner terrain. Accommodations here are generally deluxe, and there's a decent amount of après-ski activity.Copper's ski runs stretch from the easy beginner terrain at one end of this ski area, which provides some of the best terrain in the state, to the expert terrain at the far end. Lodging in the village at the base is primarily in condos, although there is a hotel and this country's only Club Med. Ski town condominiums climb up the mountain toward the slopes from the old mining town of Breckenridge. There are three peaks for skiers, opening up a lot of terrain for every skill level. Après-ski hours are a busy time in this resort.

1. Winter Park / Mary Jane

THE RESORT: Winter Park isn't a classic resort where everything is within walking distance of the slopes and there are lots of options to amuse destination visitors. Rather it's two connecting ski areas, Winter Park and Mary Jane, which jointly offer an excellent variety of terrain and a small town strung along the highway that is pushing to turn itself into a ski resort. The ski areas are owned by the city of Denver, and were once considered day areas. (In fact many skiers from Denver and other cities along Colorado's Front Range never realized there was a town of Winter Park, because it was on the road past their entrances to the ski area.) However, in recent years the skier mix has flipped from more day skiers to more destination visitors, including many Front Range skiers up for long weekends. In the town of Winter Park and the surrounding region there's a fair choice of accommodations and enough restaurants so that skiers have to think about where they want to eat.

The region is poised on the edge of growth, with a proposed new ski area, "The Vasquez," behind the existing areas which, at build-out, could more than double the current skiing capacity at Winter Park and Mary Jane. Many new condominium and hotel projects (including some with proposed lifts taking skiers directly to the slopes) have been approved by the town planning board. Some are under construction and others are in the looking-for-funding stage.

Winter Park has the largest and most comprehensive program for the disabled in the world. Carefully trained instructors provide lessons each week for more than 800 children and adults who are disabled. (During the 1986–1987 ski season $10 a day covered lessons, equipment, and lift ticket; a lift ticket alone was $12.) Zephyr Village, a housing village for the disabled, is currently under design at a nearby site.

THE SKIING: Winter Park and Mary Jane, two ski areas connected via trails and lifts, make up the Winter Park Ski Resort. And last winter this ski resort opened up the largest expansion in the Rockies: 33 new trails, some on the back side of Mary Jane and the rest on the new Vasquez Ridge at the far end of the ski area. These two ski areas complement each other: Winter Park is strong on the blue and green trails while Mary Jane is primarily blue, blue/black, and black terrain. Terrain at Winter Park is rated 32% beginner, 54% intermediate, and 14% advanced. Terrain at Mary Jane is 6% beginner, 38% intermediate, and 56% advanced/expert. There are 96 designated trails on 1,100 acres of terrain, plus guided bowl skiing at this resort. The vertical drop from the top of Mary Jane to the base of Winter Park is 2,220 feet. Twelve double, three triple, and three quad chairs open up the terrain. Because of the way the trails are laid out, the runs seem longer than one would expect with that vertical.

Winter Park has the terrain needed for beginners and all levels of intermediate to ski comfortably and progress rapidly. Advanced intermediates can explore the majority of this mountain.

Apollo Flats is a mid-mountain beginner's area for safer learning. Novices can also head up the Arrow lift and meander down Parkway or the Gnome Forest, gentle green runs. The next step is up to the top via the speedy Zephyr lift (which virtually eliminates lines from the bottom) to test March Hare, Allan Phipps, and other green runs on the far side of the mountain. The Lonesome Whistle trail, a long gentle run from the top of the Mary Jane lift following the ski area boundary back to Winter Park, provides spectacular wilderness views and few skiers. (The trail is relatively new and many skiers aren't aware it exists.)

Low intermediates should feel comfortable and all intermediates should enjoy the open, nicely pitched trails such as Cranmer, Jabberwocky, and White Rabbit around the Olympia chair. Nearby Cheshire Cat is marked blue/black because of a few steeper pitches and occasional bumps. Skiers who want to explore the black runs might start on Over N' Underwood or Engeldive, shorter black runs around the Prospector lift. They are less trafficked than Bradley's Bash, a blue/black slope, and Balch—probably the most popular advanced runs here. Bradley's Bash is blue when groomed, black when bumped up and slick from too many skiers learning how to hold an edge. Balch usually has large bumps and lots of skiers who are learning how to handle them. The blue/black Hughes under the Zephry lift is probably the longest advanced run on the mountain. Little Pierre and Mulligan's mile are interesting black runs off Hughes.

Skiers who want to explore Mary Jane can park at the base of that area or ski over. Retta's Run, a narrow bump run, might be the most difficult trail on this side of the complex.

The trails on the new Vasquez Ridge, accessed by a high-speed squad, are primarily lower intermediate with long run-outs. (If plans went as expected, the machines worked overtime last summer regrading the terrain on the run-out to make it steeper.) There are two short advanced runs, also with long run-outs back to the chair.

Skiers who want to explore Mary Jane can park at the base of that area or ski over. With the addition of key lifts in recent years, it's easy cruising between the two ski areas. (Just follow signs or read the trail maps; there are several ways to do it.) The easiest way for intermediate skiers is to take the Zephyr lift, then follow signs to the Olympia lift or take the High Lonesome lift to the top of Mary Jane. Advanced skiers into bumps can take Outhouse (185-cm or long skis only) or Drunken Frenchman, the fastest routes to the "Jane." There's also a third way over to the Jane via a long traverse that starts on the far side of Outhouse and cuts through the woods. The entrance isn't very obvious, but locals have created this route because it cuts off the need to take an extra chair lift.

One instructor who has been teaching at the Jane for years has an intriguing description for it. To paraphrase his words: It's kind of like a spouse—always changing. Another simply says: "It's unpredictable." the terrain ranges from intermediate to expert. Because it's so variable, skiers tend to take different paths when they repeat the more difficult slopes so the surface may be bumped up differently from week to week.

There's a beginner's slope sidling sideways across the base of Mary Jane, serviced by a free chair. Never-evers should get good instruction on this terrain —and possibly fewer classmates because the majority are learning at Winter Park.

There are lots of ways to meet the Jane. Intermediates should just head up the Pony Express lift, then take the Arrowhead Loop for a starter, and then move on to the Mary Jane trail, Rainbow, or Gandy Dancer.

The majority of the trails here are moguled, but there is a sort-of pecking order for skiers who want to work their way up to the toughest stuff. The ski instructors here have one or two routes that they use to introduce skiers to the varying terrain and gentle bumps. Start on the Pony Express lift, go across the trail to the open cut that takes skiers to the lower part of Golden Spike, and cut back through the trees to Arrowhead Loop. Head across that trail toward Rainbow Cut, but take the open glade between the two runs, which is called Rainbow Island.

Depending on the grooming, Sleeper, Gandy Dancer, or Narrow Gauges should have gentle easy practice bumps. The next step up could be the rock Garden (but you'll have to ask a local how to get there), the upper part of Arrowhead Loop, and sections of Golden Way. Sterling Way is popular, and the moguls in the center are often the easiest and most fun to ski. (Most skiers tend to head to either side of that trail and push up bigger, more uneven bumps).

Riflesight Notch, with a double fall line in some spots, and Drunken Frenchman usually have heavy-duty bumps where skiers can discover just how experienced they've become. The runs off the Challenger lift, including Derailler and Railbender, tend to have the shortest, choppiest moguls. Experts should know that Needle's Eye is generally awarded the honor of being the consistently roughest run on the mountain.

The back side of Mary Jane has several black runs, and open glade skiing at the top accessing a few blue runs which end at a very long run-out which brings you all the way back around to the front of the mountain. The new black runs include four steep chutes (experts only) off Derailler (on the front side), and several other interesting, but short, definitely advanced runs. Try the blue runs first, then check out the condition and steepness of the black runs, looking up from the run-out, before trying them.

Weather permitting, there is skiing in Parsen Bowl, one section of the proposed Vasquez ski expansion. Skiers are ferried by snowcats. Ask for details at the ski school or information desks.

Insider's Tips

If heading back from the far side of Winter Park (the top of the Olympia lift) at the end of the day, always hang a right when in doubt at trail intersections. The Cranmer cutoff, which takes skiers back toward the base area, is a wide road cutting across other slopes. Inevitably one skier in a group schusses straight down and must take an extra chair-lift ride to get back up to where he/she can veer toward the base lodge.

Skiers planning to spend the day on Mary Jane can park in the Utah Junction parking area and pick up their lift tickets at the base of the Challenger lift.

Take an espresso or mocha and croissant break at the Coffee and Tea Market in the Balcony House at the base of Winter Park. This tiny restuarant also serves quiche and croissant sandwiches for lunch.

Courtesy patrol members wear red uniforms marked host or hostess. They're ready to answer questions or handle problems.

Mountain Facilities

There's a cafeteria, retail shops, and ski rentals in the West Portal Station at the base of Winter Park. Ticket sales, the ski school, the emergency medical facility, and the Coffee and Tea Market are in the neighboring Balcony House. There's a mid-mountain cafeteria and pizza parlor at Snoasis. (Order on the pizza hotline phone at the top of the Zephyr lift, and it will be ready when you ski down.)

The Mary Jane Center houses a cafeteria; the Club Car, which is a sit-down restaurant open for breakfast and lunch; Pepperoni's Pizza Parlor and Sports Bar; ski school; and shops.

Snow Coverage

Snowmaking covers 22% of the mountainside, assuring a pre-Thanksgiving opening. Normally the area is open from mid-November through late April. The trails on Winter Park are groomed frequently. The blue trails at Mary Jane are groomed regularly.

Ski School

There are ski schools at the base of both areas. Group lessons several times each day and private lessons are available. Never-ever packages and NASTAR race clinics are offered. The "Jane Gang" ski school offers Ski Blast weekend workshops where advanced intermediate and expert skiers can work on the steep and deep. One-stop service for children's ski school is available in the new Children's Center, located adjacent to West Portal Station, for families with youngsters ages 3 to 13. Ski Penquins is for 3- and 4-year-olds, Ski Scouts is for 5- to 7-year-olds, and Ski Rangers is for children ages 8 to 13. Each child leaves ski school with a written progress report—very handy when moving on to another area where the new teacher wants to know how Ben or Rachel skis. Children's ski rentals, for a very reasonable fee, are available at the center.

Childcare

The new Children's Center has separate, well-staffed, and toy-stocked spacious playrooms and rest rooms for different age groups between 1 and 8. Sleeping infants have a special area which includes a quiet crib room. Advance reservations are necessary (tel. 303/726-5514).

Rental Equipment

Rentals are available at both the Mary Jane and Winter Park base lodges. Several shops in town rent equipment.

Cross-Country Skiing

There are telemarking clinics at the ski area but there are no cross-country trails. There are several operations close by. **Beaver Village** (tel. 726-8409) has 25 km (15 miles) of groomed trails, rentals, instruction, and moonlight tours. The **Experimental Forest Ranger Station** has miles of marked trails for all levels. (Ask a local for directions.) **Ski Idlewild** (tel. 726-5564) has 30 km (18 miles) of marked trails. **C Lazy U Ranch** has miles of groomed trails and runs backcountry tours, both open only for guests at the ranch. See the discussion of the C Lazy U in the Where to Stay for more information.

WHERE TO STAY: Condominiums, mountain inns or lodges with meal plans, motels, and lock-off bedrooms are the main choices for skiers staying overnight in the Winter Park area. Although the majority of accommodations are in older complexes, Winter Park is in a building mode, so ask central reservations about new lodging that has come on line in recent months. For the most current information on lodging and ski packages in Winter Park, contact **Winter Park Central Reservations**, P.O. Box 36, Winter Park, CO 80482 (tel. 303/726-5587, or 447-0588 in Denver, or toll free 800/453-2525). Central Reservations represents approximately 40 lodges and condo complexes, most on the free shuttlebus system or with their own shuttle vans. Lodging at most of the following places can be arranged through central reservations.

More Expensive

The luxurious **Iron Horse**, P.O. Box 1286, Winter Park, CO 80482 (tel. 303/726-8851), a condo/hotel set between the Winter Park and the Mary Jane slopes, is a ski-in/ski-out facility on the mountain. The units, with fireplaces, are decorated attractively but are small. There's a swimming pool, whirlpool, lounge, and restaurant. However, guests must drive to the local nightspots and other restaurants (there is van service). Prices range from $80 for a lodge room to $265 for a two-bedroom/three-bath unit.

The **Vintage at Winter Park**, P.O. Box 1369, Winter Park, Co 80482 (tel. 303/726-8801, or toll free 800/472-7017 outside Colorado), adjacent to the Winter Park base area, is a full-service resort hotel with restaurant, bar, exercise room, and whirlpool. Units range from $79 for a studio to $250 for two-bedroom suites with kitchenette, TV, and phone. There is free shuttle service to the slopes and town.

C Lazy U Ranch, P.O. Box 378B, Granby, CO 80446 (tel. 303/887-3344), is an isolated AAA five-diamond and Mobil five-star-rated guest ranch 25 miles away, where the emphasis during winter is in on cross-country skiing, but there is courtesy transportation for guests who want to spend the day at Winter Park. Guests stay in comfortable one- to three-bedroom units, and meals are eaten in the dining room in the main lodge. Amenities include superb service, fresh fruit in the rooms daily, and racquetball court, whirlpool, and sauna. See the Cross-Country section for details on Nordic skiing. There's supervision for youngsters 3 to 12 during Christmas only. Christmas and many weekends book up early. Daily rate for a three-night minimum averages $110 to $160 per person, double occupancy. The rate includes room, meals, cross-country skiing, equipment and instruction, and more.

Moderate to More Expensive

Meadowridge, P.O. Box 203, Winter Park, CO 80482 (tel. 303/726-9411, or toll free 800/525-6418), is a resort community, designed in mountain-style architecture, with one- to three-bedroom condominiums located ten minutes from the ski area. Amenities include a heated swimming pool, hot tubs, and sauna, racquetball courts in the clubhouse, and an attractive restaurant and bar. There's a full-service sport shop on the premises. Prices range from $60 to $110 for a one-bedroom to $125 to $200 for a three-bedroom unit.

The **High Country Haus**, P.O. Box 3095, Winter Park, CO 80482 (tel. 303/726-9421, or toll free 800/228-1025), has older but comfortable studio to three-bedroom condos with moss rock fireplaces in several buildings set back on a side road off U.S. 40 but within walking distance of shops and restaurants. There's a heated swimming pool and whirlpools in a glass structure, as well as a recreation center with Ping-Pong tables, pool tables, and video games. The village is on the public shuttlebus route. Units range from $70 for a studio to $288 for a three-bedroom/two-bath unit per night.

The **Snowblaze Atheltic Club and Condominiums**, P.O. Box 377, Winter Park, CO 80482 (tel. 303/726-5701, or toll free 800/525-2466 outside Colorado), includes comfortable studios to three-bedroom units. All units have microwaves, and the two- and three-bedroom units have fireplaces and saunas. The athletic club has racquetball/handball courts, an indoor pool, hot tubs, steambaths, and an exercise room. Snowblaze runs a shuttlebus to the area. Units range in price, per night, from $65 for two and $120 for four people in a two-bedroom to $180 for six people in a three-bedroom. The prices decrease per night for longer stays.

The units at the **Winter Park Tennis Club**, P.O. Box 377, Winter Park, CO 80482 (tel. 303/726-9703), located in Frasier, ten minutes from the ski area, are extremely spacious and nicely decorated. There are moss rock fireplaces in the living rooms and additional fireplaces and saunas in some larger units. The biggest units feature one-bedroom apartments on a separate floor. There's an indoor pool, Jacuzzi, public sauna, and game room. The complex is on the public shuttlebus route. Units range from $50 for a one-bedroom to $240 for a three-bedroom/3½-bath during regular season, and the minimum stay is two nights.

Less Expensive

Beaver Village Condominiums, P.O. Box 3154, Winter Park, CO 80482 (tel. 303/726-8813, or toll free 800/525-3304 outside Colorado). There are comfortable condominiums which range in size from lock-off rooms to four-bedroom units, and guests can use the pool, sauna, and whirlpool in the clubhouse. There's shuttle service to the ski area. Prices vary from $140 for a one-bedroom up to $350 for a four-bedroom. It's a popular place for groups and rates vary according to the size of the group. Call for quotes.

Arapahoe Ski Lodge, P.O. Box 44, Winter Park, CO 80482 (tel. 303/726-8222), is a cheerful, rustic place to stay. There are 14 private rooms with baths, an attractive bar/lounge, a recreation room, and an indoor spa and sauna at this lodge located on U.S. 40 in town. The daily rate per adult is $55 to $60 for a double, and the price includes lodging, dinner, and breakfast, plus transportation to the ski area.

WHERE TO EAT: Every taste from northern Italian and Swiss to subs and stews can be found in this region. The restaurants are spread out, so transportation is necessary, either by private car, public shuttlebus, or local taxi.

More Expensive

Crystal, fine linen, excellent service, and classical music are all part of the fine dining experience at the **Hideaway Ltd.,** located behind Hernando's Pizza Pub on U.S. 40 (tel. 726-9921). Meals feature carefully prepared continental dishes and good wines. Reservations are requested.

Moderate to More Expensive

Tasty German food is featured at **Gasthaus Eichler,** in a new lodge on U.S. 40 (tel. 726-5133). Wienerschnitzel, rouladen, and other German dishes, as well as American fare, can be followed by strudel or Black Forest cake and coffee. Entrees range from $12 to $22. The restaurant is open from 5:30 p.m. daily.

Fine dining, lively entertainment, and light meals and a raw bar are all available at the **Slope,** a large A-frame just down the road from the Winter Park's base (tel. 726-5727). The towering lounge with a large glass wall overlooks the slopes and holds a dance floor. Skiers in the Alcove dining area overlooking the dance floor can munch on New York–style pizzas or sandwiches, in the $4 to $6 range. A quiet corner of the building houses Expectations, with its brass and greenery, where diners can enjoy a more leisurely meal. Prices for entrees on the international menu, which includes such dishes as New Zealand lamb and seafood, range from $11 to $18 Reservations are suggested for Expectations, which is open from 6 to 11 p.m nightly. Alcove dining is from 2 p.m. to midnight. The Mary Jane Lounge is open from 2 p.m. to 2 a.m. daily, and there is live entertainment from 9:30 p.m. to closing Tuesday through Saturday.

The dining rooms at the **Shed,** on U.S. 40 in town (tel. 726-9912), are usually full on weekends. The fare at this casual restaurant includes basic, well-prepared beef and Mexican specialities. Dinner hours are 5 to 10 p.m. Burgers with trimmings go for $6, Mexican food is in the $7 to $8 range, and complete dinners go for $8 to $15.

There's authentic Swiss cuisine and American fare at the **Swiss Chalet,** on U.S. 40 in town (tel. 726-5402), where guests sit around booths and tables with

WINTER PARK / MARY JANE

checkered cloths. Fondues, quail, duckling, steaks, and lighter meals, including beef stew and fried chicken, are on the menu. There's a children's menu. Prices range from $7 to $13 at the Swiss Chalet, which is open from 5:30 to 10 p.m.

Northern Italian specialties are on the tables at the **Carousel,** located in Cooper Creek Square (tel. 726-4900), a casual but sleekly designed restaurant with its blend of green tones and brass. Pastas average $9 and entrees, including veal and steaks, go for $12.50 to $16. A children's menu is available; dinner is served Tuesday through Sunday from 5 to 10 p.m.

Deno's Swiss House and Coachman's Tavern, on U.S. 40 in town (tel. 726-5332), is a popular local spot. Steak, prime rib, and barbecue are the main items on the menu at this casual restaurant. The bar menu is $5 to $8 and entrees go from $9 to $21. There are TVs in the bar tuned to sporting events. Hours are 11 a.m. to 2 a.m. daily.

Less Expensive

Alcove dining at the **Slope** (see listing above) features New York–style pizza and sandwiches in the $4 to $6 range.

The line of skiers wanting pastry and coffee before heading to the slopes stretches through the front door at **Carver's Bakery,** on Vasquez Road next to Cooper Creek Square (tel. 726-8202), many mornings. The inside tables are filled with skiers preferring a sit-down breakfast ranging from eggs Benedict to french toast. Breakfasts go for $2 to $5 at Carver's, which opens at 6 a.m.

Pizza, spaghetti, sandwiches, and soup are served in the casual **Hernando's Pizza Pub,** located on U.S. 40 in town (tel. 726-5409). Sandwiches and pasta cost approximately $4, and pizzas begin at $6. Beer and wine are available. Hours are 4:30 to 11 p.m. daily.

The Mexican breakfasts—egg burrito or huevos rancheros—at **The Kitchen,** located in town (tel. 726-9940), will fill you up for the day. More conventional breakfasts are also available at this restaurant, where meals range from $2.75 to $5.50. Breakfast is served from 7 a.m. to 12:30 p.m.

ENTERTAINMENT: The **Slope,** on Old Winter Park Drive (tel. 726-5727), rocks both during the après-ski happy hour and later in the evening most nights. There may be a cover charge in the evening. The **Stampede,** in Cooper Creek Square (tel. 726-9433), a cavernous space with a dance floor, also has an après-ski happy hour and live entertainment many nights. The Stampede opens at 2 p.m. daily. The **Silver Screen Cinema** (tel. 726-5390) has two shows nightly.

SHOPPING: **Cooper Creek Square** has a variety of shops geared for vacationers. Choices range from a gallery to a **SportStalker ski shop** and the **Great Divide Trading Co.,** which specializes in fur and leather products. There are several small shopping plazas strung along U.S. 40.

NON-SKIER ACTIVITIES: Tubing provides a lot of laughter and some thrills. **Fraser Valley Winter Sports** (tel. 726-5954) maintains tubing hills where visitors can slide down on their rented innertubes then hitch a ride uphill on a tow for yet another slide down. There's **ice skating** in the center of the town of Winter Park (tel. 726-8334), at **Beaver Village** (tel. 726-5741), and at **Meadow Ridge** (tel. 726-9401). For information about sleigh rides, call 726-5587. **Meadow Ridge Resort** (tel. 726-9401) arranges slosh wicking (call for an explanation) and runs sleigh rides during the day and in the evening to a backcountry tent camp for chuckwagon dinners. **Snowmobilers** can explore the surroundings mountainsides. For information call 726-5587. Non-skiers can see the slopes on tours of the mountain via heated, enclosed **snowcats.** For more information, call 726-5514.

GETTING THERE: Winter Park is located 67 miles northeast of Denver via I-70 and U.S. 40 (exit 232). There is no airport at Winter Park; skiers must fly into Stapleton International Airport in Denver and proceed by rental car or bus. There are more than a dozen direct buses to Winter Park daily. The Winter Park Express (**Gray Line**) departs several times daily and **Trailways** twice daily. Call **Central Reservations** (tel. 303/726-5587) for schedules and information. Most major car-rental companies are located at Stapleton, including **National Rental Cars** (tel. toll free 800/525-5225, 800/332-0530 in Colorado), **General Rent-a-Car** (tel. 303/320-1244, or toll free 800/525-2408 outside Colorado), or **Ajax Rent-a-Car** (tel. 303/726-5408 or 303/320-8361). **Enterprise Rent-A-Cars** (tel. 303/726-1121, or toll free 800/325-8007) can be picked up at Stapleton. There is daily **Amtrak** service (tel. toll free 800/USA-RAIL) from Chicago and San Francisco. The stop is in Frazer just a few miles from the ski area. Buses meet the train.

The **ski train** continues to roll on weekends from Union Station in Denver to the resort. The train leaves at 7:30 a.m. and drops skiers off at 9:30 a.m. at the foot of the slopes. The return trip starts at 4 p.m. Cost is approximately $20 round trip. For reservations, call Select-A-Seat (tel. 303/778-6691).

MOVING AROUND: Free shuttlebuses make a loop between Winter Park, Mary Jane, and many of the condominiums and lodges approximately every 20 minutes. Many lodges have private shuttle vans for guests. Because the lodgings, restaurants, and shops are spread out along the highway and back roads, the fastest way around is via private car. However, parking at the ski areas is spread out, so arrive early on weekends or take the shuttles. The **Home James Taxi Service** (tel. 726-5060) is a local taxi operation which also has limousine and charter service.

TOURIST INFORMATION: Winter Park Central Reservations (tel. 303/726-5587, or toll free 800/453-2525) handles lodging and ski packages for more than 40 lodges, inns, and condominium complexes. For more information about Winter Park contact P.O. Box 36, Winter Park, CO 80482 (tel. 303/726-5514, or 892-0961 in Denver).

The emergency numbers are 726-5391 for **fire,** and 726-5666 for **police, sheriff,** and **ambulance.**

2. SilverCreek

THE RESORT: SilverCreek is an all-season real estate venture, and the skiing is the cold-weather amenity for condo owners and skiers staying in the Inn at SilverCreek, other condo complexes, or private homes in the area. SilverCreek is basically a beginner/intermediate area where youngsters can have some freedom because the area is small. Many skiers staying here take the shuttle to nearby Winter Park.

THE SKIING: Youngsters think "it's a great cruising area and a place where skiers can practice." Two triples and two douple chairs and a poma open up 21 trails on the 982-foot-vertical mountain. Terrain is rated 30% beginner, 50% intermediate, and 20% advanced. However, the advanced slopes are relatively short and would be rated blue/black—at best—at most resorts in the Rockies. There is night skiing on Friday and Saturday.

The majority of blue and green runs are off the Expedition lift, and the ones that bell out, including Buckhorn and Double Dealer to King of Clubs, provide surprisingly long rides for the vertical. The blue runs off the Summit lift, installed last winter, are the longest at the area. The black runs, including Widowmaker off the Conquest lift, have steep pitches varying with flatter sections.

Insider's Tips

Ask if there are any mouse races in the Secret Saloon. They're only held a few times each winter, but are definitely worth watching.

Mountain Facilities

The base lodge has a cafeteria with unusually good food (and "just out of the oven" pastries), ski school, ski shop, ski rentals, and the Secret Saloon, a lounge on the top floor.

Snow Coverage

Snowmaking covers 55% of the area at SilverCreek, which is normally open from late November to early April. Because of where the area is sited, snowmaking is a necessity during parts of the season. Because there is often a lot of man-made snow mixed with the natural, at times SilverCreek's surface may be close to New England conditions. However, management here well understands the art of grooming.

Ski School

The ski school offers group and private lessons.

Childcare

The childcare center has a play area and a quiet room with glass windows so sleeping youngsters can be watched. The center is for children between the ages of 3 months and 7 years old. Reservations (tel. 303/887-3384, ext 33, or 449-7430, ext. 33, in Denver) are required at least 24 hours in advance.

Rental Equipment

Both alpine and Nordic equipment can be rented at the base lodge.

Cross-Country

Nordic skiers have 25 km (15 miles) of trail reachable from the tops of the Expedition and Milestone lifts. The track fee includes lift rides to each trailhead. Cross-country and telemark lessons are available.

WHERE TO STAY: Skiers can stay in the **Inn at SilverCreek**, P.O. Box 4001, SilverCreek, CO 80446 (tel. toll free 800/526-0590), a large condo/hotel in the valley just a five-minute free shuttlebus ride from the ski area. The lodging rates are inexpensive and the condo units are attractive. However, skiers are constantly taken aback by such items as plastic plates and silverware in the kitchenette area and a charge for wood beyond the first bundle (which didn't have enough to make a fire). The inn has a complete health club with Jacuzzis and a heated outdoor pool. There's a casual dining area and a more formal dining room. Skiers can take a shuttle to Winter Park, 20 minutes away. The per-night price (which includes two adult lift tickets) for a room with a queen-size bed is $59.

Several condominium complexes, including some ski-in/ski-out properties, are also in the rental pool. Call central reservations for prices.

GETTING THERE: From Denver's Stapleton Airport, take one of the **Trail-**

ways (tel. 303/595-9213) twice-daily trips, or **Carey American Limousine** (tel. 303/393-0563), which leaves the airport four times daily.

If you are driving, go 79 miles west of Denver on U.S. 40, 15 miles past Winter Park.

The **Amtrak** (tel. 800/USA-RAIL) *California Zephyr* stops in Fraser daily. There is a small airport nearby for private planes.

GETTING AROUND: The **SilverCreek Shuttle**, which is free, operates within the resort area. There is daily transportation to Winter Park for a reasonable fee.

TOURIST INFORMATION: For information and lodging reservations, contact **SilverCreek Central Reservations and Management, Inc.**, P.O. Box 4001, SilverCreek, CO 80446 (tel. 303/887-2131, or toll free 800/526-0590).

3. Steamboat

THE RESORT: In spite of the condo creep around the edges of Steamboat's ski slopes, the atmosphere is still low-key, and skiers locked in the gondola together tend to chat. The lift operators usually sport a grin under their cowboy hats, and Bill Kidd, former Olympian and Steamboat's director of skiing, still meets with John Q. Skiers and families for a 1 p.m. run down the mountain whenever he's in town. The four peaks on Mount Werner are convoluted enough to keep skiers entertained. There are crusing trails for every skill level, lots of variable terrain, some highly moguled surfaces, steeps (although no super-steeps), and superb tree skiing for advanced and expert skiers.

Steamboat is actually a two-part resort. There's a vacation village wrapped around the base and the sides of the skiable mountain with enough action that many skiers never stray into town. The town of Steamboat Springs, a few miles down the road, built and still occupied by ranchers, miners, and small-town folks, also has its share of hotels, motels, trendy shops, and restaurants where locals and vacationers mix. Singles, couples, and ski groups have always vacationed here, but with the kids stay-free/ski-free program in recent years, the skier statistics are now skewed toward families. Contact central reservations for specific details, but loosely, the kids-ski-free program allows children 12 and under to ski free with parents who purchase a five- or six-day lift ticket and are staying a minimum of five nights at any participating lodging property. (Most properties in the area are involved.) Children also get ski rentals when parents rent skis for the same period of time.

THE SKIING: Knowing your way around this mountain helps, because there's a lot of good skiing spread out over 2,500 acres, but it's not always obvious how to get from one peak to another. The terrain on Mount Werner with its 3,600-foot-vertical drop is rated 15% easiest, 54% more difficult and 31% difficult. Twenty lifts, an eight-passenger gondola, a quad chair, seven triples, nine doubles, and two ski-school lifts open up the mountain.

Never-evers learn at the very base of the mountain. Beginners have a wide, open slope just above the base lodge and a few narrower but very gentle cat track/trails off the Christie II and Christie III lifts. Why Not is a winding green run that starts at the top of the gondola and feeds into Right of Way, another green run that doubles as the run-out for that side of the mountain.

Even shaky intermediates can ride up the gondola, take Spur Run down to the Priest Creek or Sundown chairs, then ride up and ski the Sunshine bowl area. This broad, gentle 400-acre section has several easy runs. Tomahawk has some interesting terrain variation (for intermediates) at the top, then becomes a very long, very gently sloped trail that ends at the short South Peak chair.

The blue runs off the Priest Creek and the Sundown chairs are a little steeper, but wide and generally well groomed. High Noon is particularly popular with its long, constant pitch. One O'Clock and Two O'Clock are shorter but as good. Other popular intermediate runs include Buddy's Run, Tornado Lane, Ego, and Rainbow, all off various chairs on Storm Peak. Wide, usually groomed carpet-smooth Heavenly Daze, under the gondola, has a steady but not-too-steep downward pitch that makes it one of the best cruising runs in the state.

If sampling black runs for the first time, try See Me and VooDoo on the bottom of the mountain. Then move onto Ted's Ridge and/or Vertigo, especially if they have just been groomed. Nearby Concentration can be very bumpy. There's a good variety of black runs off the Four Points and Storm Peak chairs, and conditions will vary because many of the runs are groomed regularly, then skiers rebuild the bumps. Hurricane, Twister, Tornado, and Cyclone are among the most popular here.

The runs in the Priest Creek area range from high-level cruising on steep but often-groomed Rolex, to midlevel bumps on Three O'Clock up to heavy-duty moguls on the Sundown Lift Line. The bumps can also get very high on White Out off the Burgess chair.

The Shadows and The Closet on the far side of the Sundown chair are where you'll find the locals. These treed areas, with occasional open spaces, are prime powder skiing after storms, then the more open (that means several feet between trees versus touching distance) sections build moguls until the next big storm. Generally the trees are tighter as you move closer to the Storm Peak area. (These runs can be reached from the top of the Sundown or the Storm Peak chairs.) There is a breakout track halfway down for anyone with tired legs.

Insider's Tips

If the gondola line is too long in the morning, take Southface lift or Headwall to Christie II or Christie III; then take Main Drag, a green cat track, over to the Arrowhead or Thunderhead lifts. Once on the mountain, there are so many chairs at Steamboat that the crowd usually thins out. Check the lift-status signs, which give the waiting time at various chairs, before heading over to a different part of the mountain. Study the trail map so you'll know where there are two lifts heading to the same spot (such as Priest Creek and Sundown) or when you can ski past a long lift line just a few hundred yards down the slope to another chair, which may open up many of the same or at least similar runs.

To make first tracks, ride the gondola at 8:15 a.m. and have breakfast at the Thunderhead facility, and be ready to go when the mountain opens at 9 a.m.

When it's cold and windy, head into Ragnar's, the sit-down restaurant in the Rendezvous Saddle mid-mountain lodge, or Hazie's in the Thunderbird Facility for a 1½-hour leisurely dining experience. (Make reservations.)

Management places a strong emphasis on friendliness and helpfulness to paying skiers. If you need help finding your way to a particular run, just ask anyone with a Steamboat cowboy hat or insignia on their clothing.

If you're the type to wrap your vacation around a wacky event, consider the Cowboy Downhill held during the week in January when Denver holds its annual stock show. Bronco busters and rodeo stars are flown to Steamboat for the day, locked into skis, then put on a downhill course. First the chaps-clad cowboys push around gates, then rope a ski hostess, saddle a horse, and ski across the finish line. Definitely a people-watcher's event.

Mountain Facilities

There's a complex of shops at the base of the gondola with everything from a retail (with rentals) ski shop to restaurants. Mid-mountain facilities at the Thunderhead, at the top of the gondola, include a cafeteria, Stoker's Bar with casual sit-down service, a sundeck barbecue, and Hazie's (tel. 879-6111) for more elegant lunchtime dining. (Hazie's is also open for special dinners several times during the winter. Ask for details.) There's a shop for quick ski repairs while you eat. Rendezvous Saddle, on High Noon at the top of the South Peak chair, houses a cafeteria and Ragnar's (tel. 879-6111), another fine sit-down restaurant with an imaginative menu. Reservations are suggested for both Hazie's and Ragnar's.

Snow Coverage

The annual snowfall is 27 feet at this ski area, which is normally open from the third week in November to mid-April. From the top of the gondola down to the base, 293 acres of skiable terrain are covered with snowmaking. The beginner and intermediate slopes are groomed continually. Some advanced runs are groomed occasionally.

Ski School

Group and private lessons are offered daily. The special ski-school programs inclued the Mount Werner Challenge, a two-day intensive program for advanced and expert skiers, two-hour experts-only classes, all-day bump classes, and early-morning powder clinics—the day after the weather person reports six or more inches of new snow! There are classes for older children and the Kiddie Corral is for youngsters ages 3 to 5. Former Olympian and Steamboat Director of Skiing Billy Kidd runs three- and six-day recreational racing camps several times a year. For information, call 303/879-6111.

Childcare

Children between the ages of 6 months and 6 years can go into the nursery (downstairs in the gondola building) for half or full days. Youngsters between the ages of 3 and 5 can go into the Kiddie Corral for a half day of lessons or a full day that includes lessons and lunch.

Ask locally for a copy of the *SKIDs* newsletter, which details activities for youngsters and teenagers. the **Skids Club**, located in Gondola Square (tel. 879-4379), is open for the 18-and-under crowd from 2 to 7 p.m. daily. They can dine at the pizza bar, watch the large-screen TV, or play video games.

Rental Equipment

Ski rentals are available at several shops including the Sport Stalker in Gondola Square at the base of the mountain, and at the Inside Edge Sports store in the Ptarmigan Inn at the base or at the store in downtown Steamboat Springs. Also at the Ski Haus, located both in the Storm Meadow complex on the mountain and on U.S. 40, Terry Sports in the Torian Plum Plaza, and at Werner's Storm Hut in Gondola Square.

Cross-Country Skiing

Miles of groomed trails are available at the **Steamboat Touring Center** (tel. 303/879-8180). Steamboat is centered in thousands of acres of national forest land so the possibilites for Nordic skiers are unlimited. Touring and telemarking on Rabbit Ears Pass are very popular. The Hogan Park trail is a local favorite. Call the **Chamber Resort Association** (tel. 303/879-0880) for a full list of certified guides and instructors. There are several ranches in the region that cater to cross-country skiers. (See, for example, Vista Verde under Where to Stay.)

Snowcat Skiing

Skier can explore the powder up near the Continental Divide via snowcat. For more information, contact **Steamboat Powder Cats**, P.O. Box 2468, Steamboat Springs, CO 80477 (tel. 303/879-5188). This operation is not connected with the ski area.

WHERE TO STAY: There's plenty of lodging at the base and strung alongside the mountain. Some skiers prefer to stay in the town of Steamboat Springs, a few miles down the road. For reservations and information about lodging at this resort, contact the **Steamboat Springs Chamber Resort Association**, P.O. Box 774408, Steamboat Springs, CO 80477 (tel. 303/879-0470, or toll free 800/332-3204 in Colorado).

More Expensive

Skiers who've stayed at the condo/hotel, the **Torian Plum**, 1855 Ski Time Square Dr., Steamboat Springs, CO 80487 (tel. toll free 800/228-2458, 800/824-5161 in Colorado), praise the spacious condos with overstuffed furniture in the living rooms and brass decorations and fixtures. Every unit has a fireplce, microwave, and whirlpool bath. Located by the base of the ski area, it's where ski school gathers—right outside the door. There's a concierge, pool, hot tubs, and sauna. Prices range from $250 for a one-bedroom to $390 for a three-bedroom condo.

Château Chamonix, 2340 Après Ski Way, Steamboat Springs, CO 80487 (tel. 303/879-7511), has attractively decorated deluxe slopeside condos. There are fireplaces and a spa bath in each unit, a heated swimming pool, an outdoor Jacuzzi, and daily maid service. Rates range from $250 for a two-bedroom to $350 for a three-bedroom unit.

You can ski in and ski out of the **Dulany**, P.O. Box 2995, Steamboat Springs, CO 80477 (tel. 303/879-7900, or toll free 800/332-5533, 800/525-5502), with its 25 privately owned, two- and three-bedroom condominiums. Each unit has a fireplace and there is also a courtyard hot tub. Prices run $200 to $400.

The **Bear Claw**, P.O. Box 774928, Steamboat Village, CO 80477 (tel. 303/879-6100), is by the top of the beginner's lift, so you can step out your back door for your first run. Units have private balconies, fireplaces, and fully equipped kitchens, plus a swimming pool, hot tub, sauna, Jacuzzi, and game room. Rates run $210 to $390.

Moderate

The contemporary **Timber Run** (tel. 303/879-7000, or toll free 800/332-5533, 800/525-5502 in Colardo), condos have an outdoor heated swimming pool, sauna, and three outdoor hot tubs. This newer facility has one-, two-, and three-bedroom/loft accommodations that run $155 to $375. Shuttle service is available to the lifts.

The **West** (tel. 303/879-4000, or toll free 800/332-5533, 800/525-5502 in Colorado) condos are a private walkway away from the gondola. Units range from studios to four-bedroom condominiums with fireplaces and fully equipped kitchens, and there is an outdoor heated pool and two hot tubs. Rates range from $90 to $260 per unit.

The **Ranch at Steamboat** (tel. 303/879-3000, or toll free 800/525-2002, 800/237-2624 in Colorado) overlooks the base area. There are 88 one-, two-, and three-bedroom condominiums with electric barbecues, private balconies, fireplaces, and a complimentary continental breakfast. Amenities include a heated outdoor swimming pool, three spas, two saunas, and an aerobics center. Rates range from $124 to $265.

The **Lodge at Steamboat** (tel. 303/879-6000, or toll free 800/525-5502, 800/332-5533 in Colorado) is located 200 yards from the base of the gondola on Mount Werner. The lodge provides shuttle service into town at night. All units have fully equipped kitchens, and there are two outdoor hot tubs, and indoor whirlpool, and a sauna. Rates run from $145 for a two-bedroom/two-bath to $375 for a three-bedroom/three-bath.

Storm Meadows (tel. 303/879-1035, or toll free 800/525-5921, 800/332-5942 in Colorado) is a ski-in/ski-out facility. Each unit has a fully equipped kitchen and a balcony, and guests will enjoy overlooking the mountains from a whirlpool. Rates run $135 to $225 for an eight-person unit.

The **Sheraton at Steamboat**, P.O. Box 774808, Steamboat Springs, CO 80477 (tel. 303/879-2220, or toll free 800/325-3535), next to the gondola has double rooms and some condos. The hotel has two restaurants, two lounges, a heated swimming pool, sauna, steamrooms, and underground parking. Rates for a one-bedroom double-occupancy unit range from $45 to $95 in peak season.

No two rooms are alike at the **Harbor Hotel** P.O. Box 774109, Steamboat Springs, CO 80477 (tel. toll free 800/543-8888, 800/334-1012 in Colorado), and each is decorated with English antiques, turn-of-the-century wall coverings, and fresh flowers. This completely redecorated hotel is in the middle of the town of Steamboat Springs, three miles from the lifts, and is serviced by a regular shuttlebus. Room rates include continental breakfasts in the Harbor Club guest lounge, a reminder of an old English pub with a wet bar for private parties. Rates for double occupancy range from $50 to $92. (Be wary of renting the condos behind the hotel, which are rented through, but not owned by, the hotel. Some are not up to par and have very noisy pipes, and the sidewalks can be covered with ice.)

The log cabins at **Vista Verde Guest Ranch**, P.O. Box 465, Steamboat Springs, Co 80477 (tel. 303/879-3858), located 25 miles northeast of Steamboat, provide comfortable relaxing places for tired cross-country skies. And the food in the main lodge, where guests chat with each other while dining at communal tables, is excellent. The ranch (a dude ranch in the summer) has 20 km (12 miles) of marked and maintained trails, but ski-touring enthusiasts will want to explore the unlimited terrain in the national forest adjoining the ranch. Lessons, and half- and full-day guided tours are available. There's a spa building with a whirlpool and a sauna. Some visitors blend the cross-country tours with a few days of alpine at the Steamboat Ski Area, or spend time ice fishing or snowshoeing. Regular season lodging packages are approximately $95 per day per cabin, double occupancy ($10 for each additional guest), plus $25 per guest for meals. For information and reservations contact the Frank Brophys, the couple who run and make this ranch such an enjoyable place to visit.

WHERE TO EAT: The restaurants are strung out in Ski Time Square, the highway to town, and in the town of Steamboat Springs. Everything from good Chinese food to fresh fish is served.

More Expensive

L'Apogee, at 911 Lincoln in downtown Steamboat Springs (tel. 879-1919), is reputed to be the best restaurant in town. It specializes in French cuisine, and one can choose a meal from a blackboard; entrees change daily. The menu includes veal, lamb, fresh fish, and game, with delicious vegetables and a salad.

Entrees range from $14.50 to $18. L'Apogee is open nightly form 5 p.m. to 2 a.m., with dinner served from 6 to 10:30 p.m. Reservations are suggested.

Ragnar's, in the Rendezvous Saddle Complex located at the midway point at High Noon in the Priest Creek area (tel. 879-6111), delivers a leisurely fine dining experience. Lunch, served from 11 a.m. to 2:30 p.m., features European and continental cuisine in an atmosphere reminiscent of the old days in Steamboat. Entrees average $5.50 to $7. It is suggested you make reservations in advance.

The tastefully turn-of-the-century-appointed **Mattie Silks,** on Times Square (tel. 879-2441), features exquisite continental cuisine, which includes fresh seafood, veal, duck, pork, lamb, and other specialties. Prices range from $8 to $22 with the chef's special priced daily. In their unique bar, one can sample more than 50 imported beers from over 20 countries. The restaurant is open for dinner nightly from 5:30 to 10 p.m.; the bar is open from 4 p.m. to 2 a.m. Reservations are suggested.

The Pine Grove Restaurant (tel. 879-1190) is housed in a beautifully converted 80-year-old barn just off the main highway near the entrance to the ski area. The restaurant features specialities such as prime rib, game, and stuffed trout. Prices range from $6 to $21, and there is a children's menu. It is open from 5 to 10 p.m. Reservations suggested.

The low-key elegance at **Cipriani's,** located in the Sheraton Thunderhead Lodge in Ski Time Square (tel. 879-8866), is conducive to good conversation and the food, northern Italian, is excellent. Entrees range from $13 to $18. Make reservations, because this is a popular place. Hours are 5:30 to 10 p.m. daily.

Hazie's, in the Thunderhead facility at the top of the gondola (tel. 879-6111), offers salads and entrees for lunch ranging from $8 to $15 in an attractive setting with spectacular views of the Yampa Valley and surrounding mountains. Lunch is from 11:30 a.m. to 2:30 p.m. Several evenings during the winter, Hazie's offers a fixed-price gourmet dinner. Cost is approximately $36 for this meal, which includes the gondola rides. Call for details.

Moderate to Expensive

Many locals rate **Giovanni's Ristorante,** 127 11th St. (tel. 879-4141), as the best dining spot in town. A cozy place with red-checked tablecloths, Giovanni's boasts of its "Brooklyn Italian-style cuisine" which includes pastas, veal, and scampi. Prices range from $7 to $15, and reservations are suggested. Hours are 5:30 to 10 p.m. daily.

La Montana Mexican Restaurant and Bar (tel. 879-5800), 200 yards from the gondola at the corner of Après Ski Way and Village Drive, offers large portions of Tex/Mex, pure Mexican, and southwestern food, washed down with margaritas. Price for meals ranging from enchiladas to beef or shrimp range from approximately $6 to $18. Happy hour is 4 to 6 p.m. Dinner is served from 5 to 10 p.m.

Dos Amigos, in Ski Time Square (tel. 879-4270), is one of the most popular restaurants/bars at the base of the ski area. There's an extensive Mexican menu with dinner specialties and à la carte choices that range from $6 to $11. They are open daily from 2:30 p.m. for drinks and appetizers, and for dinner from 5 to 10 p.m.

The **Coral Grill Seafood Restaurant and Oyster Bar,** in the Sundance Plaza on U.S. 40 (tel. 879-6858), provides Steamboat's freshest fish, obtained from the seafood market next door. Specialties include Maine lobster, grilled swordfish, Alaskan salmon, and Colorado trout. Prices range from $8 to $14, but lobster is much higher. Hours are 6 to 10 p.m. nightly.

Café Blue Bayou is an intimate, white-linen restaurant tucked in the Theisen Mall at 912 Lincoln (tel. 879-8282). The Cajun food and decor is reminiscent of New Orleans. Entrees, including blackened fish, veal Orleans, and Cajun steak, range from $11 to $18. Dinner is 6 to 10 p.m.

Less Expensive

Anderson & Friends, a tiny restaurant in Ski Time Square (tel. 879-8080), specializes in lunches and light dinners. Salads average $5; sandwiches run $4 to $6. There are also soups, pizza, and Italian dishes.

Lubins, at 617 Lincoln, beteen 6th and 7th Streets, in Steamboat Springs (tel. 879-7407), is a deli where you can find fresh cooked meats, salads, cheeses, sandwiches, a good variety of bread, and party trays. Kosher items are available, as are hot entrees and box lunches. Prices average $5. Lubins is open from 10 a.m. to 5 p.m.

The **Mother Lode,** at 628 Lincoln (tel. 879-6868), specializes in lunches and light dinners. Salads, sandwiches, some Mexican food, and Italian dinners range from $5 to $9.

The **Shack Café,** 740 Lincoln (tel. 879-9975), has good, quick breakfasts and lunches. Prices range from $2 to $6, and hours are 6 a.m. to 2 p.m.

Cugino's Pizzeria has some of the best pizza, hoagies, and strombolis in Steamboat. Pizzas begin at $5 and sandwiches run $3.75 to $7. Eat in this small restaurant from 11 a.m. to 10 p.m., or order out. Call 879-5805 for deliveries from 5 to 9 p.m.

The Tugboat, in Ski Time Square (tel. 879-9990), is another place popular with skiers and locals alike because of is western atmosphere (notice the back bar which is more than 100 years old) and friendly flavor. Open for food from 7:30 a.m. to 10 p.m., it offers hamburgers, salads, and sandwiches on the lunch and dinner menu. Dishes stretch from $2.75 to $6.

If you want to cook fresh fish in your condo, **Steamboat Seafood Company,** in the Sundance Plaza next to the post office, will deliver it, along with beef, fresh pasta, and other deli items. Stop by or call 879-3504.

ENTERTAINMENT: The hot spots for dancing include the **Inferno,** in Gondola Square (tel. 879-5111), **The Hatch,** downtown (tel. 879-8323), which has country western music, and **Hershie's,** in the Clock Tower Building (tel. 879-8701).

SHOPPING: Check out the **Steamboat Art Company,** in downtown Steamboat (tel. 879-3383), featuring Western art and American handcrafts. The **Great Divide,** in Ski Time Square (tel. 879-8495), has superb leather. **Artisans Market of Steamboat** (tel. 879-7512) is a cooperative gallery and gift shop of locally handcrafted items.

NON-SKIER ACTIVITIES: There are a number of interesting shops in this resort. Most are grouped in Ski Time Square and in downtown Steamboat Springs. The most popular après-ski spot in town is the town's year-round hot springs and water slide. The **Steamboat Springs Health and Recreation Association** (tel. 879-1828) at the east end of town pipes natural mineral springs hot water into the large soaking pool, the lap pool, and the water slide. There are changing rooms, and bathing suits and towels can be rented.

Ballooning is popular in this mountain town. There are several companies offering bird's-eye views of skiers and mountaintops. For more information contact **Balloon the Rockies** (tel. 879-7313) or the **Chamber Resort Association** (tel. 879-0880) for a list of companies.

Several companies run **sleigh rides** that include dinner. For more information, contact the Chamber Resort Association (tel. 879-0880). **Red Barn Ranch** (tel. 879-4545 or 879-4580), **All Seasons Ranch** (tel. 879-2606), and **Double Runner Sleigh Rides** (tel. 879-8877) all have sleigh rides with dinner.

Snowmobiling is very popualr in the high country here. Contact the Chamber Resort Association (tel. 879-0880) for more information.

Several local ski and sport shops rent **snowshoes.** Vista Verde Guest Ranch (tel. 879-3858) has supervised snowshoeing.

The **outside skating rink** is located at Howelsen Hill (where ski jumpers practice and youngsters sled). Call 879-4300 for more information.

GETTING THERE: Steamboat is 157 miles northwest of Denver's Stapleton Airport and 200 miles northeast of Grand Junction. **American Airlines** now provides direct service to Yampa Valley Regional Airport, 22 miles away, from Chicago and Dallas/Fort Worth, and may be adding other cities. **Northwest** flies nonstop to Yampa three times a week from Minneapolis/St. Paul. From Denver, skiers fly **United Express** or **Continental Express** to the local airport five miles from town.

Car rentals are available at Stapleton, Grand Junction, and both Steamboat airports.

MOVING AROUND: Most of Steamboat's lodging facilities are at the base of the area, and some are ski-in/ski-out. For those staying on town or elsewhere there is a shuttle service available from 7:30 a.m. to midnight. Some lodges also provide their own shuttle service. The number for **Steamboat Taxi** is 879-3111.

TOURIST INFORMATION: The **Steamboat Springs Chamber Resort Association,** P.O. Box 774408, Steamboat Springs, CO 80477 (tel. 303/879-0740, or toll free 800/332-3204 in Colorado), handles reservations for lodging in over 90 hotels, motels, condominiums, and guest ranches. The **ski report** number is 879-7300.

When in Steamboat, pick up copies of the *Whistler,* a local newspaper that includes a tourist guide, and the *Steamboat Visitors Guide* for the most current listing of restaurants, activities, and entertainment.

Dial 911 for **emergency services.**

4. Copper Mountain

THE RESORT: Copper Mountain is a made-for-skiing resort set at the base of one of the best ski mountains in the United States. The 14-year-old village has grown from a few structures to a respectably sized cluster of buildings strung along the ever-expanding base of the ski runs. Although it has all the amenities from Jacuzzis to restaurants, skiers who like to have lots of choices for après-ski should be aware that the number of options in each category is still limited. For instance there is only one posh restaurant in the village, and there are fewer than a dozen shops to explore. Although the base area of Copper doesn't have the visual charm of many long-standing ski villages, skiers keep coming because of the quality of the slopes (and the spectacular views of the surrounding mountains). The ski runs on the mountain have been developed into separate sections for each skill level, so experts can ski all day without careening into beginners, and intermediates will have their own learning bumps and medium-tough terrain. You'll find everything from hand-me-down equipment to the most expensive skis on the mountain.

The skiers are a mix of Front Range (Denver and the other cities at the edge of the Rockies) day skiers and overnight guests staying in the area.

THE SKIING: Copper Mountain is one of those ski resorts which really has lots of terrain for every level skier. The 75 trails and bowls cover 1,180 acres of astonishingly variable mountainside. A high-speed quad, six triple and nine double chairs, and four surface lifts stretch up the 2,760-vertical-foot mountain. The terrain is rated 25% easiest, 40% more difficult, and 35% most difficult. That means, looking upward from the base village, beginners have the entire right end of the ski area serviced by K and L lifts, just two of the area's 20 lifts. Intermediates and beginners share the central part of the mountain, with intermediates gravitating toward the I and J lifts. Bittersweet and Main View, off the F lift, are very popular because they are long and often have a few bumps at the top to test intermediate skills, but ease into nicely pitched smooth lanes. Advanced intermediates spend at least part of the day challenging the blue and black runs off the B and B1 lifts. Encore and Collage are among the most popular runs for this skill level because they are long cruisers. Experts expend their energy challenging the steep and/or the bump runs off the A and the Resolution lifts. Two Much, Triple Treat, and Highline will challenge most skiers' knees. The curving sides of the black-rated section of Union Bowl, at the top of the mountain, is another, shorter, play area for advanced skiers and even for the less skilled during the spring season. The Storm King surface lift opens up the double-diamond Spaulding Bowl with its very steep pitches.

Insider's Tips

The lines at F and G lifts are often long in the morning when skiers are moving onto the slopes. Try the high-speed quad. (Don't let the size of the line scare you; it moves much faster than the other lines.) Food lines at Union Creek, a base lodge below the beginner's runs, and Solitude Station, up on the mountain, are usually shorter than those at the Center.

Mountain Facilities

There are three base areas where skiers can get lift tickets, sign up for ski school, and find cafeterias or restaurants. The Solitude Station at the top of the F lift also has a cafeteria. There are several restaurants and ski shops at the base of B lift and in the main village, just a few hundred yards from the main lodge.

Snow Coverage

The average snowfall here is more than 255 inches a year. Two hundred acres of terrain under the F, G, and H lifts are covered with snowmaking facilities to ensure good coverage during the early season. Copper usually opens in early November and closes in late April. There is extensive grooming of blue and green runs but few black runs.

Ski School

Copper Mountain's ski school offers group and private lessons plus a wide range of programs from advanced skiing clinics to women's skiing seminars. Instructors here are au courant with the latest teaching techniques, because Copper's ski school director is involved in the highest levels of the Professional Ski Instructors Association, which sets the guidelines for ski instructors nationwide. Copper offers many special classes, including women's seminars, early season clinics, and beginners' workshops. There is also a complete children's ski school. Youngsters from 4 to 6 years of age join the Junior Ranch, where the day is split between supervised indoor and outdoor activity. Reservations are recommended. Children from 7 to 12 join the Senior Ranch, an all-day ski school.

Childcare

The childcare facility is in the Mountain Plaza at the base of F and G lifts. Belly Button Babies takes tots from 2 months to 2 years. At the Belly Button Bakery, which takes children from 2 years and up, the youngsters can cook, bake, do arts and crafts, and play outdoors under supervision.

Anyone using the athletic club (or the athletic club restaurant) can leave youngsters in the club's nursery.

Rental Equipment

Both adult and children's ski equipment can be rented at the Mountain Plaza and the Union Creek rental shops on a daily basis or for three days or more at a lower daily rate. High-performance rental equipment is also available at the Mountain Plaza Rental Shop.

Cross-Country Skiing

The resort maintains 25 km (15 miles) of trails threading through the backcountry around the resort. Group and private lessons are available through the Nordic center, which is based at Union Creek. Telemark clinics are scheduled regularly; a lift ticket is needed. Both track and telemark equipment can be rented.

WHERE TO STAY: Most of the accommodations are in condominiums, although there are a few inn rooms (actually lock-off condo bedrooms with baths). The lodgings owned by the ski corporation (in nine different properties) can be reserved through **Copper Mountain Lodging Services** (tel. 303/968-2882, or toll free 800/525-3878, 800/322-3828 in Colorado). Most of the other properties in this ski village (including those mentioned in this section) can be reserved through **Copper Mountain Central Reservations** (tel. 303/968-6477, or 825-7106 in Denver, or toll free 800/525-3891 outside Colorado). Generally the most expensive lodging is in the core village with ski-in/ski-out access or a two-minute walk from the slope. The outlying lodges in the central village (perhaps a five-minute walk from the lift) and accommodations in the B village area may be less expensive. (There are two restaurants in this area, and the condos look more like a group of apartment buildings clustered around a parking lot than a scenic ski village, although some of the mountain views are spectacular.)

Central reservations clerks tend to place skiers near the slopes they want to ski. That means beginners and intermediates are steered to the village, while the better skiers (and everyone else if the central village is full) are steered to the B village complex. (Intermediates familiar with Copper take the shuttle to the B lift each morning and skip the lift lines at the central village.)

The accommodations available through central reservations are managed by several different management companies and each prices the condos more by size than styling and amenities. For example, Copper Mountain Lodging Services manages five properties in which all two-bedroom/two-bath condos are the same price. That means, for example, the designer-decorated two-bedroom show unit at the new Spruce Lodge with ski-in/ski-out access is the same price as the plain two-bedroom condo in an older building.

More Expensive

During the regular season Copper Mountain Services rates average $95 per night for a basic hotel room (sleeps two) during the regular season, $120 for a one-bedroom condo (for four), and $215 for a two-bedroom condo (sleeps six). During the high season rates range from $120 for a hotel room to $350 for a three-bedroom condo. Because many of the units are owned privately, furnishings vary. Anyone staying in a property managed by Copper Mountain Services can charge everything from the athletic club to lunch at the mountain on the room bill. Properties include the Village Square: condominiums and hotel rooms in a high-rise right in the middle of the village center. The village's only posh restaurant, the shops, and casual dining are located inside this building or a courtyard away. There is a large community Jacuzzi and saunas in the building. Ask for one of the luxury condos on the top floor. The ski-in/ski-out Spruce Lodge has attractive, spacious condos with fireplaces, balconies with views, and a community Jacuzzi overlooking the woods.

Moderate

Properties located in the B lift area and managed by Carbonate Real Estate during regular season average $95 per night for an inn room (sleeps two), $135 to $145 for a studio/loft (sleeps three), $210 for a two-bedroom (sleeps six), and $300 for a three-bedroom with loft. Properties include the Anaconda, which has very attractive, rustic multilevel condominiums, many featuring dens with sliding doors (and bathrooms) closing them off from the main living room, to bedrooms with bunk beds. The Peregrine building has spacious condominiums with lots of natural wood walls and fireplaces. There are saunas and Jacuzzis at both condominium complexes.

Club Med's only ski village in North America is located at Copper. As with all Club Meds, guests pay a flat fee for the week and can put their cash away. The flat price includes six nights in a basic, twin-bedded room, all meals (and many are spectacular), and all-day ski lessons with Club Med's own well-trained ski school. Call (tel. 800/CLUB-MED) for current rates. First-timers to a Club Med village must also pay a membership fee, which allows them to stay at any Club Med in the world.

Less Expensive

The **Best Western Foxpine Lodge** is one of the better buys. Although the building is older and the decor average, the condos are slopeside and there is a swimming pool. During the regular season prices per night range from approximately $95 for a standard hotel room to $215 for a two-bedroom condo or $285 for a three-bedroom with a loft. During low season the prices range from $70 for a standard hotel room to $235 for a three-bedroom with loft.

The Lodge, located away from the main village but with ski-in/ski-out access, has a few two-bedroom condominiums with one bath that are bargains for vacationers who want to stuff a lot of skiers into one unit. There are no fireplaces and the decor is basic, but the rooms are a decent size and there is a Jacuzzi and sauna nearby. During low season the Lodge rates range from $70 for an inn room to $95 for the economy two-bedroom suite, up to $240 for a three-bedroom with loft. During regular season prices range from $95 for a room up to $285 for the three-bedroom with loft. During high season, prices range from $120 for an inn room, up to $365 for the three-bedroom with loft.

Timbercreek also offers ski-in/ski-out access via a poma lift and one of the few swimming pools in the village. Located at the edge of the slopes, it has nicely styled condominiums with small living rooms, fireplaces, and spiral staircases leading to second-floor bedrooms. However, there is no elevator, so you must carry everything up to the third-floor condos. Nightly rates during low season range from $110 for an economy (third-floor) one-bedroom with loft, which sleeps six, to $200 for a two-bedroom with loft. During regular season rates run from $150 to $260 for the same units. During high season the rates run $210 to $330.

There are two penthouses in the **Copper Mountain Inn,** each offering 28 pillows in five bedrooms set on three levels. There are five baths in the unit that has a large living room on the first floor and another living room area on the balcony area of the second floor of this chalet-style unit. During low season the unit costs $380, during regular season it's $510, and during high season it's $640.

WHERE TO EAT: There are about ten restaurants in this village offering meals ranging from deli sandwiches to Maine lobster. Anyone wanting a wider range of choices must drive to the nearby towns of Dillon or Frisco. Most restaurants expect to see diners informally dressed.

More Expensive

The **Plaza** restaurant, in the Mountain Plaza (tel. 968-2882, ext. 6505), is the only gourmet restaurant in the village. Chicken, veal, seafood, and beef are all listed on the à la carte dinner menu. The meals start around $18 per person. Diners sit at tables or booths set at different levels in this casually elegant room with its natural woods and green plants. Hours are 11:30 a.m. to 10 p.m. From 11:30 a.m. to 5 p.m. items such as pasta dishes and hearty soups are served from the lounge menu. Reduced-price meals are offered from 5 to 6:30 p.m. Meals are off the regular menu during the evening hours. The bar opens at 5 p.m.

Moderate

Rackets Restaurant (tel. 968-2882, ext. 6386), a trendy place to stop for large and elegantly prepared portions of "health-oriented" food, is located in the Copper Mountain Athletic Club. (Club facilities as well as the restaurant are open to the public, and there is a nursery on the premises, but reservations must be made in advance.) The large room is framed by glass windows with a mountain view, a rock wall blocking the pool area a level below, and a wall-length wood bar. The menu, good at lunch and dinner, ranges from pasta and salads to chicken and burgers. Prices range from $5.75 to $9. Hours are 11 a.m. to 10 p.m.

Farley's Restaurant, located in the Snowflake Building by the B lift (tel. 968-2577), is a local hangout as well as a popular spot for visitors. The paneled downstairs room is wall-to-wall locals and skiers during après-ski, when there is often live entertainment. The restaurant boasts a classic English atmosphere with comfortable captain's chairs around the wood tables. Meals—steaks, seafood, and veal—run about $10 and up. Dining is from 5:30 to 10 p.m.

The upstairs dining room at **Tuso's Restaurant,** in the Snowflake Building near the B lift (tel. 968-6090), is a great spot for two-hour lunches. The bar in this restaurant, which looks like an oversize greenhouse, is a popular après-ski spot. Prices start around $4 for finger food such as nachos and deep-fried vegetables, going up to $14 for steaks. Desserts include Irish coffee cream pie and Sicilian rum cake. Children's portions are available. Lunch hours are 11:30 a.m. to 2 p.m. Dinner hours are 5:30 to 9:30 p.m.

The **Columbine Café,** in the Village Square (tel. 968-2882, ext. 6525), is a comfortably casual restaurant with fans whirling overhead and guests seated at the blond wood tables or in burgundy wall booths. Priced for family dining, the menu offers salads, sandwiches, and burgers for lunch and dinner from 11 a.m. to 9 p.m., starting around $6. There is a full-service bar. Columbine's serves breakfast from 7:30 to 11:30 a.m.

Less Expensive

Soupy Sales (tel. 968-2629) is a family-style café featuring waffles, eggs, and freshly baked pastries for breakfast; and made-from-scratch soups, chili, stuffed potatoes, and sandwiches for lunch. Fast service is emphasized. International dinners are served weekdays at this moderately priced restaurant which opens at 7:30 a.m. Prices go from $2 to $7.

ENTERTAINMENT: The **Center** (tel. 962-2882, ext. 6510), located at the base of G lift, has live après-ski entertainment. The **Columbine Café** (tel. 968-2882, ext. 6525) also has dancing and a DJ spins records.

SHOPPING: There are a few ski shops, a drugstore, a grocery store, and several specialty shops. **Hello Colorado,** located in the Village Square, offers an excellent sampling of artwork and crafts by Coloradans. The **Scoop,** in Mountain Plaza, will satisfy any sweets lover's taste buds with ice cream and gourmet chocolate. Open daily.

NON-SKIER ACTIVITIES: The **Guest Services desk** (tel. 968-2882, ext. 6320) in the lobby of the Mountain Plaza provides resort activity information. There is **ice skating** on the outdoor lighted rink. Rental skates are available. A one-day membership to the **Copper Mountain Athletic Club** (tel. 968-2882) opens up racquetball and indoor tennis courts, a lap pool, aerobics classes, and Nautilus machines. Non-skiers can also take the Ski the Summit bus and spend the day exploring **Keystone Village** or the town of Breckenridge. **Tiger Run** (tel. 968-2882, ext. 6320) offers guided snowmobiling tours into the backcountry. Ask at Guest Services for details on sleigh rides.

MOVING AROUND: Free shuttlebuses circle the village. The majority of the lodges and condominiums are grouped around the core village located at the base of F and G lifts and the main base lodge. Even the outlying condominium complexes here are just a seven- or eight-minute walk from the lifts. The rest of the lodges and condos are clustered a five-minute shuttlebus ride away at the base of B lift, which serves the more advanced runs. Most of the restaurants, shops, and the one grocery store are located in the central part of the village. The Summit Stage takes skiers to and from Breckenridge and Keystone for the day.

GETTING THERE: Copper Mountain is located 75 miles west of Denver on I-70 off exit 195. Skiers can fly to Denver's Stapleton International Airport via most major airlines. There is a commuter connection on **Rocky Mountain Airways** from Stapleton to Avon STOLport, 35 miles west of Copper. However, most skiers use ground transportation for the 1¾-hour ride from Stapleton. **Trailways** provides daily bus service to and from Stapleton. **Carey American Limousine Service** and **Resort Express** run vans to and from Copper. Contact **Apex Travel** (tel. 303/968-2882), Copper Mountain Resort's in-house travel agency, for ground transportation schedules and reservations—which are strongly recommended. Most major car-rental companies operate at Stapleton, and car rentals are available on a daily basis at Copper for those who want to sample nearby Vail and Beaver Creek or spend the evening in the towns of Dillon or Frisco.

TOURIST INFORMATION: Information about the resort and lodging reservations at most of Copper Mountain's lodges is available through the **central reservations service** (tel. 303/968-2882, or toll free 800/525-3878, 800/332-3828 in Colorado). When at Copper, resort activity information is available at **Guest Services** in the lobby of the Mountain Plaza (tel. 968-2882, ext. 6320).

For emergency **medical, fire,** and **sheriff,** dial 911. For **security patrol** at a Copper Mountain property call ext. 6680; others call 968-2911. The **Copper Medical Center** (tel. 968-2330) in Bridge End is open during the day. During evening hours go to **Summit Medical Center** (tel. 668-3300), 0038 Summit County Road 1030 in Frisco.

5. Keystone Resort
(Includes Keystone Mountain and Arapahoe Basin Ski Areas)

THE RESORT: There's never an empty tissue box next to the chair lifts at Keystone Mountain or Arapahoe Basin, because pampering their guests has been Keystone Resort's key to success. Keystone Resort attracts many upscale, younger professionals with families who prefer substance to glitter. The lure is two ski areas—Keystone Mountain and Arapahoe Basin—plus après-ski amenities ranging from a four-star hotel and comfortable condos to such activities for non-skiers as ice skating, swimming, and sleigh rides.

THE SKIING: Ralston Purina's original acquisition was Keystone Mountain, a sleekly groomed ski area then geared for beginners and intermediates. When the more skilled skiers complained the slopes were too tame, Ralston Purina bought its "other ski experience," Arapahoe Basin, which had long been populated by Front Range expert skiers. Wisely, management cleaned up the terrain around the Pallavicini chair but basically left this part of the mountain untouched. They groomed the upper bowl and several lower runs to attract the intermediate skiers, and added a nursery.

In 1984, North Peak, with its advanced and intermediate terrain, was added to Keystone Mountain, changing the entire skiing experience. Many of the better skiers who had long ignored this mountain began coming to sample the new terrain. Furthermore, whereas novices and fast skiers had been populating many of the same slopes (creating mutual discomfort), now most of the advanced skiers move directly to the isolated North Peak area for much of the day.

KEYSTONE MOUNTAIN AND NORTH PEAK: The Keystone Mountain most skiers know is a 2,340-foot-vertical mountain with an excellent variety of beginner and intermediate runs—most groomed as smooth as a plush carpet. The Keystone Mountain terrain is rated 20% beginner, 65% intermediate, and 15% advanced. On North Peak the terrain is rated as 78% expert and 22% intermediate. (There are no beginner runs here.) North Peak, tucked behind Keystone Mountain, is visually isolated from the condos, buildings, and other signs of civilization; the views are the Continental Divide and other mountain peaks.

Access to the runs on interconnecting Keystone Mountain and North Peak is via a high-speed six-passenger gondola that moves 2,400 skiers an hour uphill; and three triple chairs, eight double chairs, and two surface lifts. Beginning and intermediate skiers can start at either base area on Keystone Mountain. Anyone who wants to go straight to the top, ski the back side of the mountain, or challenge North Peak should take the gondola out of the River Run Plaza.

Never-evers have two private sections where they can start this sport. Anyone taking a first-time lesson out of the main base area will probably learn in the Checkerboard Flats area at the bottom of the mountain. Never-evers who sign up for ski school at the River Run Plaza will take the gondola to the top of the mountain and spend the day practicing on Tip-Top, a closed-off, flat area just outside the Summit House. (They'll download on the gondola at the end of the day.)

Schoolmarm is a top-to-bottom, three-mile beginner's run pitched to ensure a comfortable, long run downhill for skiers who want to practice their turns. It's also a superb cruiser for intermediates. There are several shorter but good green runs around the Packsaddle II lift.

Intermediates have the run of most of Keystone Mountain and two good, long runs on North Peak. Paymaster is one of the most popular runs for low intermediates because it goes top-to-bottom and is comfortably pitched for tentative skiers. Spring Dipper is another challenging run that varies in pitch, so some portions are rated green and others blue. Jackwacker, Frenchman, and Flying Dutchman are other popular runs. Beginning bumpers should check out Santa Fe, where the moguls are allowed to build a little but are groomed regularly so they don't become too threatening. Go Devil and Last Hoot, the trails on Keystone Mountain with a black rating, are warm-up runs—at best—for North Peak.

North Peak has some excellent black runs—to the delight of better skiers who come to Keystone with their families. To explore the 1,600-vertical-foot North Peak, competent intermediates head down Mozart, the blue run on the back side of Keystone Mountain. It's a good intermediate run with lots of terrain variation and enough curves so the feeling is more one of skiing an open road through the woods rather than down a superhighway leading to corrals of skiers waiting to head up the lifts. Advanced skiers can head down Diamond Back, which starts out gently, then turns a corner and surprises the unwary with a steep, often moguled pitch. The Santiago lift opening up North Peak and the Ruby lift for skiers heading back up to the summit of Keystone Mountain rises out of a wind-protected clearing. North Peak's Starfire and Last Alamo are the two reasonably wide blue runs (but not as wide as most on the front face) for competent intermediates. (This area is basically for better skiers who are often moving fairly fast; shaky intermediates who need lots of turning space would be better off elsewhere.)

Perhaps the most popular run on North Peak is Geronimo, because it starts out right by the top of the chair lift. However, because it's so popular, the bumps can build in strange shapes, as often happens when less skillful skiers make large skidding turns to cope with the terrain. The bumps on Powder Cap, Cat Dancer, and Ambush (runs that begin out of sight from the top of the chair) are generally more regular and the snow is often better because it hasn't been scraped so often by skidding skis.

Night skiing here is a kick because you can ride uphill in the comfort of the gondola. Nighttime ski hours are 4 to 10 p.m. Thirteen trails, accessed by the gondola and a double chair, are open.

Insider's Tips

The gondola is usually the fastest way up Keystone Mountain. Even if the line is long, the gondola moves 2,400 skiers an hour and the ride up is only ten minutes. Riding chairs from the base lodge to the same point take more than 20 without lift lines. There are two entrances to the gondola. Look to see which one is shorter. When the mountain is crowded, often the runs to the left of the gondola, such as Spring Dipper, Swandyke, and Santa Fe, have fewer skiers.

Ski the lower mountain cautiously at the end of the day, because the blue and green runs funnel into three main run-outs: two blue trails and one green. Free shuttlebuses, which circle the area, take skiers back to the right parking lot if they end the day at the other end of the ski area.

Free ski-check corrals are located at the base of Keystone Mountain and at River Run Plaza.

Everything from soup and a cheese-and-meats tray to barbecued beef is available at various food stations in the Summit House. If you have the energy, take your lunch trays all the way to the top level, a tiny room with spectacular views of the surrounding mountains.

To avoid the end-of-the-day rush, consider staying in the Summit House until most of the skiers have ended their day. The Fondue Chessel at the Summit House serves cheese, meat, and chocolate fondues from 4 to 9 p.m.

Mountain Facilities

The base lodge at Keystone Mountain has a cafeteria, lounge, a full-service restaurant, and childcare center. Ski rental, ski repair, and other shops are located in the base complex. There's a café and a saloon in the River Run Plaza, a ski school, and a ski shop. The lodge at the top of Keystone Mountain has a cafeteria, a barbecue area, and a counter for creative sandwiches and cheese and sausage plates.

Snow Coverage

An average of 200 inches of snow falls on Keystone and North Peak each year. Of the 500 skiable acres, 395 are covered with snowmaking equipment, ensuring a Halloween opening most years. The area is usually open from mid-October to late April. Keystone has set an industry standard in snow grooming. (It's so good on most runs that some skiers tend to overestimate their skills, not realizing the difference grooming can make.)

Childcare

Children 2 months and older can go into the childcare facilities at the base of Keystone Mountain. Reservations (tel. 468-4182) are required.

Rental Equipment

Rental equipment is available at the base of the mountain and in Keystone Village. Performance rentals are available in Keystone Village.

Cross-Country Skiing

Cross-country and telemark lessons are available, as are tours for both novice and experienced skiers. Keystone maintains 33 km (20 miles) of prepared trails, some starting at the Cross Country Center which is at **Ski Tip Ranch** (tel. 468-4188). There's also a trail from the top of Keystone Mountain to the top of North Peak. (Pay a one-ride gondola fee and one-time-use fee for the trail.)

ARAPAHOE BASIN: Arapahoe Basin has some gentle runs for beginners and an entertaining range of blue slopes and an above-timberline bowl for intermediates, but the real essence of this 1,670-vertical-foot mountain is the terrain for advanced skiers. The terrain is rated 10% beginner, 50% intermediate, and 40% advanced.

Beginners and intermediates at Keystone for a week should take a day to explore Arapahoe Basin. The view from the top of the area (at 12,450 feet above sea level) will make the day! The green trails are wide enough and gentle. The blue-rated bowl at the top of the mountain opens up smooth and moguled terrain depending on the fall line chosen. The terrain for these skill levels is usually groomed Keystone style, which means extremely soft and smooth.

Advanced skiers will enjoy this mountain. The lighter blacks are rarely groomed and the Pallivicini area is never touched. Exhibition, under a lift, and the Slalom Slope, which is moguled but wide, are among the easier blacks at this area. The East Wall is the place to ski when there is fresh powder. Parts of

Pallavicini, an open bowl at the top with steep sides that narrow into a gulley, are as steep as they look from the roadside. If the way in on the top freaks you out, ski down the ridge, then cut into the gulley at an angle. The softest snow collects in the center of the trough. North Glade, Bear Trap, and the sections on one side of Pallavicini have all sorts of entertaining gnarly terrain for expert skiers. The alleys, on the other side of Pallavicini, are even steeper.

Insider's Tips

There's a free ski-check corral at the base of the mountain.

When the weather's good and the roads are clear, day skiers can get off I-70 and take the road over Loveland Pass. Views at the top of the Continental Divide are spectacular, and the ride is shorter than going through Dillon.

Mountain Facilities

There's a cafeteria, lounge, ski shop, childcare center, and ski-school office at the base.

Snow Coverage

This area so close to the Continental Divide receives an average of 360 inches annually and is normally open from late November to early June. Snowmaking covers 89 acres. The green and blue runs are groomed continually but few blacks are touched.

Ski School

The ski school offers morning and afternoon group lessons, four-hour lessons including lunch, and private lessons.

Childcare

Children 18 months and older can go into the Children's Center next to the ski-school office. Reservations (tel. 468-4182) are required.

Rental Equipment

Rental equipment is available at shops in Keystone Village, at Keystone Mountain and at River Run Plaza, and at the base of Arapahoe Basin. Performance rentals are available in the Village Rental Shop at Keystone Village, the pedestrian mall next to Keystone Lodge.

Cross-Country Skiing

See Keystone's cross-country section.

WHERE TO STAY: Skiers here can stay in **Keystone Lodge**, P.O. Box 38, Keystone, CO 80435 (tel. 303/468-4242, or 534-7712 in Denver, both for reservations only), an AAA five-diamond and Mobil four-star property and a member of Preferred Hotels Worldwide, or in the 900 condominiums and private homes in Keystone Resort. The village has a free shuttlebus system and there's a central switchboard and booking system for all activities. Guests staying here can use their special "Keystone charge card" and charge everything from meals at the ski-area restaurants to ski rentals directly to their rooms.

The mountain-contemporary Keystone Lodge has very comfortable rooms backed by the service expected at such a highly rated lodge. There are three dining areas in the lodge, offering everything from continental dining to steak and a salad bar, a comfortable lounge where guests can relax après-ski, an outdoor swimming pool, and a whirlpool. Room rates average $120 for double occupancy during regular season.

The 900 condominiums on the roads winding around Keystone Resort range from studios to four-bedroom units. Options range from standard to premium units, generally graded according to size, closeness to the village, and amenities. There are pools, saunas, and Jacuzzis spread around the village for guest use. (The **Châteaux d'Mont** is located at the base of Keystone Mountain and all units have private whirlpools. Units at the **Quicksilver**, next to the tennis center, are very spacious. **Soda Spring Townhomes** have living rooms upstairs to maximize the views.) Outline your requirements to central reservations and they'll suggest the best unit. Rates reflect the condominium size, location, amenities, and number of persons allowed. Prices range from approximately $120 for standard studios to $395 for a premium four-bedroom unit. Ask for prices on private homes.

Children 12 and under stay free in the same lodge room or condominium with their parents, providing minimum occupancy is met and maximum occupancy is not exceeded. A two-night minimum is required in the condos and during holiday weeks it may be more. Keystone offers a variety of packages ranging from two-day to week-long stays.

There are many condominium complexes and motels elsewhere in Summit County. There is bus service from many locations, but check with the lodge when making reservations. Ski the Summit buses run between the various areas, so skiers staying elsewhere can ski here.

WHERE TO EAT: There are more than 15 restaurants in Keystone Village, a pedestrian mall area next to the lodge; there are three restaurants in the lodge, and there are good restaurants on the access road and in nearby Dillon.

More Expensive

Six-course gourmet dinners are served in the rustically elegant **Ranch** (tel. 468-4161), a restored 50-year-old homestead at the edge of the golf course. Dinners are a fixed price, but with tips, tax, etc., average in the mid-$30s. Reservations are required. The food and the atmosphere are a special experience. There are two seatings nightly Monday through Sunday.

Guests enjoy leisurely fine dining in the airy **Garden Room** in the Keystone Lodge (tel. 468-2316 and ask for the Garden Room), which is filled with plants and fresh flowers. Loin of lamb, veal Oscar, fresh salmon, and roast duckling du jour are just a few of the items on the menu. Dinners range from $14 to $22. There's a champagne brunch on Sunday. Reservations are recommended. Hours are 6:30 to 9:30 p.m.

The nautical theme at the **Navigator** in the mall (tel. 468-5600) is in keeping with the menu offering fish, seafood, and beef. The Navigator is open from 5:30 to 9:30 p.m. Sunday through Thursday and until 10 p.m. on Friday and Saturday. There's a piano bar Wednesday through Sunday in season. Happy hour is from 4:30 to 6:30 p.m. daily.

Skiers can visit the **Ski Tip Lodge** (tel. 468-4202), Summit County's oldest lodge, for a four-course continental dinner backed by good wines. Reservations are recommended for dinner in this rustic lodge. Dinners average $22.

Moderate to Expensive

The **Snake River Saloon** (tel. 468-2788) is a very popular restaurant/lounge located near the entrance to Keystone. Guests relaxing in the dining room's western atmosphere work on prime rib, steak, surf and turf, or other entrees that range from $8 to $15. Dinner is served from 5:30 p.m.

The autos etched in glass and the splashy colors in **Bentley's** (tel. 468-6610) art deco dining room are eyecatching. Burgers, salads, and sandwiches averaging $5 are on the lunch menu at this restaurant in Keystone Village. Dinner entrees include prime rib, steak, seafood, and lighter fare. Entrees range from $9 to $17. Burgers and sandwiches average $6. Lunch is served from 11 a.m. to 5 p.m.; dinner, from 5 to 10 p.m.

See the section on Summit County for other restaurants.

Less Expensive

Pizza is the main staple at the **Last Chance Saloon** (tel. 468-4185 or 468-4186 for take-out), where lively bands set the mood, located in the Argentine Plaza in Keystone Village.

The **Alpentop Deli,** in Keystone Village (tel. 468-2774), a gourmet deli with an inviting atmosphere, serves three meals a day. Stews, chowders, quiche, sandwiches, and the daily special are on the menu. You can get a full dinner for under $8.

ENTERTAINMENT: The **Snake River Saloon** (tel. 468-2788) has bands on weekends. The **Last Chance Saloon** (tel. 468-3216 and ask for the Last Chance Saloon) in Keystone Village has live entertainment most nights. The **Old Dillon Inn** (tel. 468-2791) in Silverthorne is another popular spot.

SHOPPING: The three-level pedestrian mall in Keystone Village has shops stocking everything from unusual gifts and clothing to arts and crafts. Condo guests can place a grocery order at the Keystone Grocery which should be ready when they arrive. (The grocery and the Alpentop Deli have a delivery service.)

NON-SKIER ACTIVITIES: Guests staying at Keystone can arrange most of these activities through the Activities Center at the lodge. The **Keystone Tennis Center** at Keystone has indoor courts and features week-long and week-end clinics year round. There's **ice skating** on Keystone Lake next to the lodge and skate rentals are available at the Figure Skating Center. **Sleigh rides** to Soda Creek Homestead include a steak dinner. **Snowmobile tours** of the backcountry can be arranged.

GETTING THERE: Keystone is located 75 miles from Denver. Kremmling Airport is the nearest to Keystone, and it's a 45-minute ride. The best bet is to fly into Denver's Stapleton Airport and take one of the ski buses or rent a car. If you're driving, go west on I-70, 75 miles, through the Eisenhower Tunnel to the Keystone cutoff at U.S. 6, or get off the highway just before the tunnel and head over Loveland Pass, weather permitting. (If plans went as expected, part of U.S. 6, around Keystone, was turned from a two- to a four-lane road last summer.) Chauffeured van service is available through **Carey American Limousine** (tel. 303/468-4169), **Resort Express** (tel. 303/468-5579), and **Ladybug Livery** (tel. 303/453-2626); and **Trailways** (tel. 303/292-2291) offers daily service to the area.

MOVING AROUND: Free buses serve all condominiums and the two base areas at Keystone as well as Arapahoe Basin. The **Summit Stage** provides free transportation to and from Copper Mountain and Breckenridge ski areas. There is also **Summit Taxi Service** (tel. 303/668-3565) and the **Resort Express** (tel. 303/468-5579).

TOURIST INFORMATION: For more information, contact **Keystone Resort,** P.O. Box 38, Keystone, CO 80435 (tel. 524-7712 in Denver, or toll free 800/222-0188).

6. Breckenridge

THE RESORT: The central part of this former mining town has been kept in—or in some cases restored to—its Victorian style. The new condominiums cover the blocks and mountainside closest to the ski slopes that overshadow the town. The ski slopes spread over three peaks, offering a substantial amount of terrain for every skill level. Skiers here are a mixed bag. There are lots of families, budget-conscious vacationers, and other low-key skiers here for a reasonably priced good time on the slopes and some entertaining après-ski life at the restaurants and nightspots lining the town's streets.

THE SKIING: Skiers here can challenge three peaks: Peaks 8 and 9, with their range of trails from gentle beginner slopes to serious steeps and bumps for experts, and Peak 10, with its blend of intermediate runs and eastern-style steeps. The terrain is rated 23% easier, 29% more difficult, and 48% most difficult, but with three large peaks there's plenty of terrain for all levels of skiers to explore. Fourteen lifts open up more than 55 miles of trails over 1,460 skiable acres. There's a quad chair on Peak 10; a quad, a triple, and four double chairs on Peak 9; and six double chairs and a surface lift on Peak 8. Peak 8 has the longest vertical: 2,613 feet. Peak 9 has a 1,860-foot vertical and Peak 10 has a 1,389-foot vertical which stretches to 2,007 feet when skiers cruise all the way down to the base of Peak 9.

Never-evers can learn at the base of either Peak 8 or 9. Those who've already skied a few times might want to start the day on the network of trails on Peak 9, because most are a little longer than the green runs on Peak 8. Silverthorne is a good warmup. Next try Red Rover, Eldorado, and Country Boy. Then move all the way to the top of the peak and try the easier blue runs, Upper Lehman, Cashier, Bonanza, and Upper Columbia. Springmeier, Crescendo, and Pathfinder are among the popular runs for lower to middle intermediates on Peak 8. Advanced intermediates will find American, Peerless, and Gold King on Peak 9 more challenging because they are longer, a little steeper, and have more terrain variation. To get the most out of the mountain, use the interlocking lift system to move between peaks. However, spend several hours on one before moving to the other, and think about switching peaks during lunch when lift traffic is theoretically lightest.

The lighter blacks on the mountain include Rounders, North Star, and Upper Lehman, which are groomed periodically so the moguls never get too large. The runs on the back side of Peak 8 around chair 6, which begin above the timberline but funnel into cuts between trees, are steeper and never groomed. The double diamonds and yellow lines on the map indicate experts-only areas. The sides of Horseshoe Bowl are open but steep enough so that bumps rarely become very big. The smaller Contest Bowl is even steeper. The deeper black (double-diamond) runs off the north side of Peak 9 have their own character. Inferno is more open, while bumps build in the narrow gulley called Devil's Crotch. Peak 10 is for skiers who love steeps and bumps. The terrain is a combination of open slopes and glades. The bumps build on most of the black runs here, and later in the year you might have to peer over them to see the fall line on the down side of the moguls on Mustang, Dark Rider, and Black Hawk. However, there's a very long run-out back to the chair.

Insider's Tips

There are free guided mountain tours on certain days. Check locally for specific days, times, and places.

Avoid chair C on Peak 9 on a busy day.

Don't panic when you see the line at the A-1 lift. A detachable quad rising from the base of Peak 9, this chair can move 3,000 skiers an hour uphill! (In addition to being the main chair out from town, it's to be the access chair to reach the chair on Peak 10, which does not have a base area.)

Visitors should leave their cars in town lots and use the shuttlebus system to get to the base of the mountain.

Buy lift tickets the afternoon before at the ski area. Front Range skiers can pick up discount tickets in Denver.

Mountain Facilities

Breckenridge has three base areas with ticket windows. The mountain restaurants offer everything from burgers in the cafeterias to seafood at the 9,600 Foot Club in the Maggie Building. There is a cafeteria and bar at the base of Peak 8 and a restaurant at the top of chair 2. On Peak 9 there's a restaurant and bar at the base, a restaurant and bar at the base of the D lift, and a restaurant at the top of C lift. There's a general information desk outside the Maggie Restaurant at the base of Peak 9.

Snow Coverage

Snowmaking equipment can cover 300 acres, primarily on Peak 9, at this ski area that receives an average yearly snowfall of 255 inches. Breckenridge is usually open from mid-November to mid-April. There's extensive grooming, particularly on the green and blue trails.

Ski School

Adult and children's group lessons start twice each day. Private lessons are also available. The all-day program for ski school/nursery youngsters between the ages of 3 and 6 is at Peak 8.

Childcare

The childcare center (tel. 453-2368) is at the base of Peak 8 and reservations are recommended. The center takes children 2 months and older (reservations required for the very young). Youngsters between the ages of 3 and 6 can enter the ski school/childcare program. There's childcare at the Breckenridge Hilton for children ages 1 to 3.

Rental Equipment

Rental equipment is available at the base areas and at several shops in town.

Cross-Country Skiing

The Breckenridge Nordic Ski Center (tel. 453-6885) has 45 km (27 miles) of double-set tracks. Two lodges offer rental equipment, lessons, a ski shop, and lunch on the deck. Ask about night tours and fondue parties.

Helicopter Skiing

Ask at the ski area general information desk for details.

WHERE TO STAY: Skiers can choose between mountain rustic condos, miniature indoor cities, houses, and dormitories spread throughout the tiny town of Breckenridge and up the mountainside toward the ski slopes. The **Breckenridge Resort Chamber** (tel. 303/453-2918, or toll free 800/822-5381 in Colorado) has a central reservations service where skiers can reserve lodging and obtain lift ticket prices, as well as ski-school, rental, transportation, and on-the-mountain-activity information. Most of the following accommodations can be arranged through central reservations.

Moderate to Expensive

The **Tyra Summit** (book through central reservations) has ski-in/ski-out access to the ski slopes. Units range from a studio unit that sleeps four to a luxurious four-bedroom/four-bath town house sleeping up to 14. During regular season studios go from approximately $99, and the town homes go up to $425 per night.

The **Breckenridge Hilton** (tel. 303/453-4500, or toll free 800/321-8444, 800/624-4433 in Colorado) is a full-service hotel with ski-in/ski-out access. The hotel has restaurants, room service, a nightclub, a pool, hot tubs, saunas, and more. Rooms vary in size, and cost from $110 for two people to approximately $180 for six people.

Beaver Run Resort, P.O. Box 2115, Breckenridge, CO 80424-2115 (tel. 303/453-6000, or toll free 800/525-2253, 800/331-1282 in Colorado), is like a miniature indoor city located adjacent to the slopes with ski-in/ski-out accessibility. The units, which tend to have small rooms, range from one-bedroom to four-bedroom condominium suites, each with its own bath. All condos have moss rock fireplaces, private balconies, and fully equipped kitchens. A grocery and liquor store are on the premises. Other amenities include six outdoor hot tubs, a pool, saunas, and steam and exercise rooms, along with a miniature golf area. Rates range approximately from a hotel room at $110 to the four-bedroom condos at $430.

Located by Maggie Pond and close to the base of Peak 9, **The Village at Breckenridge,** P.O. Box 1979, Breckenridge, CO 80424 (tel. 303/453-2000, or toll free 800/321-8552), has comfortable, modern condos ranging from studio accommodations to four-bedroom units. The Village's facilities include conference rooms, an athletic club with indoor and outdoor pools, hot tubs, outdoor ice skating, a cinema, nine restaurants, shops, and live theater. Prices range from approximately $90 a night in a hotel room to $360 for a three bedroom that sleeps six, and children 12 and under can stay free in their parents' room.

The **Wedgewood Lodge,** P.O. Box 7489, Breckenridge, CO 80424 (tel. 303/453-1800, or toll free 800/521-2458, 800/421-7159 in Colorado), two blocks from Peak 9 with ski-in accessibility, is a blend of Victorian and mountain contemporary. There are two- and three-bedroom units with fireplaces in the town homes and studios and one- or two-bedroom units in the tower. Amenities include a sauna, exercise room, indoor and outdoor spa, and a nearby pool. There is a lobby bar and convention facilities for up to 100 people. Rates for a two-bedroom unit begin at $160 per night.

Skiside (for information, contact the Wedgewood Lodge), near the base of Peak 8, has one- and two-bedroom condominiums, some with fireplaces. You can ski home from the Four o'Clock run, but regular shuttle service is available. There are hot tubs and guests have access to a nearby pool. Prices begin at $100 nightly for a one-bedroom unit sleeping four.

Least Expensive

A charming Victorian home has been converted into the **Fireside Inn,** P.O. Box 2252, Breckenridge, CO 80424 (tel. 303/453-6456), with accommodations from dorm rooms for four, to the Brandywine Suite which sleeps four comfortably. There is a hot tub. Prices range from $16.50 per person in the dorm rooms to the Brandywine Suite at $78 per night.

WHERE TO EAT: As you'd expect in a good resort town, skiers can get any taste from barbecue to game. Of course, fresh fish, good steaks, burgers, and pizzas are available too.

More Expensive

Dine in casual elegance overlooking the Maggie Pond at the **Polo Club Restaurant** (tel. 453-2300), which serves fresh fish, beef, veal, poultry, and daily chef's specials. Entrees range from approximately $10 to $18. It's open for dinner at 5 p.m., and for a table with the best view, arrive early. Reservations are suggested.

The **St. Bernard Inn**, at 103 S. Main St. (tel. 453-2572), specializes in the cooking of northern Italy with veal, beef, lamb, game, and seafood served in light sauces. Pastas, breads, and soups are made daily on the premises. The wine cellar contains more than 175 varieties of wine, with a particular selection of Italian wines. The Victorian dining room features candlelight and classical music. Entrees range from $8 to $18, and reservations are recommended. The pub opens at 3 p.m. and dinner is served from 5 to 10:30 p.m.

Good German food is the specialty at **Weber's**, at 200 N. Main St. (tel. 453-9464), with its Victorian parlor near the entryway and Victorian dining room hinting a German influence in the decor. It's open from 5 to 10 p.m., seven days a week, and reservations are required for a party of ten or more. The menu includes dishes from Bavaria, such as sauerbraten and wienerschnitzel, and American fare, and ranges in price from $10 to $18.

The decor at **Spencer's**, in Beaver Run (tel. 453-6000), is defined by blond wood, natural wicker chairs, and striking tablecloths and napkins. The menu features European and American cuisine, including imaginative preparations of veal, seafood, and game. Soups and salads are extra. Prices run $13 to $17. Dinner is from 6 to 10 p.m.

Moderate to Expensive

Egil's, at 318 N. Main St. (tel. 453-0947), serves family style in an old-fashioned Victorian atmosphere. Entrees are limited, and accompanied by a relish tray, soup, vegetables, and real mashed potatoes and gravy. Prices range from $9 to $13, and Egil's is open seven days a week at 5 p.m. Groups can arrange for breakfasts and lunches for 20 or more.

The casual **Village Pub**, on the Bell Tower Mall (tel. 453-0369), has a view of the Maggie Pond and Peak 9. Lunches, served from 10 a.m. to 4 p.m., feature hearty sandwiches, hamburgers, and homemade soup for $4 to $7; and dinners, from 5 to 10:30 p.m., range from steaks, chicken, and seafood to Mexican and Italian specialties, from $7.50 to $15.

Diners have a top-level view of Breckenridge from **The Terrace** and **Clifton's**, atop Georgian Square (tel. 453-0989). Dinner can be continental cuisine or lighter fare. Prices range from $9 to $17. The restaurant is open nightly from 5:30 p.m.; the bar is open daily from noon until 2 a.m. Sunday brunch is from 11 a.m. to 2 p.m. Reservations are suggested.

Tillie's Restaurant and Saloon, at 213 S. Ridge (tel. 453-0669), is open from 11 a.m. and serves food until midnight. Notice the handcrafted teak back-bar with a marble bartop, and the works of stained glass. Reasonably priced sandwiches, burgers, and homemade soups are served until 4:30 p.m. Dinners are served from 5 p.m. and prices range from $4 to $15.

Least Expensive

Mi Casa Mexican Restaurant and Cantina, 600 Park Ave. (tel. 453-2071), offers a carry-out service or you can call ahead and your order will be waiting when you arrive. Happy hour, on every day, calls for inexpensive pitchers of margaritas. Prices range from $4 for Mexican food to $12 for a steak for the gringos. Lunch hours are from 11 a.m. to 4 p.m., dinner is from 4.

Zachariah's, at 111 S. Main St. downstairs in Georgian Square (tel. 453-4806), features burgers, steaks, and deep-fried vegetables, along with beer. Burgers range from $2.75 to $5. Hours are from 11 a.m. to 9 p.m.

A D.A.M. Good Pizza Place, at 111 S. Main St. downstairs in Georgian Square (tel. 453-0230), serves a "Colorado-style pizza" with the best combined from the East and the West. Prices range from $5 to $11. It also houses an ice-cream-sundae bar. Call ahead for take-outs. They are open daily from 11:30 a.m. to 10 p.m.

Fatty's, 106 S. Ridge just off Lincoln Street (tel. 453-9802), is the oldest pizzeria in Breckenridge. Italian dishes plus soups and salads are also on the menu, and prices range from $4 to $14. Fatty's is open daily from 11 a.m. to 2 a.m., serving food until 10 p.m. There is a full-service bar.

SHOPPING: Just walk along Main Street and explore the businesses set in the old Victorian buildings and the newer shopping complexes, many of which were designed to fit in with the general atmosphere.

NON-SKIER ACTIVITIES: **Tiger Run** (tel. 453-9185) bills itself as "the world's largest snowmobile touring center." Snowmobiles and appropriate clothing can be rented. Tiger Run guides will bring visitors back into the century-old mines and abandoned ghost towns in the region. Tours on heated snowcoaches are also an option. There is **ice skating** on Maggie Pond and **sleigh rides** to steak dinners. Check on the entertainment at the **Backstage Theater.** For a complete listing, contact the **Breckenridge Resort Chamber** before visiting (tel. 303/453-6018) or stop in at the office when in Breckenridge. Pick up the *Breckenridge Visitor's Guide* from the chamber and follow the walking tour of the town.

GETTING THERE: Breckenridge is located 86 miles west of Denver. **Trailways** has one daily bus going into the town of Breckenridge, and four others from Denver, Colorado Springs, and Grand Junction, taking skiers to the bus stop in Frisco, nine miles away. **Ladybug Livery** (tel. 303/668-3565, or toll free 800/321-5246) is available to pick you up at Stapleton Airport or at Frisco. Driving time is two hours from Denver. Go west on I-70, through the Eisenhower Tunnel, exit at Frisco, and go south on Colo. 9 for nine miles.

MOVING AROUND: Free in-town shuttle service is available to Peaks 8 and 9 and the D lift every 15 minutes. An evening bus runs every 30 minutes. You can also ride the Ski the Summit Stage to Copper Mountain and Keystone. Buses run between the resorts approximately every half hour from early morning until about 6 p.m. The Breckenridge Urban Circulator circles Park and Main Streets.

TOURIST INFORMATION: For general information and assistance in lodging, contact the **Breckenridge Resort Chamber,** P.O. Box 1909, Breckenridge, CO 80424 (tel. 303/453-6018 for information; 303/453-2918, or toll free 800/822-5381 in Colorado for reservations).

Call 911 for **police, fire,** and **ambulance.** The **Breckenridge Medical Center** (tel. 453-6934) handles medical emergency calls 24 hours a day.

7. Ski the Summit

THE RESORT: Summit County, often called the Top of the Rockies, boasts four ski areas carved on mountainsides that climb up to the Continental Divide. The ski areas, Copper Mountain, Breckenridge, Keystone Mountain, and Arapahoe Basin, are within easy driving distance of each other, so many skiers staying at the base of one ski area often sample another. Because Summit County is also a summer resort, there are lodging and restaurants in Dillon and Silverthorne, towns in the center of the three ski areas, utilized by many skiers. A few years ago Copper, Keystone Resort, and Breckenridge formed a marketing group called Ski the Summit to pass out information about this region. Next the group created a Ski the Summit lift ticket that rides the lifts at all four ski areas. There are four- and six-day passes for destination visitors that can be used at any or all of the four areas. Ski the Summit also has a limited number of season passes for Colorado's Front Range skiers who want to explore all four areas. The Summit Stage, a free shuttlebus, ensures skiers transportation between the ski areas from throughout the county.

SKIING: Keystone, Arapahoe Basin, Copper, and Breckenridge are all located in Summit County. See the separate sections on these resorts for details. The Summit Stage takes skiers from various stops in the county to the ski areas, and buses also take skiers from one resort to the others throughout the day.

There are several cross-country operations in the area. See the Cross-Country Skiing sections in the various resorts for details. Check with the **Summit County Chamber of Commerce** (tel. 303/668-5800) to see if the town's proposed new major cross-country skiing operation has been started.

WHERE TO STAY: Many of the skiers opt to stay in Keystone Resort, the town of Breckenridge, or at Copper Mountain. For descriptions of lodgings there, see the Where to Stay sections in each resort. There's also lodging in the Dillon/Frisco/Silverthorne area anchored by the scenic, ice-blue Dillon Reservoir. For information about lodging in all price ranges in this region, contact the **Lake Dillon Resort Association,** P.O. Box 446, Dillon, CO 80435 (tel. 303/468-6222, or 592-1428 in Denver, or toll free 800/525-9824 outside Colorado).

The **Silverthorne Comfort Inn,** P.O. Box 368, Silverthorne, CO 80498 (tel. 303/468-6200, or toll free 800/321-3509), located just off I-70 near Lake Dillon, has basic but comfortable rooms and good packages for skiers. Ask for a room on the top floor with slanted ceilings. There's a restaurant on the premises, a swimming pool, whirlpool, and saunas. Call for prices.

Studio to three-bedroom/three-bath condos are available at **Wildernest,** Real Estate, P.O. Box 1069, Silverthorne, CO 80498 (tel. 303/468-6921, or 825-4434 in Denver), a mountain contemporary-style condo complex climbing up the mountainside in Silverthorne. Amenities include a sports desk and a ski shuttle, and some rentals include access to the health club with a heated pool. Rates start at $45 a night.

WHERE TO EAT: The funky **Old Dillon Inn,** 321 Blue River Pkwy. (tel. 468-2791), is one of the hottest spots in town. The ambience here is provided by the crowd, usually pressed into the bar of this old building waiting for tables in the dining room. The fare is Mexican and prices are reasonable, generally under $11 for dinner. Dinner is from 5 to 10 p.m.

The steaks are inexpensive at the **Mint,** at 341 Blue River Pkwy., next to the Old Dillon Inn (tel. 468-5247), because you pick a steak out of the refrigerator and cook it yourself on a charcoal grill set in the middle of the room. A salad bar is included. The price of beef (which includes salad) ranges from approximately $6 to $12, depending on the size of the cut. Baked potatoes and other side dishes are extra. Dinner is from 4:30 to 10 p.m.

NON-SKIER ACTIVITIES: See the Non-Skier Activities sections in Keystone, Breckenridge, and Copper.

TOURIST INFORMATION: For information about the area—places to dine, lodge, ski, and more—stop by the **Summit County Chamber of Commerce** (tel. 303/668-5800) information booths. One is located just off I-70 at exit 203; the other is located on U.S. 6 between Dillon and Silverthorne. For information about obtaining four- and six-day passes, and purchasing season passes, contact **Ski the Summit,** P.O. Box 267, Dillon, CO 80435 (tel. 303/468-6607). Also contact the Lake Dillon Resorts Association or Keystone, Copper, and Breckenridge at the addresses listed in the Tourist Information sections for those resorts.

Chapter VI

SOUTHERN COLORADO

1. Telluride
2. Purgatory
3. Crested Butte
4. Monarch
5. Cuchara
6. Other Colorado Ski Areas

THE SKI RESORTS IN SOUTHERN COLORADO are familiar territory to many Texans and southwesterners, but the rest of the world, including Denver, is still learning about the interesting terrain and generally shorter lift lines at these ski resorts tucked into less populated sections of the Rockies where civilization's inroads aren't quite as obvious. The three major resorts in southern Colorado are Telluride, Purgatory, and Crested Butte, but there a few mini-resorts and day areas that should be noted.

Located in a remote box canyon, the town of Telluride offers skiers lodging and après-ski in the rough buildings constructed long ago as well as in sleek new condominiums. The town is overshadowed by a mountain with a good variety of terrain for all skill levels (including a lot of outstanding advanced terrain), which is being continually upgraded by a management wishing to turn Telluride into a modern ski resort.

At Crested Butte the modern ski resort called Mount Crested Butte sits at the base of a gentle mountain with a great deal of intermediate terrain. The historic town of Crested Butte, three miles down the road, keeps skiers entertained during the après-ski hours. This region is famous for the Nordic skiers (including young children) telemarking around alpine skiers face-first in the snow.

Purgatory draws a mix of locals from Durango and visitors from southwestern states. There are lots of easy, broad intermediate slopes, and advanced skiers can explore the Legends. Skiers stay in the condo complexes at the base, in resort villages along the highway, or in the town of Durango, a half hour away.

Monarch and Cuchara are two other ski areas in southern Colorado that cater to overnight guests but are too small to be called resorts. Monarch, with an amenity-loaded lodge down the road, is a small, friendly ski area. Cuchara is a resort-in-the-making with a ski area designed to double in size in future years and the beginnings of a ski village.

1. Telluride

THE RESORT: Located in a remote box canyon, Telluride was nicknamed the "city of gold" by the miners who worked in claims up around 2,000 feet above sea level. They came down into town after harsh winters to celebrate at the 30 bars, gaming houses, and bordellos. Today some of those rough buildings still house restaurants and saloons primed to feed hungry skiers, and many of the old homes have become small lodges and bed-and-breakfast inns. But there are also newer luxury condo complexes closer to the lifts and trails, one of the signs that Telluride in the wintertime is now a ski town.

The ski mountain here is good and continually getting better, as more lifts are added and more terrain is cleared. Beginners have a nice-size private section, lower intermediates have their own peak, and intermediates have the run of much of the mountain, including many long, wide trails. Advanced and expert skiers have vast, steep glades and New England–style runs topped with western powder. Well-traveled expert skiers place Telluride on that small A-1 list with Jackson Hole, Taos, and Snowbird.

THE SKIING: The 3,155-vertical-foot mountain is accessed by a quad, six double and two triple chairs, and a poma lift. There are more than 45 trails on 735 acres of skiable terrain rated 14% beginner, 54% intermediate, and 32% advanced.

This mountain has distinct sections for the various skill levels. The front face, overlooking town, blends moguls, steeps, and often powder for advanced and expert skiers. The ski terrain on the other side of the mountain stairsteps. There's superb expert terrain on the top part. The main part of the Gorrono Basin, covering the middle part of the skiable mountain, is much gentler terrain and has open terrain and wide trails pitched and groomed for intermediates and beginners. The Meadows, at the bottom, is a large, open slope with gentle glades groomed for beginners, and the gentle, wide, groomed trails on Sunshine Peak, off by itself, are for lower intermediates.

Never-evers start on the Meadows, and beginners will enjoy the easy terrain around the long (for a beginner's area) chair 1. Better beginners can move on to chair 3, the Village chair, and take the beginner's bypass down into the Meadows for a long run. Although the Telluride trail on the front face is colored green, it's not really for beginners. Novices should head off the mountain through the Meadows or download on chair 7, the Coonskin lift.

Lower intermediates have wide runs off chair 3, ranging from the Lower See Forever to Misty Maiden with its gentle rolls and Sunshine Peak. Intermediates can explore the complex of runs around chairs 3 and 4, the Gorrono lift. Chair 5, the Palmyra lift, also has good intermediate terrain including Palmyra, which is a wide, open trail with one side kept smooth and the other side left moguled for advanced intermediates. Intermediates who want to go all the way to the summit can take See Forever, a comfortable cruiser with good terrain variation, back down.

The terrain around chair 7, the lift that climbs from the far edge of town, has both open slopes for advanced intermediates and some tighter trails for advanced skiers.

Advanced and expert skiers have fast access to their turf via the Oak Street and the Plunge lifts which climb up the front face. They open up the infamous Plunge and the equally notable Spiral Stairs, both of which have made many of the "toughest" and "most terrifying" lists regularly published by ski writers. In keeping with a ski-area trend to groom steep slopes regularly for "aging" knees, bumps on the Plunge are knocked down on a regular basis, so some expert skiers like to cruise it. Skiers who like to make bank turns should try Mammoth Slide, a steep, narrow gulley.

The expert terrain off chair 6, the Apex chair, at the top of the mountain, could take days to explore. Allais Alley and Zulu Queen are steep, narrow mogul chutes, reminiscent of eastern trails but with Rocky Mountain snow. Apex Glades is a vast expanse with lightly treed areas, open spaces, and tight tree stands, all intermixed.

Insider's Tips

Take the shuttlebuses to the slopes so you don't have to worry about parking a car.

The runs around chairs 3 and 4 are in the sun most of the time. Advanced skiers will find sun around chair 5. To catch the sun on the trails off chair 6, ski there early in the day. The front face gets sun later on.

When everyone has rushed to the top on a powder morning, check out the trails around chair 7.

Mountain Facilities

The Meadows Day Lodge, at the base of chair 1, has a cafeteria and bar. The Coonskin base has ticket offices, ski rentals, a ski shop, a restaurant, bar, and retail shops. Gorrono Restaurant and Bar, located at mid-mountain, has a cafeteria, a self-serve deli, barbecue, and a bar. The Plunge Restaurant on top of chair 9 has pizza and sandwiches.

Snow Coverage

Snowmaking equipment covers approximately 120 acres of the area with heavy skier traffic and sun exposure. An average of 300 inches falls on this ski area, which is normally open from before Thanksgiving to mid-April. There's a strong emphasis on grooming beginner and lower intermediate trails. Other intermediate trails are groomed regularly. The Plunge is groomed approximately three times a year when the moguls become too choppy.

Ski School

The ski school offers half- and full-day group lessons and private lessons. There are women's weeks, men's weeks, and mountain workshops for the steep and deep or moguls. There are special children's programs, including one where the ski school handles rentals as well as lessons and lunch.

Childcare

The "Wildbunch" Nursery accepts youngsters from 2½ months old. Childcare plus skiing is an option for 4- and 5-year-olds.

Rental Equipment

Rental equipment is available at the Coonskin and Meadows base areas. Several ski shops in town have rentals.

Cross-Country Skiing

The Telluride Nordic Center maintains 10-km (6-mile) and 20-km (12-mile) trails off the Meadows access road. Track and telemark lessons and rentals are available. There's a track in the town park.

TELLURIDE   103

Helicopter Skiing

Contact **Heli-Trax** (tel. 303/728-4904 or 728-3369) or **Sidewinder Ski Tours** (tel. 303/728-4944) for more information about heli-skiing in the San Juans.

WHERE TO STAY: Skiers can stay in accommodations ranging from a renovated brothel to a plush contemporary condo with a private whirlpool. **Telluride Central Reservations**, P.O. Box 1009, Telluride, CO 81435 (tel. 303/728-4431, or toll free 800/525-3455), will arrange for everything from one night of lodging to a weekly package complete with lodging, lift tickets, rentals, ski school, nursery, and transportation. **Resort Rentals**, P.O. Box 1278, Telluride, CO 81435 (tel. toll free 800/538-7754, 800/835-7433 in Colorado), handles more than 150 condominiums in town, and has a travel desk. All of the following may be booked through these sources.

While the ski corporation has been upgrading the mountain, developers have been renovating older properties and adding new condo complexes. Skiers now must choose between several new comfortable to luxurious condominium buildings near the slopes or just a short shuttle ride away. There are many lift/lodging packages. When making your reservations, ask if there are any special deals for the time you intend to visit Telluride. (In some cases it might be cheaper to take a three-day lift/lodging package than to pay for two nights' lodging.)

More Expensive

There are several liftside condominium complexes, or buildings within a five-minute walk, with amenities including whirlpools in the unit. The luxurious, individually owned, **Lulu City** condominiums, many with steam cabinets and solariums with spas, are near the Coonskin lift. The three-bedroom **Etta Place** condos have Jacuzzi spas and gas fireplaces. Both have outdoor pools. Prices vary greatly depending on the number of persons in the unit and the time of year. Call central reservations for quotes. The regular season rates for a one-bedroom condo at Etta Place or Lulu City, for example, are $130 a night; a two-bedroom is $230 a night.

There are also ski-in/ski-out condos available at the mid-mountain village. The attractive **Telemark** units overlook the intermediate beginner terrain (a car is needed to go into town at night). Ask for prices.

Moderate

There are several condominium complexes for more restricted budgets. The comfortable **Boomerang Village** units, within walking distance of the Coonskin lift, are popular with families and groups. The compact **Muscatel Flats** condominiums, with a contemporary decor, are in town. (It's a hike to the third floor with luggage at some of the complexes without elevators.) Again, rates vary. Regular season prices for a one-bedroom condo at either place is $110 a night.

The **Coonskin Inn** has rooms and one-bedroom apartments, located at the base of the Coonskin lift. Amenities include a hot tub and a Jacuzzi. Room rates run approximately $67 for double occupancy.

The **Best Western Tomboy Inn** has standard rooms and studio condominiums. There's also a sauna at this motel located several blocks from downtown. Room rates begin at approximately $58.

The **New Sheridan**, 231 W. Colorado (tel. 303/728-4351), provided the finest lodging and cuisine between Denver and San Francisco in the 1880s. It was renovated in 1977, and today guests have a choice of private rooms, room with bath down the hall, or even the William Jennings Bryan Suite decorated in antiques. If you like to sleep, make sure your room isn't over or too near the bar. The New Sheridan is in the center of town. Room rates begin at $35 a night, the exact rate depending on the type of room and whether it has a private bath.

Less Expensive

The **Dahl House** is a charmingly decorated guesthouse in the center of town. Each room is decorated differently in Victorian style. The bath is down the hall. Rates run approximately $45 a room.

The restored **Johnstone Inn** is three blocks from the Coonskin lift. The European-style lodge includes continental breakfast, après-ski refreshments, and hot tub rental. Room rates range from approximately $45 to $50 a night.

WHERE TO EAT: Most of the restaurants are located in the small, central part of town. Choices range from pizza to fresh fish and steaks.

More Expensive to Moderate

Annabelle's, 123 S. Spruce St. (tel. 728-4080), serves char-broiled selections, seafood, and Annabelle's specialties in a historic Victorian building with a fascinating history. Entrees run approximately $9 to $20. Reservations are recommended at this restaurant open for dinner nightly from 5 to 10 p.m. and also for lunch Monday through Saturday.

Leimgruber's Bierstube, 573 W. Pacific (tel. 728-4663), offers German food washed down with imported German beer on tap. This restaurant, near the Coonskin lift, is open for breakfast, lunch, and dinner, and is a popular après-ski spot. Entrees range from $6 to $15.

Julian's, at the New Sheridan, 231 W. Colorado (tel. 728-3839), is a sparsely elegant dining room with excellent dinners. Entrees feature northern Italian cuisine, including pasta and veal. Pasta starts at $8, and beef and other dishes run $11 to $20.

The Silverglade, 115 W. Colorado (tel. 728-4943), on the main street, still offers mesquite-broiled fresh fish. Steak, lamb chops, and duck are also on the menu. Hours are 6 to 10 p.m. daily, and entrees run $10 to $20.

Less Expensive

Sofio's, 110 E. Colorado (tel. 728-4882), a casual restaurant on the main street, is a popular breakfast place and an even busier dinner spot. The dinner menu is primarily Mexican food. Prices range from $3 to $7 for breakfast and from $7 to $12 for dinner. Breakfast is served from 7 to 11:30 a.m. Monday through Saturday and from 8 a.m. to 12:30 p.m. on Sunday. Dinner, ranging from $6 to $13, is served nightly from 5:30 to 10 p.m.

Soup, salad, and a variety of creative sandwiches and burgers with gourmet toppings are the fare at the **Floradora Saloon,** 103 W. Telluride Ave. (tel. 728-3888), a laid-back eating and drinking establishment on the main street. Most meals are under $10. Hours are from 11 to 2 a.m. Breakfast is served from 7 to 11 a.m.

The **Excelsior Café,** 200 W. Colorado (tel. 728-4250), is more of a European-style café on the main street that has mouth watering pastries and excellent coffee or cappuccino. Fondues, sandwiches, and other light meals are available for lunch and dinner. Prices range from $3 to $10. Hours are 11:30 a.m. to 10:30 p.m. daily.

Cheap Eats

Pick up baked goods, deli stuff, and some grocery items at **Baked in Telluride,** 127 S. Fir (tel. 728-4775). Hours are 6 a.m. to 10 p.m.

The Underground, 121 W. Colorado, has an ice-cream parlor, hamburger grill, and video games. Hours are 11 a.m. to 9 p.m. Sunday through Thursday, to 10 p.m. on Friday and Saturday.

ENTERTAINMENT: The **Last Dollar** (tel. 728-9922), 100 W. Colorado, a popular locals' spot, has live music, a pool table, and dart board. **Fly Me to the Moon Saloon,** 132 E. Colorado (tel. 728-MOON) has live music, a spring-loaded dance floor for your tired feet, and an adult game room.

SHOPPING: Just wander down the main street. The number of shops is limited but there is everything from T-shirts to trendy fashions in the windows.

NON-SKIER ACTIVITIES: There are movies and live productions at the **Nugget Theater** (tel. 728-3030). Wednesday nights there are skating parties at the town rink, which is open all week. For information about **sleigh rides** along the San Miguel River, call 728-3200. For information about the ice-climbing and mountaineering schools, call the **Telluride Chamber of Commerce** at 728-3041.

GETTING THERE: Telluride, located in a remote box canyon in the San Juan Mountains, boasts the highest commercial airport in the country. (It's on a mesa more than 10,000 feet above sea level. Takeoffs and landings here provide a unique view of the surrounding mountaintops.) Last year **Continental Express** and **Mesa Airlines** flew special planes into this airport and are expected to continue to do so. When the weather's bad, planes land in Montrose, 64 miles away, and skiers are bused to Telluride. **United Express** also lands at Montrose. Most skiers from major cities fly into Denver's Stapleton International Airport, then connect to Telluride or Montrose. The airlines and flight schedules into Telluride for this winter weren't finalized at the time this was written. Call **Telluride Central Reservations** and ask for the travel desk, which will have the current schedule and fares, and be able to make your reservations. The **Telluride Transit Company** (tel. 303/728-4105) meets flights.

For anyone driving, Telluride is on Colo. 145, 64 miles south of Montrose, 127 miles south of Grand Junction, 79 miles north of Cortez, and 125 miles from Durango.

GETTING AROUND: Free shuttlebuses circle the town approximately every 12 minutes. Check locally for the schedule on the Coonskin–Meadows shuttle that stops at those base areas and at the Nordic Center.

TOURIST INFORMATION: Contact **Telluride Central Reservations,** P.O. Box 1009, Telluride, CO 81435 (tel. 303/728-4431, or toll free 800/525-3455 outside Colorado), for information about the resort and reservations.

2. Purgatory

THE RESORT: Well along in the process of turning from a day area to a resort, Purgatory draws a mix of locals and visitors from southwestern states to its ski slopes. The mountain, which boasts a lot of good ballroom terrain, has a new section called the Legends for upper intermediate and advanced skiers. Visitors can stay in condo complexes at the base of the mountain in the Village Center area, at various condo complexes or lodges on the highway leading into Durango, or in that southern Colorado town. Skiers here tend to be "laid-back" both in dress and style, as one local explained.

THE SKIING: Purgatory is popular with southwesterners, especially those from New Mexico and Texas, because there is so much good intermediate terrain on this 2,022-vertical-foot mountain. However don't assume the black slopes are empty, because there's a strong local contingent that frequents that type of terrain on this mountain, which is actually rated 20% beginner, 50% intermediate, and 30% advanced. Purgatory has four triple chairs and five double chairs opening up the mountain.

Beginners have a private area, Columbine Station, set away from the main ski area so other skiers won't come rushing through. Once comfortable, beginners can move onto the main mountain to open runs like Mercy and Demon, or to Walk-A-Lot, a gentle road.

Much of the terrain here, as on What, West Fork, and Limbo, is benched so on many trails skiers ski steeper pitches, coast along on more level ground, then slide back onto steeper ground. However, the most popular intermediate run, Dead Spike, has a consistent pitch. Boogie and Peace are also popular because their "benches" are more subtle.

Skiers trying advanced runs for the first time might consider Pandemonium or Lower Hades. They both have good bumps but they are shorter than most of the other black runs. Many of the better skiers tend to spend much of the day exploring the runs around chairs 3 and 5 (and they even have an on-mountain restaurant nearby). Wapiti, which follows a lift line, is the showcase bump. However, Styx will probably have less traffic, because it starts way off to the left of chair 6 and takes an effort to find. The Legends is a 120-acre high intermediate and advanced area.

Mountain Facilities

Everything from restaurants to a ski school and ski rentals is housed in the Village Center and Kendall Mountain Buildings at the base of the ski slopes. There's also a pub in the old base lodge and food services in the Powderhouse, located midway up chair 2, and in Dante's, midway up chair 5, which has a sit-down restaurant in a greenhouse setting.

Snow Coverage

Purgatory receives an average of 300 inches each year and is normally open from mid-November to early April. Snowmaking equipment covers 100 acres, primarily beginner and some intermediate terrain. There is extensive grooming, with the emphasis on the beginner and intermediate trails.

Ski School

There are half- and all-day group lessons and private lessons, as well as racing and advanced skier clinics. Groups of up to 12 skiers can "rent a coach." Children go into the all-day ski school and youngsters from the ages of 2 to 6 can go into the Teddy Bear Camp.

Childcare

There is a nursery in the Village Center for children 2 years old or older. Youngsters between the ages of 2 and 6 can go into Teddy Bear Camp, which combines ski lessons with childcare and lunch.

Rental Equipment
Both alpine and Nordic (including telemark) rentals are available at Purgatory Sports in Village Center.

Cross-Country
The Purgatory Ski Touring Center, located across the highway from the ski area, has 15 km (9 miles) of groomed track. Both cross-country and telemark lessons are available. The touring center directors are members of the Professional Ski Instructors of America Nordic Demonstration Team. Rentals are available at Purgatory Sports at the base area.

Helicopter Skiing
Durango Helicopters takes skiers into the San Juans. For more information, contact the guest activities desk at the ski area through the main number.

WHERE TO STAY: Skiers can stay in the new condominiums at the base of the ski area; along U.S. 550; at nearby Tamarron, a luxury resort; or in Durango, a small western town 25 miles away. Many accommodations, including most of those listed below, are available through **Purgatory/Durango Central Reservations,** 546 Main Ave., Suite C, Durango, CO 81301 (tel. toll free 800/525-0892, or 800/358-3400 in Colorado). This service offers one-stop shopping for visitors who want to arrange for lodging, lift tickets, rentals, ski school, and even side trips. Winter is high season pricewise at the ski area, and low season in Durango —just the opposite of summertime. (If you're heading to or from the ski area early in the morning or at twilight, be sure to watch for elk in the fields.)

More Expensive
The **Village Center, Kendall Mountain,** and **Eolus** (book through central reservations) are the condominium complexes at the base of the ski area with ski-in/ski-out access. Lock-offs to more spacious two-bedroom units are available in the Village Center, identified by its southwestern architectural styling and copper roofs. The Eolus has smaller units. In the studio apartments murphy beds come down at night, then go up in the daytime, and a table comes out of the back of the bed!

There are studio to three-bedroom units and underground parking at Eolus, located up the mountain from the Village Center. The Eolus has an indoor/outdoor pool and whirlpool, but the Village Center and Kendall Mountain have rooftop Jacuzzis. Guests at all three complexes can use the facilities at the others. A lock-off at the Village Center runs $80, a studio (with a kitchen area) at the Eolus or Kendall Mountain runs $90, and a two-bedroom, which sleeps six, costs $220.

The elegantly rustic **Tamarron,** P.O. Box 3131, Durango, CO 81302 (tel. 303/247-8801, or toll free 800/525-5420, 800/525-0493 in Colorado), is an AAA four-star resort. Accommodations run from spacious rooms in the main lodge to condominiums and three-bedroom town homes spread around the property. There is shuttle service to the ski area, 15 minutes away, and to Durango. Known for its magnificent golf course, Tamarron turns one section into a 500-foot-vertical beginner's ski hill during the winter. The health club area has a heated pool, saunas, whirlpool, and hot tub, and there's skating on the pond, sleigh rides, and snowmobile tours. Purgatory Sports has a shop in the main lodge with ski rentals. There's a family restaurant, a gourmet dining room, and a lounge. Room rates range from $85 for a studio to $235 for a three-bedroom condo that sleeps six, and package plans are available.

You can't downhill ski at Purgatory when staying at **Tall Timbers Resort,**

SSR Box 90, Durango, CO 81301 (tel. 303/259-4813), because it's accessible only by helicopter. However, cross-country skiers should know about this one. It is a very highly rated hideaway in the beautiful Animas River Canyon, containing just a few elegant units with fireplaces. Amenities include a heated pool, a sauna, and whirlpool, with cross-country ski trails. A three-day minimum stay is required and rates are available on request. The winter rate includes all meals and a daily morning helicopter shuttle to Purgatory and an afternoon return.

Moderate

Cascade Village, located one mile from the ski area, has deluxe studio to three-bedroom condos with fireplaces and Jacuzzi tubs. There's an indoor pool, outdoor hot tubs, a restaurant and lounge, and a free shuttle to the ski area. Room rates go from $75 for a studio to $210 for a three-bedroom unit for six.

The **Strater Hotel,** 699 Main Ave., Durango, CO 81301 (tel. toll free 800/247-4431, 800/227-4431 in Colorado), built in 1887, is located in the historic heart of Durango, two blocks from the Silverton Train Depot. The hotel's 93 rooms are furnished with Victorian antiques. The restoration included modern bathrooms in single rooms and the suites. The Diamond Belle Saloon features live ragtime music. Room rates begin at approximately $54 for a double.

Less Expensive

The **General Palmer House,** 567 Main Ave., Durango, CO 81301 (tel. 303/247-4747), is a renovated Victorian hotel, built in 1898, containing 39 beautifully appointed rooms separated by fairly thick walls. It's located next to the historic station of the Silverton train. Excellent dining places are nearby. Room rate for double occupancy starts at $45. A continental breakfast is included.

WHERE TO EAT: There's enough competition between restaurants in this region to keep the chefs in top form. Although there are restaurants at the mountain and along the highway, the majority are in Durango.

More Expensive

Sample steaks to Colorado trout in an elegant Victorian atmosphere at the **Palace Restaurant** (tel. 247-2018), located next to the train depot. Prices range from $10 to $18. Hours are 11 a.m. to 2:30 p.m. for lunch and 5:30 to 10 p.m. for dinner. Reservations are suggested.

Hunters Restaurant, 992 Main Ave. (tel. 385-4737), offers steaks, seafood, home-style game, and nightly specials. Entrees range from $10 to $16. The lounge at this downtown Durango restaurant is a popular spot. Dinner is from 5:30 to 10 p.m.

Moderate to Expensive

The **Ore House** (tel. 247-5707) in Durango has a casual, rustic atmosphere where guests can dine on steak and seafood. A children's menu is available. Prices range from $10.50 to $16 for steak and up to $21 for lobster and crab. Dinner is from 5:30 to 10:30 p.m.

Ariano's, 150 E. 6th St. (tel. 247-8146), is a small, pleasant restaurant that features northern Italian fare. Pasta goes for around $8 to $11. Veal, beef, and steak specialties run $13 to $15. Hours are 5:30 to 11 p.m.

At the **Red Snapper,** 144 E. 9th St. (tel. 259-3417), diners can explore the underwater world in many saltwater aquariums set around the restaurant while waiting for their seafood, steak, or prime rib. Most entrees fall between $9 and $15. There's a children's menu at this restaurant in downtown Durango. Dinner is from 5 to 10 p.m.

Moderate

The **Olde Tymers Café,** 1000 Main Ave. (tel. 259-2990), serves sandwiches, soup, and salads for lunch and dinner. Prices range from $4 to $7 at this locals' gathering spot.

There are two **New York Bakery** restaurants, one located in Durango (tel. 259-1007) and the other at the base of the ski area (tel. 259-6477). Breakfast, lunch, and dinner are served. Breakfast costs up to $5. Lunch is from $3 to $7. Dinner includes different types of pasta, seafood, and steak. Prices range from $7 to $14. Hours are 6:30 a.m. to 10 p.m. daily.

Less Expensive

Clancy's Pub, below the Abbey Theater (tel. 247-2626), is an Irish pub complete with dart boards. It serves sandwiches, fish and chips, and ribs. Prices run $3 to $6.

Pronto Italian Café and Market, at 160 E. 6th St. (tel. 247-1510), is a popular pizza and spaghetti restaurant, with black-and-white tile floors, white Formica tables, and the smell of Italian seasonings from specialty items sold at the deli counter. A spaghetti dinner is $4.50 and up. Pizzas run $7 and up. Hours are 5 to 10 p.m.

B.W. Shay's, 948 Main Ave. (tel. 247-4144), serves salads, sandwiches, and inexpensive food for lunch and dinner. This restaurant is casual with large booths, nice woodwork, and lots of plants. Lunch is 11 a.m. to 3 p.m.; dinner is 5:30 to 10 p.m.

ENTERTAINMENT: The **6th St. Parlour,** 110 W. 6th St. (tel. 259-2888) and **Farquharts,** 725 Main St. (tel. 247-9861), have live music many evenings ranging from reggae to rock. Country and western sounds come from the **Sundance Saloon** 601 E. 2nd Ave. (tel. 247-8821); be sure to look at the mural on the back wall. For musical comedies and olios—or occasional straight theater—check the schedule at **Abbey Square** (tel. 247-9083).

SHOPPING: Wander along the Main Street area and around the train depot area to explore the shops and galleries. Stop by Durango Stockman, A & B Clothing, and Hogan's, where the locals buy western gear. **Piedras,** 1021 Main Ave. (tel. 247-9395), and in the Village Center at the ski area, has western art, unusual jewelry and glasswear. **To-atin** at 145 W. 9th St. (tel. 247-8277) displays American art and artifacts. **Gallerie Marguerite,** 144 E. 8th St. (tel. 259-2377), displays Indian and western art.

NON-SKIER ACTIVITIES: The topography in this part of Colorado changes from canyon to 14,000-foot mountains within a driving hour or two. Drive southward for about an hour toward canyon country until you see a lone mesa stretching off in the distance. It holds **Mesa Verde,** designated a world cultural site by the United Nations because of the cliff dwellings built by the Anasazi Indians, then abandoned mysteriously 700 years ago. Parts of Mesa Verde are open year round so visitors can explore the excavated archeological sites tracing the evolution of the ancient ones from pit dwellings to the "apartment houses" built in caves half way down sheer cliffs.

Information about Mesa Verde is available through the **Durango Chamber of Commerce** (tel. 247-0312 and ask for the activities information desk) at Purgatory. Other activities, from snowmobiling and snowcat tours to sleigh rides, can be arranged through the activities desk too.

Downtown Durango is a registered national historic district. Take a walking tour, stopping in the lobbies of the Strater and General Palmer Hotels. If you have a car, drive along **Third Avenue** (roughly from 6th to 15th Streets), another registered historical district, to see the Victorian mansions built by wealthy residents many years ago.

GETTING THERE: LaPlata Airport at Durango is the nearest airport to Purgatory, which is served by **America West, Continental Express, Mesa Airlines, Trans-Colorado,** and **United Express.** From there, regular shuttle service takes passengers to Durango and Purgatory. Car rentals are also available at the airport and in Durango.

If you're driving, Purgatory is 25 miles north of Durango via U.S. 550, 150 miles south of Grand Junction via U.S. 50 and U.S. 550, and 210 miles north of Albuquerque via U.S. 44 and 550; from Denver, it's 340 miles southwest via U.S. 285, 160, and 550.

MOVING AROUND: The Lift, a regularly scheduled bus shuttle, takes passengers from Durango to the slopes daily. Schedules are available at most lodging facilities. Many condominiums operate their own shuttle service.

TOURIST INFORMATION: For information and reservations in either nearby Durango or Purgatory, contact **Purgatory/Durango Central Reservations,** at 546 Main Ave., Suite C, Durango, CO 81301 (tel. 303/247-8900, or toll free 800/525-0892, 800/358-3400 in Colorado).

Dial "0" (zero, or operator) for **emergencies. LaPlata Community Hospital** (tel. 259-1110) is at 3801 Main Ave. at the north end of town.

3. Crested Butte

THE RESORT: This is a two-part resort! There is a collection of condominiums, lodges, and restaurants on a flank of the ski mountain which is topped by a massive, jagged stand of rock promoting the name of the resort and the mountain: Mount Crested Butte. The rest of the après-ski life, shops—many run by local craftspeople—and a few motels and lodges with baths down the hall are in the town of Crested Butte, a registered national historic district three miles down the road. There never seem to be lift lines on this gentle mountain where there are many well-groomed trails for intermediates and beginners. There is good acreage for advanced skiers and experts. And if the proposed surface lift was installed last summer, the 440 acres of double-black-diamond terrain in the Outer Limits, formerly reachable only by trekking, will be instantly popular with all good skiers. Often compared to Aspen 20 years ago, the Crested Butte regulars tend to be easy-going. Ultra-high-fashion outfits are still a rarity on the slopes. Much more common are the three-pinners telemarking around downhill skiers floundering in the snow. Even youngsters can be seen sliding down the hill on metal-edged cross-country skis in this region where postmen delivered the mail on skis during the late 19th century.

THE SKIING: There are nine chairs and a T-bar opening up this 2,150-foot-vertical mountain. Usually the mountain opens in mid-November and closes in early April. The terrain is rated as 27% easiest, 53% more difficult, and 20% most difficult, excluding the North Face section of the Outer Limits (which now has a lift if last summer's plans went as scheduled), which is 100% most difficult. The maintenance crew spends a lot of night hours grooming the slopes at this resort so beginners and intermediates will have carpet-smooth runs. The complex of green trails off the Keystone lift offer gentle, open slopes for beginners. Intermediates and cruisers gravitate toward the Paradise lift. Many of the runs vary challenging pitches with plateaus where skiers can rest and enjoy the panoramic view. Upper Treasury has some of the steepest pitches and keeps powder longer than most of the runs off this lift, because the entrance is off the popular track. Advanced skiers will enjoy skiing most of the blue runs on this mountain because the pitches are good for comfortable, controlled cruising. Keystone, Twister, and other runs off the top of the Silver Queen lift are excellent for advanced skiers because they offer steep pitches split by cat tracks where skiers can rest or cut to another run. There is good expert terrain in bowls, chutes, and glades in the North Face section of the Outer Limits, 440 acres now accessed by a poma lift if plans went as scheduled last summer. This terrain is strictly for very advanced skiers. The Outer Limits off the Silver Queen lift includes the Upper Forest, a cut in the trees that narrows down to Forest (strictly tight tree skiing), and a few other steep runs under the mountain's peak.

Insider's Tips

The mountain stands alone; no other mountains overshadow it, blocking the sun. To follow the sun, start on the East River chair lift and work around the mountain to the Silver Queen lift on the front side.

Crested Butte is considered a hot spot for telemarkers, so rent a pair of mountaineering skis, take a lesson, and spend a day telemarking down the slopes.

Snow Coverage

Snowmaking covers more than 300 acres reachable via seven lifts. The annual snowfall is 300 inches.

Ski School

The ski school offers two sessions daily. In addition to the regular classes, there are learn-to-ski packages and bump and powder clinics for advanced skiers. The area offers NASTAR racing clinics and races, and Star Test. There is a self-timed dual format race course. Butte Busters is all-day ski school with supervised lunch for children between the ages of 7 and 12. There's a new program opening up skiing experiences for the physically handicapped.

Childcare

Childcare is available for babies from the age of 6 months up through 6 years old. Children from 6 months to 3 years stay in the infant-care room, staffed by a professional nurse, at Buttetopia Ski and Day Care Center located in the Whetstone Building at the base of the Silver Queen lift. Youngsters from the ages of 3 to 8 have a different play area and can spend part of the day in ski classes. In Buttetopia's ABC on Skis, the staff, all members of the Professional Ski Instructors of America, teach the children basic skiing skills so they can easily move into regular ski-school classes when they get older. Buttetopia runs a special parent/child class during which parents are taught how to ski safely with their children. To ensure space, make childcare reservations in advance through the toll-free number, 800/525-4220. Children between the ages of 7 and 12 can go into Butte Busters, an all-day ski-school program.

Rental Equipment

Equipment is available at the Crested Butte Ski Rental and Repair. High-performance equipment and overnight repair and storage service are also available at this shop open from 8 a.m. to 5 p.m. Sunday through Friday, to 8 p.m. on Saturday.

Cross-Country Skiing

Crested Butte bills itself as the home of telemarking, and there are often as many cross-country skiers on the slopes as downhill skiers. Both set track and telemarking classes are available through the ski school. The resort maintains more than 13 km (8 miles) of groomed trails, but the backcountry is waiting to be explored by skiers on guided tours that go past mining ruins. Cookouts and moonlight tours are other options for cross-country skiers. Lift tickets can be exchanged for Nordic equipment rental and lessons.

The Irwin Lodge also offers guests cross-country skiiing. See the description of the lodge in the Where to Stay section.

Snowcat Skiing

The Irwin Lodge snowcats run guests up the mountainside for up to 2,000-foot-vertical runs. See the Where to Stay section for more information.

WHERE TO STAY: The village at the base of the mountain was started in 1974 so the lodges and condominiums are in good condition. There are several condo complexes with ski-in access or within a three-minute walk of the slope. There are dorm-style lodging and comparatively inexpensive rooms in the town of Crested Butte. For **lodging reservations** at the following properties, call toll free 800/525-4220 from anywhere in the continental U.S.

More Expensive

The **Grande Butte Hotel** (tel. toll free 800/341-5437, 800/441-2781 in Colorado) is a luxury hotel with kitchenettes and Jacuzzi tubs in each of the 262 rooms. There are six restaurants, a pool, tub, sauna, and more in this full-service hotel with ski-in/ski-out access. Regular season prices range from $100 to $120 for a hotel room depending on the view; suites are $150 to $165.

Some of the most luxurious accommodations in Mount Crested Butte are called the **Penthouse Condominiums** (tel. 303/349-7555, or toll free 800/282-2013, 800/521-5970 in Colorado) and are located in the ski-in/ski-out Crested Mountain Village Conference Center. Interior designs here had to pass a board approval. Primarily one-bedroom units, each has a microwave, Jacuzzi tub, and fireplace, and some have fireplaces in the master bedroom. Ask for a top-floor unit; the rooms have slanted, wood ceilings. Guests use the indoor pool and hot tubs in the lodge next door. One of the premier properties on the mountain is the three-bedroom/three-bath condominium on top of the mini-mall next door, considered one of the Penthouse units. The 2½-story living room has a rock wall fireplace; there's a hot tub, a private deck overlooking the slopes, and a sauna off the master bedroom with its own Jacuzzi tub. Prices for the Penthouse condominiums range from $140 for a studio/bath to $360 for a three-bedroom/three-bath.

Many of the spacious condominiums at the **Buttes,** just up the mountainside, have hot tubs in the condos. These condos are spread over several levels and the larger ones even have separate sitting areas beyond the living room, a dining room, and a table in the kitchen. Guests can use the heated indoor pool, hot tub, and sauna at the main lodge. Prices range from $142 for a studio with private bath to $319 for a three-bedroom/three-bath.

The condominiums in the **Crested Mountain North** (tel. toll free 800/282-2013, 800/521-5970 in Colorado) property are comfortable and nicely decorated. Each has a fireplace and a microwave, and all master bedrooms have Jacuzzi tubs. Guests have the use of an indoor pool and hot tub in a nearby building. Prices range from $145 for a two-bedroom/two-bath to $263 for a three-bedroom/2½-bath.

For a unique experience, visit the **Irwin Lodge,** P.O. Box 457, Crested Butte, CO 81224 (tel. 303/349-5140), located in the wilderness, accessible only by snowcat or snowmobiling during the winter months. Guests are picked up for a minimum of a three-day stay at the rustic lodge. Visitors have their choice of downhill skiing via snowcat (with 2,000-foot-vertical runs often in fresh powder), snowmobiling with tour guides, or cross-country skiing with guides. Meals are included. Contact the Irwin Lodge for details and prices.

Moderate

The **Mountain Sunrise Condominiums** are actually attractive town houses with garages. They are located several blocks from the slopes so skiers must take the shuttlebus, walk, or drive their car and park in the main lot. There is an outdoor Jacuzzi and a sauna. Prices range from $136 for a two-bedroom unit to $183 for a three-bedroom unit.

The **Plaza,** at the base of the mountain, has deluxe two- and three-bedroom condominiums. Amenities include elevators, underground parking, on-site grocery delivery, hot tubs, sauna, and steam room. Rates run $210 to $275.

The **Gateway** condominiums (tel. toll free 800/821-3718, 800/349-2448 in Colorado) are located at the base of the Peachtree lift, offering ski-in/ski-out access but a short uphill walk to the base area. The units have large living room/dining areas and are nicely decorated. There are outdoor Jacuzzis in the complex. Prices range from $110 for a one-bedroom/one-bath to $185 for a three-bedroom/three-bath.

The **Crested Butte Lodge** (tel. toll free 800/282-2013, 800/521-5970 in Colorado) is right next to the slopes, and has a 24-hour front desk, a restaurant on the premises, and an indoor heated pool and Jacuzzi. Rooms start at $59.

Less Expensive

Rozman's, at the edge of the town of Crested Butte, has basic motel rooms, many with kitchenettes. The motel, which has a restaurant and lounge, is within walking distance of main street, but skiers must take the shuttle or drive to the ski slopes. Rooms start at $38.

The **Elk Mountain Lodge** is a renovated historic miners' hotel located two blocks from main street and the nearest shuttle stop. There are 19 Victorian-style rooms with queen-size beds and private bath. There is a communal whirlpool. During regular season rooms cost $55 to $78 a night.

WHERE TO EAT: There are several restaurants in Mount Crested Butte and a much larger selection in the town of Crested Butte. Many skiers spend the day and après-ski hour in the ski village, then come down to the old town for dinner. Unless listed as being on or near the slopes, the restaurants and bars below are in the town of Crested Butte.

More Expensive

A locals' favorite is **Le Bosquet,** 201 Elk Ave. (tel. 349-5808), the town's French restaurant. Guests relax in the intimate dining area around attractively set tables in this rustic older building. Located at the corner of 2nd and Elk, Le Bosquet's hours are 5:30 to 10 p.m. for dinner. Reservations are requested. House specialties range from $10 to $20.

Penelope's Restaurant and Greenhouse, 120 Elk Ave. (tel. 349-5178), is one of the most popular spots in town. Guests dine in rooms decorated in keeping with the style of this century-old house or in the large, airy "no-smokers" greenhouse. Entrees on the continental American menu, such as scampi, fresh trout, and steak, range from $8.75 to $16.75. The bar opens at 5 p.m., and dinner is served from 5:30 to 10 p.m.

The **Soupçon,** 127A Elk Ave. (tel. 349-5448), is a charming gourmet restaurant located in an old log cabin in the alley behind the Forest Queen. The longtime specialty is roast duck with plum sauce, but there's fresh seafood and innovative presentations of steak and veal. Entrees range from $15 to $18. Hours are 6 to 10 p.m. daily, and reservations are recommended because the place is small.

Moderate

Slogar, housed in a Victorian building on the corner of 2nd and White Rock (tel. 349-5765), offers family-style food at family prices. There's steak and skillet-fried chicken, and the dishes are all made from scratch at the restaurant. Dinner is from 5 to 9 p.m.

Skiers park their skis next to the **Artichoke** (tel. 349-5400), at the base of the lifts, and run inside for a leisurely lunch or après-ski activity in this restaurant with high wood ceilings, plants, and glass windows for ski-slope viewing. The lunch menus range from the infamous "stuff it" burger to veggie sandwiches, while the evening meals run from prime rib to steaks. Lunch is served from 11:30 a.m. to 3 p.m. and dinner is served from 6 to 10 p.m. daily. Lunch is from $5.50 and dinner from approximately $8.

Donita's Cantina, 330 Elk Ave. (tel. 349-6316), is a local institution, although it was moved to a new building a year ago. Mexican food is served from 5 to 10 p.m. nightly.

The "souper, stew-pendous" salad bar at the **Tin Cup Café,** in the mall at the base of the mountain (tel. 349-7555), is a tasty bargain. The reasonably priced buffet includes soups, chili, stew, pastas, and salads. Actually the restaurant serves three meals a day, and all items are available for take-out. Breakfasts can range from build-your-own omelets to hotcakes. There is a complete burger and sandwich lunch menu, and dinner entrees range from barbecued chicken to beef stew. Prices go from approximately $5 to $15. Breakfast is served from 7 to 10:30 a.m., lunch is from 11:30 a.m. to 3 p.m., and dinner is from 5:30 to 9 p.m. daily.

The **Gourmet Noodle,** 411 3rd St. (tel. 349-7401), creates unexpected combinations with success. Diners choose from a variety of pastas, ranging from egg and herb to tomato, and the many sauces including pesto, Italian sausage, and red clam sauce. Sauce and pasta starts at $7, and entrees start at $10. Winter hours are 6 to 10 p.m.

The **Wooden Nickel,** 222 Elk Ave. (tel. 349-6350), promises hearty portions ranging from one-pound steaks to steamed clams. Prime rib, ribs, and live lobster are featured on different nights of the week. The bar in this old, weathered-wood saloon opens at 3 p.m. and meals are served from 5:30 to 10 p.m.

The **Rafters** (tel. 349-2298), located in the top of the Gothic Building next to the slopes, serves appetizers and a variety of hamburgers from 11 a.m. to 3 p.m. and from 5 to 9 p.m. Prices go from $5 to $10. There is a children's menu too.

ENTERTAINMENT: The **Rafters** (tel. 349-2298), topping the Gothic Building at the base of the mountain, is a barn-size room where skiers congregate when the slopes close for après-ski and an early dinner. There is usually live entertainment. Check for hours and talent. **Kochevar's Saloon and Dance Hall,** 127 Elk Ave. (tel. 349-6745), is the ultimate authentic western saloon where locals and visitors mingle at the pool table, playing darts or watching the evening's entertainers. Big names, such as Richie Cole, have been known to stand in for a set or two. Check for talent and hours. The **Eldorado Café**, 215 Elk Ave. (tel. 349-6306), upstairs next to the post office, is a long, rustic room offering burgers and dinners, ranging from $3 to $9, with pool tables and live entertainment several nights a week. Food is served from 11 a.m. to closing. The **Saloon**, a small watering hole in the Convention Center at the base of the slopes, is well populated during the après-ski hours. Parents talk and hungry children wolf down hot dogs.

SHOPPING: There is a mini-mall at the base of the mountain, but the most interesting shops and galleries are on the main street (Elk Avenue) in the town of Crested Butte. The **Company Store**, on Elk, once was the place where miners and their families shopped. The renovated building houses several shops, including an art gallery and a gift store with many interesting, handmade items. **Mountain Tops of Crested Butte,** 302 Elk Ave., sells silk screened and monogrammed shirts and caps. Hours are 9 a.m. to 8 p.m. daily. Stop by the **Hardware Store** (and Conoco Station) at the corner of 4th and Elk, to see the world-record elk, shot in the early 1900s. Built in 1883, this place still sells everything from knives to gas.

NON-SKIER ACTIVITIES: At the chamber of commerce office in the Town Hall, pick up a map that outlines a **walking tour** of this town, which is a designated historic district. Many artists and craftspeople live in Crested Butte and display their works in small galleries on or near Elk Avenue. **Just Horsin' Around** (tel. 349-6821) also offers sleigh rides leaving from town, and snowmobiling tours are popular. There are films at the **Princess Theater** and plays at the **Mountain Theater.**

GETTING THERE: Crested Butte is 28 miles from Gunnison, via Colo. 135. **American Airlines** has daily nonstop flights from Dallas to the Gunnison/Crested Butte airport. **Trans Colorado Airlines,** a commuter line, flies into Gunnison. Skiers from other cities connect via **United Express** and **Continental Express** through Denver (230 miles away). The **Crested Butte Taxi** (tel. 349-5789) and **Crested Butte Limousines** (tel. 641-5074) run from the airport to the resort. **Hertz** and **Budget** rental cars are available at the Gunnison Airport.

MOVING AROUND: Mount Crested Butte is small, so most of the lodges are within easy walking distance of the slopes. There is a free resort shuttlebus service that operates daily from 7 a.m. to midnight. Buses make a tour of the condos at Mount Crested Butte every 20 minutes and run every half hour between the towns of Crested Butte and Mount Crested Butte.

TOURIST INFORMATION: For information about or reservations in Crested Butte, contact the **Mount Crested Butte Resort,** P.O. Box A, Crested Butte, CO 81224 (tel. toll free 800/525-4220). When in the area, brochures and a map of a walking tour of Crested Butte are available at the chamber of commerce offices (tel. 349-6438) in the Town Hall at 2nd and Elk, Monday through Friday.

For **emergencies** call 911, which will bring help from the fire station, ambulance service, police, sheriff, state patrol, and search and rescue.

4. Monarch

THE RESORT: Monarch Ski Resort encompasses a day area with one of the best 360° views in the Rockies (and good views are too numerous to calculate in Colorado) from the top, and an amenity-loaded lodge three miles down the road. Although the vertical here is just 1,000 feet, short by Colorado's standards, there's plenty of well-pitched terrain for beginners and intermediates. The area draws day skiers from Colorado Springs, Pueblo, and nearby Gunnison, as well as overnight visitors from Texas and Oklahoma. The inexpensive lodging/lift packages provide a low-cost way to spend the weekend skiing on Rocky Mountain snow.

THE SKIING: Laid out in the conventional superhighway style, the 50 runs come off four double trail lifts. The trails are rated 20% beginner, 52% intermediate, and 28% expert. They are spread around the sides of a bowl (which means there is always a run in the sun), and they all end close to the base lodge, a plus for families. Beginners can enjoy the spectacular scenery from the top by taking the Tumbelina and Panorama chairs, then skiing down Skywalker, which follows the rim of the Continental Divide. (Five major ranges—the Elk Mountains, San Juans, Sangre de Cristos, the Sawatch Range, and the Front Range, which includes Pike's Peak—are visible from here.) Then they pick up a meandering run that starts as Sleepy Hollow and turns into Glade. Most of the intermediate and advanced runs are short; they end on run-out terrain, which takes skiers back to the base of the chairs. The most notable exception is the long, nicely pitched intermediate run called Slo-motion that borders one side of the ski area. There are some good steeps here—Sheer-Rock-O and High Anxiety are appropriately named—but unfortunately the runs are quite short. Bumps build up on Mirage but are cut down on most of the other black runs. When there is good powder to be found (and that's often here), it's on Out Back, a wide, open piece of black-rated turf where skiers can make giant slalom turns without crossing over other skier's tracks.

Mountain Facilities

The base lodge has one of the most attractive dining areas found in any ski resort of this size. Skiers sit around butcher-block tables in the eating areas or in the greenhouse area with skylight and hanging plants. The upstairs bar is startingly trendy for a family ski area.

Snow Coverage

There are no snowmaking machines here. The base lodge is at 10,800 feet, and the area averages 350 inches of snow each winter, so management doesn't believe falsie flakes are needed. The grooming crews work constantly to keep the trails in good condition.

Ski School

The school runs regular half- and full-day adult ski-school classes, and private and children's lessons. In addition to the regular children's classes, Monarch runs a KIDski program for children ages 6 to 10. The classes, which run from 10:30 a.m. to 3:30 p.m., include lunch with the instructor. The school also offers the two-hour Explorer program, a chance to ski with an instructor as a guide, which does include line-cutting privileges. The Supreme program places skiers of the same level together for an all-day ski lesson and lunch with the instructor. Videotaping and critiques by an instructor are also offered.

Childcare

The Jellybean Jungle is a childcare center at the ski area for children from ages 6 months to 6 years. There is indoor/outdoor play, and all-day or half-day care if available, with or without ski instruction.

Rental Equipment
Regular ski equipment and demos are available at the rental shop in the main lodge. There is a daily and a multiple-day rate.

Cross-Country Skiing
The Monarch Touring Center, headquartered in the base lodge, maintains ten kilometers of trails. Cross-country lessons and rentals are available. Backcountry tours, overnight tours, and cookouts are all offered.

WHERE TO STAY: The **Monarch Lodge,** three miles down the road, is a popular pit stop for travelers driving through this section of the Rockies. But stepping beyond the coffeeshop, there is a lodge that offers all the amenities, from an outdoor Jacuzzi, an indoor swimming pool, and racquetball courts to an arcade area and live entertainment during holidays or recorded music during weekends in the lounge. The 100 rooms aren't fancy but they're comfortable. Ask for a room on the fifth floor (on the back side because they overlook the mountainside instead of the highway) because they've pushed out the walls for windows so there is more space. The efficiency units cost approximately $10 more but they have kitchenettes. (Again, the units on the fifth floor in the back have the most space and the better view.) Rates per room per night during the regular season are $64. There are lodging and lift packages. Children 6 years and under stay and ski free.

There are other motels in Poncha Springs and Salida, approximately 18 miles east of the ski area.

WHERE TO EAT: The attractive dining room at the Monarch Lodge, the **Syncline Room,** has a brick fireplace, blue-patterned wallpaper, and large windows offering a mountainside view. The menu runs the gamut from prime rib to fried chicken. Entrees range from $8 to $16.

ENTERTAINMENT: There is entertainment on the weekends and après-ski all the time in **Taylor's Upstairs Bar.** There is a small game room nearby.

GETTING THERE: Monarch Ski Resort is on Monarch Pass, 157 miles from Denver via U.S. 285 and U.S. 50. It is 120 miles from Colorado Springs via Colo. 115 and U.S. 50. Some skiers fly into Denver or Colorado Springs and get a rental car. Shuttlebuses run between the lodge and the ski area, three miles away. However, skiers usually come here by car, and a car is a necessity for skiers staying in nearby Poncha Springs or Salida.

TOURIST INFORMATION: For reservations, contact **Monarch Ski Resort,** Garfield, CO 81227 (tel. toll free 800/525-9390, 800/332-3668 in Colorado).

5. Cuchara

THE RESORT: Cuchara, just six years old, is more accurately a resort-in-the-making. The drive through the spoon-shaped Cuchara Valley, past the wind-blasted ridges and by rushing streams, to reach this "resortlet," makes the visit. The ski area is small, 120 acres, but scheduled to double in size and climb several hundred vertical feet, according to future expansion plans. Care is being taken to create attractive facilities in the base area. There's a small mall with a few shops and restaurants, and several condo complexes nearby. Cuchara is popular with Texans because it's one of the closest ski areas to parts of Texas (just 272 miles from Amarillo), Oklahoma, and Kansas.

THE SKIING: Four chairs and a tow open up the 1,562 vertical feet of primarily intermediate terrain. Terrain is rated 25% beginner, 50% intermediate, and 25% advanced, although the black trails would be blue/black or light black at many bigger areas in the Rockies.

The area is frequented primarily by beginning and intermediate skiers so the easier slopes may get crowded, although the advanced slopes are often close to empty. Beginners can work off the small lifts at the base of the mountain. The trails around chair 5 are wide and comfortably pitched for intermediates. More advanced skiers head to Rattlesnake or Bear Bumps off chair 3, then move on to Ultima, a short, open black run that may not be groomed. Black-rated El Diablo is a genuine cruiser, with fun-size bumps on the lower half.

Mountain Facilities

There's a clean, pleasant cafeteria in the warming hut at the foot of the main lifts. The mall, with several shops and a deli, and a fancier lounge/restaurant are located a few steps away.

Snow Coverage

Snowmaking covers 85% of the Cuchara, which is normally open from the end of November to April. Grooming is very sophisticated at this area, which has an average snowfall of 190 inches.

Ski School

The ski school offers group and private lessons. Children under 6 ski free.

Cross-Country Skiing

Cross-country skiers can explore miles of trails in and around Cuchara. Equipment rentals and lessons are available.

WHERE TO STAY: Housing here ranges from deluxe multilevel town houses with private spa rooms to more basic condominiums. There are five complexes, two close to the slopes and the others in a more secluded area less than a five-minute drive away. A horse-drawn sleigh takes skiers from some of the accommodations to the base lodge. Rates range from $85 a night for a basic Aspen Leaf Village condo for two up to $205 nightly for the plush Panadero Villas, which sleep up to six.

GETTING THERE: Cuchara Valley Resort is located 185 miles from Denver via I-25 south to U.S. 160 west, to Colo. 12 south to Cuchara. It is 70 miles from Pueblo and 270 miles from Amarillo, Texas, and less than three hours from the borders of Oklahoma and Kansas. **Rocky Mountain Airways** flies to Pueblo and Alamosa. **Trailways** goes to La Veta, 14 miles away. Check with Cuchara about using **Amtrak**.

TOURIST INFORMATION: Contact **Cuchara Valley Central Reservations**, Resort Box 10, Cuchara, CO 81055 (tel. 303/742-3163, or toll free 800/227-4436 outside Colorado).

6. Other Colorado Ski Areas

LOVELAND BASIN AND VALLEY: One of the most popular Front Range day areas, and just 56 miles from Denver on the close side of the Eisenhower Tunnel butting up to the Continental Divide, this ski area gets dumps of snow ensuring mid-October openings and May closings. Five double chairs, two triples, and a poma access the wide slopes and trails at this 1,430-vertical-foot ski area. Terrain is rated 25% easiest, 50% more difficult, and 25% most difficult. There are good slopes for beginners and intermediates in the basin, open slopes above timberline for intermediates, and challenging trails for advanced and expert skiers. Loveland is just off I-70 via exit 216, the last exit before the tunnel entrance. For information contact **Loveland**, P.O. Box 899, Georgetown, CO 80444 (tel. 303/569-2288, or 571-5580 in Denver).

SKI SUNLIGHT: Ski Sunlight, a 2,010-vertical-foot ski area, ten miles southwest of Glenwood Springs on County Road 117, is geared for friendly, family crowds and skiers on a budget. Two double chairs and a surface lift open up lots of cruising intermediate runs. Terrain is rated 20% easiest, 58% more difficult, and 22% most difficult. Cross-country skiers can try 24 km (14½ miles) of machine-groomed trails. There's a wide range of lodging in the area, and skiers often end the day with a dip in the world's largest hot-springs pool, located in Glenwood Springs. For information, contact **Ski Sunlight**, 10901 County Road 117, Glenwood Springs, CO 80601. The central reservations number in Colorado is 800/221-0098 toll free; outside Colorado, call 303/945-7295.

BERTHOUD PASS: Berthoud Pass is the oldest ski area in Colorado, and has one of the longest seasons. Only 57 miles west of Denver, it's a good family day area. Sitting on top of Berthoud Pass, one can experience top-of-the-world views at its highest elevation of 12,015. Their 993-foot vertical provides 40% beginners, 40% intermediate, and 20% advanced terrain. They also have bargain prices. For information, contact P.O. Box 3220, Idaho Springs, CO 80452 (tel. 303/572-8014).

CONQUISTADOR: Located in south-central Colorado, Conquistador is in the San Isabel National Forest, five miles west of Westcliffe. Four lifts open up the 1,200-foot vertical. The 15 runs are on terrain rated 30% beginner, 55% intermediate, and 15% expert. A Nordic center offers instruction in trail skiing and telemarking by reservation. There are base-area accommodations. Contact P.O. Box 347, Westcliffe, CO 81252 (tel. 303/783-9206).

SKI COOPER: Another long-established ski area located on the Continental Divide, Ski Cooper is ten miles from the historical town of Leadville. It is 100 miles from Denver and 129 from Colorado Springs. The uncrowded slopes have a vertical drop of 1,200 feet and three lifts open up terrain rated 30% beginner, 40% intermediate, and 30% advanced. Contact P.O. Box 896, Leadville, CO 80461 (tel. 303/486-2277).

WOLF CREEK: More than 450 inches of snowfall per year makes Wolf Creek the ski area with the most snow each season, the reason for its deserved reputation as a powder haven. Though served by five lifts, snowcats take advanced skiers into more vertical for virgin powder (only on weekends). Terrain is 25% beginner, 45% intermediate, and 30% advanced on this 1,125-foot-vertical mountain. Contact P.O. Box 1036, Pagosa Springs, CO 81147 (tel. 303/264-2533).

HIDDEN VALLEY: Located in the Rocky Mountain National Park, just outside the summer resort of Estes Park, Hidden Valley is an inexpensive place for families, church groups, and clubs. It serves the population of northeastern Colorado, but is also a destination area for some skiers on a budget. The area is divided into two sections, the lower one for all skiers, and the bus-served upper mountain is more for the experts and advanced intermediates. Terrain on the 2,000-vertical-foot mountain is 30% beginner, 40% intermediate, and 30% advanced. Contact P.O. Box 1379, Estes Park, CO 80517 (tel. 303/586-4887 or 303/586-4165).

POWDERHORN: Powderhorn, located 45 minutes from Grand Junction, is in the middle of an expansion and renovation. This 1,600-vertical-foot mountain, rated 15% beginner, 65% intermediate, and 20% advanced, is noted for powder skiing and tree bashing. If plans went as expected last summer, one of the two existing chairs was replaced by a quad chair and a double chair replaced the poma on the beginner's lift. There is childcare for ages 2 to 7 and nursery ski school for ages 3 to 9. Lodging is in Mesa and Grand Junction. For information, contact Powderhorn, P.O. Box 1826, Grand Junction, CO 81502 (tel. 303/243-5637 or 303/268-5812).

Chapter VII

UTAH

1. Park City
2. Deer Valley
3. Snowbird
4. Alta
5. Salt Lake City Area
6. Interconnect Tour
7. Golden Spike Empire
8. Southern Utah: Brianhead
9. Other Utah Ski Areas
10. Utah Liquor Laws

THE SNOW HAS BEEN AIR-DRIED by the time it reaches Utah. It usually comes from storm systems that first pass over the Pacific coastal mountain range, which leaches out much of the moisture, and then passes over the desert. What's left falls on the high country around Salt Lake City as powder: the powder captured in photographs of skiers drifting thigh-high in snow trailing white plummage.

Little Cottonwood Canyon, where Snowbird and Alta are located, usually grabs the white stuff first. The dumps are measured in feet there more often than in inches. Next the storms spill over the ridge into Big Cottonwood Canyon to cover Solitude and Brighton. Parley's Canyon, where the Park City, Park West, and Deer Valley ski areas are set, gets what's left—and that's still a respectable amount.

As the helicopter (probably carrying skiers) flies, these three canyons and very narrow valleys in between line up like rows of houses separated by city streets. However, the only backyard shortcut to Park City is just an hour long. So while some skiers prefer to stay at the base of ski areas in a major resort like Park City, the more streamlined Snowbird or rustic Alta, others choose to bed in Salt Lake City, where each of these resorts and several others are less than 40 minutes away.

There are ski areas elsewhere in Utah. The Golden Spike Empire, down near Ogden, boasts three ski areas, and although there is lodging nearby, they are primarily day areas. Another almost unknown is Sundance, owned by actor Robert Redford, who has fought to keep this area in its beautiful natural state, is on the verge of being expanded. Down in southwest Utah, there's a sleeper called Brianhead that is drawing skiers from Las Vegas and southern Californians who've learned there's not too much difference between driving here and to the northern California resorts—and the lift lines may be shorter.

This obviously doesn't apply to most skiers, but those few whose blood pressure rises when confronted with the steeps (even those you are looking at but not actually skiing on) should seriously think about where in Utah they are going to ski first. Those skiers who come from flatland homes may be psychologically intimidated by the overall impression of extreme steepness at such areas as Snowbird and Alta, even though the blue and green slopes they are sliding over are no steeper than what they are used to and the snow is probably much better. If you have this problem (and it's not an uncommon one for Midwesterners and Easterners who ski West the first time), consider spending the first day or two skiing at an area, or at least a section of a ski area, where you can build your comfort level against skiing surrounded by steeps. The topography of the land in Parley's Canyon is fairly open. When skiing on the runs at Deer Valley, ParkWest, or Park City (with the exception of the bowls), less than advanced skiers don't have to deal with that problem. The chairs on the back side of Alta and chairs in the Gad Valley bowl are less intimidating than the face of Alta or the slopes under the tram at Snowbird. The topography at Solitude and Brighton in Big Cottonwood Canyon, where many locals learn to ski because it's so inexpensive, is even more "friendly."

1. Park City

THE RESORT: Main Street in Park City will remind you of "main street" in many western flicks. That's because through the years motion picture companies have sprinkled dirt over the pavement, shot films, and rode off into the sunset back to the studio! But the three ski areas—Park City Ski Area, ParkWest, and Deer Valley—that surround the town are strictly contemporary. Park City Ski Area rises directly up from the edge of town; ParkWest, the smallest of the three areas, is a few miles down the road; and Deer Valley resort backs up against one end of town. Skiers staying in town, where the accommodations range from spartan rooms to plush condos, have easy access to all three resorts via their own cars or the public shuttlebus system. The après-ski life thrives here.

SKIING: Skiers staying in Park City can easily sample Park City Ski Area, ParkWest, and Deer Valley. The skiing at Park City and Park West are covered in this section. For a description of Deer Valley, see the following, separate section on that resort. To encourage skiers to sample all nearby ski areas, there is an interchangeable pass between these three, plus Alta, Brighton, Solitude, and Snowbird.

PARK CITY SKI AREA SKIING: Park City is one of those ski areas that honestly offers a lot of "something for everyone." There are 82 designated trails, a number that aren't on any map but have been carved by locals, and steep open bowls for advanced skiers. A gondola and 13 chairs move skiers around the mountain, opening up more than 2,200 acres with ridge skiing; broad open runs; steep, moguled bowl sides; and treed slopes. From the top of Jupiter Bowl to the base lodge, the vertical measures 3,100 feet. However, most runs head off the tops of ridges and end at the base or feed into run-outs so they have shorter—but still respectable—verticals.

PARK CITY SKI AREA & PARKWEST 123

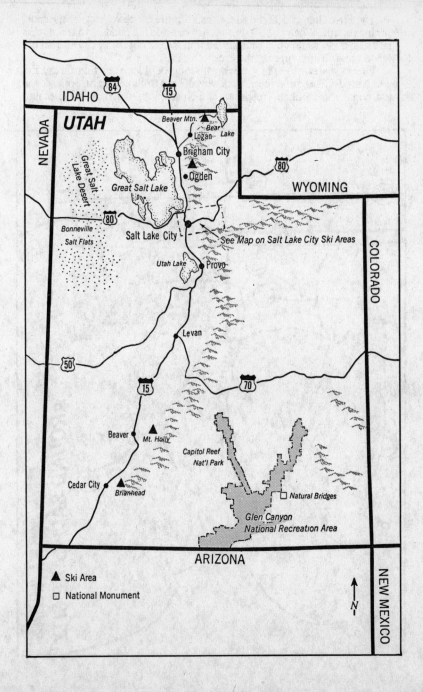

The First Time and Three Kings chair lifts are for newcomers to the sport learning to turn. When under control, they can ride the gondola to reach trails that are at times wide, open cat tracks. From the gondola, they can also ski the Meadow and Claimjumper to the Prospector lifts.

Intermediates can take a week exploring the blue runs that thread the mountainside. There are, literally, dozens of runs to choose from. Some of the most popular are around Prospector and King Consolidated chairs. (Because

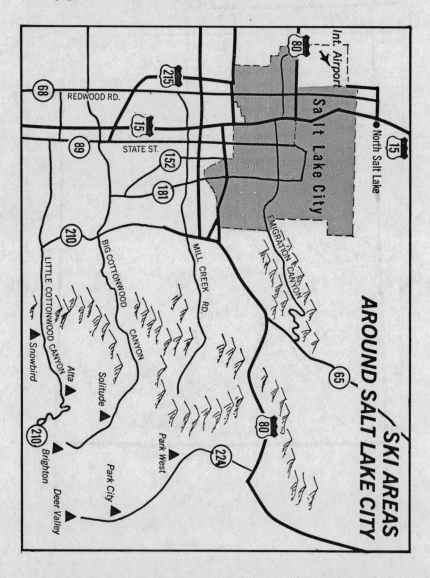

Park City is built over old silver mines, many of the runs have names from the mining era.) The runs off the Pioneer lift, such as Comstock and Red Fox, are broad and groomed to provide good cruising terrain. This lift is accessible from the top of the gondola. Some of the runs off the Thaynes chair can be an introduction to more advanced skiing. Try the intermediate-rated Single Jack, then move onto the advanced run called Double Jack.

Experts have several runs off the Ski Team chair, which are used by the U.S. Ski Team members for training at various times of the year. The bumps are also allowed to build up on Silver Skis and Crescent by the neighboring Crescent chair. Ford Country and Glory Hole, which both cut under the Motherload chair, have steady, large bumps to challenge the legs and skier's skills. The Blueslip Bowl is a good introduction to bowl skiing. The Hoist is open only to skiers on 190-cm skis or longer.

Experts and/or skiers who can honestly rate themselves as advanced may want to head up the access trail to the Jupiter Bowl lift. Before tackling this bowl, look up and make sure it's for you. Once on the lift (where the sign reads "for advanced and expert skiers only") the least difficult way down is a deep shade of black, and the hardest ways down, through the chutes and over cornices, are as black as a slope can be! (Somersaults in the air—before hitting the ground a few bumps downhill—are not unknown.) McConkey's and Puma Bowls have their fans, but it's a hike to reach these wide, open spaces.

The Town lift, from the site of the old historic Coalition building on Park Avenue to a point near the angle station of the gondola, provides easy access to the mountain for skiers staying in the downtown area.

Insider's Tips

The fastest way up the mountain is a ride on the Ski Team chair. From the top there's an easy cat track to Claimjumper and the Prospector lifts, a blue route to the King Consolidated chair, and of course, the black Ski Team runs are in front of you.

Some skiers complain they spend too much time here on cat tracks getting to or out of runs. There's truth in that statement! To beat the cat track syndrome, ski the runs directly off the various chairs and use those chairs for transportation rather than riding uphill on the gondola and working your way to the lower ski runs.

The easiest way down, a 3½-mile run, is well marked by an orange dotted line on the map. It can also be the most crowded way down, so better skiers might want to bypass parts of the trail by taking regular ski runs such as Silver Queen and/or Treasure Hollow, which intersect with the run-out trail.

Sunbathing while skiing isn't hard at Park City. The runs off the Pioneer lift are in the sun much of the day, although parts of the chair are always in the shade. There's sun over the Prospector lifts in the morning and early afternoon, but move to the Motherload and King Consolidated chairs for the rest of the day.

Bilingual hosts and hostesses are available for groups free of charge. Arrangements must be made at least two weeks in advance.

Mountain Facilities

There are three restaurants on the mountain: the Summit House, the Snow Hut, and the Base Cafeteria. There are restaurants—cookie and candy shops—and other businesses in the mall area at the base of the gondola.

Snow Coverage

The average annual snowfall is 350 inches at this area, which is usually open from mid-November to late April. There is snowmaking for 330 acres. The snow grooming is sophisticated here.

Ski School

The Park City Ski School offers half-day, all-day, and multiple-day group lessons, as well as private instruction and race clinics. The Mountain Experience classes are for high intermediate and advanced skiers who want to try Jupiter Bowl, off-trail, and powder skiing. The 1½-hour Kinderschule lessons are for youngsters from 3 to 6 years old. Combined Kinderschule with day care is available on a half- or full-day basis.

Childcare

There is childcare for those in the **Kinderschule** (tel. 649-8111, ext. 314). **Merry Pop-ins** at Central Check-in (tel. 649-1701), in the Park Meadows Plaza, cares for infants and children any time of day or night in your hotel room or condo. **Miss Billie's Kids Campus** (tel. 649-9502), across from ParkWest Ski Resort, cares for newborns to 9-year-olds. Call each center for more information, prices, and reservations.

Helicopter Skiing

Utah Powder Guides offers daily helicopter skiing in the Wasatch and Uinta Mountains. The helicopter departs from Park City and the full-day program includes seven runs. For more details, see Chapter XVIII on helicopter skiing or contact the **Utah Powderbird Guides,** P.O. Box 1760, Park City, UT 84060. During ski season, call 801/649-9739 or 801/742-2800 between 3 and 7 p.m.

Cross-Country Skiing

The Park City Ski Area doesn't have a cross-country operation, but there are cross-country touring centers located in town.

The **White Pine Touring Center** (tel. 649-8701) utilizes the Park City Golf Course. There are daily lessons and guided tours ranging from half-day trips geared for beginning and intermediate skiers to full-day trips geared for better cross-country skiers. Telemark lessons are held twice weekly, utilizing ski lifts to maximize downhill practice. The retail shop has a "try before you buy" program with high-performance equipment. White Pine also runs overnight trips in the High Unitas. Contact the **Touring Center** (P.O. Box 680393, Park City, UT 84068) for a brochure.

Balloon the Rockies (tel. 645-8188) offers remote ski-drop adventures where cross-country skiers are ballooned to and dropped in the wilderness for a tour back to civilization, led by a qualified guide.

Piute Creek Outfitters (tel. 783-4317) takes skiers three-quarters of a mile in from the road to a base camp where they have lessons, hot lunch, and guided tours.

PARKWEST SKIING: This ski area is a surprise to visitors who glance at it as they're driving into Park City and often dismiss it because only the smallest of beginners' runs are in view. On the way out of town, the long, wide groomed ridges and the other runs come into view! ParkWest has long been popular with locals because the snow is the same as that on the slopes of the neighboring resorts, but the lift tickets cost less. The management actively pursues destination visitors with the interchangeable lift ticket. (Because this area's lift ticket costs less, the difference is made up in ParkWest dollar bills to spend at the ski-area restaurants and shops or for lessons.)

The seven double-chair lifts access more than 50 trails with a rating of 33% easiest, 30% intermediate, and 37% advanced. There's a strong emphasis on grooming here. Beginners have that tiny section off the Green Horn and Tumbleweed lifts at the base of the area, as well as several longer runs off the upper lifts. There is a top-to-bottom green run open to anyone who can turn comfortably starting off the Ironhorse chair. The 2,200-foot vertical includes Maverick, a well-groomed blue-colored ridge run that provides some of the best cruising in the valley. Stampede and Bronco are other popular blue runs. Advanced skiers will enjoy some of the smooth, well-groomed steeper runs, such as Slaughterhouse, or the moguled runs like the one appropriately named Massacre. Smaller moguls punctuate runs like Hombre Ridge.

There is a lot of off-trail tree and powder skiing. Experts should check out the powder chutes on the south side of the Ironhorse lift or hike to Murdock Peak above that lift.

Insider's Tips

On weekends and holidays attendants will carry your skis up the front step and leave you by the lifts with a trail map.

To follow the sun, spend much of the day on the Iron horse lift, which opens up the longest runs for both novices and intermediates as well as several interesting expert runs.

Mountain Facilities

There is a base lodge with the Chuckwagon Coffeeshop and a cafeteria. The Branding Iron Restaurant and Bar is also located at the base of the mountain. The Lookout House is located mid-mountain. Soup's On, a soup kitchen, is at the base of the Ironhorse lift.

Snow Coverage

The base here is at 6,800 feet above sea level, and the area gets an average of 280 inches of snow each winter. Snowmaking covers 5% of this area, which is usually open from December to early April. The runs are groomed as needed.

Ski School

The Ski School has half- and full-day group lessons as well as private lessons and race clinics. There are special three-day learn-to-ski packages. Kinderschool has full-day lessons with supervised lunch for children from the ages of 3 to 9.

Childcare

There is childcare in the town of Park City. See the Park City Ski Area childcare section.

Rental Equipment

The Red Pine Sports shop has both high-performance and regular rentals available in daily and multiday packages.

Cross-Country Skiing

See the Park City Ski Area section on cross-country skiing.

WHERE TO STAY: With thousands of pillows in this region, guests can stay in anything from a basic hotel room to an ultraplush condominium with a glassed-in private Jacuzzi. There is limited ski-in/ski-out lodging, but the town's shuttlebus system places every bed within a three- to ten-minute ride from the Park City Ski Area slopes and a little farther for the other ski areas.

Lodging prices vary dramatically and there can be more than a $100 difference in the rate for the same unit between low and holiday seasons, while others have the same prices throughout the year. According to the chamber of commerce spokesperson, single unit hotel rooms can go from $35 a night for a shared bath up to $150 a night. Studios range from $50 for a basic one in the center of town up to $150 a night for a deluxe unit near the slopes. Two-bedroom condos start around $80 a night and go up to $400 a night for super-deluxe.

The majority of beds are in condominiums, so your best bet is to deal with one of the central reservation services, outlining your price range and personal requirements such as ski-in/ski-out access, older lodge in town, daily maid service or biweekly, and so on. Several of the properties listed below can be booked directly or through the central reservation services, as well as numerous others.

For general questions, prices, and a winter vacation guide, call the **Park City Area Chamber of Commerce/Convention & Visitors Bureau** (tel. 801/649-6100, or toll free 800/453-1360).

Central Reservations Services

Some of the central reservation services (many of which can arrange your entire trip from flights to lift tickets) include:

Park City Ski Holidays, P.O. Box 4409, Park City, UT 84060 (tel. toll free 800/222-PARK or 800/222-7275), can book the trip, from lodging and lift passes to rental equipment and ski-school lessons. They can also arrange airfare-inclusive packages.

Advance Reservations, Inc., P.O. Box 1179, Park City, UT 84060 (tel. 801/649-7700, or toll free 800/453-4565), offers all-inclusive trips to 21 western resorts. This group can also arrange a complete trip from lodging and transportation to lifts and lessons.

Jupiter Property Management (tel. 801/649-9598, or toll free 800/453-5789) probably has the largest selection of accommodations in Park City. Lodging in rooms for the budget-minded to homes for the affluent is available.

ParkWest Information Center (tel. toll free 800/392-9378) has information about the region and specializes in lodging reservations near the ski area, approximately three miles north of town. The office is located at the ParkWest Resort office by the main parking lot.

Upper Bracket

Silver King (tel. 801/649-5500, or toll free 800/331-8652), just across the street from the base of the Park City ski area's lifts, is a luxury condominium complex with accommodations ranging from well-furnished studios to penthouses. There's 24-hour front desk service, valet and laundry service, an indoor/outdoor swimming pool, spa, and sauna.

The **Park City Resort Center Lodging** (tel. 801/649-0800, or toll free 800/824-5331 outside Utah) offerings range from comfortable hotel rooms to two-bedroom/loft condos with fireplaces and microwaves, located in the plaza at the ski-area base. There are communal Jacuzzis, an ice-skating rink, and shopping and dining in the complex.

There's a variety of deluxe and ultra-deluxe condominiums at Deer Valley. See the lodging section in the Deer Valley description for details.

Moderate

There are hundreds of condominium units and hotel rooms (many are lock-offs) in this price range. Deal directly with the chamber of commerce or one of the central reservation services to find a unit to fit your needs. The following complexes offer comfortable lodging and a good range of amenities for moderate prices.

The **Prospector Square Hotel and Conference Center**, P.O. Box 1698, Park City, UT 84060 (tel. toll free 800/453-3812 or 801/649-7100), has hotel rooms and comfortable one-, two-, and three-bedroom condos. There is a complete athletic club on site with an indoor pool, racquetball courts, and a Jacuzzi. The Grub Steak restaurant is open for breakfast, lunch, and dinner. Prospector Square vans provide free shuttle service to Park City Ski Area and the center of town.

The **Yarrow Hotel and Conference Center**, P.O. Box 1840, Park City, UT 84060 (tel. 801/649-7000, or toll free 800/327-2332), is located within walking distance of some shops and restaurants and on the town's shuttlebus system. The rooms range from comfortable to deluxe and vary in configuration from two double beds to suites with two queen-size beds and a queen-size sofa-sleeper. Amenities include a restaurant, Jacuzzi, and swimming pool. Room rates range from $87 for a double to $200 for a suite.

The **Snowflower Condominiums** (tel. 801/649-6400, or toll free 800/852-3101 outside Utah), located right next to the Three Kings chair lift, push the upper end of the moderate range. The deluxe units include private hot tubs and fireplaces, and there are also outdoor hot pools.

The condominiums in the **Blue Church Lodge**, P.O. Box 1720, Park City, UT 84060 (tel. 801/649-8009), built as the town's first Mormon church in 1897, are all different. Furnished in country style, the one- to four-bedroom units have fireplaces. Amenities include a lounge area, indoor spa, game room, and continental breakfast (although the kitchens are completely equipped). The lodge and the Blue Church Townhouses across the street, which have two-bedroom condominiums, are a block from the restaurants and shops on Main Street. The minimum stay required varies according to season. Rates range from $69 to $247.

The rooms at the **Old Miners' Lodge**, P.O. Box 2639, Park City, UT 84060 (tel. 801/645-8068), a bed-and-breakfast spot, are named after local characters from the city's mining days. Located in the historic district, it's close to the nightlife in the center of town. There are individually decorated suites, and rooms with private bath and shared bath. Lodging rates start at $70 and include breakfast and refreshments.

Less Expensive

Château Après, P.O. Box 579, Park City, UT 84060 (tel. 801/649-9372), an older lodge offering rooms, at $39, with private baths and dormitories, is located close to the lifts. Extremely reasonable meals are available.

The historic **Washington School Inn**, 543 Park Ave. (P.O. Box 536), Park City, UT 84060 (tel. 801/649-3800), set in a 100-year-old schoolhouse, offers bed-and-breakfast. Amenities include an indoor spa. Rooms are $60 to $150. Call for more information.

WHERE TO EAT: Dining in the Park City area ranges from gourmet food in a fern-bar-modern atmosphere to steaks and ribs in mining-days-rustic buildings along Main Street.

Upper Bracket

Swiss specialties and other continental meals are on the menu at **Adolph's** at 1541 Thaynes Canyon Rd. (tel. 649-7177). Guests relax in this restaurant, which has a Swiss decor and overlooks the golf course. Entrees such as roast rack of lamb, veal Cordon Bleu, and coquilles St. Jacques range from approximately $15 to $19. Hours are from 6 p.m. Tuesday through Sunday. Reservations are recommended.

See the Deer Valley section for information about dining at the Glitrend in Stein Ericksen's Lodge, the elaborate buffets at the Huggery, and the Café Mariposa. Also see Deer Valley for information about Philippe's, a longtime favorite of discerning Park City locals, which has moved to the Stag Lodge in Deer Valley.

Moderate

Cowboy western describes the decor in the **Claimjumper Restaurant**, 536 Main St. (tel. 649-8051), where the menu ranges from baseball and teriyaki steak to buffalo steak and prime rib. Prices range from $9 to $25. This restaurant in the old Park City Hotel is open daily from 6 p.m.

The **Grub Steak** in Prospector Square (tel. 649-8060) is a casual restaurant offering a basic American menu including beef, ribs, chicken, and seafood. Breakfast hours are 7 to 10 a.m. Monday through Saturday; lunch is served from 11:30 a.m. to 2:30 p.m. Monday through Friday, and dinner is served from 6 to 10 p.m. Monday through Thursday, to 11 p.m. on Friday and Saturday, and from 5 to 10 p.m. on Sunday. There's a Sunday brunch.

Less Expensive

The **Baja Cantina** in the Park City Resort Center (tel. 649-BAJA) is an ongoing "in" spot with locals who work on the margaritas while waiting for their food. There are no reservations taken at the Baja Cantina with its Mexican/fern-bar decor. The Mexican fare ranges from $3.50 to $12, and the majority of dishes are around $6 to $8. Check locally for hours at this restaurant, which is open for lunch and dinner.

The **Eating Establishment,** 317 Main St. (tel. 649-8284), serves breakfast all day, plus regular lunches and dinners, in a casual coffeehouse atmosphere. Evening house specials range from pasta du jour to catch of the day. Soup, salad bar, and sandwiches are also on the menu. Prices range from approximately $4 to $15. The restaurant is open from 8 a.m. daily.

The **Stew Pot,** in the Plaza Building on Deer Valley Road (tel. 645-STEW), offers stew, soups, fish, wursts, and sandwiches. Prices at this informal, small spot range from $3.50 to approximately $6.25. Hours are 11:30 a.m. to 9 p.m.

ENTERTAINMENT: This is a party town. Just scout out the beer and wine bars and private clubs on Main Street or at the Park City Ski Area base plaza. (Remember to review the liquor laws listed at the end of this chapter. Also check the laws locally—they're available at most lodges—in case there have been any changes, so you'll know where you can get in.)

Some of the local hot spots include **The Alamo** (tel. 649-2380) and **The Club** (tel. 649-6693), both on Main Street and both private clubs; and **The Steeps** (tel. 649-3500), a lounge/beer bar at the base of the ski area.

Check locally for the schedules at the lounge/beer bars, which often have live entertainment. Popular private clubs (where you can buy a reasonably priced "temporary" membershop) include **Sneakers**, at the Park Meadows Racquet Club (tel. 649-7742).

PARK CITY SKI AREA & PARKWEST

The **Claimjumper Saloon** features live entertainment four to six nights a week during ski season. There is a large-screen TV for sports events, and watchers can order off the Claimjumper Restaurant menu.

SHOPPING: Boutiques, galleries, and interesting shops are located on Main and nearby streets. There are several shops—ranging from a cookie store to a ski shop—in the plaza at the base of the Park City Ski Area.

NON-SKIER ACTIVITIES: Everything from club-hopping to sleigh rides is an option for those who don't ski or who need a day off their boards. Sleigh rides through the countryside are scheduled by **Park City Sleigh Company** (tel. 649-3359, or toll free 800/453-5757).

Casino Caravans (tel. 649-DICE) offers gamblers tours to the Silver Smith Casino and to the State Line Casino in nearby Wendover, Nevada. (The "party" bus ride is approximately 2½ hours each way.) Tours for groups of 25 or more can be arranged to other places, such as Temple Square to hear the Mormon Tabernacle Choir.

There are more than a dozen **art galleries** in town. For a specific listing, see the Winter Visitors Guide. Most are on or close to Main Street.

Park City Performances presents light entertainment, such as *Dracula* and *Come Blow Your Horn,* in the renovated Egyptian Theater on selected weekends during the winter. Call 649-9371 or check the local papers for the schedule.

Ballooning over the skiers is another possibility. **Balloon the Rockies** (tel. 645-8188) offers champagne flights over Park City and Deer Valley. (They also drop cross-country skiers off with a guide in remote areas.)

GETTING THERE: Park City is 27 miles east of Salt Lake City via six-lane I-80. Many of the major **airlines,** including United, American, Delta, Eastern, Northwest, Transworld, America West, and Continental service Salt Lake City. **Amtrak** also stops in Salt Lake City. Many of the major **car-rental companies** operate out of the Salt Lake City airport. Both **Trailways** and **Greyhound** bus lines stop in Salt Lake City.

Shuttle service from the airport to the resort is provided by several companies. **Lewis Brothers Stages,** 549 W. 500th St. South, Salt Lake City, UT 84104 (tel. 801/359-8677, or toll free 800/826-5844), runs regularly scheduled buses and has mini-vans for special runs. For group and individual transfers, also contact **Park City Transportation Services,** P.O. Box 126, Park City, UT 84060 (tel. 801/649-8567, or toll free 800/637-3803).

MOVING AROUND: The Park City Transit has a **no-fare bus system** in operation from 7:30 a.m. to 12:30 a.m. daily. Buses run by each stop on the three routes approximately every 20 minutes up until 10 p.m. and less frequently afterward. The buses go to both Park City Ski Area and Deer Valley. Transportation to and from ParkWest is via a complimentary van which circles the town and Deer Valley. Schedules for both bus systems should be on hotel/lodge front desks.

There are two taxi services in town. For a ride, call **Park City Transportation Service** (tel. 649-8567) or **Park City Taxi** (tel. 649-8567).

Skiers staying in Salt Lake City can utilize the **ski buses,** which move between downtown hotels and the ski areas daily. When making reservations, ask the hotel for specific details. The buses are equipped to handle mountain weather and hold skis.

TOURIST INFORMATION: For information about the Park City area, contact the **Park City Area Chamber of Commerce/Convention & Visitors Bureau,** 528 Main St. (P.O. Box 1630), Park City, UT 84060 (tel. 801/649-6100, or toll free 800/453-1360 outside Utah). When visiting the resort, pick up a copy of the Park City, Utah, Winter Visitors Guide, which outlines everything from local transportation to restaurants.

Emergency medical attention is available at the **Holy Cross Family Health and Emergency Center** (tel. 649-7640) or the **Park City Emergency Center** (tel. 649-HELP). **Police, fire, ambulance,** and **sheriff** can all be reached through 649-9369 in Park City and 649-9561 outside of Park City.

2. Deer Valley

THE RESORT: Deer Valley is considered the country club of ski resorts, an approach its marketing department pushes with good reason. A class act, this resort is defined by amenities such as an attendant at the base lodge who takes your skis while you park the car, elaborate buffets in the cafeteria, deck chairs set so skiers can enjoy the sun, and slopes as smooth as a well-tuned ski bottom. When not on the slopes, guests are ensconced in wood-and-stone buildings, many of which could grace an architectural magazine. Such service isn't cheap, however, and a stay at this resort is priced accordingly. The less expensive category doesn't apply here. However, there is lodging in that price category in Park City, literally next door, and skiers can—and should—spend a day on the slopes here.

THE SKIING: Deer Valley is an ego-building mountain. The runs are so well groomed that most skiers perform better on these trails than they would on similar terrain at other resorts. The skiers who visit here are as interested in social times as they are in skiing, and the majority aren't really interested in steep, tough ungroomed runs. The terrain on the mountain reflects that belief. Most of the runs are beginner and intermediate. Even many of the black runs are really blue/black or light black, with the definite exception of the Mayflower Bowl. Technically the rating is 15% easiest, 50% more difficult, 35% most difficult.

The 41 runs are spread over Bald Mountain, where the runs drop 2,040 vertical feet, and Bald Eagle Mountain, where the runs drop 1,200 vertical feet. Three triple chairs and a double chair access primarily beginner and intermediate runs on Bald Eagle. The lifts start at the Snow Park base lodge. The beginner runs wind downward at a steadily comfortable (for novices) pitch. Skiers can even ski around trees left in the runs but set so there is little danger of making tree stops. They add to the experience of being outside with nature. Success, listed as the easiest way down, is one of the most popular runs.

The midway lodge, Silver Lake, is located at the top of Bald Eagle Mountain—and at the base of the chair lift accessing Bald Mountain. (Skiers heading back down from the Bald Mountain runs to the base lodge must take the Homestake lift, or download on the top part of the Clipper lift, to get over a tiny ridge so they can ski back down to the main lodge. The addition of the Clipper lift a few years ago eliminated the lines of skiers waiting to ride up in the morning and cross over the ridge in the afternoon.) Three triple chairs and a double chair open up primarily intermediate and advanced terrain. There are several broad, smooth blue runs off the Sterling and Wasatch chairs. Birdseye, a cruiser for comfortable intermediates, is the most popular run in this area, although Nabob and Tycoon have their fans. Most of the black runs are off the Sultan and the Mayflower chair lifts. The Ruins of Pompeii is one of the most challenging off the Sultan chair. Grizzly, Timberline, and Blue Ledge, all short black runs that feed into intermediate terrain, can be challenging when there are moguls. The Mayflower lift (built in response to skier request for more difficult terrain) has several long black runs. The Orient Express, which is usually well groomed, has proved to be the most popular. The bumps are allowed to build on Paradise and Fortune Teller. Skiers seeking steep, ungroomed terrain should test the top of the Mayflower Bowl. Intermediate skiers should pay attention to signs. The Morning Star run, colored blue on the map, has a black-rated entrance (through the Mayflower Bowl) many days and is signed at the top accordingly. Experts with sharp eyes will find several tree runs. Generally the openings are tight (to discourage the timid) but the trees open up once inside. Look in the bottom section between the Orient Express and the Mayflower lift, between Morning Star and Paradise, and around the trees between the blue and black versions of Hawkeye.

Insider's Tips

Drive up to the base lodge and an attendant will help you unload and watch your equipment while you park.

Lift ticket sales are cut off here at a certain number, so the lift lines never get too long.

Don't expect to find a greasy burger and fries here. Deer Valley is the creation of the Royal Street Corporation, owners of the Stanford Court Hotel in San Francisco, and the same high standards apply. Management's goal is to provide a relaxing vacation, not the hustle-bustle experience offered at many resorts. For instance, lunch in the cafeterias can rival a meal in many city restaurants. The food stations here offer barons of beef, roast leg of lamb, a natural salad buffet, and more. For a memorable dining experience, make reservations at the Café Mariposa, given top ratings by many restaurant critics.

Powderhounds should ask a local how to get into the Son of Rattler or the treed area between Reward and the Sultan lift.

Check your skis at the free ski corral at the base lodge when taking a lunch break or for overnight storage.

Mountain Facilities

There are two day lodges, Snow Park Center at the base and Silver Lake Lodge at mid-mountain, which will become the nucleus of a mid-mountain community, Silver Lake Village. The base lodge has all the expected facilities wrapped in a striking decor of brass fittings, paneled walls, and fireplaces, that provides an elegant backdrop for skiers. There is a buffet restaurant and a lounge, a ski shop, ski-rental area, a photo shop, the childcare center, lift-ticket office, and ski-school office. The Silver Lake Village, as superbly decorated, houses another buffet restaurant, a ski shop, and the Café Mariposa, a gourmet sit-down restaurant open for dinner. The "cafeterias," the Huggery and the Snuggery, both have elaborate buffets which may vary from day to day but include choices ranging from baron of beef to a health-food salad bar.

Snow Coverage

Deer Valley averages 300 inches during the winter. The exceptional grooming efforts at Deer Valley keep the snow soft and smooth. There is snowmaking on the entire mountain.

Ski School

The ski school offers half- and full-day group and private lessons and racing clinics. Group classes average six to eight persons. There are half- and full-day group lessons for children. For youngsters age 4 or younger, lessons must be private.

Childcare

The childcare center in the base lodge is larger and has separate areas for the different age groups. Children from the age of 3 (must be toilet trained) to 12 are accepted. There's a daily schedule of indoor and outdoor activities appropriate for the age group. Lunch for the youngsters is prepared in the cafeteria and eaten in the dining area of the childcare center.

Rental Equipment

The high-performance and regular rentals are available at the base lodge. Half-day rentals are available after 12:30 p.m.

Cross-Country Skiing

Cross-country operations are located in Park City. See the Cross-Country Skiing in Section 1 on the Park City Ski Area for details.

WHERE TO STAY: The condominiums here range from deluxe to posh. Guests can stay in anything from a comfortable one-bedroom condo to a designer-decorated five-level condo with a private outdoor Jacuzzi.

Most Expensive

The **Stein Eriksen Lodge,** located in Silver Lake Village (at mid-mountain) (tel. toll free 800/453-1302), deserves the superlatives usually tossed into any description of this mountain retreat. The suites are spacious, beautifully decorated with designer furnishings including hand-carved furniture and custom European kitchens; many also have private Jacuzzis. The communal areas are rustic but very classy, with stone fireplaces and massive beams supporting the ceiling several stories overhead. The emphasis in this lodge is old-world elegance from afternoon tea to having a valet take your skis in the afternoon and return them tuned the next morning. There is a health spa with an indoor/outdoor pool, a lounge, and two restaurants. There is ski-in/ski-out access. A deluxe room at this lodge runs $245 to $375 per night, and a two-bedroom suite runs $630 to $935. Accommodations here can *only* be booked through the above toll-free number.

Deer Valley Central Reservations (tel. toll free 800/424-3337) handles the majority of condos for rent at the resort. Even though the condos are spread in clusters in Snow Park Village at the base of the resort and in Silver Lake Village at mid-mountain, concierge, and valet and daily maid services are provided. The available condos vary in style and decor, but all are above average. The most inexpensive rentals are at the base of the resort, while the ones at mid-mountain are generally higher. **Lakeside,** in Snow Park Village, has the only swimming pool. The three- and four-bedroom units at the **Pinnacle,** in Snow Park Village, are among the most elaborate. The living space is spread on four or five levels and each has a private Jacuzzi set on a protected deck. **Cache,** in Silver Lake Village, has attractive three-bedroom condos with a Jacuzzi in a glassed-in area. Prices range from $360 for a two-bedroom to $640 for a four-bedroom at the Pinnacle, to $650 for a four-bedroom with Jacuzzi at **La Maconnerie,** set on the side of a ski trail.

The **Pine Inn** is a complex of deluxe condos right next to the base lodge. The luxurious one- to three-bedroom units each have an outdoor hot tub and spa tubs in the units. The multi-level three-bedroom units have two master bedrooms. During regular season prices range from $275 for a one-bedroom to $485 for a three-bedroom unit. For reservations at these ski-in/ski-out units, call Jupiter Property Management (tel. toll free 800/453-5789).

DEER VALLEY

Moderate and Less Expensive Lodging

Deer Valley is in Park City, and there is lodging in every price range in this ski town. The local shuttle-service route encompasses both Deer Valley and Park City. Lodging in Park City puts skiers just a five- to ten-minute drive from the ski slopes.

WHERE TO EAT: There are six restaurants in Deer Valley—and they are outstanding. Of course, a smörgåsbord of tastes is available just across the resort line in Park City.

The **Café Mariposa** in the Silver Lake Lodge (tel. 649-1000) has received high ratings from a variety of restaurant critics who have never been on skis. It's open only for dinner (reserve well in advance), and the chef prepares both classic and innovative dishes. Although the wood walls and fireplace create a rustic look, it is tempered by the carefully set tables and the mouthwatering pastry tray near the entrance. Leisurely lunches of the daily pasta, a seafood stew, or a sandwich with unexpected but well-matched ingredients could slow down your return to the slopes. Dinner here is a good example of fine dining with entrees ranging from rack of lamb al presto to roast squab. Dinner is a prix-fixe menu at $32. Reservations are usually necessary. Hours are 6 to 9:30 p.m.

Formal dinners and lunches with flair are available in the informally elegant **Glitrend Gourmet Room** at the Stein Eriksen Lodge (tel. 649-3700). Entrees range from $16 to $25. Reservations are necessary. Check for current hours.

There are specialty buffets several evenings a week in the **Huggery** at the Snow Park Lodge and the **Snuggery** at the Silver Lake Lodge. Call 649-1007 for details and reservations.

Phillippe's, now in the Stag Lodge (tel. 649-2421), formerly located in Park City (as this restaurant's devotees know), delivers creative and classic cuisine at lunch and dinner with menus that change weekly. Reservations are recommended at this restaurant which won the 1983 Silver Spoon award from the Gourmet Diners Club of America. Hours are 6 to 10 p.m.

Moderate

The **Birkebeiner** (tel. 649-3700) is the Stein Eriksen Lodge's version of a family restaurant. More than a step up from the typical family restaurant, entrees here range from $14 and $20. Check for current hours.

The **Stew Pot** in the Plaza (tel. 645-STEW) offers light meals in a casual atmosphere. Stews average $5 and sandwiches start at $3. Hours are 11:30 a.m. to 9 p.m. for lunch and dinner.

Less Expensive

Eat in Park City!

ENTERTAINMENT: Nightlife in the resort means getting together with friends for dinner or a drink in a condo. There's a lot of action in Park City, accessible to anyone with private transportation. (The shuttlebus service doesn't go to the mid-mountain village in the evening.)

SHOPPING: As in most resort towns, the shops in Park City offer everything from crazy T-shirts to designer clothes and ski equipment to toys.

NON-SKIER ACTIVITIES: Guests at the Stein Eriksen Lodge can utilize the health spa under the exercise instructor's direction. There's a wide range of activities from skating to racquetball and gallery exploring in Park City. Read the Non-Skier Activities section in Park City resort.

GETTING THERE: Deer Valley is a 45-minute drive from the Salt Lake City International Airport and a 40-minute drive from downtown Salt Lake. It is located at the edge of Park City, 28 miles up I-80 and seven miles in on fairly flat, all-weather roads.

MOVING AROUND: There is a shuttlebus service between the ski lodges and the condominiums during the day. The Park City bus system stops at several points in Deer Valley. However, it's easier to move around with a private car. Skiers staying at the mid-mountain lodges definitely need a car if they want to visit Park City in the evenings.

TOURIST INFORMATION: Contact **Deer Valley Resort Company**, P.O. Box 1525, Park City, UT 84060. For **general resort information** call 801/649-1000. For **ticket information** call 801/649-4149. For **snow** and **weather conditions** call 801/649-2000. The toll-free **Deer Valley Lodging** number is 800/424-3337. The toll-free number for the **Stein Eriksen Lodge** is 800/453-1302.

Contact the **police, fire, ambulance,** and **sheriff** through 649-9410 in Park City and 649-9561 outside Park City. Twenty-four-hour health-care service is available at the **Holy Cross Family Health and Emergency Center** (tel. 649-7640).

3. Snowbird

THE RESORT: Snowbird is a 20th-century resort, from the lean, concrete buildings that fill most of the canyon floor at that point to the tram rising up one side of the dramatically narrow Little Cottonwood Canyon. Advanced skiers know that this is one of the ultimate mountains, but there's plenty of good terrain for intermediates and beginners. The clientele comes from all over the country, and the dress is a blend of high fashion with a touch of out-of-date ski jackets. Après-ski choices are limited, but those choices are usually packed. Anyone staying at Snowbird can sample the skiing at Alta, a mile away.

THE SKIING: A tram and seven chair lifts service the runs and open terrain in the two large bowls, Peruvian Gulch and Gad Valley, which contain the majority of Snowbird's terrain. The runs off the chairs in the Gad Valley area are primarily beginner and intermediate. The slopes off the tram in those bowls and the run in the Peruvian Gulch bowl are mainly for competent intermediate, advanced, and expert skiers. Terrain is rated 20% for beginners, 30% for intermediates, and 50% for advanced and experts.

Snow cover on the upper part of this 3,100-vertical-foot mountain is usually enough to provide a summer skiing season from Memorial Day through mid-June.

Many first-time visitors claim that the ski slopes, especially those under the tram (black runs), look "heart-stoppingly" steep. However, the chairs open up all of the green and most of the blue runs and some black runs. Chair-lift-only tickets are available for beginners and intermediates and anyone else who doesn't want to use the tram.

Never-evers learn around the Chickadee chair in an area well protected from other skiers. Then they move onto the Wilbere Ridge and the Mid-Gad chairs. West Second South and lower Big Emma, from the midway unloading point on the Mid-Gad chair, are popular green runs. The full length of Big Emma, a broad, gentle swath, has been described by many skiers as one of the better beginner runs in the Rockies.

Wilbere Ridge is a very popular blue run on the lower part of the mountain because it's open and has a gentle grade. The slightly harder intermediate runs off the Gad 2 lift, Bananas, Election, and Bassackwards, are popular because they're wide enough for comfortable turning, or cruising, and high enough on the mountainside for great views. Intermediates who get tram tickets can take Chip's Run from the top for an up-close look at what they'll ski when they become more advanced. The run is almost a wide cat track on the very top (to ease skiers down the steepest section), then follows the most gentle line through the open bowl. It is a run for competent intermediates on the top; shaky intermediates enjoy the lower half from the top of the Peruvian chair.

Advanced skiers will want a tram ticket to reach the majority of the tougher terrain. Newcomers to the area might consider taking Chip's Run down the first time to view the black turf, because it crosses over or comes within view of many of the slopes used by advanced and expert skiers. Primrose Path, straight down the center of the Peruvian Gulch bowl, is a popular route for a first black. There are bailout spots where Chip's Run crosses over. Other hot runs on this side include the Peruvian Cirque and Blackjack, a wide, wide piece of never-groomed, very lightly treed area on the lower half of the mountain.

Regulator Johnson, a broad, open face at the top of the Gad Valley bowl, with a fairly steady, medium-black downward pitch, challenges legs. The bumps build big, but it's groomed occasionally so skiers may be able to find smooth sections. The entire upper part of this bowl, around the Little Cloud lift, is prime territory on powder days. Skiers into very steep slopes should check out Silver Fox, Great Scott, and Upper Cirque (marked with yellow caution triangles on the map) on the upper half of the mountain. Dalton's Draw, Mach Schnell, and Wilbere Bowl will all entertain expert skiers. They blend serious steeps; some have no bailout sections, all have variable snow conditions, and some have bumps, depending on the day. There is some terrain outside the ski area boundaries which locals ski that some visiting experts might want to try. The tram operator will announce what's open and closed that day. Ask a local about these runs, including the route (with chutes) to Alta, before deciding whether you should try them.

Insider's Tips

Snowbird has free guided tours which match visitors with the runs and lifts that best match their abilities. Tours depart from the Plaza Deck at Snowbird center at 9 a.m. and 1 p.m. daily.

If the snow is really "hard pack" at the bottom of the mountain, try runs on the upper half. It might just be softer.

Snowbird offers both morning and afternoon half-day tickets.

For a fast, good breakfast, try the Plaza Restaurant. If you're there on Sunday, catch the brunch.

Mountain Facilities

Several restaurants, shops, the ski-school office, and the ski shops with rentals are in the Snowbird Center, the Cliff Lodge. There's a cafeteria restaurant at the top of the Mid-Gad lift.

Snow Coverage

The snowfall averages 500 inches yearly at this area, which opens in mid-November, runs through mid-May; weather permitting, the Gad 1 and Little Cloud lifts reopen for a summer season from Memorial Day through mid-June. Most of the beginner and intermediate runs are groomed at night and packed after heavy snowfalls.

Ski School

This school offers group and private lessons as well as a variety of special programs, including several for better skiers. In the Advanced Skiing Classes good skiers work with members of the PSIA Intermountain Team, receiving advice on developing techniques and the mental attitude needed to ski difficult terrain. The Mountain Experience is a guide service for adults who want to experience off-trail and powder skiing on steep terrain. Kinderbirds is open to 4½- and 5-year-olds; older children go into regular ski-school classes but have instructors who specialize in teaching children.

Childcare

There is childcare for youngsters 3 and older (who are toilet trained) for Snowbird Lodge guests. Hours are 8:45 a.m. to 5 p.m. for this center located in the Cliff Lodge. Private in-room sitting for younger children is available upon request to your lodge's front desk. An hourly fee is charged for private day and evening babysitting.

Rental Equipment

The Cliff Rental Shop, Breeze Ski Rental, and the Sport Stalker Ski Shop have alpine rental equipment. High-performance demos are available at these shops located in the Snowbird Center.

Cross-Country Skiing

Equipment rentals are available at the ski shops in the center. There's good terrain in the canyon to explore.

Helicopter Skiing

Wasatch Powderbird Guides (tel. 801/742-2800) runs daily helicopter trips in the region. See Chapter XVIII on helicopter skiing for details.

WHERE TO STAY: Snowbird Ski and Summer Resort runs its own lodges at the base. There is a **central reservations number** (tel. toll free 800/453-3000) to handle your needs. The four lodges include:

The **Cliff Lodge** is Snowbird's only full-service hotel. With the new wing, opened in December 1986, the Cliff now boasts 532 deluxe guest rooms, eight restaurants and lounges, a health spa, and a conference center. There's an outdoor heated pool, a day-care center, a ski-school office, and more. Prices for one-bedroom units run approximately $150 per night, double occupancy.

The **Iron Blosam Lodge** is an owner-shared condo complex with 195 units, each with its own balcony and view of the mountains. This is a good place for families, as there are amenities such as a year-round heated outdoor pool, a large Jacuzzi, a weight room, saunas, and a game room with Ping-Pong and pool tables. It also contains the Wildflower Restaurant and Lounge.

The **Lodge at Snowbird** is comfortable mountain rustic, with 160 condo units. There are bedrooms, studios, efficiencies, and suites. All but the one-bedroom units have kitchenettes. There is an outdoor heated pool and whirlpool. The Lodge Club is the restaurant and lounge.

The Inn has 73 deluxe condo units with private balconies. It is within easy walking distance of the Snowbird Center, the complex serving the skiers. However, it has no restaurant. Amenities include a heated outdoor pool, saunas, and card room.

Prices for one-bedroom units in all three condominium lodges run approximately $300 per night, double occupancy. There are package plans that include lifts, lodging and ski school.

SNOWBIRD

WHERE TO EAT: Guests may choose from 17 restaurants and lounges at Snowbird. There's a wide variety of food offered, ranging from Mexican to continental cuisine. These restaurants, except when noted, can be reached through the Snowbird main number: 801/742-2222.

More Expensive

The **Golden Cliff Dining Room** in the Cliff Lodge is a large room, open to the second floor, with a warm relaxed atmosphere. Entrees include veal Oscar, champignon noir, and Pacific salmon, and range in price from $10 to $18. There is quiet dinner music in the background. The buffet breakfasts take up a 12-foot table.

The **Lodge Club,** a private club on the first level of the Lodge at Snowbird, is decorated colorfully with burgundy chairs and blue tablecloths. In the separate bar area you can enjoy interesting hors d'oeuvres while slaking your thirst. The selected dinner menu is in the $9 to $16 range.

The **Steak Pit,** in Snowbird Center (tel. 521-6040), is one of the most popular restaurants in the resort and well worth the wait often necessary. The menu is mainly high-quality basic beef and some seafood simply prepared, with a side of unlimited salad. The food is presented with flair. Reservations are suggested.

The **Wildflower,** in the Iron Blosam, is more family oriented and it has a separate children's menu. The dinner menu emphasizes Italian cuisine with fresh pasta and daily specials. Entrees range from $10 to $14.

The **Aerie Restaurant,** located on the top floor of the Cliff Lodge, offers elegant gourmet dining with a view of the canyon. In addition to regular menu items, the Aerie serves food choices for guests following the Spa menu plan. Entrees range from $6 to $16.

Less Expensive

The **Atrium Lounge,** in the 11-story atrium at the Cliff Lodge, has a light menu for three meals daily. There is live piano entertainment daily in this restaurant with an indoor garden atmosphere. Prices range from $5.50 to $7.75.

The **Spa Café** has healthy, low-calorie choices. Vegetarian selections, fish, and blended smoothies range from $2.75 to $9.75.

The **Plaza Restaurant,** on level 2 in the Snowbird Center, offers breakfast and lunch, cafeteria style. Hamburgers, pizza, a salad bar, and daily specials range from $2 to $5.

Design your own hamburgers at the **Forklift,** located on level 3 of Snowbird Center. Prices run $3.50 to $11.

The **Mexican Keyhole,** also in the Cliff Lodge, offers Mexican fare for $6 to $12. Inlaid wood in the tables adds to the cozy decor.

Cheap Eats

The **Ice Cream Shop** on level 2 of Snowbird Center has soup, sandwiches, and pizza, plus ice cream. Prices range from $1.50 to $5.

The **Birdfeeder,** on the Plaza Deck of Snowbird Center, has burgers, hot dogs, fries, cinnamon rolls. The fast food goes for $1.75 to $4.50.

ENTERTAINMENT: The **Eagle's Nest Lounge** features a raw seafood bar for après-ski and overlooks the Golden Cliff dining room. You can sit by the fire on comfortable couches and chairs to relax after a hard day of skiing. The **Tram Room Bar** in Snowbird Center rocks with live music most nights. The **Lodge Club** and the **Eagle's Nest Lounge** have solo or duo musicians many nights. While there, consult Snowbird's "What's up at the Bird" weekly flyer to see what's happening.

SHOPPING: Shops in the Snowbird Center range from a pharmacy with a post office to a gift shop. There's a small grocery store, a tailor, a sweet shop, and more.

NON-SKIER ACTIVITIES: The **Cliff Spa** is novel to the ski world. Occupying the top two floors of the new wing at the Cliff Lodge, the spa offers "pampering" treatments and exercise programs. Try a parafango wrap, massage, herbal wrap, hydrotherapy, or some of the hair, nail, and skin-care treatments. There is a weight room and lap pool. The staff offers facials, personal fitness consultations, daily aerobics and stretching classes. Snowbird offers packages that include both skiing and spa-ing. Call 801/742-2222, ext. 5900, for more information.

GETTING THERE: Snowbird is located in Little Cottonwood Canyon, 31 miles from the Salt Lake International Airport. Many major airlines fly to Salt Lake City, and many major car-rental companies are located at the airport. In recent years there has been a group transportation desk at the airport near the baggage carousels. Ask there about transportation to the resort. Some of the many companies providing transportation, upon arrangement, from the airport to Snowbird include **Trailways Bus System** (tel. 801/328-8121) and **Lewis Brothers Stages** (tel. 801/359-8677, or toll free 800/826-5844). Taxi service can run approximately $40 one way. The **Utah Transit Authority** (tel. 801/531-8600) has daily service from the airport and from downtown Salt Lake City. Call UTA or Snowbird for schedules and fares.

MOVING AROUND: There's no need for a car at Snowbird because everything is within easy walking distance. Snowbird runs a free shuttlebus service for day skiers and lodge guests to and from parking lots to the Snowbird Center throughout the day. There is also regular shuttle service to Alta, a mile away, for a minimal fee.

TOURIST INFORMATION: For information, contact **Snowbird Ski and Summer Resort**, Snowbird, UT 84092 (tel. 801/742-2222). For reservations only, call toll free 800/453-3000. Call Snowbird's **Adventure Travel** (tel. 801/742-2222) for air and ground transportation arrangements.

4. Alta

THE RESORT: Alta has long had the reputation of being a laid-back, "we never will enter the 20th century" resort. Everything from their lift ticket—one of the lowest priced in the country—to the superb variety of runs is understated. The area and the lodges where guests stay are as timeless as the area's base facilities (actually located in one of the lodges). Skiers who want a slicker atmosphere stay at Snowbird, just a mile down the canyon.

THE SKIING: The approach here was not to put up so many lifts that skiers, on a crowded day, would mob the slopes. (Management thinks you would rather wait in line than have the quality of skiing down the runs spoiled.) There are eight chairs and two rope tows opening up the 2,000 vertical feet of mountainside. Terrain is rated 25% beginner, 40% intermediate, and 35% advanced. Intermediates shouldn't freeze when they first look at the mountain. The front side is primarily black terrain. The out-of-sight lifts open up excellent blue terrain.

Beginners have their own lifts at the far end of the ski area above the Albion parking lot. The runs off Albion and Sunnyside are gently pitched. The slopes are open.

Intermediates have runs on the front face off the midway unloading point of the Wildcat lift and the Collins lift. They are broad enough swaths cut down the mountainside in between the steeper runs. The runs off the Germania lift, Mambo and Ballroom, can be danced down by competent intermediates. The treasureload of blue runs is off the Supreme lift. Big Dipper and Challenger, lightly gladed areas that crews have thinned and widened, and the gladed section called Sleepy Hollow provide an unlimited number of fall lines for intermediates. The terrain undulates across this section of mountainside, especially on Rock 'n Roll next to Big Dipper, but always stays comfortably within an intermediate's skill level. Devil's Elbow and Roller Coaster are rolling blue trails off the Sugarloaf chair. The Sunset and So Long area off the Supreme lift have intermediate backcountry-like skiing because the terrain is ungroomed.

Alta is prime turf for advanced and expert skiers. Most of it is directly accessible from lifts. Some of the best powder areas require a hike. Basically, what you see is what you'll find under your skis. If you question whether you have enough control for runs such as High Rustler, try easier slopes first. Sunspot is a good one to test yourself on because the sun usually keeps it soft later in the day, and it's light black in comparison to many of the other slopes at this area. The slopes past that, Stone Crusher and Alf's High Rustler, are much steeper and the only way out is down. (Word of warning: When the ski patrol says the snow conditions aren't right for skiing some of these runs, pay attention.) Punch Bowl, on the other side of the front face, is the local bump run. Rock Gully, a light black, is a long narrow chute where bumps can build. Wildcat is more difficult because it's a little more open but steeper. Greeley Bowl is the easier of the bowls off the back side because it's not as steep. These bowls are never groomed and Glory Hole, Yellow Trail, and East Greeley are quite steep. They are as close as one would come inside the ski-area boundaries to back-country conditions. Around and under the Supreme lift, expert skiers will find tight chutes, close woods, and other gnarly terrain. On powder days, many of the locals traverse (and then hike up if they have enough stamina) to kick up snow on Devil's Castle. There are expert-only out-of-area trails, including a ski route to Snowbird. Check with the ski patrol to see if these are open and to obtain exact directions.

Insider's Tips

On busy days when there are lines on the two lifts out of the base, all these skiers must form a single line to go up the Germania lift. Consider taking an extra run on the Wildcat face or Collins while the line at the Germania chair thins.

Mountain Facilities

Ticket offices are located near the main and the Albion parking lots. The new Albion Day Lodge houses the Albion Grill and Alta Sports, and the Goldminer's Daughter also doubles as another base lodge with food service. The Watson Shelter and the Alpenglow Inn are mid-mountain facilities with cafeterias.

Snow Coverage

Alta receives an average of 15 feet of snow annually, and is usually open from mid-November to May. The beginner and intermediate runs are groomed regularly and many are packed after a storm. However, some open slopes, as well as the chutes and forested glades, aren't touched so powderhounds will find plenty of terrain.

Ski School
This school pioneered powder techniques by Alf Engen, and many of its alumni run ski schools elsewhere in the nation. Group and private lessons are available. The Vesle Barne is the little children's ski school for ages 3 through teens.

Childcare
There is a childcare center in the Albion Ticket Office building for youngsters 3 months old and up. There is a combination ski school/day-care day.

Rental Equipment
Rental equipment is available at four shops: the Goldminer's Daughter, the Deep Powder House, Alta Sports in the Albion Day Lodge, and the Ski Rack in the Peruvian Lodge.

Cross-Country Skiing
There's plenty of terrain for cross-country skiers in this canyon. Cross-country instruction is available through the ski school.

WHERE TO STAY: There are four lodges and four condominium complexes in the base area. All the lodges offer both modified American plan and full American plan. Lodging prices are quoted in three-, five-, and seven-day packages and vary dramatically depending on the quality of the lodge or condominium complex. Meal plans add between $30 and $38 a day per person. For specific prices, contact these lodging places directly or contact **Alta Reservation Service** (tel. 801/742-2040).

The **Alta Lodge,** Alta, UT 84092 (tel. 801/742-3500), with ski-in/ski-out access, has been considered a classic ski lodge for years. Everything from dorm space to bedroom-sitting rooms is available at this lodge with a four-star AAA rating. The lounge has a fireplace, and there's a bar, hot pools, and saunas.

The rustic **Alta Peruvian Lodge,** Alta, UT 84092 (tel. toll free 800/453-8488), is a favorite with skiers who return to Alta yearly. The lodge rooms are spartan but comfortable, and there are two-bedroom suites. All guests dine on the full American plan and mingle at the tables during meals. Reserve early for holiday weeks.

The **Rustler Lodge,** Alta, UT 84092 (tel. 801/742-2200), is another classic ski lodge with standard and deluxe rooms, good food, an outdoor swimming pool, saunas, and a Jacuzzi. Guests can ski to Alta's lift and the lodge shuttle takes skiers to Snowbird for the day.

At the **Hellgate** condominium complex, Alta, UT 84092 (tel. 801/742-2020), there are two-, three-, and four-bedroom condos. It is located halfway between Alta and Snowbird. The **Blackjack Condominium Lodge,** Alta, UT 84092 (tel. 801/742-3200), is also located approximately halfway between Snowbird and Alta. Units range from studios to three-bedroom units. There is a lounge and saunas, and a free shuttle to the slopes.

WHERE TO EAT: Many of the skiers at Alta arrange for meal plans with their lodging. The **Shallow Shaft** (tel. 742-2177), with its 1870s mining decor, is a popular place. Entrees range from steak to stuffed trout and there are nightly specialties. It's open daily, and dinners run approximately $7 to $15. Reservations are accepted.

The Rustler and other lodges are open to skiers unless full with houseguests. There are several restaurants at Snowbird, a mile away.

GETTING THERE: Alta is located 25 miles southeast of Salt Lake City, a mile past Snowbird Ski and Summer Resort. Rental cars, limousines, buses, and helicopter service are available from the airport. (See the list of transportation companies in the Getting There section in Snowbird.) The Utah Transit Authority runs buses to Alta from downtown locations and from the airport.

MOVING AROUND: Guests in most lodges can ski or walk to the slopes. Skiers staying in the condos should have cars, especially if they intend to eat out at night. Snowbird runs a regularly scheduled bus to and from Alta for skiers who want to try the other area's slopes.

TOURIST INFORMATION: Contact **Alta Reservation Service**, Alta, UT 84092 (tel. 801/742-2040), or **Alta Ski Lifts**, Alta, UT 84092 (tel. 801/742-3333).

5. Salt Lake City Area

THE RESORT: Salt Lake City is the place for skiers who want to explore several of the ten ski areas within an hour's drive of the downtown area. It's also a good resting point for any party with members who don't like to ski. Non-skiers can spend the day exploring Temple Square and other tourist sites in this city. Evenings can be spent anywhere from the symphony to a professional sporting event, depending on what's available that night and your mood.

Contact **Ski Utah**, 307 W. 200 South, Suite 5005, Salt Lake City, UT 84101 (tel. 801/534-1779), for the annual Ski Utah Planner, which lists the hotels and motels in Salt Lake that court skiers.

The **Utah Transit Authority** (tel. 801/263-3737) has bus routes to Little Cottonwood and Big Cottonwood Canyons that stop at many of the listed hotels. **Park City Transit** (tel. 801/649-8567, or toll free 800/637-3803) and **Lewis Brothers Stage** (tel. 801/359-8677, or toll free 800/826-5844) go to Park City.

The Golden Spike Empire ski areas are an easy hour's drive. Trapper's Loop Road, expected to open this fall, will offer direct access to the three ski resorts in Ogden Valley from the Salt Lake City airport in less than an hour. For complete details on Park City, Deer Valley, Snowbird, Alta and the Golden Spike Empire, destination resorts to out-of-state skiers but day resorts to Salt Lake City residents, see the separate sections for each one. Information is listed below about the smaller day ski areas, Solitude and Brighton.

SOLITUDE SKIING: Solitude is one of those day areas frequented by Salt Lake locals because the snow is excellent, there's lots of good terrain for novices, intermediates, and advanced skiers—and there are no lift lines. Destination skiers rarely come into this canyon; they are lured elsewhere by the flashier resort names. However, a Big Cottonwood ticket that opens up both Solitude and Brighton (via the interconnecting SolBright trail) opens up a lot of skiing for very little money when compared with the going lift-ticket rates at major areas. Skiers who are staying in Salt Lake City and are new to the Rockies should consider utilizing the Big Cottonwood ticket for a day before moving on to the other canyons. (Just be aware that you must end up at the resort where the car is parked, or you'll have to hitch a ride back to the right parking lot.)

Five chair lifts open up 51 runs and open slopes. The 2,000-foot vertical has the expected beginner and intermediate terrain and some very intriguing terrain for advanced skiers. The ski area is built on moraines (like giant steps left by an ancient glacier), which means the steepest sections are at the top, then there is a gentle plateau area, another steeper section, and another gentle plateau near the bottom of the slopes. Beginners have several open runs off the Moonbeam and Sunrise lifts. Wander, a run that does as it says, is the longest run. Intermediates have a variety of runs off all lifts. Some, such as Sundance and Sunshine, are actually the same run; half is always smoothly groomed but the other half has beginner bumps. Because the area is underutilized (translate that as too few skiers for serious lift lines), especially during the week, skiers can find powder many days after a storm.

There's some interesting advanced terrain here. The open area, which has been arbitrarily split into runs with names ranging from Vertigo to Paradise, has wide-open bump and powder fields. The Summit chair (which takes skiers to the SolBright trail) heads up to a high canyon, where advanced skiers can traverse around the sides and pick their own lines down. Intermediate skiers can cruise the gully. The novel feature at this resort is the Honeycomb Canyon, a canyon just over the ridge from the front face and accessible via openings at the tops of three chair lifts. Although the map has a blue rating for the gulley, this canyon is only for strong intermediate—or better—who can parallel. The terrain is rough and never groomed.

Mountain Facilities

The Main Street Grill is at the base of the Moonbeam lift, Inspiration Station is at the base of the Inspiration lift, and there is a cafeteria downstairs in the main lodge and Houlihan's Bar upstairs. The Mountain Shop sells ski accessories and there is a ski rental and repair shop.

Snow Coverage

There is no snowmaking at this area, which receives an average of 410 inches of snow each year. The area is usually open from mid-November to May. There is snow grooming as needed.

Ski School

There are reasonably priced half- and full-day group lessons and private lessons. Children can go in the SKIwee program.

Childcare

Children can go into the all-day SKIwee program.

Rental Equipment

Both regular rental and demo equipment is available at the shop at the base area.

GETTING THERE: Solitude is in Big Cottonwood Canyon, 23 miles from downtown Salt Lake City. Skiers come by private car or the Utah Transit Authority's regularly scheduled buses. Check locally for the schedule.

TOURIST INFORMATION: For information, contact **Solitude Ski Resort Company**, P.O. Box 17557, Salt Lake City, UT 84117 (tel. 801/534-1400).

BRIGHTON SKIING: Brighton, the other day area located in Big Cottonwood Canyon, promises good beginner and intermediate terrain for exceptionally reasonable—and on some days cheap—prices. Skiers who buy the Big Cottonwood lift ticket can also use the trails at Solitude, reachable via the interconnecting SolBright trail. Because most of the terrain is so gentle, many Salt Lake skiers come here to learn to ski. There's night skiing several evenings a week.

The 1,445 feet of vertical at this primarily beginner and intermediate ski area is serviced by five chair lifts. The terrain is in two major sections: trails cut through woods off three lifts and open mountainside off two other lifts. Terrain is rated 26% beginner, 44% intermediate, and 30% advanced.

Beginners start on the runs off the Mary lift, but those with turning control can quickly move onto the Majestic lift, with longer, open runs. The most entertaining runs, for all levels of intermediates and advanced skiers who like to cruise, are off the Snake Creek chair. These runs are carved like eastern trails, wide enough but not too open, but have western snow. Sunshine, One Star, and others are up to a mile long and curve gently through the woods, so there's a feeling of privacy unless a gaggle of other skiers comes along. Scout, the intermediate access trail back to the base area, is a good cruising run. Most of the advanced terrain is in the light- and medium-black range. The largest section is in a relatively short open bowl area off the Millicent lift.

Mountain Facilities

The Alpine Rose lodge is a day lodge at the base with a cafeteria and a ski shop with rental equipment. The Millicent Chalet, at the base of the Millicent and Evergreen lifts, serves food all day.

Snow Coverage

There is no snowmaking at this area, which receives an average of 428 inches of snow each year. The area is normally open from mid-November to early May. Grooming is taken very seriously here, and the slopes usually reflect it.

Ski School

Intro-Ski packages and Intro II packages are big here. There are regular classes three times a day, private lessons, and learn-to-ski nights. The Kinderschool is for 4- to 6-year-olds. There are also parent/child private lessons for 2- to 4-year-olds where the parents attend the last 15 minutes and learn how to work with the child.

Childcare

There isn't a nursery, but 2- to 4-year-olds can take private lessons and 4- to 6-year-olds can go into Kinderschool.

Rental Equipment

Rental equipment is available in the Alpine Rose day lodge.

Cross-Country Skiing

The **Brighton Touring Center** (tel. 801/649-9156) nearby has 15 km (9 miles) of track, ski school, guided tours, and rentals. Ask about the overnight treks where skiers stay in a yurt in the backwoods.

GETTING THERE: Brighton is located in Big Cottonwood Canyon, approximately 25 miles from downtown Salt Lake City. Check locally about buses to the ski area.

TOURIST INFORMATION: For information, contact **Brighton Ski Bowl,** Brighton, UT 84121 (tel. 801/359-3283).

SALT LAKE CITY LODGING: There are 10,000 beds for visitors in Salt Lake City, but several hotels court skiers with special packages.

For the price of a basic room at one of the resorts, skiers can stay in luxurious comfort at the Salt Lake Sheraton Towers, the upper floors of the **Salt Lake Sheraton Hotel and Towers** (tel. 801/328-2000, or toll free 800/325-3535). Visitors to the Towers register at a private desk, then are escorted to spacious rooms with such amenities as terrycloth robes and fresh flowers. Tired skiers can have cocktails and complimentary hors d'oeuvres in the private lounge, and stop by in the morning for a complimentary continental breakfast. (They can also arrange to have that breakfast sent to their room.) The price: approximately $100 a night. Rooms in the regular section of the hotel run $85 a night. There's a health club with a large spa and indoor pool, as well as several restaurants on the lower floors. The hotel is just a few blocks from Temple Square.

The rooms at the **Marriott** (tel. 801/531-0800, or toll free 800/228-9290) are the quality expected from this fine chain. There is a health club with a whirlpool and an indoor pool, as well as several restaurants. The hotel is connected with the Crossroads Plaza, one of the largest indoor shopping centers in the country, which has a variety of stores, restaurants, and more. The Marriott is located a block from Temple Square. Check for current ski-package prices.

The comfortable rooms at **Little America,** 500 S. Main, Salt Lake City, UT 84101 (tel. 801/363-6781), are individually decorated. There's an indoor/outdoor pool, a whirlpool, and restaurants on the premises. The hotel is located five blocks from Temple Square. Ask about the current ski packages.

WHERE TO EAT: As you'd expect in a big city, there are many good restaurants. Ask locally for current favorites.

Among the more popular spots in the middle to upper ranges are the **Market Street Grill** (tel. 322-4668), **Café Central** (tel. 531-0895), the **Devereaux** (tel. 575-5200) for French cuisine and the **Lamb's Grille** (tel. 364-7166), which has been around since 1919.

Rio Grande (tel. 364-3302), which serves Mexican food, the **Dodo Restaurant** (tel. 328-9348), with entrees such as herbed chicken and clam sauce with spinach pasta, and **Pasta Mulino** (tel. 364-8066) are less expensive.

SHOPPING: The **Crossroads Plaza** near Temple Square is one of the nation's largest shopping centers. Inside, you'll find everything from department stores and boutiques to restaurants and food stalls. **Trolley Square** has dozens of shops, including several trendy boutiques, many restaurants, and several theaters, all set in renovated turn-of-the-century trolley car barns.

NON-SKIER ACTIVITIES: Salt Lake City is, of course, the focal point of the Church of Jesus Christ of Latter-Day Saints. Visitors may want to explore **Temple Square,** the religious and symbolic center of Mormonism. There's a visitor's center and frequent tours. Check on the schedule for organ recitals in the Tabernacle and concerts by the Mormon World Tabernacle choir. The **Beehive House,** home of the former church leader, Brigham Young, is open daily. The **Daughters of Utah Pioneers Museum** is nearby. Check the local papers for current events at the **Salt Palace,** a sporting event, entertainment, and convention center. Pick up the local visitors guides, available at most hotels, for a complete listing of places to explore and current happenings.

6. Interconnect Tour

Locals skied backcountry shortcuts between several of Utah's major ski resorts in the Wasatch range for years. However, few vacationers inching along on snow-covered canyon roads realized the hour-long drive between Alta in Little Cottonwood Canyon and Brighton in neighboring Big Cottonwood Canyon could be shortened to a 50-yard climb and a long glide on skis over a mountain pass. The Interconnect Adventure changed that! The Interconnect tours are a blend of backcountry skiing over mountain passes and skiing on groomed runs at four or five ski areas in the canyons. With the installation of critical lifts at Alta and Solitude a few years ago, bringing skiers very close to the ridges dividing the canyons, the long-dreamed concept of interconnecting the canyons became a reality. Weather conditions permitting, a guide leads advanced skiers in good physical condition on the five-area tour, which includes Park City, Solitude, Brighton, Alta, and Snowbird; or the four-area tour which begins at Snowbird and includes Alta, Brighton, and Solitude. It is being touted as the U.S. answer to the European concept of skiing from town to town, but the trips are more of a novelty adventure than a serious day of skiing because much of the backcountry experience includes a lot of hiking and traversing at high altitudes.

However, the trip does show skiers a number of resorts they might not otherwise see. Although the route between the ski areas is now well marked, it should never be attempted without a qualified guide. (In fact, it may be illegal to ski certain parts of the route without guide service.) For additional information about the Interconnect Adventure, contact **Ski Utah, Inc.,** 307 W. 200 South, Salt Lake City, UT 84101 (tel. 801/534-1779). There are both day trips and an extended trip which allows skiers to travel to different resorts via the Interconnect route and spend the night. The luggage is transferred by car.

7. Golden Spike Empire

THE RESORT: There are three areas in the Ogden Valley—Snowbasin, Powder Mountain, and Nordic Valley—that promote themselves as the Golden Spike Empire. If construction went as scheduled, the Trapper's Loop Road should have opened by the 1987–1988 ski season, making the trip from Salt Lake City Airport to the Ogden Valley, weather permitting, less than an hour. For the current status of the road, general information about the three ski areas, lodging reservations, and restaurant information, contact the **Golden Spike Empire,** P.O. Box 1601, Ogden, UT 84402 (tel. 801/399-8288, or toll free 800/255-8824).

THE SKIING: Snowbasin is often touted as Utah's "secret" area because there's good skiing here, but not too many skiers outside Utah know about it. There are 40 designated runs, up to three miles in length, on the 1,300 acres serviced by four triple chairs and a double chair. Terrain is rated 20% beginner, 60% intermediate, and 20% advanced on the 2,400-vertical-foot mountain. Snowbasin is an excellent family place, and in the process of becoming a significant ski area since the Sun Valley Company bought it and is renovating it. For information, contact Snowbasin, P.O. Box 348, Huntsville, Ut 84317 (tel. 801/399-1136, 801/399-0198 for the snow line).

Powder Mountain is a local area with a short vertical by Utah standards, 1,300 feet, and short lift lines. Terrain is rated 10% beginner, 70% intermediate, and 20% advanced on the terrain serviced by three chair lifts. Ski here in a snowstorm to learn how the area earned its name. The backside has powder runs up to 2,000 vertical feet, ending in a canyon. A shuttlebus brings skiers back to the base area. There's day and night skiing on one lift pass. For information, contact Powder Mountain, P.O. Box 68, Eden, UT 84310 (tel. 801/745-3771).

Nordic Valley is a small family-oriented area with two chairs climbing the 1,000 vertical feet. There is night skiing at this inexpensively priced ski area. For information, contact Nordic Valley, P.O. Box 178, Eden, UT 84310 (tel. 801/745-3511).

WHERE TO STAY: Lodging in the valley is mainly in condominiums or bed-and-breakfast places, while lodging in Ogden ranges from economy to luxury motels and hotels. Contact the Golden Spike Empire (address above) for a lodging list. Many skiers stay in Salt Lake City.

WHERE TO EAT: Choices range from fast food to fine dining. When making reservations through the Golden Spike Empire, this organization will suggest restaurants.

TOURIST INFORMATION: The **Golden Spike Empire**, P.O. Box 1601, Odgen, UT 84402 (tel. 801/399-8288, or toll free 800/255-8824). Ask for a copy of the "Travel, Ski, and Entertainment Guide."

8. Southern Utah: Brianhead

THE RESORT: Brianhead is a friendly, low-key resort peopled primarily by families. Approximately 40% of the skiers come from Las Vegas, 3½ hours away. Slopes rise up from both sides of the road along which the lodging and restaurants are situated. There's a hotel and a good number of very attractive condominiums here, more than one would expect in a relatively remote resort with a gentle but entertaining mountain. Snowmobiling in the surrounding mountains and up to nearby Cedar Breaks National Monument runs a close second to skiing.

THE SKIING: The vertical is only 1,200 feet here, but there's a fair amount of mountainside to explore. Seven lifts open up the terrain, rated 20% beginner, 40% intermediate, and 40% advanced. Beginners have their piece of mountainside behind the large main base lodge. The Riviera lift, opening up a gently tilted slope, is good for starters. Once comfortable with turning and stopping, skiers move onto the Stardust chair with nicely graded, wide beginners' trails called Maryland Parkway and Paradise. Intermediates can ski off the top of the Stardust lift and head over to the more open blue terrain on Sioux Face and Cheyenne around the Navajo lift. The rest of the ski complex is across the road, rising above the other base lodge. Intermediates can explore most of this terrain from the popular Second Step and Third Step (the First Step is black) under the Giant Steps lift to the network of runs off Roulette. The runs around the Roulette chair have a steady intermediate-skill-level pitch. However, when bumps build at the top of Straight Up and others, a black-diamond sign is stuck in the ground to warn skiers the run is tougher. The blue runs off the Dunes lift are often less busy than other areas, and the views of the Cedar Breaks National Monument are terrific. The advanced terrain here is very limited, and the stretches are short. The bumps can build on the First Step, while cruisers will enjoy floating down Engens, especially after a powder storm.

Mountain Facilities

The main base lodge is an attractive, open building with a cafeteria, ski shop with a stone grinder for working on ski bottoms in the repair department, and a very workable rental area. There's a small lodge at the base of the Giant Steps chair lift with a restaurant next door.

Snow Coverage

There is no snowmaking at this area, which receives an average of 450 inches of snow each year. Snow grooming is emphasized here and the slopes are worked on regularly.

Ski School

Beginners are treated well here. They start out in the main lodge by meeting their ski instructor, who will ease them through a well-thought-out rental shop to get their equipment and step outside to put on skis, then start the on-snow lesson. There are regular group and private lessons. Kinderschool is for youngsters between the ages of 5 and 8.

Childcare

Kindi Kare is a combination ski school and/or day-care service for youngsters of all ages. Half- and full-day care is available. Call the ski school (tel. 677-2035) for details.

Rental Equipment

Rental equipment is available on the lower floor of the main lodge. **Crystal Mountain Recreation** (tel. 677-2-FUN) rents snowmobiles and runs guided tours.

Cross-Country Skiing

The **Brianhead Cross Country Ski Center** (tel. 801/677-2012) is located in the mall. Touring near the rim of Cedar Breaks National Monument is a popular tour for beginners. Cross-country skiers head out around the resort to explore the countryside.

WHERE TO STAY: Skiers have their choice between a comfortable hotel and condominiums ranging from plush with private Jacuzzis to more spartan but adequate units. When compared to similar condominiums at megaresorts, most of the units are in the moderate price range.

Many of the condominiums in the **Copper Chase** are decorated in furnishings more expected in an elegant home than a condo, and several have private Jacuzzis. The complex is ski-in/ski-out from some slopes, and there's an indoor pool, saunas, and an exercise room in the dramatically designed main lobby area. Prices range from approximately $55 to $190, depending on the size of the unit.

The **Timberbrook** condominiums are nice, clean units with fireplaces, microwaves in the kitchens, and a standard floor plan. Skiers take shuttles to the slope. The recreation building includes an indoor pool and a Jacuzzi. Units range from studios to one-bedrooms with lofts, but they are on the third floor and there is no elevator. Unit rates stretch from approximately $53 on weekends to $82, depending on the size.

Many of the attractive condominiums in the **Giant Steps** complex have underground parking and ski-in/ski-out access. (The units at the far end are popular with snowmobilers because they can unload and drive their machines away.) Units have fireplaces and microwaves. Condo prices range from $81 to $158 on weekends, depending on unit size.

Central reservations agencies that represent properties at these and other complexes at Brianhead include the **Accommodation Station** (tel. 801/677-3333, or toll free 800/572-9705) and **Brianhead Condominium Reservations** (tel. 801/677-2045, or toll free 800/722-4742).

WHERE TO EAT: There are approximately ten restaurants in the area. Most are in the moderate and less expensive categories.

Moderate to More Expensive

The Edge (tel. THE-EDGE), where the menu is printed on a paper bag, is one of the most popular restaurants in town. Notice the curiosities on the walls, ranging from creative posters to ski boots. Entrees are basic beef, seafood, veal, and chicken, ranging from $13 to $18. Dinner is served from 5 to 10 p.m.

Cosmos (tel. 677-3663) has good Italian food.

Less Expensive

Shep's (tel. 677-2587) half and whole sandwiches are popular with skiers. It's a very casual tiny place where ski boots are okay. Prices run approximately $2.50 and up for sandwiches to $15 for a large, special pizza.

The **Tele Deli** (tel. 677-2258) is the spot for breakfast and lunch, although some skiers stop by for an early light dinner. Breakfast is served all day, and sandwiches range from a variety of vegetarian choices to clubs. Omelets average $3.75, quiche averages $4, and sandwiches are $4.

NON-SKIER ACTIVITIES: Snowmobiling is almost as popular here as skiing. Many guests bring their own machines.

GETTING THERE: Brianhead is 190 miles north of Las Vegas. **Skywest** has flights to nearby Parawan Airport in Cedar City, 30 miles away, from both Salt Lake City and Las Vegas. **Chartered buses** are available from Las Vegas.

MOVING AROUND: Guests staying at some of the condominiums are shuttled to the slopes. (Check when making reservations.) Other condos are ski-in/ski-out, but a car (or strong legs) is needed to reach restaurants.

TOURIST INFORMATION: For more information about Brianhead, try the central reservations agencies listed above and/or contact **Brianhead Ski and Summer Resort,** P.O. Box F, Cedar City, UT 84720 (tel. 801/677-2305 or 801/586-4010).

For medical emergencies contact the **Brianhead Medical Clinic** (tel. 677-

2700) in the day lodge at the base of the number four and six chair lifts. After hours, call the **town sheriff** (tel. 677-2043).

9. Other Utah Ski Areas

SUNDANCE: Home of Robert Redford's Sundance Institute, this ski area and arts community is nestled in a canyon at the base of 11,750-foot Mount Timpanogos. Two double chairs and two triple chairs open up 2,150 vertical feet and 34 trails, including Bishop's Bowl. Night skiing is available from 4 to 9 p.m. Tuesday through Saturday evenings. There's fine dining in the Tree Room and the Grill restaurants, located at the base lodge. Lodging is available in the Mountain Inns, private homes set in the canyon and managed by Sundance. For information, contact **Sundance**, RR 3, Box A-1, Sundance, UT 84604 (tel. 801/225-4107).

BEAVER MOUNTAIN: Beaver Mountain is primarily for beginners and intermediates, but powder skiers should enjoy the acres of lightly treed areas. Terrain is rated 25% beginner, 35% intermediate, and 40% advanced at this 1,600-vertical-foot ski area. For information, contact **Beaver Mountain Ski Area**, P.O. Box 3455, Logan, UT 84321 (tel. 801/753-0921).

MOUNT HOLLY / ELK MEADOWS: These two ski areas, located in the Tushar Mountains of southern Utah about half a mile apart, operate as one resort. At Elk Meadows, with its 850-foot vertical, the trails and open bowls serviced by a two chairs are primarily beginner and intermediate terrain. The double chair and T-bar at Mount Holly, with its 1,135-foot vertical, access terrain rated 10% beginner, 20% intermediate, and 70% advanced. Almost 400 beds are available in Mount Holly Village, and each area has a base lodge with food service. Rentals, ski accessories, a mini-mart, bar, and other services are available. For information and reservations, contact **Mount Holly / Elk Meadows**, P.O. Box 511, Beaver, UT 84713 (tel. 801/438-5030 or 801/438-5544).

10. Utah Liquor Laws

Visitors to Utah soon learn that all those cracks about this being the "driest state in the Union" couldn't be farther from the truth! The reality is: Liquor flows steadily in this Mormon state—it simply flows in a manner unlike liquor is poured anywhere else.

Check locally for any changes, but basically a brown-bag guide to this state reads as follows: The minimum legal drinking age in Utah is 21. There are three ways to purchase liquor in Utah:

1. Buy it in a bag—in state liquor stores and package agencies. (These stores can be large, but the package agencies will offer just a few brands of each type of booze.)

2. Buy it in a bottle. Mini-bottle stores are located in many restaurants. (These can be just a closet behind the cash register in a restaurant or a tiny room near the lounge in a hotel.) You must buy the mini-bottle of booze (think inflight liquor bottles to visualize the size) or mini-splits of wine and take them into the lounge. The set-ups (tonic for gin, bloody mary mix, etc.) cost extra and must be bought in the lounge. Although the liquor prices appear inexpensive at first, when you add on the price of the set-up, the complete drink cost is comparable to most resorts. They even charge a "corkage fee" to uncork your wine bottle and give you a glass. Visitors can brown-bag their own liquor. However, they will still be charged a "set-up" or "corkage fee." Restaurants are allowed to open regular size bottle of wines.

3. You can buy liquor by the drink—in a private club. Private clubs have a different meaning in this state—they are places where members can legally order a premixed drink. These "clubs" offer yearly and reasonably priced two-week "temporary" memberships, which are available to any visitor. Anyone can visit a lounge/beer bar and buy beer by the glass or brown-bag their liquor.

Most resorts have an explanation of the liquor laws within easy reach of every visitor. The tourist guides to restaurants and entertainment spots usually mark where you can buy it by the bottle and where you need a membership to buy it by the drink.

Chapter VIII

THE LAKE TAHOE AREA

1. Mount Rose
2. Slide Mountain
3. Ski Incline
4. Homewood
5. Tahoe Ski Bowl
6. Alpine Meadows
7. Sugar Bowl
8. Sierra Ski Ranch
9. Squaw Valley
10. Kirkwood
11. Northstar-at-Tahoe
12. Heavenly Valley
13. Smaller Ski Areas Around Lake Tahoe
14. Cross-Country and Other Facilities
15. Lodging and Dining
16. Practical Matters

SOME 20 SKI AREAS ARE CARVED into the mountainsides surrounding Lake Tahoe, which straddles the California/Nevada state line. Staying in one state allows you to play in both. The ski slopes are located in both states—but the gambling and big-name shows are in Nevada. Skiers can mix their ski days at Heavenly and other California ski areas on the south shore with nights of fine dining and gambling, because the two states butt against each other here. The north-shore areas, including Squaw Valley USA, Alpine Meadows, and North-at-Tahoe, are in a quieter locale. There's lodging and après-ski in the summer/winter vacation towns on the lake. Anyone staying on the north shore who wants Nevada's nightlife stays closer to the Nevada line or in Reno. The Nevada ski areas are near Reno and open to skiers trying the Lake Tahoe resort "experience." Mount Rose and Ski Incline are compact ski areas that have been in operation for years but are continually modernizing their operations.

THE RESORT: Lake Tahoe, which spreads into both California and Nevada, is the center of a destination region—versus a destination resort—and skiers tend to sample more than one set of ski slopes during their stay. Although several of the more than 20 ski areas have lodging at the base of the slopes, the majority of visitors tend to bed down in the summer/winter lakeside vacation towns or in Reno. Staying in Reno places the nearby areas a short drive away, and all of the north shore ski slopes within a 1½-hour drive. Lodging in Tahoe City, Incline Village, or other towns right on the lake, in the Truckee area, or at Northstar places most of the north-shore areas within a half-hour drive. Skiers on the south shore have easy access to Heavenly and three other areas. However, during the winter the most direct road between the ski areas on the south and north ends of the lake is often closed, so skiers will have a 1¾-hour journey to ski the runs at the other end. There is a modernized version of the old-fashioned paddleboat that takes skiers from the south shore to Alpine or Squaw Valley several days each week.

THE SKIING: The ski area verticals here range from 300 feet at tiny Granlibakken to 3,600 feet at Heavenly Valley, and cater to everyone from never-ever locals, to yuppies and the upper-crust crowd from the West Coast. Skiers new to the region tend to gravitate toward the better-known resorts—such as Heavenly Valley and Squaw Valley USA—but there are several other lesser-known ski areas with exciting runs (and often shorter weekend lift lines!). The ski areas are grouped in clusters. Mount Rose and Slide Mountain, which share a ridge, and Ski Incline area are all located just southwest of Reno. Northstar-at-Tahoe, Alpine Meadows, Squaw Valley USA, Sugar Bowl, and several other smaller areas are located off the north shore of Lake Tahoe, each about an hour's drive from Reno. Heavenly Valley stretches upward from the most populated part of the south shore, while Kirkwood is an hour's drive and Sierra Ski Ranch is 25 minutes from South Lake Tahoe, California / Stateline, Nevada, the two adjoining cities where the majority of the accommodations and après-ski activities for that region are located.

Obviously there is something for everyone at all the ski areas to be listed. However, several have—to me—either better than average, or more than average, terrain for various skill levels.

At Squaw and Heavenly the beginner's terrain is part way up the mountain opening up the views. At Squaw, beginners take the tram to the beginners' area at mid-mountain, while at Heavenly they take the gondola up to the green runs. These skiers can eat lunch at the mid-mountain lodges and download at the end of their day. Never-evers might try one of the smaller ski areas such as Mount Rose, because they often offer bargain-basement prices on lift/lesson and even rental packages for newcomers to the sport. Most first-timers—and even second- or third-timers—use so little terrain that the quality of the instruction is more important than the number of green runs available.

Obviously there's good intermediate terrain at most of these areas; however, skiers who want "endless" amounts (or at any rate more than they can ski in a day) should steer toward Alpine Meadows, Northstar-at-Tahoe, or Heavenly Valley. Heavenly probably has the largest number of longer intermediate runs, but Alpine Meadows and Northstar have some of the most interesting terrain with lots of terrain variety with an intermediate's comfort-level pitch. All three have a variety of blue slopes, where barely intermediates can progress to almost advanced.

Advanced and expert skiers have all heard about the infamous KT22. It, of course, is the focal point of eyes looking out from the tram rising up the cables at Squaw Valley USA. KT22—as promoted—has the lion's share of the toughest skiing in the region. However, there are several other slopes at this area that will keep advanced skiers intrigued. Advanced skiers should also check out Alpine

INTRODUCING LAKE TAHOE

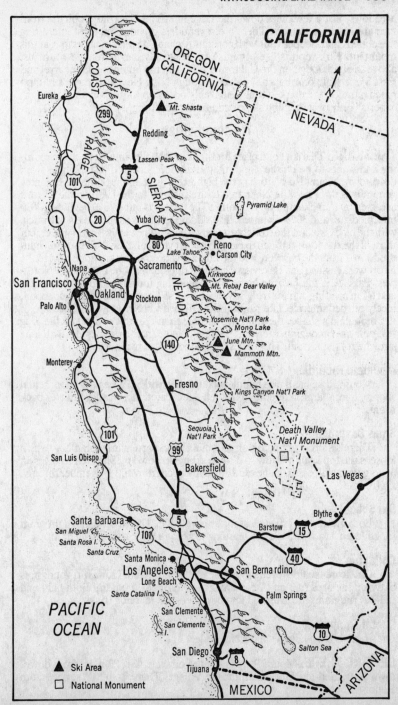

Meadows, just a few miles down the ridge line. The black slopes on the front face are good for starters. There are several less obvious but most interesting treed areas and steeper runs with constantly changing terrain underfoot at this mountain. Kirkwood is like a mini-Alta. Heavenly has its toughest turf just above the base lodge on the California side, and the bumps on Gunbarrel and East Slope will go on most any skier's "tough" list. However, there's not too much more on the marked trails. Heavenly opens up Mott Canyon "for super-experts" only, weather and slope conditions permitting.

1. Mount Rose

THE SKIING: This is a good place for the skier who flies into Reno in the morning and wants to be on the slopes that afternoon. Located just 22 miles from downtown, Mount Rose is one of the highest ski areas in the Sierra, so the snow generally is drier here (as compared to areas closer to the lake) on the 27 runs accessed by four chair lifts and a poma. The terrain is rated 30% beginner, 40% intermediate, and 30% advanced. The skiable terrain is shaped like a half circle with the black trails at the straightest, longest part. The vertical is 1,440 feet, but most of the runs don't stretch the length of that vertical. Skiers hike several hundred yards from the base lodge to the lifts. Advanced skiers gravitate toward the Northwest Passage and Lakeview chair lifts that open up the black runs. Northwest Passage is the favorite here: it's challenging for advanced intermediates and a fun cruising run for truly advanced skiers. There are several wide, open, nicely pitched intermediate runs off the Lakeview chair. However, because of the mountain's shape, the trails are shorter than the black runs and the long run-outs are on beginner terrain. Beginners have their own two lifts with long stretches of flat terrain. The longest run is more than two miles.

Mountain Facilities

Mount Rose has a nice multilevel day lodge with an accessory shop, rental shop, a bar, a large cafeteria, and a deli line located in a smaller, quieter back room.

Snow Coverage

There's a strong emphasis on grooming here, particularly rotatilling, which loosens the top layer of snow so it's like skiing on powder. The area receives an average snowfall of 400 inches and is usually open from mid-November through April.

Ski School

Both group and private lessons are available. The Rosebuds is a program for children 3 to 7 who are just learning to ski or unable to ride a chair lift.

Childcare

Childcare facilities aren't available on the mountain. However, youngsters between the ages of 3 and 7 can enter the Rosebuds program. Both half- and full-day programs are available for youngsters just learning to ski.

Rental Equipment

Rentals are available in the base lodge.

GETTING THERE: Mount Rose is located on Nev. 431, 22 miles from downtown Reno and ten miles from Incline Village. There is shuttle service from Reno.

MOUNT ROSE / SLIDE MOUNTAIN 157

TOURIST INFORMATION: For more information, contact **Mount Rose Ski Resort,** P.O. Box 2406, Reno, NV 89505 (tel. 702/849-0704). Snow report number is 702/849-0706. For information on **ski/lodging packages,** call toll free 800/824-8557, 800/822-5959 in California.

2. Slide Mountain

Note: Slide Mountain was only open for part of the 1986–1987 season and its status was uncertain. Call the ski area or the **Tahoe North Visitors and Convention Bureau** (tel. 702/583-3494) before going.

THE SKIING: The locals refer to Slide Mountain as "steep and cheap." Located on the flip side of the mountain from Mount Rose (they share a common ridge), this area has the steeper runs for intermediates and advanced skiers. Although there is a small beginner's area at the bottom, it's also the run-out for many of the trails, so many skiers fly through it heading for the lift. (The tiny never-evers area is protected.) The terrain is rated 10% beginner, 40% intermediate, and 50% advanced. The skiable terrain, accessed by three chairs and a few surface lifts, is developed in a shallow sort of half bowl so skiers can move from one open run to the next, starting with Washoe Zephyr and moving over to the open Silver Dollar as the sun changes the snow conditions. Gold Run, with its steep grade and trees making an informal slalom course, is for advanced skiers. There is good tree skiing here in between the big cedars that dot the landscape. Reno is a 24-hour town, and locals make the 25-minute drive to this area when they want a few hours on the slopes.

Mountain Facilities
The lodge houses a cafeteria, bar, and ski shop.

Snow Coverage
This area has a southeast exposure, so a lot of snow is needed to cover the steeper slopes adequately. Rock skiing early in the season or during a slow snow year is a possibility. The annual snowfall is approximately 200 inches, and the area is usually open from mid-November to late April. There is snowmaking equipment used when needed.

Ski School
The Slide Mountain ski school offers both half- and full-day group lessons and private lessons. There are specialty programs in powder skiing, mogul skiing, race clinics, telemark skiing, and snowboarding.

Childcare
There is no childcare facility on the mountain.

Rental Equipment
Rentals are available in the base lodge.

GETTING THERE: Slide Mountain is on Nev. 431, 22 miles from Reno via U.S. 395 and 12 miles from Incline Village via Nev. 432. The ski area runs a shuttle service from Incline Village, Lake Tahoe, and Reno. Call for a specific schedule.

TOURIST INFORMATION: For information, contact **Slide Mountain**, P.O. Box 11156, Reno, NV 89510 (tel. 702/849-0303). For a report on **snow conditions**, call 702/849-0304.

3. Ski Incline

THE SKIING: If plans went as scheduled, the vertical at Ski Incline more than doubled last summer! The expected installation of a new quad to open up an entirely new section of mountainside ups the vertical from 900 to 1,840 feet. The new section is a mix of intermediate and advanced terrain with a combination of trail and tree skiing.

The area was developed with destination families in mind and draws visitors from the West Coast who prefer skiing at a compact area. Some vacationers staying in Reno spend a day or two here before moving on to larger ski areas. The chance to sit on the sun-drenched porch of the cabin atop the mountain and watch the changing colors in Lake Tahoe's water, less than a mile away, is worth the price of the lift ticket. A quad chair and six doubles open up 30 runs, if the expansion came through as scheduled.

Beginners utilize the Blue Bell chair, set off to one side so better skiers shouldn't come schussing through. Intermediates can move over most of the mountain's terrain. The runs off the Yellow Jacket lift and the Red Fox lift offer everything from straight shots downhill to curving trails. Advanced skiers gravitate toward the runs off the Yellow Bird lift, including Oh God and G.S. They'll also want to challenge the runs around the new quad chair.

Mountain Facilities

The attractive base lodge has a cafeteria offering more than the usual ski-area fare and the upstairs cocktail area in the lodge is a pleasant place to sit. The ski shop and lockers are on the lower floor. The lodge at the top of the slopes has a spectacular view of Lake Tahoe.

Snow Coverage

The average annual snowfall is 300 inches because the area is in a banana belt, so snowmaking equipment covers approximately 200 acres. The machines are used constantly, and the snow is continually groomed. The area is usually open from mid-November to mid-April.

Ski School

Ski Incline's ski school offers both half- and all-day lessons and private lessons. Young children who can stop can go into ski school; others must be in private lessons. SKIwee is for ages 5 to 12.

Childcare

The new childcare facility is the place for youngsters of all ages. Policies were still being outlined at the time this was published. Call for hours and ages.

Rental Equipment

Regular and demo rentals are available in the rental shop in the base lodge.

GETTING THERE: From Incline Village, take Nev. 28 to Country Club Drive to Ski Way. Ski Incline is on the edge of Incline Village and 45 minutes from Reno. The ski area runs a free shuttle service in the Incline Village area.

TOURIST INFORMATION: For more information, contact **Ski Incline**, P.O. Drawer AL, Incline Village, NV 89450 (tel. 702/832-1177). For information on **lodging** and **ski packages,** call Incline Village reservations (tel. toll free 800/242-SNOW, 800/60-TAHOE in California). The 24-hour **snow phone** is 702/831-3211.

4. Homewood

THE SKIING: Homewood is a locals' area with a few cheap, mid week price breaks for skiers who want to ski cheaply. Lift tickets are limited. The slopes are more protected from the wind than those at other nearby ski areas, and the view of Lake Tahoe, across the road, is impressive. Three chairs, three platters, and a T-bar open up 22 runs on the 1,650-vertical-foot mountain. However, the only top-to-bottom run is down upper Rainbow Ridge and off the face onto a black run or down Lombard Street, a track for intermediates. The runs below the Madden Ridge chair are all short open faces with a black-diamond pitch. (And can surprise the shaky intermediate who drops over the ridge instead of taking the Lombard trail.) Off the Madden Canyon quad chair there are several intermediate runs, including the popular Bonanza. The advanced runs off this chair include Juniper and Nugget, with steeper pitches at the end where bumps can build. Tahoe Ski Bowl shares a ridge with Homewood, but as of this writing there are no interchangeable lift tickets.

Mountain Facilities
There is a rustic base lodge with a restaurant, a cocktail lounge, a ski shop, and a rental shop. The Warming Hut on the mountain has a food area and a bar.

Snow Coverage
There is no snowmaking here. Most of the runs are groomed carefully and frequently. Homewood is usually open from Thanksgiving to Easter.

Ski School
Group lessons are offered twice a day. Private lessons are available.

GETTING THERE: Homewood is on Calif. 89 on the west shore of Lake Tahoe. There is public bus service to the area.

TOURIST INFORMATION: Contact **Homewood Ski Area,** P.O. Box 165, Homewood, CA 95718 (tel. 916/525-7256).

5. Tahoe Ski Bowl
Note: Tahoe Ski Bowl did not open during the 1986–1987 season and its status is uncertain. Contact the **Tahoe North Visitors and Convention Bureau,** P.O. Box 5578, Tahoe City, CA 95730 (tel. 916/583-3494), for more information.

THE SKIING: When open, this locals' ski area has skiing for all levels off two chairs, a T-bar, and rope tows. The lift tickets are cheaper here, and lift-ticket sales are limited. The terrain is rated 40% beginner, 40% intermediate, and 20% advanced. The mountain has 1,630 feet of vertical, but most of the runs don't stretch that length. The longest run is a green one that starts out as the Rainbow Ridge run at the top of the upper lift and winds its way to the bottom. (Any skier using the upper lift must take this green track partway to get back to the lower chair.) Of the two chairs, the longest runs are off the upper triple chair. Many, such as the popular Dutch Treat, are rated black at the top and blue halfway down, but are usually groomed so competent intermediates can handle them. The lower chair, which opens up a different set of runs, has several short, steep black runs on the face.

6. Alpine Meadows

THE SKIING: Alpine Meadows has long had the reputation of being "that area down the road from Squaw," mainly for beginners and intermediates. That's not exactly true. Alpine Meadows is down the road from Squaw, but in its 2,000 acres of skiing, there is a lot of exciting terrain for advanced skiers as well as for the less skilled. Two triple chairs, nine double chairs, and two pomas open up 100 designated trails, including six open bowls spread across two mountains. Terrain is rated 25% beginner, 40% intermediate, and 35% advanced/expert. Every skill level has a large variety of terrain at this ski area, with a 1,797-vertical-foot drop off one mountain and slightly less off the other. (And there are many runs that grab the full vertical off each mountain without ending on run-outs.)

The terrain at Alpine Meadows has texture. Of course there are runs that have a smooth, steadily downward pitch (translate that as the generic ski run that can be found anywhere). But there are also many runs with varying pitches —steeper, then smoother—and stretches that even slant at times from one side to the other, so the skier has the challenge of dealing with the mountain itself instead of just cruising down a superhighway. Beginners work off two short chairs and a poma set away from the main trails. Their area is smooth, well groomed. Intermediates have trails all over the front side of the mountain, including such popular runs as Yellow Trail and Dance Floor, although the Red/Green trail has a similar pitch and usually far fewer skiers. The runs off the Lakeview triple chair on the south ridge of Scott Peak are similar to those off the Roundhouse and Yellow chairs on the front face, and several are good cruising intermediate runs.

Advanced skiers and experts will gravitate toward the Sherwood, Alpine, and Summit chairs. The Sherwood Bowls have wide, open spaces where skiers have space to traverse if needed. (However, barely advanced skiers should make sure they can handle the snow conditions in this area.) This is the prime turf on the mountain during spring skiing. (Even competent intermediates may be able to handle this terrain then.) On the front side, advanced skiers can explore the terrain under the Summit chair, because there's enough space in the Wolverine Bowl and Three Sisters to maneuver. The chutes, D-8 and D-7 (next to it but not on the map), have some steeper spots to challenge the more skilled advanced skiers. Alpine Meadows is one of those "follow-a-local" areas to get the last bits of powder or reach the most exciting areas for expert skiers. Gentian Gully and Promised Land, off the Scott Chair, are away-from-it-all treed runs that eventually break into more open areas for the skiers who like to track down that last bit of powder. Wolverine Bowl is another popular area with powderhounds. The Alpine Bowl chair opens up Palisades and other cliff areas that are all double-diamond runs on the map and definitely experts-only turf. Among the other intriguing marked runs not so easy to find are Art's Knob and, for experts only, Our Father (and the neighboring unmarked Hail Mary).

Insider's Tips

For a fast entry onto the slopes, visit the ticket booth at the base of the Subway chair, which is halfway back on the parking lot next to the slopes.

There are free guided tours of the mountain on intermediate terrain. Check with the Information Desk in the base lodge for the schedule.

To follow the sun, especially in the spring, start on the Sherwood Bowls area, then ski the Lakeview chair and then the front side.

The check room in the base lodge offers 24-hour storage of ski equipment and clothing.

Mountain Facilities

The base facilities include a day lodge with a cafeteria, full-service restaurant, bar, cocktail lounge, a repair shop, and a ski shop, plus a mid-mountain chalet.

Snow Coverage

Alpine Meadows, which averages an annual snowfall at the base of 350 inches, is open from November to Memorial Day. There is snowmaking on the beginner and some intermediate slopes. This area has an intensive grooming program that even utilizes a snow mover.

Ski School

Full- and half-day group and private lessons are available. There are special ski-school programs throughout the year, including recreational racing clinics and the Sierra Holiday, in which students (no more than five in a class) get lessons, pre-ski stretching sessions, luncheon seminars on topics such as sports psychology, and more. The Children's Snow School is a well-developed (and copied) program for youngsters from 3 to 6, which combines indoor activities and ski lessons. There are half- and full-day programs.

Childcare

Supervision is available only for youngsters ages 3 to 6 in the Snow School and in regular ski-school lessons. They are supervised while not in class and escorted to and from class.

Rental Equipment

High-performance and regular equipment can be rented in the Alpine Meadows Rental Shop.

GETTING THERE: Alpine Meadows is on Calif. 89, 12 miles south of I-80 off the Truckee interchange. The area operates a free daily shuttle with pickups at several spots on the north and south shores of Lake Tahoe. There is also public transportation on a regularly scheduled basis in the North Lake Tahoe area.

TOURIST INFORMATION: Contact **Alpine Meadows**, P.O. Box 5279, Tahoe City, CA 95730 (tel. 916/583-4232). For **lodging** arrangements, call toll free 800/824-8557, 800/822-5959 in California. The **snow phone** is 916/583-6914.

7. Sugar Bowl

THE SKIING: A classic mid-size ski area, the runs offer a reasonable amount of terrain for every skill level from beginner to advanced. The novelty here is an access gondola that brings skiers and overnight guests from the parking area over a gully holding the railroad tracks to the ski area. (Ask an old timer about the years spent climbing over the snow sheds protecting the tracks—and how they coped when the trains roared by—to get to the ski slopes.) At the area seven chairs open up the runs on two peaks. On Mount Lincoln, a quad opens the 1,502-foot vertical drop, the black runs offer a variety of increasingly steep pitches from the smoothest trail, Shute One, to the bumps on Vanderbilt and the path through cliffs in Steilhung Gully. Intermediates cruise down the popular Lakeview Run and California Street. Beginners have their own terrain off the Christmas Tree and Lincoln Access chairs. The intermediate and advanced runs off Mount Disney are more wide open. Crow's Traverse, which winds across the mountain, is the longest run. Both the Mount Disney and the Crow's Nest chairs open up all of the intermediate terrain on this part of the mountain. There is night skiing on Saturday and Tuesday.

Insider's Tips

When the lines on Lincoln Two are long, head over to the Disney lift, and if that's crowded, keep going to the Crow's Nest chair.

Sugar Bowl was started by members of the San Francisco Bay area society crowd almost 50 years ago. Through the years many built vacation homes at the base, and several of these houses are in a rental pool. (There are also bare-bones rooms in the main lodge.) Ask about ski weeks.

For a leisurely lunch on weekends, visit the dining room in the main lodge.

The fare—mostly sandwiches—is simple but well prepared, and the desserts are good. (The dining room is small, so be prepared to wait in front of the fire in the nearby living room.)

Mountain Facilities

The base lodge houses a cafeteria, the **Belt Room** bar, the dining room, and the Company Store, which has deli items, snacks, and souvenirs. There is a ski shop with rental equipment and ski clothing next door and the Chalet Bar nearby, which is open after skiing during the week and at 11 a.m. on weekends and holidays.

Snow Coverage

This is a high snow area: the annual snowfall averages 500 inches and Sugar Bowl is normally open from November to April. There is no snowmaking. The area grooms the beginner, intermediate, and many advanced runs regularly.

Ski School

Half- and full-day group lessons and private lessons are available. Racing clinics are on Saturday.

Childcare

There is no childcare facility.

Rental Equipment

Regular and high-performance rentals are available at Klein's Ski Shop just up the slope from the base lodge.

GETTING THERE: Sugar Bowl is three miles east on old U.S. 40 off the Soda Springs/Norden exit of I-80. The ski resort is 11 miles from Truckee.

TOURIST INFORMATION: Contact **Sugar Bowl**, P.O. Box 5, Norden, CA 95724 (tel. 916/426-3651). For information about **staying at the lodge** in the private chalets or condominiums, also call 916/426-3651.

8. Sierra Ski Ranch

THE SKIING: Sierra Ski Ranch has a long time clientele of skiers who are convinced they get as much—or more—for their money at this resort than at comparable ones that charge much higher lift-ticket prices. The nine chair lifts open up 2,000 acres of terrain rated 20% beginner, 60% intermediate, and 20% advanced. The vertical drop is 2,212 feet and skiers can find a five-mile-long run.

Beginners have two chair lifts at the bottom, but as soon as they can make wedge turns and stop, they head to the top for a gentle 3½-mile trip down. (Head to the top of the King or Queen lift and take Sugar N' Spice down.) Lower intermediates head for Lower Main Street, Aspen West, and other runs around the Knob Hill and Rock Garden chairs. More competent intermediates head for the backside (called the sunnyside by many) to try the runs off the Eldorado chair. Advanced intermediates challenge the runs off the Cougar and Puma chairs because they are open, long, and might even be considered black at some other ski areas. Advanced skiers start out on Eastabout, then move onto Preachers Passion, and finally the steepest run—the often bumpy (it's too steep to groom) Dynamite.

Insider's Tips

For a five-mile warmup run that starts on green trails, graduates to easy blue terrain, and then to a more difficult blue trail, take Sugar 'N Spice, cut over to Spur, ski onto Corkscrew, and end up on Beaver.

There are no bars at Sierra Ski Ranch, but skiers may bring their own beer or wine.

Mountain Facilities

There are three base lodges and a mountaintop building, all with cafeterias. In good weather, there are barbecues at the lodges. Ski rental, repair, and accessory shops are located in the base area.

Snow Coverage

The annual snowfall on this area, which is open from November to April, averages 450 inches. There is no snowmaking.

Ski School

Half- and full-day group lessons are available at this PSIA ski school. Children go into Super Skiers.

Childcare

There is no childcare facility on the mountain, but the ski area management will recommend one on the road leading up to the area.

Rental Equipment

Both adult and child equipment rentals are available at the rental shop in the base area.

GETTING THERE: Sierra Ski Ranch is on Sierra Ski Ranch Road off U.S. 50, 12 miles west of South Lake Tahoe. The ski area runs shuttle buses daily in the region. For time schedule and location of stops, call 916/659-7453.

TOURIST INFORMATION: Contact **Sierra Ski Ranch**, P.O. Box 3501, Twin Bridges, CA 95735 (tel. 916/659-7453). For **snow information,** call 916/659-7475.

9. Squaw Valley

THE SKIING: This mountain lives up to its billing! Site of the 1960 Olympics, Squaw has long had the reputation for being a unique ski mountain. There are 27 lifts, including a cable car, a gondola, and two high-speed quads to spread skiers over the vast amount of terrain, which ranges from the barely downhill novice slopes at mid-mountain to the world-famous steeps on KT 22. The terrain is rated 30% beginner, 40% intermediate, and 30% advanced. The vertical off Squaw Peak, the highest of the five peaks covered with lifts, is 2,700 feet.

Imagine a champagne glass and you've envisioned the major part of Squaw's terrain. The gondola and cable car rise up the stem, and many of the chairs, including the beginners' lifts, bell out from the bowl of the glass. Beginners and intermediates ski on the middle and the upper part of the mountain. Advanced skiers have the run of most of the terrain, and expert skiers have more terrain then they'll tackle in a day, especially on KT 22 and Red Dog peaks.

Squaw's trail map only lists the ski lifts because the terrain is so open. However, there are local names for most of the trails. Pay strict attention to the black, blue, and yellow ratings. (There is a run off KT 22, for instance, that is rated blue but would be black at almost any other area in the country. It is the easiest way down off that lift—but only very, very surefooted, experienced intermediates should consider taking it.)

Beginners take the tram up in the morning, ski off several lifts set in the widest, most gentle part of the mountain, then download at the end of the day. Intermediates who know the area take the tram or gondola, then pop over the backside to the Granite Chief area—bowl-shaped terrain with intermediate skiing in one part and advanced terrain on the rest. (This section is wind-protected and the front is not.) There are several open trails cut through the woods with nicely pitched terrain for intermediate skiers off the Solitude and Shirley Lake chairs. Skiers who want to graduate to black runs should try the nearby Granite chair but pick the route down carefully. There are some where the pitch is steeper than on the nearby intermediate runs, but the terrain is open enough so a skier could traverse. There are also several tougher sections with interesting, varied turf (which may require some tighter turns) for advanced skiers.

On the front side of the mountain, the Newport, Mainline Gold Coast, and Emigrant chairs open up a gentle bowl at the top with groomed blue runs. The Cornice I and Super Squaw lifts access wide, open, groomed blue-rated terrain in the middle and lower parts of the mountain. Intermediates could spend most of a day in this area without getting bored.

Skiers used to the black ratings at smaller areas should eyeball the black runs here carefully before heading down. Locals suggest the open area under the Siberia chair as the place to test one's skills. From there, progress to the Granite Chief area or Sun Bowl, a bowl not visible from the front but located off the top of the Cornice II chair. The face of Headwall, under the Headwall chair, is a classic long, steep bump run. The terrain between Squaw peak over to KT 22 is primarily for very advanced and expert skiers. There is some "gnarly" (as one expert skier put it) terrain like the Enchanted Forest, where stopping isn't a luxury at times because the pitch is too steep. (This is definitely follow-a-local turf.)

KT 22 is the peak that put Squaw on every expert's personal ski map. Looking up will help tell if you've the head and skills to ski it. Anyone backing out on top can take the easier way down (that blue run, which would be a black elsewhere). The bumpy west face is a test of any skier's skills. It's one of the longest, steepest bump runs in the country. (There are downsides on some of the bumps taller than many skiers.) A PSIA examiner once commented that he takes ski instructors vying for their pins down the neighboring 75 Chute, and "if they hesitate," they lose. (And, of course, the "only one unforgiving way in" is just what challenges the super-experts who ski this run!)

Insider's Tips

Either the gondola or the tram takes skiers to mid-mountain, so take whichever one has a shorter waiting time.

If the Shirley Lake lift is crowded, take the neighboring Solitude lift, which accesses much of the same terrain and usually has a shorter line.

When the KT 22 chair line is long, take the Olympic Lady or the Red Dog chairs. They are shorter, but they open up good advanced terrain and there's time for an extra run while others are still in line.

Sno-hosts and hostesses located throughout the area are trained and ready to answer questions about the skiing and offer first aid or other reasonable assistance.

Dining with a panoramic view is part of eating at High Camp. If sit-down service appeals but you don't want to go to the base area, try Alexander's. (The cheese plate is fruit and French bread surrounding a complete wheel of Brie.)

Mountain Facilities

At the base, there is the Olympic House, which has an Oyster Bar, Bar One, and Jimmy's sit-down restaurant; the Olympic Plaza and Bar, which houses a deli, a taco, and a hamburger place; and the Squaw Valley Mall, with several shops and restaurants.

Snow Coverage

The annual snowfall averages 400 inches at Squaw, which is usually open from mid-November through early May. There is no snowmaking. This area's grooming fleet is big enough to maintain the snow on several smaller areas.

Ski School

The PSIA ski school offers group and private lessons. There are many specialized programs, including five-day advanced skiing seminars, Woman's Way seminars, the Beginners Junior Ski School for youngsters 6 to 12, and the Ten Little Indians Snow School for children 3 to 6. Reservations are recommended for the **Ten Little Indians Snow School** (tel. 916/583-4743 or 916/583-0119). There are half- and full-day sessions that include ski instruction and indoor supervised activities. A and B ski-school classes don't need lift tickets.

Childcare

Ski lessons and indoor supervised activities are part of the Ten Little Indians Snow School (see ski instruction).

Rental Equipment

Rentals are available at the Company Store, located near the Clocktower at the entrance to the Squaw Valley Mall.

GETTING THERE: Squaw Valley is on Calif. 89, off I-80, seven miles north of Tahoe City. There is limited shuttlebus service to the mountain from properties in Tahoe City and Truckee.

TOURIST INFORMATION: Contact **Squaw Valley USA**, P.O. Box 2007, Olympic Valley, CA 95730 (tel. 916/583-6985). Squaw Valley has a **central reservations service** that handles a variety of accommodations in Squaw Valley and Lake Tahoe. For information call 916/583-5585, or toll free 800/824-7954, 800/545-4350 in California.

10. Kirkwood

THE SKIING: Kirkwood is an area with a lot of exciting terrain. Ten chairs and a platter open up 60 runs, including several open-bowl areas spread over 2,000 skiable acres. The terrain is rated 15% beginner, 50% intermediate, and 35% advanced at this area, where the vertical drop is 2,000 feet.

There's gentle novice terrain off the Hay Flat lift near the main base lodge, as well as off the Bunny and the Hole 'N Wall chairs near the Timber Creek base lodge. There are blue runs off most of the chairs, but intermediates tend to congregate at the Solitude chair near the base area and the Sunrise chair in a basin at the far end of the skiable terrain. The runs off the Solitude chair are groomed, wide enough to make comfortable turns, and with good downward pitches. It takes a couple of chair rides to reach the runs off the Sunrise chair (not in sight of the base area), but it's worth the time. Elevator Shaft and Happiness Is, off the Sunrise chair, are cut in a low timber area, and there's lots of room to make wide, wide turns on these runs, all more than a mile long.

One former Utah resident who works at Kirkwood noted that the black terrain here is similar to that at Alta. Lots of good steep pitches, a few chutes, and some tree skiing characterize the advanced terrain. The terrain for better skiers is off the Cornice, the Wagon Wheel and the Sunrise lifts. Many of the black runs start above timberline in steep, open bowls whose sides become more gentle midway down the mountain.

Traversing to the right off the Cornice chair opens up Olympic, a piece of bowl with moguled steep sides open enough to traverse a little if necessary. Sentinal, down the ridge, also has a respectably steep pitch and it leads into Stumps Run, a beautifully pitched black trail ripe for cruising when well groomed. There's a wide, open treeless bowl on the other side of the Cornice chair. Skiers can head under the chair to enter Zachary, usually a bump run, or Monty Wolfe on an angle, or head farther down the ridge and slide down or jump over the lip. Skiers who want to try the chutes keep heading down the ridge. The open skiable area under the top of the advanced-skiers-only Wagon Wheel chair has a steep pitch and often there are lots of moguls. (It's a powder run immediately after storms.) The skiing stays tough as the treeline forces skiers into cut runs with the names of Short Spoke and Conestoga.

Insider's Tips

To follow the sun in the winter, start on the Sunrise chair and later in the afternoon ski off the Cornice chair, then come down to the Cables Crest chair.

To avoid lift lines, use the Sunrise chair until 10:30 or 11 a.m. and then come back to the Cables Crest, Iron Horse, or Wagon Wheel chair. After a late lunch, ski the Solitude chair and end up at Cables Crest.

There's a sushi bar and a deli counter in the main lodge!

Mountain Facilities

The food is upscale here, in both taste and presentation. There's a sushi bar and a deli bar in the Red Cliff Lodge. Between the Red Cliff Lodge and the Timber Creek Lodge at the other end of the base, skiers also have two cafeterias, an ice-cream parlor, and a pizza parlor. The Cornice Café Restaurant and Bar, across from chair 6, offers "California cuisine" at lunch and dinner, and live music after dinner on weekends. Each base lodge has a rental and a ski shop.

Snow Coverage

Kirkwood averages 425 inches of snow annually and is open from mid-November through early May. There is no snowmaking.

Ski School

Group and private lessons are available, as are special programs for youngsters ages 4 to 12. (Ski instructors will take the young ones to and from the nursery for class.) There are advanced workshops and recreational racing clinics.

Childcare

The Rainbow Day Nursery is in the Red Cliff building adjacent to the main lodge. Children from 3 to 8 are accepted on a daily and hourly basis.

Rental Equipment

Regular, demo, and high-performance rental equipment is available at both base lodges.

GETTING THERE: Kirkwood is on Calif. 88, 30 miles south of Lake Tahoe.

168 DOLLARWISE GUIDE TO SKIING USA—WEST

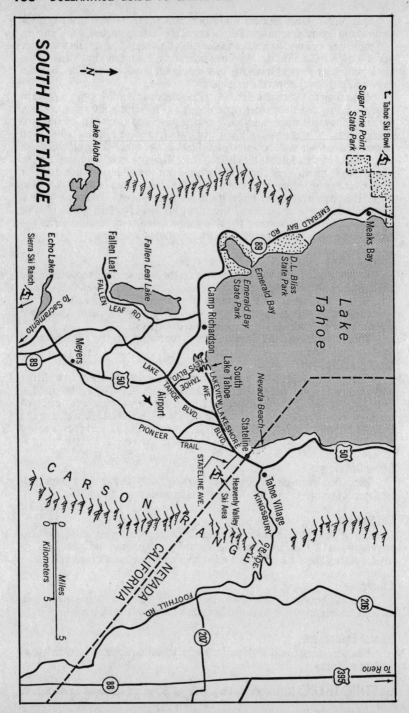

(Take Calif. 89 from Tahoe to Calif. 88.) The ski area offers bus service to and from South Lake Tahoe.

TOURIST INFORMATION: Contact **Kirkwood**, P.O. Box 1, Kirkwood, CA 95646 (tel. 209/258-6000). The **snow phone** is 209/258-3000. There is lodging in condos at the base of the mountain. For information, contact **Kirkwood Central Reservations** (tel. 209/258-7247).

11. Northstar-at-Tahoe

THE SKIING: Northstar-at-Tahoe is a ski area with ego runs for most skiers. Novices can graduate to blue runs quickly because of the grooming (definitely some of the best in the region) and the mountain's topography. Intermediates will be able to test some of the black runs as soon as they can do stem turns comfortably and control their speed, and barely advanced skiers may be able to challenge many of the black diamond trails. A gondola, eight chairs, and two surface lifts open up more than 48 runs on 1,700 acres of mountainside with a 2,200-foot vertical drop.

Beginners work around the day lodge and on the well-groomed, almost flat runs off the Big Springs gondola. Northstar's day lodge and the ski school are located at mid-mountain; there's a mall with shops, restaurants, and a deli at the base.

Better skiers take the Echo lift or gondola from the base and spend the day skiing the runs above the day lodge. They only use the lower trails for a run-out at the end of the day. The runs off Forest, Aspen, and Lookout chairs are all intermediate terrain. Almost all of them are wide enough for skiers making wedge turns, and the downward pitches are steady but relatively gentle. Lumberjack, Main Street, and West Ridge are the most popular runs. Runs such as Sunshine and the Gully are a little off the tracked-up paths but offer the same good terrain and fewer skiers. The Comstock lift is popular because it opens up a variety of blue and black runs.

Advanced skiers head to the backside of the mountain for the runs off the Schaffer Camp chair. Ironhorse is an open, usually groomed-smooth, advanced run. Some locals consider Rail Splitter, Sierra Grande, and Burn Out more difficult. Rapids, a moguled, often-narrow run mostly under the lift, is the most difficult. When there are long lines at this lift, advanced skiers may head to the Rendezvous lift, where the waiting time may be shorter—but the black runs are shorter too.

Insider's Tips

This ski area is below timberline and more protected from the wind than many of the others in the region, a point to keep in mind when it's really blowing off the high ridges at other areas.

A 2.9-mile top-to-bottom end-of-the-day run-out on blue and green terrain (which might avoid some of the crowd) is West Ridge to Luggi's to Cascades, then Main Street to The Gulch to Village Run.

Northstar limits lift-ticket sales, and management strives to keep lift lines no more than 20 minutes long.

Mountain Facilities

The Big Springs day lodge, at mid-mountain, has a cafeteria, deli, bar, and sundeck barbecue. There is a wine and cheese house nearby. In the mall at the base of the ski runs, there is a deli, for fast sandwiches (no seating space); Schaffer's Mill Restaurant and Lounge, which serves three meals daily; a pizza parlor; and the Rendezvous Sports Pub. In the mall there is a ski shop, a ski rental shop, a gift shop, and a general store.

Snow Coverage

The annual snowfall averages 400 inches, and there is snowmaking on some slopes. Northstar is open from Thanksgiving Day through Easter.

Ski School

This **PSIA** ski school offers a variety of group lessons, from three-hour beginner classes to three-day programs, and private lessons. Star Kids is available for youngsters from 5 to 12. Peewee is for children 3 to 6.

Childcare

There is a childcare center in the base village. They only take children ages 2 to 6 who are potty trained. Youngsters from 3 to 6 can take the peewee ski-school option. Children from 7 to 12 can enter Star Kids, which runs from 10 a.m. to 3:45 p.m.

Rental Equipment

Rental equipment is available from the Northstar ski rental shop in the base village.

GETTING THERE: Northstar is on Calif. 267, halfway (six miles) between Truckee and the north shore of Lake Tahoe.

TOURIST INFORMATION: Contact **Northstar-at-Tahoe**, P.O. Box 129, Truckee, CA 95734 (tel. 916/562-1010, or toll free 800/824-8516, 800/822-5987 in California). For information about **lodging** at this ski resort, call the toll-free numbers. The **Snophone** number is 916/562-1330.

12. Heavenly Valley

THE SKIING: An aerial tram, 16 chairs, and nine surface lifts open up Heavenly Valley's 20 square miles of skiing terrain sprawled over the state line between Nevada and California. The terrain, covering nine mountain peaks, is rated 25% beginner, 50% intermediate, and 25% advanced, but its reputation as an "intermediates" mountain is well deserved. The vertical is 3,600 feet on the California side, slightly less on the Nevada side, and intermediate skiers can utilize it all skiing top to bottom.

The terrain at Heavenly is flip-flopped with the advanced slopes near the bottom, beginners in the middle, and intermediate at the top and all over on the Nevada side. Beginners here have a compact mid-mountain section at the top of the aerial tramway. (They download at the end of the day.) They also have a long run around the Boulder chair on the Nevada side.

Intermediates can ski for days without taking the same trail twice. Many spend half the day on slopes in one state and the rest of the day in the other. (The time it takes to move from one side to the other is minimal if you're going to spend hours on each side, but it's a lot of trucking for just a run or two.) On the California side, intermediates gravitate toward the Canyon, Sky, and Ridge chair lifts. The most spectacular views of the lake are off Ridge Run, an open, frequently groomed trail along one portion of the ski area's perimeter.

Liz's, Betty's, and Canyon runs are all popular, rolling blue runs in this area. To reach the Nevada side, take the Sky chair, ski to the left, and follow the Nevada signs that lead to the Skyline trail (a very gentle green trail with some stretches where you might have to pole). The blue runs are longer on the Nevada side (the vertical here is 2,700 feet), wide, and usually less crowded, and there is a lot of easy intermediate skiing. Orion, Big Dipper, and the long Olympic Downhill are just a few of the gently pitched blue trails on the Nevada side.

To return to the California side, take the Dipper chair and follow the signs to the California trail, or take the East Peak chair and follow the signs to California and take the Von Schmidt trail, which includes some walking. Be sure to allow time for lift lines when heading back to the other state. Intermediates heading down at the end of the day on the California side can take the Roundabout trail, which cuts across the steep runs on the face, or they can download in the tram or chairs.

Advanced skiers can test their skills on the Big Dipper or the Little Dipper on the Nevada side, or Ellie's—a bump run on the California side. When comfortable on those runs, consider challenging Gunbarrel and East Bowl, the steep, moguled runs on the face overlooking the California base lodge. (Tired skiers are encouraged to download on the tram or chairs at the end of the day.) They're mean and steep, and the moguled sides can drop quite deep. Super-expert skiers have complained that there's not enough for them, so Heavenly opened an area "for super-experts" only! Called Mott Canyon (on the Nevada side neighboring the Milky Way Bowl), this area with steep bowls, canyons, and chutes is reached through control gates. Snowcats shuttle skiers back to the groomed terrain.

Heavenly is touted as a mountain for powder skiing. On powder days, there are often more skiers in the open treed areas (especially on the Nevada side) between the runs than on the trails.

Insider's Tips

Most skiers (especially vacationing tourists) start the day on the California side. Actually, the base lodges in California and Nevada are equidistant for anyone staying in the casino area, and Nevada's day lodges are rarely crowded. (But keep in mind it is up a steep road, which can be a problem in bad weather.) Often skiers at the California base are still standing in line while those who parked at the Boulder or Stagecoach base lodges in Nevada are already on their second run. Intermediates can ski to the bottom on the Nevada side but might have to download in California.

Read the back side of the trail map. It's full of tips on moving around this ski area—tips that will help keep you from wasting a day just trying to figure out how to get around the 20 square miles of skiable terrain.

To follow the sun, spend the morning on the Nevada side and the afternoon on the California slopes.

On sunny days, skiers can bring their meat and use the barbecue grills set up (with supplies) on the Sky Meadows and East Peak decks.

Mountain Facilities

On the California side there's a day lodge with a cafeteria, a ski shop, a rental shop, and an attractive cocktail lounge with live music and dancing. There's a cafeteria, sit-down restaurant, and lounge, all with great views, in the Top of the Tram. Sandwiches are available at Sky Meadows, at the base of the Sky chair.

In Nevada there are cafeterias, bars, ski shops, and rentals at both the Boulder and the Stagecoach lodges. The East Peak mid-mountain lodge has a cafeteria and a wine and cheese bar. There are "cook your own" barbecues at the East Peak and Sky Chair lodges. (You buy raw steak, a burger, or chicken and cook it on the grill.)

Snow Coverage

The snowfall averages between 300 and 500 inches yearly at Heavenly Valley, which is open from mid-November through mid-May. Snowmaking covers many of the high-skier-usage areas.

Ski School

Ski-school lessons are available in both California and Nevada. The all-day lessons begin at 10 a.m. and the half-day lessons begin at 2 p.m. Youngsters ages 4 to 12 can join SKIwee for half- or all-day lessons and lunch.

Childcare

Childcare is available at ten different facilities in the shore area. Call the south shore visitors center or the ski area main number and ask for childcare recommendations. Several are within a half mile of the area and take children from infants on up.

Rental Equipment

Rental equipment is available at all three base lodges.

GETTING THERE: To reach the California base area, follow the signs up Ski Run Boulevard, off U.S. 50. To reach Nevada base lodges follow Nev. 207 (the Kingsbury Grade) to the top and follow the signs. The ski area runs complimentary shuttles between the California base lodge and lodging properties in the area, and from the casinos to the Boulder base lodge in Nevada.

TOURIST INFORMATION: Contact **Heavenly Valley**, P.O. Box AT, South Lake Tahoe, CA 95705 (tel. 916/541-1330). For current **ski conditions,** call 916/541-SKII. For information about lodging, contact **Heavenly Valley Central Reservations** at 702/588-4584, or toll free 800/648-3383 for ski packages, 800/822-5922 for lodging only.

13. Smaller Ski Areas Around Lake Tahoe

BOREAL SKI RESORT: After-dark skiing is an option at Boreal Ski Resort almost every night of the season. There are more than 30 slopes at Boreal, and the longest run is one mile. There are nine lifts on the 600-vertical-foot mountain. Terrain is rated 35% beginner, 50% intermediate, and 15% advanced. The Animal Crackers Center has day care for youngsters ages 2 to 12. Snackbar and cafeteria service are available. It's located ten miles west of Truckee, and you can get there via I-80, using the Castle Peak exit. For information, contact **Boreal Ski Resort,** P.O. Box 39, Truckee, CA 95734 (tel. 916/426-3666).

DONNER SKI RANCH: Located near Norden, rustic and homey Donner Ski Ranch offers night skiing on Friday and Saturday. There are four lifts servicing the 825-foot vertical drop with 25% beginner runs, 50% intermediate, and 25% advanced. There is a cafeteria, snack bar, lounge, and dining room. Contact **Donner Ski Ranch,** P.O. Box 66, Norden, CA 95724 (tel. 916/426-3635).

SKI TAHOE/DONNER: Served by three lifts, Ski Tahoe Donner, a beginner/intermediate mountain, is part of a resort development and is used mainly by residents, although it is open to the public. The ski area has a vertical drop of 600 feet, and the terrain is rated 50% beginner and 50% intermediate. Two double chairs and a rope tow open up 120 acres of bowl skiing. Children ages 3 to 6 can enter the Snowflakes skiing program. There is a snackbar and a restaurant. For information, contact **Ski Tahoe/Donner**, P.O. Box 11049, Truckee, CA 95734 (tel. 916/587-9444).

14. Cross-Country and Other Facilities

CROSS-COUNTRY: Royal Gorge, reputedly the biggest and one of the best cross-country operations in the country, is the best-known cross-country area in the region, but there are several others with groomed trails threading through the mountains surrounding Lake Tahoe. Contact the north and south shore tourism centers (see Tourist Information section at the end of this chapter for addresses) for a complete list of Nordic centers.

Royal Gorge

Royal Gorge, in Soda Springs, has 62 trails, 255 km (155 miles) of groomed track, and seven warming huts on the trails spread over a wooded Sierra plateau, just 45 minutes from Reno. There are all-day, half-day, twilight, and children's track fees. French country cuisine, ski lessons, and more are part of the multiday packages for guests in the Royal Gorge Wilderness Lodge, reachable by a three-mile sleigh ride. There are two rental shops, a retail shop, two cafés, and a bar at Royal Gorge. For information, contact **Royal Gorge Cross-Country Ski Resort**, P.O. Box 178, Soda Springs, CA 95728 (tel. 916/426-3871).

Northstar-at-Tahoe

Northstar-at-Tahoe has 40 km (25 miles) of groomed trails with skating lanes and set tracks winding from the Big Springs day lodge (midway up the mountain) to the base area and around the backside of the mountain. The trail fee includes the use of the Big Springs gondola to take skiers to the Nordic center located near the day lodge. (Cross-country and downhill skiers can meet at lunchtime here.) Telemark lessons are available. The center has a ski shop, ski school, and rental equipment. For information, contact **Northstar Cross Country and Telemark Ski Center**, P.O. Box 129, Truckee, CA 95734 (tel. 916/562-1010).

Kirkwood

Kirkwood has 75 km (45 miles) of groomed trails dotted with four huts where skiers can get warm. There's a ski school with lessons, including advanced telemarking and video lessons, and guiding services. Regular and demo rentals are available at the Nordic Center. For information, contact the **Kirkwood Touring Center**, P.O. Box 77, Kirkwood, CA 95646 (tel. 209/258-6000).

Other Areas

Experienced cross-country skiers may want to explore some of the underdeveloped areas. For a list of places ranging from Nevada Lake Tahoe State Park to Desolation Wilderness, ask the local visitors bureaus. Skiers must check with the **U.S. Forest Service** (tel. 916/573-2600) before heading into the backcountry for the latest snow condition report and/or warnings.

NON-SKIER ACTIVITIES: Harrah's Automobile Collection boasts more than 1,000 antique, classic, vintage, and unusual cars ranging from a 1906 Compound with power brakes to the first car with air conditioning, a 1940 Packard. For directions to the collection, the schedule for the free double-decker bus that runs from Harrah's Hotel to the collection, and ticket prices, call 702/355-3500. The collection is open daily from 9 a.m. to 6 p.m.

The **Reno/Tahoe Gaming Academy** offers 1½-hour lessons on the fundamentals of various games of chance from blackjack to craps. Call 702/329-5665 for more information.

The growth of **Virginia City,** 23 miles southwest of Reno, was fueled by silver from the Comstock mine in the 1800s. Today tourists can stroll along the boardwalks, take an underground mine tour, and explore the old mansions, the Opera House, the churches, and the saloons so popular when it was a city of 30,000 in the 1870s. From Reno, take I-395 south, then go east on Nev. 17.

Horse-drawn sleigh rides are available on the south shore through Borges Sleigh Rides in South Lake Tahoe. Call 916/541-2953 for details.

There is **ice skating** on Lake Christopher and in the Tahoe Keys area, weather conditions permitting. For additional information, contact the South Lake Tahoe Chamber of Commerce at 916/541-5255.

Snow play is an option at Hansen's Resort (tel. 916/544-3361) and at Winter Wonderland (tel. 916/544-7903). Rental equipment is available.

Off-road and backcountry **snowmobiling** is limited, but there are several companies that offer guided tours and rent snowmobiles. Tour prices range widely, and clothing rentals are available at some companies. Contact the local visitors bureau for a list of snowmobile tour operators.

15. Lodging and Dining

WHERE TO STAY: Skiers bed down all over the region from Reno, Nevada, to South Lake Tahoe, California, and drive, or take one of the many shuttlebuses provided by the ski areas and many lodges, to the slopes. There is some lodging within walking distance of the lifts at Squaw, Northstar-at-Tahoe, Sugar Bowl, Heavenly, and Kirkwood.

Skiers who stay in Reno have the cheap food and nightlife attendant to a 24-hour town where casinos fill the main floor of every major hotel and big-name entertainers appear nightly. They have a 20- to 30-minute ride to the areas southwest of town (Mount Rose and Ski Incline), a 45- to 60-minute ride to the ski areas on the north shore (Northstar-at-Tahoe, Squaw, Alpine Meadows, and Sugar Bowl), and a 1½-hour ride or more to the south-shore areas (Heavenly, Kirkwood, and Sierra Ski Ranch).

Skiers staying at Incline Village are a few miles from Ski Incline, 15 to 20 minutes from Mount Rose, between 30 and 45 minutes from the north-shore ski areas, and about an hour or more from the south-shore areas. Incline Village, Nevada, is a high-rent district for permanent homes and a popular summer resort town, so many of the restaurants are big-city sophisticated in style and food quality. Anyone staying at the properties that line the north shore from Kings Beach (next to Incline Village) to the Tahoe City area is bedding down in California.

South-shore lodging is concentrated in South Lake Tahoe, California, and Stateline, Nevada. (To realize how close they are, understand that one major hotel casino is in Nevada, but the area where guests give their cars to parking attendants is allegedly in California!) Heavenly Valley's lower ski slopes are in view as you walk down the street in South Lake Tahoe. Kirkwood is an hour south and Sierra Ski Ranch is 25 minutes away.

Staying in Reno

Wintertime is the down time in Reno's casinos, and so many of the hotels topping these gambling halls offer ridiculously low prices to draw in skiers, many of whom spend the evenings gambling and watching shows.

There are more than 20,000 rooms in the Reno area, and the number of motor lodges and hotels offering special ski packages—including a variety of items from cheap lodging and a cabaret show to reduced lift tickets and transportation to the ski areas—keeps changing. For the most current information, contact the Tourism Department, **Reno/Sparks Convention and Visitors Authority,** P.O. Box 11430, A 16-01, Reno, NV 89510 (tel. toll free 800/FOR-RENO).

Staying in a downtown hotel opens up the action in all the big hotels located within a few blocks of each other. That also means lots of cheap buffets and food bargains designed to draw in diners who drop coins in a slot machine on the way in and stop by a blackjack table on their way out. Deciding which big-name entertainer to watch can also be a problem, since there are usually several performing within the five-minute walk. About the only problem with staying in this downtown area concerns the trains that move through once or twice during the night. Ask for a room on the upper floors!

Among the hotels offering price breaks for skiers are: **Harrah's Reno** in the downtown area, which has rooms and service that have earned a Mobil four-star and an AAA four-diamond accommodation award. There's a 24-hour casino, celebrity entertainment, health spas, and five restaurants and bars including the Harrah's Steak House.

The **Hilton** in downtown Reno has nicely decorated rooms, and the service and amenities, from 24-hour room service to shampoo and shoeshine cloths, are as expected from this chain. There's a 24-hour casino and big-name entertainment in the evenings. The lounge on the 21st floor has comfortable chairs and a panoramic view of the area.

Circus Circus, also in the downtown area, has compact rooms and cheap buffets where the food is unlimited but the quality is less than inspiring. Most evenings there are aerial circus acts on the second floor and a midway to keep youngsters entertained.

The **MGM Grand Hotel,** located about ten minutes from downtown, has large, comfortable rooms. (If you're willing to spring for a little decadence, rent a suite reminiscent of a movie set with a round bed and mirrored ceiling or a sunken Roman tub.) This hotel also has RV hookups on the premises. There's a casino bigger than a football field, a bowling alley, and health spas in the underground shopping center, and a variety of live entertainment in the evenings. *Hello, Hollywood, Hello,* a two-hour extravaganza featuring showgirls parading to various musical hits interspersed with acts such as gauchos and an aerialist directly overhead, has been drawing visitors for years. There are seven restaurants, and the food prices tend to be higher than in the downtown area, where there is more competition.

The **Nugget,** one of the biggest hotels in the area since a recent 28-story tower addition, has attractive rooms, a 24-hour casino, live entertainment nightly, ten restaurants, and daily shuttle service to several ski areas. This hotel is located on I-80, five minutes east of downtown.

Staying on the North Shore

Many of the condominiums, lodges, and hotels on the north shore of the lake stretching from Incline Village to Tahoe City were built for summer vacationers, but skiers are needed to fill the beds during the wintertime. Several properties have lodging packages that include an interchangeable lift ticket good at seven ski areas: Alpine Meadows, Squaw Valley USA, Northstar-at-Tahoe, Homewood, Ski Incline, Mount Rose, and Sugar Bowl. For specific information about the establishments offering such packages, contact the **Tahoe North Visitors and Convention Bureau,** P.O. Box 5578, Tahoe City, CA 95730 (tel. 916/583-3494, or toll free 800/824-8557, 800/822-5959 in California). Ask for the booklet describing many of the lodges and restaurants on the north shore. Lodging possibilities range from bed-and-breakfast inns to condominiums and first-class chain hotels. Contact the visitor's bureau with your specific requirements. They should have plenty of suggestions, and they can make the reservation through their computerized central reservation service that represents more than 80% of the lodging on the north shore.

Although the following list of accommodations (which can all be booked through the toll free numbers) lists the per-night price, the north shore visitors bureau sells lots of packages that include lodging and lifts. Three-day/three-night package prices for skiers staying in motels or hotels range from $136 to $219 per person, double occupancy. Week-long packages range from $232 to $426. Three-day packages in condos range from $200 to $318 per person, double occupancy in a studio, and the price for six skiers in a three-bedroom condo ranges from $115 to $188 per person. The week-long packages range from $377 to $712 in a one-bedroom and from $275 to $393 in a two-bedroom.

Moderate to Expensive: The **Olympic Village Inn,** near the base of Squaw (tel. toll free 800/VILLAGE), designed along the lines of a European inn, has deluxe suites, hot tubs, a heated outdoor swimming pool, and two restaurants. Suites run about $175 a night. For information contact the visitors bureau or call the above toll-free number.

The **Tavern Inn** condominiums, just minutes from Squaw's lifts, are one-, two-, and three-bedroom luxury town houses with fireplaces. Rates range from $150 a night for a one-bedroom up to $200 for a three-bedroom. There's a communal Jacuzzi.

Located on the lake in Incline Village, the 460-room **Hyatt Lake Tahoe,** P.O. Box 3239, Incline Village, NV 89450 (tel. 702/831-1111), or toll free 800/228-9000), has attractive rooms and suites with fireplaces. A full-service Hyatt, there is a casino, room service, several restaurants, and bars. Rooms range from $94 a night to $137 for a Regency suite.

Studios to four-bedroom condos and houses are set on the ski runs and nearby at **Northstar-at-Tahoe,** P.O. Box 2499, Truckee, CA 95734 (tel. 916/562-1113, or toll free 800/824-8516, 800/822-5987 in California; or call North Tahoe Central Reservations). There is a shuttle service for guests, and transportation to and from the airport is available if prearranged. Lodging ranges from $97 a night for a studio to $207 for a four-bedroom unit.

Granlibakken Resort (tel. 916/583-4242, or toll free 800/543-3221 in California) has motel-style rooms in a main lodge and studio to three-bedroom condominiums in the mountain-style buildings once a conference center for a college. There is a 300-foot ski hill on the premises. Good complimentary breakfasts are part of the price. Lodging prices range from $70 for a motel room to $260 for a four-bedroom condo.

The **Squaw Ridge complex** has deluxe condominiums with shuttle service to Squaw, a mile away. The condos run $175 a night in high season for a three-bedroom.

The **River Run condominiums** are located on the access road to Alpine Meadows, set by the Truckee River. In high season, condo rates range from $145 a night for a one-bedroom to $200 for a three-bedroom with a loft.

Less Expensive: The mountain-style **Kingswood Village condominiums** are located on Calif. 267 halfway between the lake and Northstar. Two-bedroom condos run $85 a night, and four-bedrooms average $117 a night.

The rooms have river views and antique furnishings, but the service is strictly luxury modern at the **River Ranch,** P.O. Box 197, Tahoe City, CA 94730 (tel. 916/583-4264), set at the edge of the Truckee River one mile from Squaw Valley. A complimentary breakfast is brought to your room each morning at this ranch where rooms go for $60 and up.

The renovated rooms in the **Cal/Neva Lodge,** P.O. Box 368, Crystal Bay, NV 89402 (tel. 702/832-4000, or toll free 800/CAL-NEVA), are comfortable. There's a casino, restaurant, and bar in this lakeside hotel. Rates range from $60 for the older rooms to $90 for the renovated ones. Ask about skier packages.

The **Truckee Hotel** has been hosting travelers for more than 100 years. Skiers stay in rooms reminiscent of the Old West, complete with creaky floors, on the upper floor of this Victorian-era hotel. There is a lounge and restaurant in the hotel, and guests receive a complimentary box brunch when they leave for the slopes. Rooms start around $67 a night; both shared and private bath are available.

Staying on the South Shore

There are 10,000 beds in the Stateline, Nevada / South Tahoe, California, region so the best way to find lodging to suit your vacation style is to call the **South Lake Tahoe Visitors Bureau** (tel. toll free 800/824-5150, 800/822-5922 in California) and outline your needs. The bureau won't actually make the reservation, but you'll be directed to an appropriate lodge—whether you're looking for clean, bug-free cheap rooms, or a five-star hotel.

Heavenly Valley Central Reservations (tel. toll free 800/648-3383) will make reservations for ski packages in many of the major hotels with casinos, and in lodges and condominiums throughout the area, including several within walking distance of the lifts. Heavenly Valley, Kirkwood, and Sierra Ski Ranch all have buses picking up skiers from various properties in this resort region, and many of the properties have courtesy shuttles to take guests to Heavenly's ski slopes. (Vacationers who want to gamble at the major casinos in the area simply have to call, and a courtesy shuttle will pick them up and later return them to their lodging.)

Most Expensive: Harrah's Lake Tahoe, P.O. Box 8, Stateline, NV 89449 (tel. 702/588-6111, or toll free 800/648-3773), has earned Mobil's five-star and AAA's five-diamond awards for its service and amenities in the rooms. The extras in these luxurious, attractively decorated rooms range from mini-bars (just insert the room key, the mini-bottle drops out, and the price is recorded automatically on the bill) to the most complete vanity amenities packages around, wrapped in a black leather traveling case. Each room has two bathrooms and a console by the bed with switches to control the radio and television. There's a 24-hour casino, several restaurants, 24-hour room service, a health club, and more. Write or call for prices.

Most of the standard rooms in **Caesar's Tahoe,** P.O. Box 5800, Stateline, NV 89449 (tel. toll free 800/648-3353), boast round beds, circular Roman tubs, and two televisions. The luxurious suites have master bedrooms and living rooms with large-screen TV and a dining area with a wet bar. Rated five stars by Exxon Travel, this hotel has concierge service, a casino, several restaurants, big-name entertainers in the Cascade Room, 24-hour room service, and a health club with a swimming pool designed to look like a miniature lake with lagoons, waterfalls, and spas. Room rates begin at $105 per night. Ski packages with lodging, lifts, and more are available.

Rated four diamonds by AAA and four stars by Mobil Travel Guide, the deluxe rooms at **Harvey's Hotel/Casino,** P.O. Box 128, Stateline, NV 89449 (tel.

toll free 800/648-3361 or 800/553-1022), are smaller than the rooms at some of the other casino/hotels but attractively decorated. The hotel has a 24-hour casino and 24-hour restaurants, and the El Dorado Room has a buffet with mouthwatering desserts. Standard rooms start at $80 a night and go up. Small suites are available.

Lake Tahoe Accommodations specializes in luxury vacation rentals. The homes, condos, and cabins are in the South Lake Tahoe area. For information, contact Lake Tahoe Accommodations, P.O. Box 7722, South Lake Tahoe, CA 95731 (tel. 916/544-3234).

Moderate to Expensive: Oak, cedar, and tile help create the attractive interiors of the remodeled units at the **Tahoe Beach and Ski Club,** 3601 Lake Tahoe Blvd. (P.O. Box 1267), South Lake Tahoe, CA 95705 (tel. 916/541-6220, or toll free 800/822-5962). The one-bedroom condos have large jet-spray tubs, a king-size or two double beds, and well-equipped kitchens. Regular hotel rooms with king-size or two double beds are also available. There is a communal hot tub and heated swimming pool. Rates average $68 a night for a hotel room and $115 a night for a one-bedroom condo.

Rooms at the **Del Webb's High Sierra** (tel. toll free 800/648-3395 or 800/648-3322) are compact, comfortable, nicely decorated, and priced lower than at the other casinos. The hotel has a 24-hour casino and several restaurants including the Chuckwagon Buffet and Stetson's for gourmet fare in a casual setting. Big on a western motif, the hotel holds Lily's Dance Hall/Restaurant/Saloon with dancing most evenings. Room rates start at $65 a night but go higher for mini-suites.

The **Best Western Station House Inn,** 901 Park Ave. (P.O. Box 4009), South Lake Tahoe, CA 95729 (tel. 916/542-1101 or the Best Western toll-free 800/528-1234) is an AAA four-diamond property with attractive, comfortable rooms located two blocks from the casinos. There is a restaurant, bar, and hot tub on the premises.

Opened in 1862 for wealthy travelers, **Walley's Hot Springs Resort,** P.O. Box 26, Genoa, NV 89411 (tel. 702/782-8155 or 702/833-6556), is unique! Today, bed-and-breakfast guests stay in cottages (one is a former jail) at the reconstructed resort. Guests have use of the hot mineral spas and a small swimming pool, all set on a patio area overlooking a stream. There is a good restaurant at the resort, which is located in a quiet spot about 20 minutes from Heavenly Valley. Bed-and-breakfast in the cottages (double occupancy) begins at $70.

Less Expensive: The **Tahoe Valley Motel,** P.O. Box 7702, South Lake Tahoe, CA 95731 (tel. 916/541-0353), is an excellent choice for the price. The basic, clean motel rooms, with showers, include drip coffee makers to get skiers going in the morning. There is an outdoor whirlpool in a private enclosure that guests can reserve. There are a few rooms with whirlpool tubs. The price per night averages $50 for two persons in a room. The price per night drops for two- and three-day stays.

The **Timber Touch Lodge,** P.O. Box 343, South Lake Tahoe, CA 95705 (tel. 916/544-2036, or toll free 800/822-5922 and ask for Timber Touch lodge between 9 a.m. and 5 p.m.), has basic motel rooms (some have waterbeds) with showers. There is a hot tub and sauna on the premises and a shuttlebus to the casinos a mile away. Rooms go from $42 on weekends and $34 during the week. Ski packages are available.

The **Crystal Range Motel,** P.O. Box 7302, South Lake Tahoe, CA 95731 (tel. 916/541-1866), has basic, clean rooms, and kitchens are available.

WHERE TO EAT: Cheap eats in the hotel/casinos (to lure gamblers) and French cuisine served by attentive waiters describes the variety of dining available to skiers vacationing around Lake Tahoe. Many of the restaurants will deplete your pocket a little—or a lot—depending on what you order. The ones in this group are listed in the moderate to expensive range.

Expensive on the South Shore

Nouvelle, California, and French cuisine are prepared and served with flair at **Maison Marguite,** 901 Park Ave., South Lake Tahoe (tel. 916/542-1072), which has earned the Silver Spoon Award from the Gourmet Diners Club of America. Breakfast, lunch, and dinner from 5:30, are available in this stylish restaurant where the rich wood walls are covered with prints and plants. Luncheons range from a low of $5 for a club sandwich to a fancier Italian sandwich for $1.50 more. Dinner selections range from $11 to $18.

The **Christiania Inn,** located across the road from Heavenly Valley's tram (tel. 916/544-7337), promises gourmet cuisine served fireside. This country-style inn is considered one of the finer restaurants in northern California and has been featured in several national publications. A continental menu includes veal Oscar, roast duck, and steaks ranging from $13 to $24. Dinner is from 5:30 to 10:30 p.m. Reservations are suggested.

Stetson's, in Del Webb's High Sierra Hotel/Casino (tel. 702/588-6211), is simply decorated with Stetsons hung up on the walls—but the food is fancy both in presentation and taste. Specialties include mesquite-broiled beef and seafood specialties such as the sinfully rich lobster "Stetson's." Reservations are suggested. The restaurant is open from 6 to 11 p.m.

Moderate to Expensive on the South Shore

Aged steaks, seafood, and seasonal game are all on the menu in the **Zephyr Restaurant,** at Walley's Hot Springs Resort (tel. 702/883-6556). Entrees range from $12 to $19. The dining area, with its warm peach tones, stone, and floor-to-ceiling tree trunks that double as supporting beams, is a pleasant place to eat. If you have a large group, try to book the side room—its stone walls and fireplace date from 1812 and come from the original building. Come early and use the outdoor mineral hot tubs (see Non-Skier Activities in Section 14). Zephyr is located on Genoa Foothills Road on the back side of Heavenly Valley. Lunch is from 11 a.m. to 3 p.m. and dinner is from 5 to 10 p.m.

The **Fresh Ketch Lakeside Restaurant,** 2435 Venice Dr. East, South Lake Tahoe (tel. 916/541-5683), at the Tahoe Keys Marina, offers dockside views of the lake along with tasty fish dinners to guests relaxing around tables in the restaurant's polished-wood-accented-with-brass interior. Open for lunch, brunch, and dinner, it has a good selection of fresh fish from $11 to $16, and goes up to $20 for filet mignon and lobster. Lunches feature hamburgers in the $4 range and seafood salads for a few dollars more. Dinner from 5:30 to 10 p.m. daily.

At **Nephele's,** 1169 Ski Run Blvd., Lake Tahoe (tel. 702/544-8130), you can indulge in a hot-tub soak before or after dinner! If you choose the former, they will deliver cocktails to your "private room" hot tub. Dinners, from salads to a steak, range from $2.50 to $14. Dinner is from 6 to 10 p.m. Hot tubs must be reserved.

Less Expensive on the South Shore

Oversize omelets, bacon or apple pancakes, and Belgian waffles are just a sampling of what's available at **Heidi's,** on U.S. 50 on the Bijou Center, South Lake Tahoe (tel. 916/544-8113), a popular breakfast spot. At brunch-lunch you can build your own "frikandelle burger," starting at a little over $4 and adding extra change for each added item. Other sandwiches are available in the $4 to $5 range. Hours are 7 a.m. to 9 p.m.

The portions are huge and tasty at **Tep's Villa Roma,** 3544 U.S. 50, South Lake Tahoe (tel. 916/541-8227). The antipasto salad bar is loaded and the soup is good. Pizzas begin at $5.75, spaghetti at $7.50, and entrees with veal, chicken, or seafood run $9.50 to $19. Hours are 5 to 11 p.m.

The **Donner House,** 2600 Lake Tahoe Blvd., in the Town and Country Mall, South Lake Tahoe (tel. 916/541-9610), is a casual restaurant good for family dining. The menu lists a wide variety of food from sandwiches and spaghetti to fish and steak. Sandwiches go from $2.70 and entrees start at $6. Hours are 6:30 a.m. to 11 p.m. daily.

Residents and visitors mix during the breakfast and lunch hours at **Michel's,** in the Fremont Mall, South Lake Tahoe (tel. 916/544-6963), an inexpensive and consistently good coffeeshop. Breakfast at Michel's begins at approximately $2 for pancakes and lunch sandwiches average $2.50.

Expensive on the North Shore

Le Petit Pier, 7252 North Lake Blvd., Tahoe Vista (tel. 916/546-4464), is a classic French restaurant that features fixed price gourmet dinners. The à la carte menu starts at $16.50; the more elaborate menu gastronomique is $35 per person. Each has a selection of dishes from which to choose during a leisurely meal in this restaurant where understated quality—from attentive service to flowers on the well-set tables—is the operating mode. Make reservations.

Moderate to Expensive on the North Shore

Steven at Incline Village, 341 Ski Way, in the Bullwheel Building (tel. 702/832-0222), has the type of sophisticated decor and menu designed to make big-city residents feel at home. The view of Lake Tahoe from here is worth the price of an après-ski drink, and the food is terrific. Steven is open for lunch from 11:30 a.m. to 4 p.m. and for dinner from 6 to 10 p.m. Luncheons feature salads from $5, sea foods at the market price, and beef for $8. The same salads are served at dinner, and entrees, which include lemon chicken and New York sirloin, range from $15 to $18. Try the mozzarella sauté.

Jakes-on-the-Lake, Boatworks Marina, 780 N. Lake Blvd., Tahoe City (tel. 916/583-0188), is a trendy spot, and reservations are a must on busy nights if you don't want to wait. (Only part of the restaurant is reserved; the rest is left for open seating.) Even in the winter, diners can sit in Jakes (which looks like an Eastern Seaboard restaurant moved west) and watch the changing colors in the lake right outside the restaurant window. Seafood from $9 to $19 is the main fare here, although there are steaks. Jakes is open from 4:30 to 11 p.m. for dinner.

Unwinding after a rugged day on the slopes is a sure bet watching the sunset, Irish coffee in hand, in **Captain Jon's bar,** 7220 N. Lake Blvd., Tahoe Vista (tel. 916/546-3185), at the edge of the lake. Stay for a seafood or beef dinner in the restaurant next door. Entrees range from $12.75 for fresh fish to $26 for filet and lobster tail. Reservations are suggested at this restaurant, open Tuesday through Saturday, from 6 a.m.

Swiss Lakewood, six miles south of Tahoe City on Calif. 89 (tel. 916/525-5211), serves dinners only, opening at 5:50 p.m. One of Lake Tahoe's oldest restaurants, it is housed in a quaint Swiss chalet-type building. This four-star restaurant features European cuisine, with prices ranging from veal and dumplings at $13.50 to pepper steak flambé at $18. Specialties for two feature fondue bourguignonne, fresh quail, and chateaubriand.

The old European atmosphere at the **Pfeiffer House,** 760 River Rd., a half mile south of Tahoe City on the main route (tel. 916/583-3102), a long time favorite with skiers who frequent the Tahoe area, is reflected in the menu's specialties such as Vienna schnitzel garnie and sauerbraten. Meals range from $10 to $18 at the Pfeiffer House, which opens at 5:30 p.m. daily for dinner during the winter.

The new **Rosie's Café**, 571 N. Lake Blvd., Tahoe City (tel. 916/583-8504), is one of the busiest and best breakfast spots in the region. Skiers group here for your basic breakfast, with just-baked breads or pastries, to more sophisticated variations from blintzes to eggs Benedict. You can also order a bag lunch for the slopes when you order your breakfast. Rosie's serves breakfast until 11:30 a.m. weekdays and until 7 p.m. on weekends. There's a luncheon menu from 11:30 a.m.

Both the room with the big wood bar and the wood booths and stove fireplace in the dining rooms highlight the Tahoe-casual atmosphere at **Emma Murphy's** and the **Avalanche Sushi Bar,** 425 N. Lake Blvd., Tahoe City (tel. 916/583-6939). Sushi is on the menu and entrees are seafood, pasta and beef, ranging from $9 to $16. Hours are 5:30 to 10:30 p.m. There's live music in the bar many nights.

Less Expensive on the North Shore

Squeeze In, on Truckee's main street (tel. 916/587-9814), is appropriately named because hungry skiers and locals are packed in this narrow restaurant demolishing omelets. The omelets—filled with an amazing variety of edibles—are named after area locals. Prices are $3 to $7. The restaurant is open from 7 a.m. to 2 p.m. daily.

The **Donner Lake Kitchen,** 13440 Donner Pass Rd. (tel. 916/587-3119), is open seven days a week from 7 a.m. to 2 a.m. The counters and few tables may fill up fast with regulars and skiers ordering from the breakfast menu, which has entrees ranging from flapjacks for $2.25 to $4 with trimmings, to scrambled eggs with sausage or bacon for about $4.50.

Expensive in Reno

Harrah's Steak House, on the lower level of Harrah's Hotel in downtown Reno (tel. 702/786-3232), is a quiet oasis in the middle of this frenetic town. Guests can enjoy leisurely dinners featuring steak Diane, roast leg of lamb, and other well-prepared dishes served by attentive help from 5 p.m. to midnight.

Moderate to Inexpensive in Reno

Check the local tourist guides for the many specials. All the major hotel/casinos have several restaurants, and the food in many is reasonably priced. Most of the casinos advertise at least one cheap dinner—be it prime rib or New York steak.

Buffets are a fixture at the hotel/casinos in the downtown area. They range in price from $2.50 for breakfast up to approximately $13 for the more elaborate ones. Some are good; others are simply filling. The **Hilton** has a very good breakfast buffet.

ENTERTAINMENT: Gambling is the most popular form of nightlife in this region. However there's plenty of entertainment for skiers who don't want to slide their money into a slot machine or place chips on a roulette table. Nightlife around Lake Tahoe ranges from watching big-name entertainers like Joan Rivers and Sammy Davis, Jr., in one of the hotel/casino show rooms, to quiet drinks at lounges overlooking the lake. The best way to discover exactly what's happening when is to pick up a *KEY,* the weekly entertainment guide for the region, or one of the local newspapers, which should have the latest schedule for entertainment in the smaller lounges.

In the Reno area, famous names usually perform in the **Headliner Room** at Harrah's Reno and in the **Opera House Theatre** at the Reno Hilton. *Hello, Hollywood, Hello,* a musical extravaganza with showgirls is the long-running hit at MGM. There's usually musical entertainment in other lounges at these hotels as well as in the other casinos, including the **Peppermill,** the **Ramada Reno,** and John Ascuaga's **Nugget.**

On the south shore, headliners perform in the **South Shore Room** at Harrah's Lake Tahoe and the **Cascade Showroom** at Caesars Tahoe. There's also musical entertainment in other lounges in these hotels and at the **High Sierra** and **Harvey's. Hodges** and **Yesterday** at the Tahoe Sands Inn and **Carlos Murphy's** are popular evening spots.

On the north shore, the **Cantina los Tres Hombres** in Kings Beach is a popular nightspot where skiers can down pitchers of fruit margaritas. The **Olympic Village Inn, Emma Murphy's** in Tahoe City, and the **Tahoe Biltmore** in Crystal Bay are other popular spots. The **Passage** in the Truckee Hotel is a popular nightspot. Skiers gather here to down imported beers, wine by the glass, or espresso drinks while listening to live entertainment on weekends.

16. Practical Matters

GETTING THERE: Several of the major **airlines** including Air Cal, American, Continental, Delta, Eastern, PSA, Republic, and United fly to Reno-Cannon International Airport. Limousines, taxis, and hotel-operated mini-vans are available for transportation to the Reno area from the north end of the terminal. Limousine services to the north and south shore of Lake Tahoe are also available (see below).

The Lake Tahoe region is approximately four hours **by car** from the San Francisco Bay area. By automobile, South Lake Tahoe is 58 miles from Reno via I-395 through Carson City to U.S. 50, west over Spooner Summit. (For **road conditions,** contact CalTrans at 916/577-3550 or Nevada Road Conditions at 702/793-1313).

The **LTR Stageline** (tel. 702/323-3088 in Nevada or 916/588-6633 in California) provides airporter service between Reno and the south shore. **Air Cal** and **Wings West** have direct service to the South Lake Tahoe Airport from several cities in California. **Dial-A-Ride** (tel. 916/577-7000) provides regular service between the South Lake Tahoe Airport and the south shore. **Sunshine Taxis** is at 916/544-5555.

The north Lake Tahoe region is approximately 30 miles from the Reno airport via I-80, and transportation is available via shuttlebus, chartered limousine service, or rental car from the airport. **See Tahoe Tours** (tel. 702/832-0713) provides regularly scheduled shuttle service to the north shore. **Trailways** and **Greyhound** provide east- and westbound service to Truckee. The Truckee-Tahoe general aviation recreation airport is two miles east of Truckee. **Thrifty Car Rental** (tel. 916/587-4119) is located at the airport.

Amtrak stops in Reno and in Truckee. For information and reservations, call toll free 800/252-2231 or 800/USA-RAIL.

MOVING AROUND: In the north Lake Tahoe area, there are free ski shuttle services offered by Alpine Meadows, Northstar-at-Tahoe, Ski Incline, and Squaw Valley USA. Local lodgings should have the schedules, or contact the **North Lake Tahoe Chamber of Commerce,** P.O. Box 884, Tahoe City, CA 95730 (tel. 916/583-2371).

TART (Tahoe Area Regional Transit) operates a public bus in the northshore area from 6:30 a.m. to 6:30 p.m. Monday through Saturday throughout the year and on Sunday from mid-December to mid-April. For information about the route, which includes several ski areas, call 916/581-6365. In the south Lake Tahoe area, Heavenly runs a regular shuttle, while Kirkwood, Alpine Meadows, Squaw Valley, and Sierra Ski Ranch have buses bringing skiers to the resort in the morning and back to town in the afternoon. The local lodges should have the details or contact the resort of your choice. Many of the hotels and lodges have free courtesy vans for their guests.

The major casinos will pick up vacationers who want to gamble from their accommodations and return them in courtesy vans. (Just call the hotel/casino. Many lodges in the area have boards with the numbers listed and a free courtesy phone.) The **South Tahoe Ground Express (STAGE)** (tel. 916/573-2081) runs 23 hours a day on both the U.S. 50 corridor and in some residential areas.

Skiers staying in Reno really need a car for the freedom to visit several resorts. There is a Ski Bus service that stops at several Reno hotels and takes skiers either to Squaw or Mount Rose for the day. When booking lodging, ask for participating hotels.

If you're staying on the south shore, consider taking the *Tahoe Queen,* a glass-bottom paddleboat, across the lake for a day of skiing at Alpine Meadows or Squaw. The ski day will be shorter, but it will be wrapped in a boat ride that includes breakfast, bus transfer to the mountain, dinner, and dancing. For details, days of departure, and prices, contact **Lake Tahoe Cruises, Inc.,** P.O. Box 14327, South Lake Tahoe, CA 95702.

TOURIST INFORMATION: There are several visitors information centers in the region. All will mail information about their specific area and answer telephone inquiries, and most have displays manned by informed personnel for walk-in visitors. Those with toll-free numbers for lodging reservations or lodging referrals are listed in the Where to Stay section. The **South Lake Tahoe Visitors Authority,** 3066 U.S. 50 (tel. 916/541-5225), is open from 8:30 a.m. to 6 p.m. Monday through Friday and from 9 a.m. to 5 p.m. on weekends. The **North Tahoe Chamber of Commerce,** 950 N. Lake Blvd., in the Lighthouse Shopping Center in Tahoe City (tel. 916/583-2371), is open from 9 a.m. to 5 p.m. Monday through Friday. The **Incline Village Chamber of Commerce** at 999 Tahoe Blvd., (Nev. 28), Tahoe Shores Center (tel. 702/831-4440), is open from 9 a.m. to 7 p.m. Monday through Friday, to 5 p.m. on Saturday and Sunday. The information center at the **Reno/Lake Tahoe Visitor Center,** 133 N. Sierra St. (tel. 702/786-3030), is open from 9 a.m. to 5 p.m. Monday through Saturday.

CalTrans has a toll-free number for **weather:** 800/952-ROADS. Local numbers for **road conditions** are 916/587-3806 in Truckee, 916/577-3550 in South Lake Tahoe, and 702/793-1313 in Nevada.

The Kiwanis of Lake Tahoe has published a **directory of facilities and information for the handicapped.** Contact the South Lake Tahoe Visitors Authority for a copy.

On the north shore, dialing 911 will get the **sheriff's department** or the **fire department** in Incline, Northstar, Tahoe City, Truckee, Northshore, and Squaw Valley. The South Lake Tahoe **police** number is 916/573-2100. **Hospital and emergency clinics** include **Barton Memorial Hospital** (tel. 916/541-3420) and **Stateline Emergency Clinic** (tel. 702/588-3511). The **Barton Kingsbury Clinic** at 200 Kingsbury Grade in Stateline, Nevada (tel. 702/588-6284), is open daily from 8 a.m. to 6 p.m.

Chapter IX

CENTRAL CALIFORNIA

1. Mammoth Mountain
2. June Mountain
3. Mount Reba / Bear Valley
4. Other California Ski Areas

LOS ANGELES SKIERS board buses and cram into cars for the ride up to Mammoth Mountain, which is by far the most mammoth of the ski areas in this state. The 32-lift system for ferrying skiers around the terrain has overtones of an elaborate freeway interchange at times, but when used wisely, opens up more than 150 runs, slopes, and bowls. Nearby June Mountain is a very much smaller ski area—fun for families. There are other mid-size family areas in central California, including Mount Reba / Bear Valley, a family-oriented resort set in the Mokelumme Wilderness in the Central Sierra.

1. Mammoth Mountain

THE RESORT: Los Angeles skiers are willing to drive six or more hours straight (depending on weather) to get to this—literally—mammoth ski complex. It's one of the largest in the country and the major ski area closest to L.A. The mountain, serviced by so many lifts that some slopes look like super freeway complexes with chairs and gondolas running in every direction, is massive enough that once skiers have spread out there is usually room for everyone. (Mammoth's record day saw slightly more than 20,000 skiers. On these slopes 16,000 skiers is considered a comfortable day when the lift lines are reasonable.) Keep in mind that, as crowded as Mammoth can be on weekends and holidays, the place is virtually empty during weekdays and skiers can often jump right on lifts.

Lodging and après-ski life here are spread from the ski area down to the town of Mammoth Lakes. They're available in minimal doses up near the base area; the maximum dose is in town. (The ski area's main base is four miles up the road from the town of Mammoth Lakes. However, Warming Hut II, which is larger than the base lodges at 90% of the ski areas in this country, sits by several condominium complexes at the edge of town.)

Spring skiing is hot here! May and June are prime months at this resort. But the weather is notoriously variable here anytime during the year. Always be pre-

MAMMOTH MOUNTAIN

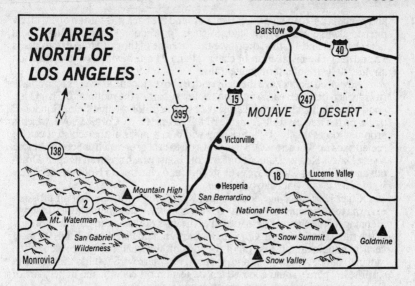

pared to strip down if the weather turns hot, or suit up if brutal winds begin blowing.

THE SKIING: I had heard all the jokes about the friends who say to each other: "Ski gondola 1, chair 10, then 4. With luck we can meet at Warming Hut II anywhere between noon and 1:30 for lunch depending on the lift lines!" My first ride uphill, on chair 1, my lift mate said to me: "Oh! You like to ski. You have to try chair 22. Take 1, go down Over Easy, then up 10 and go down Roller Coaster to the base of chair 22. Later work your way back to Chair 1, then up gondola 2 and over. . . ."

If you don't understand how the 32 lifts in this system interconnect, you may never get from here to there—although you'll still have fun skiing. Mammoth is a place where skiers study the trail map carefully and don't hesitate to question those employees in the Mammoth ski jackets about the best ways to reach certain lifts. On weekends stay with your friends. Don't plan on meeting them somewhere on the slopes.

There's more skiing for every skill level here than most skiers could enjoy in a weekend or even a week, according to the Los Angeles skiers who migrate here every weekend. Here's just a sampling of what is available on the more than 150 open bowls and trails rated 30% beginner, 40% intermediate, and 30% advanced. Beginners have chairs 7 and 11. Low intermediates who can turn and stop have plenty of gentle terrain off gondola 1—just watch the trail signs—and off chairs 6, 13, and 15.

Stronger intermediates can tackle almost any of the blue runs on the lower two-thirds of the mountain, reachable via gondola 1 or many of the chairs. Chair 19 has good (but comparatively short), not-too-wide but definitely blue runs. Broadway, off chair 1, and Stump Alley, off chair 2, are probably the most popular intermediate runs on the mountain. (That means they are also often the most crowded. Instead, try Mambo, which parallels Stump Alley, or Bowling Alley, which parallels Broadway.) The runs off chair 14 (in a wind-protected area around the backside of the mountain) are excellent intermediate terrain. (To reach this area, strong intermediates can take gondolas 1 and 2—or chair 1 and gondola 2—then take the cat track around the back side into an open, nicely pitched skiable area, which leads to chair 14. Middling intermediates should take chairs 11 and 12, then drop over the backside of the ridge to use both chairs 12 and 13.) The installation of chairs 24 and 25 a few winters ago opened up another network of intermediate trails.

Advanced skiers have the entire ridge above treeline as well as many black runs tucked between easier runs on the lower part of the mountain. Chair 3 is a good place to match your skills against black runs for the first time. Gondola 2 opens up the treeless walls from the rim. As a starter, try Cornice Bowl, which is groomed occasionally (by a machine wired to a pillar at the top so it can be reeled back up if necessary). Then move on to other runs such as Scotty's before trying Dave's Run and Climax or Paranoid Flats, which are even steeper. Dropout and Wipe Out Chutes are even steeper, and Hangman's Hollow is definitely just for those into one-way-out chutes.

Chair 23 is space-age architecture, with its top enclosure that protects skiers from the elements on the ridge and the chair itself from being buried in snow. Stepping off the chair, skiers slide out of the enclosure and can go onto most any of the runs stretching from Cornice Bowl to Paranoid Flat. Chair 22 has the most vertical underneath it. Several of the runs off this chair are quite steep, often moguled but never groomed and, in spots, very narrow. Shaft has a few built-in surprises. There's some good advanced terrain off chair 9: the upper part of Richochet and Dragon's Back are open and steep.

Insider's Tips

Prod a regular here and you'll get a new insider's tip. Some of the best known are:

Dress in layers and be prepared for fast weather changes.

On a busy day, try skiing the chairs farthest from the base areas in the morning, then use chairs 1, 2, and 3 during the lunch hours.

The busiest lifts, most of the time, are chairs 3 and 5 because they open up so much of the mid-mountain terrain.

If there is a long line on gondola 2, advanced skiers can reach many of the rim runs from chair 23.

When it's too windy to ski the top part of the mountain, advanced skiers stay near chairs 3 and 5, although chair 22 is another good choice for experts.

Chair 16 at Warming Hut II is busiest in the morning and after lunch. Try chair 7 or 17 to chair 4 to get back on the slopes faster.

To follow the sun, take chair 8 and warm up on chair 15. By then the sun should be high enough that you can ski anywhere.

The fastest way from the Main Lodge to the Warming Hut at the end of the day just might be T-bar 2 down Mambo to Over Easy to chair 21; then up chair 21 and down Roller Coaster to Downhill or Spring Canyon.

The fastest way from the Warming Hut back to the main base area might be chair 16 down Come Back to Easy Ride, to chair 18; then up chair 18 and down Saddle Bowl to Broadway.

Take chair 21 as an alternative to 10, and take chair 20 as an alternative to 4. These chairs aren't as long, but the lines are often shorter and they open up many of the same runs.

Parking near the lifts can be a problem. If you are near the shuttle or ski area routes, leave your car at the condo/lodge and take a shuttlebus to the lifts. (Ask locally for the route map.) Ask if your lodge has a shuttle service. If you end up at the wrong base area at the end of the day, hop a Mammoth shuttle to the right one. If you drive, park the car close to chair 2, 4, 10, or 15 and ski to the car at the end of the day.

Senior citizens 65 and older, as well as children 3 and under, can ski free. Show proof at the courtesy counters at either lodge.

Come to the Main Lodge before the lifts open and have a mountain muffin for breakfast.

Mountain Facilities

Mammoth has a Main Lodge which is bigger than many major hotels. Inside there are cafeterias, retail and rental ski shops, a ski school, lift-ticket windows, and lots of lockers. The same services are available at Warming Hut II, located at the second major base area. Continental breakfast and lunch are available at the mid-chalet.

Snow Coverage

Many of the ski areas measure new snow in inches; Mammoth often measures it in feet. This ski area is sited in a natural snow-dump zone. The average annual snowfall is 500 inches. There is no snowmaking equipment at this area, which stays open normally from November to June.

Ski School

More than 200 instructors are available for a variety of classes ranging from half- and full-day group and private lessons to advanced skiing clinics. Youngsters 6 to 12 years of age go into the Children's Ski School. Your 4- and 5-year-olds can try Funland, a preschooler's ski school. There are ski-school offices at both lodges. The race department, headquartered at Warming Hut II, runs racing classes with video analysis.

Childcare

The **Small World Day Care Center,** located in Mammoth Inn across the parking lot from the Main Lodge, takes newborns to 12-year-olds. Reservations are necessary so the appropriate number of staff people will be available. The children are separated according to age groups into different play areas, and there are organized activities throughout the day. For information on day care or children's ski lessons, as well as reservations, call 619/934-2581 and ask for the day care center.

Rental Equipment

Rental shops are located in the Main Lodge and Warming Hut II. There are several ski-rental shops located in Mammoth Lakes.

Cross-Country Skiing

There are track trails around **Tamarack Lodge and Sierra Meadows** (tel. 619/934-6161). Both operations offer rentals, lessons, and special tours. Many skiers stop along the Mammoth Scenic Loop and head into the country on cross-country skis. There are also trails around Rock Creek Canyon 20 miles away. Contact the local chamber of commerce for more information.

Heli-Skiing

Mammoth Heli-Ski takes skiers into the Sierra Nevada. (See the heli-ski section in Chapter XVIII for details.) For information, contact **Mammoth Heli-Ski,** P.O. Box 600, Mammoth Lakes, CA 93546 (tel. 619/934-4494).

WHERE TO STAY: Skiers who want to stay within walking distance of the ski lifts can choose the inn or condos owned by the ski resort that are located near the Main Lodge, four winding miles from town. However, nightlife is very limited. Another option is to stay in one of the condominium complexes within walking distance of Warming Hut II, which is at the edge of town. There's a variety of accommodations in town, where the majority of restaurants are located.

Expensive to Moderate

The **Mammoth Inn,** P.O. Box 353, Mammoth Lakes, CA 93546 (tel. 619/934-2581 or toll free 800/228-4947), on the mountain, has very comfortable, attractive hotel rooms and a complex of condominium units next door. Guests are just a few hundred yards from the ski area's main lodge. There's a dining room, Mountainside Bar and Grill, in the hotel and a less formal restaurant, the Yodler, nearby. Three indoor Jacuzzis are located in the building with the condominium units, a short walk from the main lodge. Lodging prices per night range from $55 to $175 for hotel rooms to condominiums.

The **Snowcreek Resort,** P.O. Box 657, Mammoth Lakes, CA 93546 (tel. 619/934-3333), boasts luxurious mountain-architecture condominiums set off by themselves at one end of town. There's an athletic club on the premises and cross-country skiing outside the door. The price range for units is from $90 to $230, plus tax.

The large units at **Mountainback at Mammoth,** Mountain Management Service, P.O. Box 1437, Mammoth Lakes, CA 93546 (tel. 619/934-4549, or toll free 800/468-6225), are luxurious with stone fireplaces, natural-wood walls, and complete kitchens. There is a heated pool and Jacuzzi. Mountainback is located near Warming Hut II, and the shuttlebus stops at the complex. Rates go from $110 for two bedrooms with two baths for four to six persons, to $250 for a two-bedroom unit plus loft and den with three baths.

Many of the units in the **1849 Condominiums,** P.O. Box 835, Mammoth Lakes, CA 93546 (tel. 619/934-7525, or toll free 800/421-1849), 200 yards from the Warming Hut II area, have rough-sawn natural-wood walls and rock fireplaces. The units are graded A and B, depending on decor, but all are the same price, so ask for an upgraded unit. This complex has three Jacuzzis and a courtesy van to take guests to and from the village. Condominium prices range from $120 for a one-bedroom to $300 for a four-bedroom.

Sierra Megeve, Mammoth Properties Reservations, P.O. Box 378, Mammoth Lakes, CA 93546 (tel. 619/934-4242, or toll free 800/227-SNOW), has luxurious condominium units within walking distance of Warming Hut II. Most have rough wood walls and brick fireplaces; some have brass beds. There is a Jacuzzi. The two-bedroom units start at $160.

The **Mammoth Lakes Resort Association** (tel. 619/935-2712, or toll free 800/FOR-MLRA), offers accommodations in several condo complexes. Most are either on the shuttle route or close to Warming Hut II or chair 15. The condos are priced in three ranges and can be rented either with or without linens. The standard units are pretty basic and some are without dishwashers. Most have a Jacuzzi, sauna, and rec room in the complex, and they are on or near the shuttle route. The deluxe units have upgraded furnishings and more amenities, including two TVs. Most have fireplaces and dishwashers, as well as a Jacuzzi, sauna, and rec room in the complex, and are also on or near the shuttle routes. The premium units are the more luxurious in decor and amenities such as color TVs in the living room and the master bedroom, microwave ovens, fireplaces, and dishwashers. Jacuzzis, saunas, and rec rooms are in the complexes. These units are in the best locations. Standards cost from $48 for a studio weekdays to $148 for a three-bedroom with loft on weekends. Deluxe units range from $58 for a studio on weekdays to $168 for a three-bedroom/loft on weekends. The premium units run from $68 for a studio on weekdays to $190 for a three-bedroom with loft on weekends. There are five-day rates.

The **Mammoth Reservations Bureau**, P.O. Box 8, Mammoth Lakes, CA 93546 (tel. 619/934-2528, or toll free 800/462-5571 or 800/462-5585), books skiers into a variety of condominium complexes ranging from luxurious accommodations near the slopes to more basic condos in town. This company lists units in more than 35 condominium complexes, so call explaining what you want and they'll match you with the appropriate unit. Prices range from $80 for a studio up to $200 for a three-bedroom unit. There are a few larger units.

The **Sierra Nevada Inn**, P.O. Box 918, Mammoth Lakes, CA 93546 (tel. 619/934-2515, or toll free 800/824-0583, 800/824-5132 in California), is located in the central part of town near restaurants and shops. There is shuttle service to the ski area. The inn has standard lodge rooms, rooms with free-standing fireplaces, and family rooms with kitchenettes and suites. There is a heated pool and Jacuzzi. Room rates begin at $74. Children 6 and under are free.

Moderate to Less Expensive

Both of the above central reservation services have condominiums listed in the moderate to less expensive price range as well.

The **Alpine Lodge**, P.O. Box 389, Mammoth Lakes, CA 93546 (tel. 619/934-8526), located in town, is within walking distance of several restaurants and is on the bus route to the ski area. There are king-size, queen-size, or double queen-size beds in the rooms in the main building, and there are two-bedroom housekeeping cottages. The Jacuzzi is indoors. Room prices run from $42 midweek and $90 on weekends and holidays.

The **Mammoth Mountain Travel Lodge**, P.O. Box 360, Mammoth Lakes, CA 93546 (tel. 619/934-8576), has basic motel rooms with a king-size or two queen-size beds. There is a small indoor pool and a Jacuzzi at this motel located in town within walking distance of several restaurants. Rooms go from $63 to $95 for an apartment.

WHERE TO EAT: There's limited dining at the mountain base areas. In town, however, the restaurants serve everything from fast food to creative gourmet.

Expensive

Informally elegant **Roget's**, on the corner of Calif. 203 and Minaret Road (tel. 934-4466), is considered to be Mammoth's finest dining experience. The cuisine is continental and prices range from $15 to $20 for entrees including fresh fish, lamb, and veal. Reservations are needed; plan on a leisurely two-hour meal once you are there. Roget's is open from 5:30 to 10 p.m.

The **Mountainside Bar and Grill** (tel. 934-2581) is the open, raftered dining room in Mammoth Inn across the parking lot from the ski area's Main Lodge. The menu ranges from prime rib and fresh fish to pasta, and there's an extensive wine list. Prices range from $10 to $17. Reservations are recommended.

Expensive to Moderate

Whiskey Creek, on the corner of Main Street and Minaret Road (tel. 934-2555), the closest thing to a fern-bar/restaurant in this town, is a trendy spot. It's open from 5 to 10 p.m., and dinner prices range from $8 to $16 for entrees such as garlic prawns and chicken caliente. The upstairs **Creekside Café and Oyster Bar** has lighter meals. Live dance bands provide music for dancing in the upstairs bar most evenings.

Rafters, just south of Calif. 203 on the Old Mammoth Road (tel. 934-2537), with its mountain rustic charm and dramatic high ceilings is a pleasant place to dine. The cuisine is basically American, and prices run from $10 to $19 for entrees such as petite top sirloin, crab, and a fish combo. It's open only for dinner, and there's live entertainment from 9:30 p.m. to 1:30 a.m.

Slocum's Bar and Restaurant, on Main Street (tel. 934-7647) with its turn-of-the-century decor, features affordable continental cuisine. Open from 5:30 p.m., Slocum's is a hangout for many ski area employees during happy hour. Prices range from $9.75 to $17 for fresh fish, and steaks.

The **Yodler** (tel. 934-2581) is a woody, casual dining room and lounge just across the parking lot from the ski area's main lodge. At lunchtime the place is filled with skiers wanting a sit-down lunch. Salads and sandwiches are served at lunchtime, and dinner dishes, which range in price from $3.50 to $8.75, include burgers, ribs, and chicken.

The **Mogul,** on Old Mammoth Tavern Road, across from Mammoth Mall (tel. 934-3093), is another popular restaurant where diners start with home-made soup, move to the salad bar, and then on to steaks, seafood, or chicken. There is a children's menu. Dinners range from $8 to $16. The Mogul opens at 5:30 p.m. Monday through Friday and at 5 p.m. on Saturday and holidays.

Less Expensive

Las Montanas, on Main Street (tel. 934-9014), serves "the best margarita in town" and the food comes in generous portions. The combination plates range from $7.75 to $9.50, and there are à la carte selections. Guests can enjoy the heat from the large central fireplace at dinner, which is served from 5:30 p.m. daily.

The **Stove,** on Old Mammoth Road (tel. 934-2821), is one of the most popular breakfast restaurants in town. Their morning specials include huevos rancheros, pancakes, and the usual egg dishes, in the $4 to $7 range. Burgers and sandwiches are available at lunch. Hours are 6:30 a.m. to 2 p.m.

Berger's, Minaret Road (tel. 934-6622), has, locals say, the best burgers in town. Besides burgers, one can order pork ribs, barbecued beef, and chicken. The jumbo burger is only $3, and prices for other entrees go up to $10.50. Berger's is open for lunch and dinner.

Skiers head to the **Swiss Café,** on Old Mammoth Road south of Meridian Boulevard (tel. 934-6196), for an early breakfast before heading up to the ski slopes. Fresh croissants and blueberry muffins and more are on the menu with the expected eggs, pancakes, and waffles for breakfast. This cozy café also serves moderately priced lunches and dinners. Hours are 6:30 a.m. to 9 p.m. daily except Wednesday.

Angel's Restaurant, on Main Street next to the Motel 6 (tel. 934-RIBS), is a family restaurant boasting of large portions for reasonable prices. Fare ranges from Mexican to barbecue followed by desserts like chocolate Hot N' Gooie. Prices range from $4 to $11. Lunch from 11:30 a.m.; weekends dinner only from 4:30 p.m. Call for take-out.

NIGHTLIFE: Nightlife here is limited. Après-ski at the mountain is at the **Yodler.** The **Creekside Café** at Whiskey Creek is usually full of dancers moving to a live band, and there's often live entertainment at the **Rafters.** The **Village Inn Saloon** and **Ocean Harvest** have a band playing for dancing most nights. Check locally for hours and entertainers.

SHOPPING: There are several shopping centers in Mammoth Lakes with some interesting shops including the **Minaret Shopping Center** on Mammoth Road and Meridian Boulevard, and the **Old Mammoth Mall** on Old Mammoth Road at Mammoth Tavern Road.

NON-SKIER ACTIVITIES: **Ice skating** is best at Convict Lake. Rent skates at the Ski Surgeon (tel. 934-6376). For **snowmobiling** information, contact DJ's Snowmobile Rentals (tel. 935-4880), or for tours call 619/935-4480. Sierra Meadows (tel. 934-6161) has **sleigh rides. Sleds** and **discs** are available at Kittredge Sports (tel. 934-7566) or Filson's (tel. 934-2290).

GETTING THERE: From the record number of skiers who find their way here, it's easy to see that Mammoth Mountain is most accessible.

By Car

From the south, skiers reach Mammoth by taking U.S. 395 north and turning at the Mammoth Lakes junction. From the bay area, Mammoth is reached via I-80 then U.S. 395 south, and then turning at the Mammoth Lakes junction. (In good weather, take I-80 to U.S. 50, and go over Calif. 19 or Calif. 89 to U.S. 395 south. Driving time from Los Angeles is approximately six hours. Driving time from the San Francisco Bay area (which means going around the Lake Tahoe region during the winter because the mountain passes are closed) is also approximately six hours.

By Bus

Greyhound buses run both north and south into Mammoth daily. Charter buses also leave from various locations in southern California.

By Air

There is no major airport near Mammoth. However, **Mammoth Air Shuttle** (tel. 619/935-4737, or toll free 800/446-4500) has regular service between Mammoth and Burbank. **Alpha Air** (tel. toll free 800/421-9353) has service between Mammoth and Oakland and Los Angeles International, West Imperial Terminal. **Sierra Mountain Airways** (tel. toll free 800/AIR-9299) has service between Mammoth and Burbank, San Diego, and Oakland.

MOVING AROUND: Mammoth runs a shuttle service throughout the main lodge parking lots daily. **Mammoth Area Transit** will take you to the mountain from town, from the Old Mammoth Road area, or the Warming Hut II area for a minimal fee. Obtain a schedule locally to verify the route map and times.

TOURIST INFORMATION: For general information about the ski area, contact **Mammoth Mountain**, P.O. Box 24, Mammoth Lakes, CA 93546 (tel. 619/934-2571). For information about lodging, ask for the Mammoth brochure that describes the ski area and lists accommodations. The **snowline numbers** are 213/935-8866 in Los Angeles and 619/934-6166 in Mammoth. Information about the region is also available from the **Mammoth Lakes Resort Association**, P.O. Box 123, Mammoth Lakes, CA 93546 (tel. 619/934-2712, or toll free 800/FOR-MLRA). The **emergency number** here is 911. There is emergency service at the **Mammoth Hospital**, 85 Sierra Park Rd. (tel. 934-3311).

2. June Mountain

THE RESORT: June Mountain ski area is located up above the tiny town of June Lake, a popular summer spot ringed by mountains. The area is small when compared to its neighbor Mammoth Mountain approximately a half hour away, but there's honestly something for every skier here from gentle beginner terrain to steep, tight tree skiing.

It has been upgraded since Mammoth Mountain bought the ski area a few years ago, and even more changes are planned. The first change was the installation of a tram to upload and download skiers to the day lodge at mid-mountain. Most of the beginner and intermediate skiing is above that point; with the exception of an intermediate trail to the bottom and a small slope, the lower portion of the mountain is for advanced skiers. (Future plans include creating a better trail to the bottom of the mountain for less experienced skiers.)

This is a family area, and the atmosphere in the mountain lodge and on the slopes is low-key—and the crowds are much lighter than at its sister resort. There are some condos, motels, and restaurants close to the base.

THE SKIING: What you see from the parking lot is not what you have to ski. Some of the best advanced terrain stretches across the bottom half of the mountain—but many skiers just look at it as they take the chair lift up to the main lodge. (And they look at it again when they download at the end of the day.) The 2,562-foot vertical drop at this ski area stairsteps! There is some good steeper and intermediate terrain on the top third, gentle almost flat terrain in the middle, and steep terrain on the bottom third. (There is an intermediate cat track from the lodge to the base of the mountain.) Five double chairs, a quad, and a tram open up the 30 runs on terrain rated 30% beginner/novice, 45% intermediate, and 25% advanced (which includes 12% expert).

The runs around chair 2, starting just above the main lodge, are gentle beginner terrain. The slopes are wide and quite flat. The two peaks on the upper third of the ski area have a good variety of intermediate to very advanced terrain. There's a 2½-mile run winding around the edge of the ski area starting at the top of chairs 4 and 6. Bodie and Rosie Mae are other popular intermediate cruising runs off this chair. Sunrise Ridge to Sunrise is a cruising blue run off chair 3.

Advanced skiers have a lot of terrain on this mountain. Skiers should test their skills on Sunset or Schatzi off chair 3 before moving on to other black slopes here. There are several steep chutes around the upper half of chair 4, and there is good tree skiing off the ridge around Schatzi. The black runs on the lower face are steep enough so that they are only open when there's enough snow to cover them properly, usually after the rest of the area has been open for some time.

Insider's Tips

When it's sunny, try chair 3 in the morning and chairs 4 and 6 in the afternoon.

Mountain Facilities

There's a ticket office and an après-ski bar at the base of the mountain. There's a large cafeteria in the main chalet at mid-mountain.

Snow Coverage

This area is usually open from Thanksgiving to Easter. There is snowmaking over 40 acres, mainly high-traffic areas. There is a strong emphasis on grooming, particularly the beginner and intermediate trails.

Ski School

This ski school offers group instruction in small classes as well as privately. They have a special multiday program, June Way I, which is designed to move beginners along quickly. June Way II is for skiers who want to refine their skiing techniques. Both of these programs include lift tickets, ski lessons, and equipment. These programs are open to children 6 and older. Youngsters 4 to 12 years of age can join the SKIWEE program.

Childcare
There is no childcare facility. Youngsters 4 and 5 years old can join the Snow Playground program. Children 6 and older may also go into regular ski school.

Rental Equipment
Rental equipment is available in the June Chalet, the main lodge located at mid-mountain. Skiers can take chair 1 or the tram to reach the lodge.

Cross-Country Skiing
There are no groomed trails at the mountain, but telemarking is allowed on the slopes.

WHERE TO STAY: Lodging in June Lake, where the ski area is located, is in a variety of lodges, condominium complexes, and cabins. Places are listed in the Mammoth/June brochures. Write **Mammoth/June Ski Resort,** P.O. Box 24, Mammoth Lakes, CA 93546 (tel. 619/934-2571), for a brochure. During weekends, some skiers staying in Mammoth Lakes head to June Mountain for the day.

WHERE TO EAT: There are several restaurants in June Lake, from inexpensive coffeeshops to inns offering more elaborate meals. **Schat's,** a superb bakery that bills itself as the home of the original sheepherder bread, is the spot for hungry skiers to pick up a sampling of delicious baked goods.

GETTING THERE: June Mountain is located in the eastern Sierra Nevada Mountains, 20 miles north of Mammoth Lakes. The ski area, a 2½-hour drive from the Lake Tahoe area, is on Calif. 158 approximately three miles off U.S. 395.

TOURIST INFORMATION: For more information about the area, contact **Mammoth/June Ski Resort,** P.O. Box 24, Mammoth Lakes, CA 93546 (tel. 619/934-2571). For **motel and condominium reservations,** call the telephone numbers listed in the Where to Stay section. The June Mountain **snow report** telephone is 619/934-6166 or 213/935-8866.

3. Mount Reba / Bear Valley

THE RESORT: Skiers have to want to drive to Mount Reba / Bear Valley, a family-oriented resort surrounded by the Mokelumme Wilderness Area in the Central Sierra. Skiing on the slopes of Mount Reba is the main activity here. Lodging is in Bear Valley, a town four miles away.

THE SKIING: More than 21 miles of runs interconnect on Mount Reba. Two triple and seven double chairs open up the 2,100 vertical feet of terrain rated 20% beginner, 50% intermediate, and 30% expert. The skiable terrain is divided into three sections. The front face above the main lodge (at mid-mountain, but skiers drive to it) has terrain for every skill level. Advanced skiers have the lower half of the mountain and ski directly down from the lodge. The backside of the mountain is primarily intermediate terrain. Beginners start out on Cub Meadow, then move up to Rodeo. Lower intermediates head for Hog Back and Water Tank off the Koala chair. Mokelumme West off the Kuma chair, and most of the runs on the backside off the Pooh bear and Hibernation chairs are good middle-level intermediate terrain. Advanced skiers have the lower portion of the mountain serviced by the Grizzly and Kodiak chairs. Most test their skills on the runs in the Snow Valley bowl, the terrain around the Kodiak chair, before trying the even-steeper runs in the Grizzly bowl accessed by the Grizzly chair. There are steeps, chutes, and other bits of "interesting" terrain in these bowls to entertain expert skiers.

Mountain Facilities

Skiers drive up to the day lodge, located at mid-mountain. The Hungry Bear cafeteria and the Bear Paw lounge are located in the day lodge.

Snow Coverage

Mount Reba receives an average of 450 inches of snow each year. There is no snowmaking at this area, which opens normally from November to the end of April. Slopes are groomed as needed.

Ski School

There are group and private lessons in the regular school and the Kinderschool for children. The Skiing Bears Ski School is open to children 3 to 7 years of age. It includes all-day care, up to four hours of lessons, lift ticket, rental equipment, and lunch.

Childcare

There is a day-care facility for children 2 and older in Bear Valley Lodge (tel. 753-2301), in the town where all the lodging is located. Youngsters 3 to 7 can enter the Skiing Bears school, and older children can go into Kinderschool.

Rental Equipment

Demo and regular rental equipment is available on the mountain.

Cross-Country Skiing

Some 90 km (55 miles) on 30 trails wind through meadows and forests, and by creeks or cliffs around the Bear Valley Nordic Ski Area. Lessons in set track, the skating technique, and telemarking are available. Rentals and demos are available at the Bear Valley Sport Shop. Skiers on the multiday cross-country ski packages can stay in log cabins. The Powder Bears offers cross-country trips starting from secluded log cabins. Rates for trips begin at approximately $100 per night, plus the fee for the snowcat ride to the cabin. Contact the ski area for details.

WHERE TO STAY: Accommodations are in the town of Bear Valley, four miles away. Lodging choices available through **Bear Valley Condominium Management** (tel. 209/753-BEAR) include the **Lodge at Bear Valley** with its hotel room/condominiumized units and a limited number of condominiums or homes in the area.

The **Red Dog Lodge** (tel. 209/753-2344) and the **Tamarack Pines Lodge** (tel. 209/753-2080) are European-style lodges, both with restaurants and bars. The Red Dog has shared baths, but the Tamarack Pines Lodge has both shared and private baths. Lodging prices range from $45 for a room with a shared bath to $185 for a three-bedroom home.

For a brochure describing what's available above, contact **Mount Reba Ski Area**, P.O. Box 5038, Bear Valley, CA 95223. For general information about lodging, call the **central lodging number** (tel. 209/753-BEAR). For reservations, contact the specific property.

WHERE TO EAT: The restaurants in town serve everything from pizza to gourmet food. Try the **Altitude** for family-style dining and the **Lodge** dining room for California French cuisine.

GETTING THERE: Mount Reba / Bear Valley, located 52 miles east of Angels Camp, is closer to San Francisco than Lake Tahoe. Skiers must drive here. The ride on Calif. 4 includes spectacular views of the Gold Rush country and the Stanislaus National Forest.

MOVING AROUND: Once in the region, skiers can take the shuttle, which goes between the ski area and the town. Intermediates or better can ski off the backside of the mountain down to town on Home Run, a groomed patrolled trail.

TOURIST INFORMATION: For information about Mount Reba / Bear Valley, contact **Mount Reba Ski Area,** P.O. Box 5038, Bear Valley, CA 95223 (tel. 209/753-2301).

4. Other California Ski Areas

SIERRA SUMMIT: Sierra Summit, 67 miles northeast of Fresno, is a mid-size area that is being continually upgraded. Five chair lifts, two T-bars, and two tows open up 230 acres of cleared runs on the 1,679-vertical-foot mountain. Terrain is rated 40% beginner, 35% intermediate, and 25% advanced. There is lodging in the Sierra Summit Inn at the base and in other lodges and condos nearby. For information about skiing/lodging packages, contact **Sierra Summit Accommodations,** P.O. Box 236, Lakeshore, CA 93634 (tel. 209/893-3305). Lift tickets are available through Ticketron and Teletron as well as at the ski area. The Sierra Summit **snow report line** is 209/893-3311.

DODGE RIDGE: Seven chairs and three tows open up the terrain at Dodge Ridge in Pinecrest, approximately 160 miles from San Francisco. Terrain is rated 15% beginner, 65% intermediate, and 20% advanced on the 1,600-vertical-foot ski area. Although this is basically a day area, there is lodging and dining nearby. For information, contact **Dodge Ridge,** P.O. Box 1188, Pinecrest, CA 95364 (tel. 209/965-3474).

Chapter X

SOUTHERN CALIFORNIA

1. Mtn. High
2. Snow Summit
3. Snow Valley
4. Goldmine
5. Other Ski Areas
6. Lodging, Dining, and Other Practical Matters

THE DAY AREAS within two driving hours of Los Angeles are prime skier spawning grounds. Many southern Californians first put on skis at areas such as Goldmine, Snow Valley, Snow Summit, and Mtn. High. The terrain is geared for beginners and intermediates; the slopes are usually very well groomed. Once past the novice stage, many of the skiers move on to the mid-size resorts for the weekend or head up to Mammoth for a "resort experience."

THE RESORT: Terming southern California as a resort area for skiers takes more nerve than I have. It is far more accurate to say that there is a group of ten day ski areas, classic skier spawning grounds with verticals stretching up to 1,800 vertical feet, all within a 2½-hour drive of Los Angeles. These areas range from older ski hills where the atmosphere is still reminiscent of skiing in the '60s, to modern plants with astonishing amounts of snowmaking equipment and lift-ticket sales systems so sophisticated that you can pick up a ticket at department stores. There is lodging near several of these areas; however, most skiers just drive up for the day or a few hours of night skiing.

In spite of the belief held by many, these ski areas are attempting to hold the weekend lines to a maximum of 25 minutes (and skiing the right lifts might shrink that time somewhat). During weekdays the lines are often nonexistent. That the lines aren't horrendously long is due both to the increasing use of triple and quad chair lifts and to the U.S. Forest Service limit on the number of skiers allowed on the slopes. (The ski areas here are all on land managed by the U.S. Forest Service, which controls the development of the land and the number of skiers allowed on the slopes at any one time.) That there aren't near riots (as one ski area spokesperson claimed once happened when the skiers sitting since 3 a.m. got tickets and those who came at 4 a.m. didn't) is due to a novel ticketing system—advance reservations. Southern California skiers are probably the only ones in the country who book their space on the ski slopes through Ticketron, Teletron, or ski areas' private reservation numbers earlier in the week.

The southern California skier has a unique profile, according to one better-left-nameless ski-area employee. He simply whispered that many of these skiers race the one or two hours up to the mountains at least a day or two—each year—take a lesson or two, decide they are advanced skiers and proceed to "ski fast and fall down a lot" to get their kicks. "Ski defensively" is the watch phrase for the more cautious on those southern ski slopes.

The snow this close to the coast is wet—but a strong emphasis on grooming at the major areas usually keeps the slopes very skiable. In some cases the machines provide runs where you feel like you're skiing on a hint of fresh powder. Snow conditions on the slopes can vary greatly. Low temps followed by 70° or 80° weather followed by a drop back below freezing is not unheard of here. This is when the ski areas with the best grooming crews win. When Mother Nature is stingy with the white stuff, the ski areas turn on their snowmaking equipment. They run some of the more elaborate systems in the country, so it's not uncommon to ski on more falsie flakes than on the real stuff.

THE SKI AREAS: The ski areas here are geared toward beginners and intermediates. With the exception of Goldmine, the verticals go 1,200 feet or less. Most of the runs are very short, although at many areas skiers can cruise from one straight to the other, working their way downhill. The "advanced" terrain on the runs here is—with few exceptions—simply steeper than the other terrain (although when some of the steeper sections are iced they are definitely "difficult" runs). When set in many of the Sierra or Rocky Mountain major resorts, most of southern California's black turf would be classified blue.

Four of the ten areas located in the San Bernardino and San Gabriel Mountains—Mtn. High, Snow Summit, Snow Valley, and Goldmine—grab more than 90% of the skier days. Snow Valley is close to, and Snow Summit and Goldmine are located at Big Bear Lake, a quiet town with some basic motels and skier-rustic condos to house skiers who don't want the two-hour drive back to the coast at night. Mtn. High is located near Wrightwood, an easy 1½-hour drive (on empty expressways) from downtown Los Angeles. The smaller ski areas are also spread around the San Gabriel and San Bernardino Mountains.

1. Mtn. High

THE SKIING: Mtn. High encompasses two separate ski areas, a short, free shuttlebus ride apart, which can be skied on the same lift ticket. A quad, three triples, and six double chairs, and a poma access the 19 miles of ski runs rated 25% beginner, 55% intermediate, and 20% advanced at Mtn. High. The vertical at Mtn. High East is 1,600 feet; the vertical at Mtn. High West is less. Among the busiest day areas, this one has some of the most challenging runs for advanced skiers. A day area located just 1½ hours from Los Angeles, Mtn. High (on Calif. 2, approximately three miles west of Wrightwood) has escalated its skier day count by imaginative ways that skiers can obtain discounted lift tickets (good primarily during weekdays and slow periods). Children 10 and under ski free when accompanied by a paying adult (one child per adult). There is night skiing seven days a week.

Coming up from Wrightwood, the steepest slopes on Mtn. High East are the first terrain skiers see. But there's a 1½-mile intermediate run here, among the longest ski trails in this section of the state. Part of the beginners' terrain at

Mtn. High East is at the bottom, but there is also novice terrain around chair 8 at the top. (There is downloading.) From the top, intermediate skiers tend to veer left heading downward; advanced skiers steer toward the trails on the right. Advanced skiers tackle the open Olympic Bowl, which can build heavy-duty bumps.

Mtn. High West, less than a mile up the road, has a good variety of runs, but many are short. Beginners and novices practice on the gentle terrain around chair 3. Intermediates and advanced skiers have runs off all the other chairs. Upper and Lower Chisolm are popular with lower intermediates. Red Eye to Wyatt Earp is steeper. Advanced skiers slide down Gunslinger and Calamity. The bumps are allowed to build on Silver Spur and Wild Bill.

Insider's Tips

The way up from the coast is via major highways and a relatively level road as compared to the steep, curvy roads that access most of the other areas.

Mountain Facilities

The two base areas have restaurants, retail and rental ski shops, and ski schools, and there are a few cabins at Mtn. High West. The Bull-Wheel Saloon is in the Big Pines Lodge at Mtn. High West.

Snow Coverage

The majority of the skiable terrain, or 180 acres, is covered with snowmaking equipment. The ski area is normally open from mid-November to mid-April and usually utilizes a lot of man-made snow. More than 80% of the skiable terrain is groomed most nights, weather conditions permitting.

Ski School

There are regular group and private lessons. The Children's Buckaroo Ski School, which includes lifts, lesson, and lunch, is for youngsters from the age of 3 to 7.

Childcare

There is no childcare facility. Youngsters between the ages of 3 and 7 can join the Buckaroo Ski School.

Rental Equipment

Rental shops are located at both base areas.

CONTACT NUMBERS FOR TICKET/TOURIST INFORMATION: Advance credit card reservations for Mtn. High can be made through **Teletron** (tel. 213/410-1062 or 714/634-1300). Tickets are also available through **Ticketron** or **Ticketmaster.** Lift-ticket advance sales are also available by calling the **snow report number** (tel. 714/972-9242) and staying on the line after the report to make lift-ticket purchases via credit card. For information about lodging in the **Mtn. High / Big Pines Lodge Cabins,** contact Mtn. High, P.O. Box 993, Wrightwood, CA 92397 (tel. 619/249-5471).

2. Snow Summit

THE SKIING: Don't expect to buy a lift ticket at the base of this ski area on prime Saturdays during ski season. They've probably been gone since Thursday! The skier capacity limit here is 5,200 at this 1,200-foot-vertical ski area located by Big Bear Lake. Two quad, two triple, and six double chairs open up the 30 runs on terrain rated 10% beginner, 25% low intermediate, 40% intermediate, and 25% advanced. The longest run is 1¼ miles. There is night skiing, but always call that day to verify that the slopes will be open.

The front section of the ski area has wide, open slopes. The trails off to the sides are wide but cut through the trees. Beginners can work off chairs 4 and 8 all day. (Some days they can get a ticket just for those chairs.) Low intermediates can spend most of a day on the gentle runs off chair 9. There's more of a feeling of being in the woods here, because the trails are bordered by trees and you can see fewer skiers than on the open front area. Miracle Mile is particularly popular with intermediates. Advanced skiers head toward chair 6, which has the area's steepest—but short—runs. Log Chute and Side Chute, both longer, open runs off chair 5, are also popular with more competent skiers. Bumps are rarely allowed to build here, but when they do they'll probably be on the Wall.

Insider's Tips

Ski hosts are available at the bottoms most weekends and busy days to answer questions about the many different lift-ticket options available. They will also steer skiers toward less populated chair mazes and encourage skiers to stay on the top half of the mountain where the lines may be shorter.

Although skiers can reach all the runs from chair 2, on crowded days it may be faster to take chairs 4 and 5 to get up to the runs off chairs 6 and 7.

Mountain Facilities

There's a cafeteria, a bar, and a rental shop in the Summit Inn at the base. The Bear Bottom Lodge, a short hike up the slope, has lockers, a cafeteria, a beer and taco bar, and a full bar. The mountaintop restaurant has hot food.

Snow Coverage

Snowmaking covers 94% of all cleared runs at this area. Grooming is intensive. The area is usually open from mid-November to mid-April.

Ski School

In addition to the regular group and private lessons and the Kiddie Ski School, the Snow Summit ski school runs several imaginative programs. The free Beginner's Orientation session every morning is not a replacement for ski school, but the ski instructor does offer sound tips on everything from using a chair lift to basic ski positions. At midday there's a Ski with a Pro session, when the instructor offers tips on progressing to the real advanced skiing level. There are also recreational racing clinics and a daily Hot Skiers Contest Run, where entrants are judged on their ability and prizes are awarded. Check the exact times for these various programs. On anticipated sell-out days, the ski school reserves a limited number of lift tickets for skiers in classes.

Childcare

There is no childcare facility. The Kiddie Ski School takes youngsters from the ages of 4 to 8 for a half or full day class.

Rental Equipment

Regular and demo rentals are available at the rental shop in the Summit Inn. On anticipated sell-out days, the rental shop reserves a limited number of lift tickets for skiers who use rentals.

CONTACT NUMBERS FOR TICKET/TOURIST INFORMATION: Tickets can be reserved through Teletron or Ticketron, through the Snow Summit **credit card reservation service** (tel. 714/866-5841) and at the Snow Summit ticket office. Tickets can also be reserved with lodging through Big Bear Central Reservations (tel. 714/866-5878). On anticipated sell-out days, the ski school and rental shops have a limited number of tickets for customers who also want to attend ski schools or rent equipment. The **snow report number** is 714/866-4621. For more information, contact **Snow Summit**, P.O. Box 77, Big Bear Lake, CA 92315 (tel. 714/866-5766).

3. Snow Valley

THE SKIING: Snow Valley is a 1,143-vertical-foot ski area with a lot of good terrain for beginners and intermediates and a separate peak for advanced skiers. It's the first area skiers pass when heading into this section of the San Bernardinos; it's another half hour to the other ski areas around Big Bear Lake. Five triple and eight double chairs take skiers up to 35 runs on terrain rated 35% beginner, 35% intermediate, and 30% advanced. There is night skiing several days a week.

Beginners have their own open terrain, which includes just about the entire lower mountain. Intermediates have the run of most of the mountain. Bear Canyon and Mambo are among the most popular blue runs on the open face. There is good skiing for competent intermediates off chair 5 hidden from the base; some of the terrain is lightly gladed. The black runs on the front are light black at best, so the better advanced skiers head over to Slide Peak. Slide Peak West is easier and is more of a trail than an open slope. Slide Peak East is a short, open mogul field.

Insider's Tips

Reserved ticket holders get priority parking in the 3,000-car parking lot at the base.

Mountain Facilities

At the base there is a lodge with a cafeteria, a bar, and a retail/rental shop. The snackbar is mid-mountain.

Snow Coverage

This ski area boasts that it can blow more snow per minute than any other ski area in the country. Snowmaking equipment covers approximately 40% of the mountain, which is normally open from mid-November to the beginning of May. Grooming is an art here; most of the runs are groomed nightly or as needed.

Ski School

The school has regular group and private lessons as well as a special school for youngsters age 3 to 5. No lift ticket is required for this Snow School where youngsters are introduced to skiing skills in a specially groomed area.

Childcare

There is no childcare facility at the area, but youngsters age 3 to 5 can be placed in the Snow School.

Rental Equipment

Both regular and demo equipment rentals are available in the rental shop at the base.

CONTACT NUMBERS FOR TICKET/TOURIST INFORMATION: Lift tickets can be purchased through **Ticketron** or through **Snow Valley's reservation service** (tel. 714/867-5111 or 714/625-6611). The **snow report number** is 714/867-5151 or 714/625-6511. To contact **Snow Valley,** located on Calif. 18, five miles east of Running Springs, write P.O. Box 8, Running Springs, CA 92382 (tel. 714/867-2751).

4. Goldmine

THE SKIING: The Goldmine ski area is the biggest in southern California since a lift was added during the summer of 1985, raising this ski area's vertical to 1,800 feet. This would make Goldmine the major southern California area with long runs and some solid advanced terrain. Five double and three triple chairs open up the terrain, rated approximately 30% beginner, 40% intermediate, and 30% expert. The terrain is varied from open, gentle slopes for beginners to steep narrow trails for expert skiers. This area is more family oriented than the others in this region.

Novices can play on most of the bottom half of the mountain. The gentle open terrain under chair 5 is popular, as is Old Miner's. The longest green runs away from the mainstream of skiers is off chair 6. Intermediates can head all the way up the longest chair, chair 1, then take their choice of runs back down to the bottom. Upper Claimjumper to Marion's Run to Gambler is the most popular way down because it combines comfortable trail skiing with open slopes. Advanced skiers can start out on Outlaw, a well-groomed slope (often used for races) by chair 3. Then they can move to Sluice or Quick Silver (where bumps are allowed to build), relatively long runs off chair 6. The Geronimo lift on Geronimo Peak opens up the expert terrain, including tree skiing. Snow conditions permitting, a lot of skiers here must challenge the treed areas between the runs if the ski tracks are an indicator.

Insider's Tips

Management here doesn't believe in discounting lift tickets, but they want to offer skiers who pay for a full-price lift ticket good bargains. Every week there is a premium day when skiers are given gifts ranging from goggles to poles, a ladies day when women receive free lessons and have a cocktail party, and a race day when skiers can join in a free race clinic and try NASTAR.

When the area is filled to capacity, the lift lines are longest on chairs 1 and 2. Lower intermediates should try chair 6, while intermediates should try chair 3, and advanced skiers should try chairs 4 and 8.

Mountain Facilities

In the older base lodge there's a cafeteria, a deli/pizza room where skiers can order a variety of deli sandwiches, and a barbecue grill on the outdoor patio. There's an attractive second-story bar in a high, raftered room overlooking the ski slopes. The rental and ski accessory shop is located at the new base.

Snow Coverage

Snowmaking equipment covers 100% of the skiable terrain at this area which is normally open from Thanksgiving to Easter. The runs are groomed as needed.

Ski School

The ski school runs full- and half-day group and private lessons, recreational racing, and advanced skiing clinics. The Miner's Camp, for children between the ages of 5 and 12, is a full-day session which includes lunch. (It is a SKIwee program.)

Childcare

There is no childcare facility at the mountain. Children from the ages of 5 to 12 can go into the Miner's Camp.

Rental Equipment

Regular and top-of-the-line rental equipment is available in the rental shop at the base.

CONTACT NUMBERS FOR TICKET/TOURIST INFORMATION: Reserved tickets are available through **Ticketron, Teletron,** or through **Goldmine's reservation system** (tel. 714/585-2518). For **general information** and **snow conditions,** call 714/585-2517. For more information, contact **Goldmine,** P.O. Box 6812, Big Bear Lake, CA 92315-6812 (tel. 714/585-2519).

5. Other Ski Areas

SNOW FOREST: Snow Forest's 17 runs, accessed by a chair and three surface lifts, is located on the south shore of Big Bear Lake. Skier terrain is rated 25% beginner, 45% intermediate, and 30% advanced at this 1,000-foot-vertical ski area. There are restaurants and a ski-rental facility where Scorpian skis are available. For information, contact **Snow Forest,** P.O. Box 1711, Big Bear Lake, CA 92315 (tel. 714/866-8891). Lift tickets may be purchased through Ticketron and Ticketmaster. The 24-hour **ski report phone** is 714/866-5503.

MOUNT BALDY: Mount Baldy, a name long familiar to Los Angeles skiers, is just a 45-minute drive from the downtown area. The terrain off the four double chairs is mixed on this 2,100-vertical-foot mountain. There is an extensive racing program for recreational skiers as well as serious young skiers. Lift tickets may be purchased through Ticketron or Ticketmaster as well as at the area. For information, contact **Mount Baldy,** P.O. Box 459, Mount Baldy, CA 91759 (tel. 714/946-9653). The **snow report number** is 714/981-3344.

MOUNT WATERMAN: Mount Waterman is another local area long familiar to Los Angeles skiers. It is only 43 miles from the downtown area. Three double chairs open up the 25 trails on this 1,600-foot-vertical mountain. This area has a discounted lift-ticket program. For information, contact **Mount Waterman Ski Lifts, Inc.,** 817 Lynnhaven Lane, La Canada, CA 91011 (tel. 818/790-2002).

SKI SUNRISE: Ski Sunrise boasts a few very steep runs off the quad chair and four surface lifts opening up the ski trails and an open advanced bowl at this 800-vertical-foot ski area. Groups get a good break on lift tickets here. For information about this area, located an easy 90 minutes from Los Angeles (up the road from Mtn. High), contact **Ski Sunrise,** P.O. Box 645, Wrightwood, CA 92397 (tel. 619/249-6150).

6. Lodging, Dining, and Other Practical Matters

WHERE TO STAY: These are really day ski areas, but because Snow Summit and Goldmine and smaller Snow Forest are located two hours from the coast, many skiers decide to stay overnight on a weekend. There is lodging in the Big Bear Lake region, most of it in skier-rustic condos or motels. For a luxurious mini-vacation, check into the Arrowhead Hilton on Lake Arrowhead, which runs a shuttle to Snow Valley.

Accommodations in the Big Bear Lake area can be arranged through the **central reservations office** (tel. 714/866-5878 or 714/866-4601) in the Big Bear Lake Tourist and Visitors Bureau. There are some condos at the bases of Goldmine and Snow Valley; the other lodges and motels are located around the lake. Only a few of the facilities have spas or pools. Question carefully what you are getting so you're not surprised with the reality. Ask about lodging/lift ticket packages.

The **Big Bear Inn,** which opened last winter, has 80 comfortable rooms, several with Jacuzzi tubs and fireplaces. Rooms and suites range from $45 to $65 in midweek and $65 to $105 on weekends. For reservations, contact the Big Bear Inn, P.O. Box 655, Beverly Hills, CA 90213 (tel. 714/866-3471, or toll free 800/BEAR-INN in California).

The **Arrowhead Hilton Lodge** (tel. 714/336-1511, or toll free 800/223-3307 in California), located at the edge of Lake Arrowhead, is a particularly attractive property, and room or ski package rates fall in the expensive (for the area) category. The nicely decorated rooms have the expected Hilton amenities, and there are two restaurants in the hotel and several others within walking distance. There is an outdoor pool and Jacuzzi, and a health club with an instructor on tap to show guests how to use the various Nautilus and Universal machines. (Exercise clothes are available.) Ski packages combining lodging, continental breakfast, and lift tickets at Snow Valley are available and there is shuttle service to the ski area approximately 12 miles away via a winding road. Contact the Hilton through the national reservation number (tel. toll free 800/HILTONS) or call the lodge directly for prices.

WHERE TO EAT: Top on the list of locals' favorites in the Big Bear region is the **Iron Squirrel,** 646 Pine Knot, Bear Lake Village (tel. 866-9121), a country French restaurant where the chef utilizes some traditional and some of his own recipes. Reservations are a must on holidays and busy weekends if you want a seat in the small, cozy dining area where the tables are elegantly set on blue and white tablecloths. Entrees such as scallops provençale and escalopes de veau normande range from $11 to $16.50. Hours are from 5:30 p.m. daily for dinner. Sunday brunch is from 10 a.m. to 2 p.m.

Less expensive but filling meals are set on the tables at the **Blue Ox,** 441 W. Big Bear Blvd., Big Bear City (tel. 585-7886), where peanut shells on the floor best describes the decor. Try the Big Swede Ole Dinner, a giant baked potato stuffed with Hungarian goulash. Meals range from $6 to $12. Hours are 11 a.m. to 11 p.m. Sunday through Thursday, to midnight on Friday and Saturday.

Inexpensive family dining is the approach at **Ronardo's,** 553 S. Pine Knot, one block south of the signal in the village (tel. 866-7676), where the soup comes in a big tureen and the salad is passed in a large bowl. Ronardo's is open from 4 to 8:30 p.m. Monday through Thursday, to 10 p.m. on Friday and Saturday, and to 9 p.m. on Sunday for dinner. Prices run $5.50 to $8.50.

On the way up to the Big Bear area, pick up some pastries or a sandwich-to-go at **Grumpy's Bakery & Deli** in the center of Running Springs (tel. 867-4277). It's a small store with no seating but the pastries are delicious.

SHOPPING: More than a dozen merchants in the Big Bear area rent ski equipment. The price wars can give the consumer equipment for approximately $7.50

for skis, boots, and poles. Check that the equipment is in good condition and all the safety features are working.

NON-SKIER ACTIVITIES: The choice is very limited in the Big Bear region. There are snowmobiling tours of the Big Bear area. Contact **Adventure Expeditions** (tel. 866-7216 or 583-5453) for details. The **Snow Play Recreation Area** is a tubing hill open daily. One fee includes the tube rental and use of the hill. For information, call 585-2698.

The Ice Castle has a covered outdoor skating rink in Blue Jay Village near Lake Arrowhead. For information and hours, contact the **Blue Jay Ice Castle,** Calif. 189, Blue Jay, CA 92317 (tel. 714/33-SKATE). The Arrowhead Hilton Lodge has ice-skating packages.

ENTERTAINMENT: Several of the bars around Big Bear Lake have live entertainment on weekends and during some weekdays. Pick up the local guide to see what's happening. Places promising entertainment include the **Prospector's** (tel. 866-6696) and the **Red Baron** (tel. 585-2583).

GETTING THERE: The best way to reach these ski areas is by private car. A few, such as Goldmine, run buses from stores in Los Angeles and Orange County. Check with the local ski shops and with the ski areas regarding bus transportation to the bigger ski areas. The **Mountain Area Transit Company** (tel. 714/866-4440) offers charters to groups and shuttle service to and from the airport.

For information on the best way to reach the various ski areas, contact the ski areas. There are three ways to get to the Big Bear region. The most popular is Calif. 330 through Running Springs, then Calif. 18 past Snow Valley. Calif. 38 through Redlands is longer but apt to be less congested. Many skiers recommend Calif. 18 through Lucerne Valley when the weather is bad. Skiers heading for Mtn. High can take Calif. 138 to 2 and follow the signs. Private planes can land at the small airport in Big Bear.

MOVING AROUND: Private car is the best means of transportation. To reach the **Dial-A-Ride shuttle,** call 866-4444.

TOURIST INFORMATION: The best source of information about the ski areas in this region is the **United States Recreational Ski Association (USRSA),** P.O. Box 15486, Santa Ana, CA 92705 (tel. 714/641-0724). Membership in the USRSA includes various discounts and benefits on skiing and lodging throughout the United States. Call or write for information.

Chapter XI

IDAHO

1. Sun Valley
2. Ski Schweitzer
3. Bogus Basin
4. More Idaho Ski Areas

IDAHO HOUSES one of the country's best-known resorts—Sun Valley. However, there are other virtually unknown mid-size and smaller ski areas in this state which offer skiers good times for exceptionally reasonable prices. Ski Schweitzer, located close enough to the border that Canadians bus down to ski every weekend, is a mid-size area with lots of attractive terrain. Some visitors stay in the limited lodging on the mountain, but most bed down in the summer resort town down the mountain. Another is Bogus Basin, often touted by ski writers as a "find" because there is more entertaining skiable terrain for every skill level than skiers would, or should, expect to find at a day area (with very limited lodging) perched on a mountainside overlooking a city.

1. Sun Valley

THE RESORT: This ski resort has been serving the rich and famous since the 1930s, but it's definitely a fun spot for the rest of us. The first poster of a man stripped to the waist skiing downhill on good snow in sunny weather popularized Sun Valley to a wealthy crowd who loved "roughing it" as long as there were luxuries such as wind-protected outdoor pools, fine dining, and an orchestra playing nightly. After *Sun Valley Serenade* was filmed on site, celebrities began making the ski resort a regular winter vacation spot. (The old photographs of visiting celebrities on the walls in the lodge and mountain restaurants is a who's who of visitors.) The first narrow racing trail was cut in 1939 and skiers were pulled uphill on tractor-drawn sled.

Today there are 12 lifts ferrying skiers up Bald Mountain to explore a network of trails for every level of intermediate skier. Dollar Mountain, a small treeless bump a few miles away, is the teaching site for lower levels and the practicing area for skiers who want lots of space. The resort actually encompasses several living areas: Sun Valley, Warm Springs, Elkhorn Village, and the town of Ketchum, which are all wrapped around the skiing mountains. Sun Valley is a plush, well-designed, and well-run complex that includes a luxurious lodge, an inn, condominiums, and a mall with shops and restaurants. Of course, Sun Valley owns the ski mountains: Baldy and Dollar. However, many skiers stay in

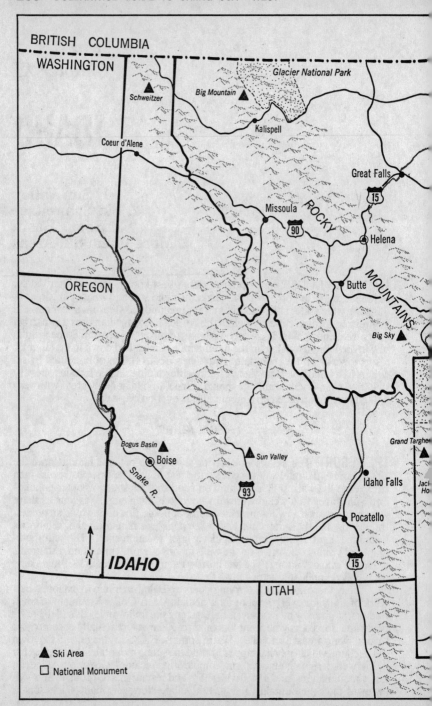

SUN VALLEY 207

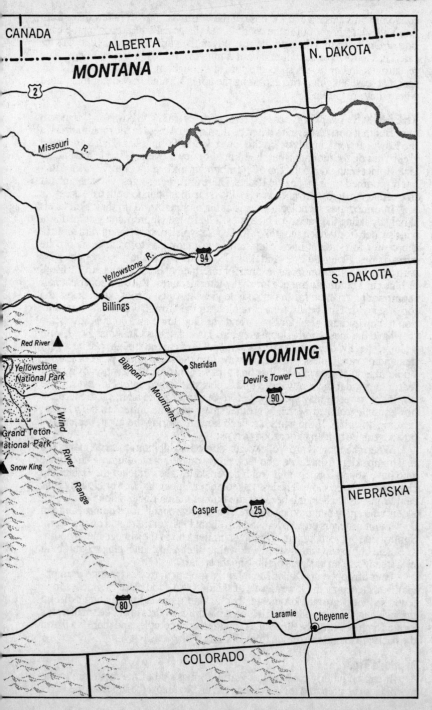

condominiums clustered at the base of the Warm Springs lift (a few miles from Sun Valley). Others opt for the condo/hotel village called Elkhorn on the back side of Dollar Mountain, and the rest stay in the various hotels and lodges located in the town of Ketchum, about a mile from the Sun Valley Lodge. The restaurants and après-ski spots are spread throughout the region. Most skiers spend at least a night or two exploring the après-ski amenities other than those where they are based.

THE SKIING: Twelve lifts access the 750 acres of trails and bowls on this mountain. But that doesn't begin to describe the skiing. Access to the mountain is via the Lower River Run lift or on the lower Warm Springs lift. There are many green runs on the mountain but they aren't for never-evers. (They learn on Dollar.) Novices can ride to the top of the mountain and explore the wide, immaculately groomed trails off Seattle Ridge. There are green routes (via trails and cat tracks that cut across advanced runs) down the mountain to both base areas.

Intermediates spending a week on this mountain will up their skill levels simply by skiing the variety of blue runs. The Ridge, appropriately named, is a wide swatch from which runs take off. The Canyon is a wide trough with room in the center for straight-line skiing, although many like to bank turns off the curved sides. Flying Squirrel and Blue Grouse are two of the more popular runs with a predictable, comfortable pitch for intermediates. The bowls are all listed as blue runs but many are not for shaky intermediates. Ride on Lookout chair (appropriately named for the incredible views), which ferries skiers across the top of several of the bowls, for a closer look at the terrain. For an easy introduction to bowl skiing, head for Siggi's and Far Out Bowl; on a comparative scale they have the most gently sloping terrain. The infamous Christmas Bowl, with its long, steadily downward pitch and mogul fields in the trough, can be a very demanding run. Unless you cut sideways into the steep upper parts of Easter, Lookout, and Mayday Bowl, that first turn will lower your elevation by a lot of feet. On powder days, advanced and expert skiers race here. However, these bowls are so vast it may take days before the surfaces are all tracked. Since the bowls aren't groomed, watch how other skiers do in the untracked snow before heading downhill. If the wind has been howling during the night, yesterday's powder can be hidden under today's crust.

When the moguls are Volkswagen-size on Exhibition, this run marks the real bump skiers from those who look pretty on the smaller bumps—and those who have young legs. Even if you'll never ski it, take a ride up the Exhibition chair to watch the show. The less talked-about Upper and Lower Holiday runs can be just as challenging because the bumps march down a double fall line. Skiers who enjoy bump skiing but prefer more reasonably sized bumps, and can do without watchers on an overhead lift, should test International on the Warm Springs side of the mountain. Limelight, under a lift of the same name, is another classic bump run with a steady, downhill pitch and challenging moguls built by a steady stream of skiers "following their line."

Four lifts open up Dollar Mountain, a groomed, treeless mound used primarily for teaching the lower levels of skiing. It's a good place to practice for a few days but it grows old quickly. The terrain there is for teaching skills up through beginning parallel, and it is possible the class sizes might be smaller. It's located at the edge of the Sun Valley condominium complex and there is a lift on the backside for skiers coming from Elkhorn Village.

Insider's Tips

It can be bitterly cold on the Warm Springs side of the mountain in the morning, so be prepared for the ride up the lift. To follow the sun, take the River

Run lift in the morning, then the Sunnyside lift and the cat track to the Round House, and the Christmas Bowl lift to the mountaintop. Ski the River Run side and the bowls until the sun reaches the Warm Springs face.

Because more skiers seem to start from the double chair on the Warm Springs side, take the River Run triple-chair lift on busier days. If the lines at the Limelight lift are long, head for the Flying Squirrel lift 100 yards below, and from the top of that lift take the cat track to the base of the Christmas lift, which goes to the top of the mountain.

When it's snowy and visibility is bad in the bowls, try the more protected runs set between trees on the front side of the mountain.

The ski school often uses Upper College between 10 a.m. and noon and between 2 and 4 p.m., so use the Flying Squirrel lift instead of the Limelight lift, which carries classes.

Try the brownies and cookies in the cafeterias on the mountains. The mountain lodges, with etched-glass dividers between tables surrounded by benches and stools covered in real leather, are very attractive. However, with the exception of the baked goods, the rest of the offerings are nothing special and are expensive when compared to other resorts.

Sun Valley's information boards on the mountain list the groomed runs with the "best" skiing of the day.

Mountain Facilities

There are lift-ticket windows at both base areas at Baldy and at Dollar Mountain. There are three mountain restaurants at Baldy and a base lodge at Dollar.

Snow Coverage

Sun Valley receives an average of 200 inches annually and is usually open from December to mid-April. There is snowmaking on 197 acres. Most of the equipment is aimed at high-traffic areas such as run-outs to lifts, although there is top-to-bottom coverage in one area.

Ski School

Never-evers and tentative novices take lessons at Dollar; intermediates and better usually take ski-school classes on Baldy. (The ski school at Dollar can teach intermediates and upper intermediates at Dollar.) The Sun Valley Ski School has desks at Dollar Mountain, at Look-Out, the lodge at the top of the mountain (the North Face Hut), and in the Sun Valley Mall. The school offers class and private lessons, and racing classes. Youngsters 6 and older can join the children's ski school where ski/play activities are emphasized when appropriate. The graduated-length approach is suggested for beginners.

Childcare

The childcare setup at Sun Valley receives rave reviews from parents. It's in a separate house, the blue building off a side path in the Sun Valley Mall, and there are many rooms for children to play in and others where they can rest. Although the majority of youngsters are between the ages of 2 and 6, all ages are accepted. The winter program includes a variety of activities scaled to meet the youngsters' age levels. Ice skating is available for an additional charge. There is a special two-hour ski program for an additional fee. Children's equipment can be rented at any of the ski shops in the mall. Call 622-4111, ext. 2288, for more information and the daily and hourly rates.

The **Great Escape Babysitting Service** (tel. 726-8666) has daytime, evening, and 24-hour babysitting care in the area's condo and hotels. The sitters are at least 20 years of age. There is a four-hour minimum, and rates run approximately $4.75 per hour and up, depending on the number of children.

Edgar's Place is another day-care center located in the Elkhorn Village Mall. They accept toddlers and older from 8 a.m. to 6 p.m.

Helicopter Skiing

Heli-skiing in the Sawtooth Range is an option when the weather conditions are good and the snow is stable. Tours are open to advanced and expert skiers. There are also drop-offs with a guide for a day of cross-country skiing. For more information about a day of heli-skiing in the backcountry, call **Sun Valley** (tel. 208/622-4111, ext. 2493). (See the Heli-skiing section in Chapter XVIII for details.)

Rental Equipment

Rental equipment is available in most ski shops in the area. Regular rentals and high-performance demo equipment are both available at the **Pete Lanes** in the Sun Valley Mall, the **Snug Ski Shops** (tel. toll free 800/223-7684 for advance ski rentals) in the Sun Valley Mall, Elkhorn Village, and Ketchum, and at the **Paul Kenny's Ski Shop** at the base of the Warm Springs lift. **Pro Select** has a toll-free number (tel. 800/262-6319) for ski rentals, which are picked up at Pro Select/Jolers of Sun Valley in Ketchum.

Cross-Country Skiing

There is excellent backcountry skiing less than a mile from Sun Valley—in any direction. Contact the **Cross Country Ski Association**, P.O. Box 3636, Sun Valley, ID 83353 (tel. 208/726-3266), for a free map and Nordic guide to the Sun Valley/Ketchum area. There are several good cross-country centers in the region offering groomed trails, guided tours in the backcountry, overnight trips with lodging in huts, and lodging/cross-country packages. Contact the association for a list. The **Sun Valley Nordic Touring Center** (tel. 208/622-4111, ext. 2251) has 30 km (18 miles) of groomed trails and a ski school run by Leif Odmark, a former U.S. Olympic coach. Also contact **Wood River Nordic at Bigwood**, P.O. Box 3637, Ketchum, ID 83340 (tel. 208/726-3266).

WHERE TO STAY: Lodging is grouped in four loose pods around the mountain. The most luxurious accommodations are in Sun Valley, a tiny village with a posh lodge, an inn, condominiums, and a mall. Guests are transported to the ski area, about ten minutes away, via Sun Valley's shuttlebus system. Skiers who like to walk to the lifts in the morning stay in the complex of condos and lodges at the base of the Warm Springs lift. Yet others stay in Elkhorn Village, at the base of Dollar Mountain but a short ride from Baldy. The most reasonably priced hotel and motel rooms are in the town of Ketchum, also a short shuttlebus ride from the slopes. Reservations for lodging in the Sun Valley Lodge and Inn can only be made through the toll-free number listed below. Reservation numbers for other lodges discussed are also listed below.

There are central reservations-numbers for bookings in a variety of lodges in the region. One is **Sun Valley Area Reservations**, P.O. Box 1710, Sun Valley, ID 83353 (tel. 208/726-3660, or toll free 800/635-1076); the other is **Sun Valley Ketchum Central Resort Reservations**, P.O. Box 979, Sun Valley, ID 83353 (tel. 208/726-0147, or toll free 800/635-4156).

Expensive

The deluxe rooms in the **Sun Valley Lodge and Inn**, Sun Valley, ID 83353 (tel. 208/622-4111, or toll free 800/635-8261), are luxurious, with comfortable

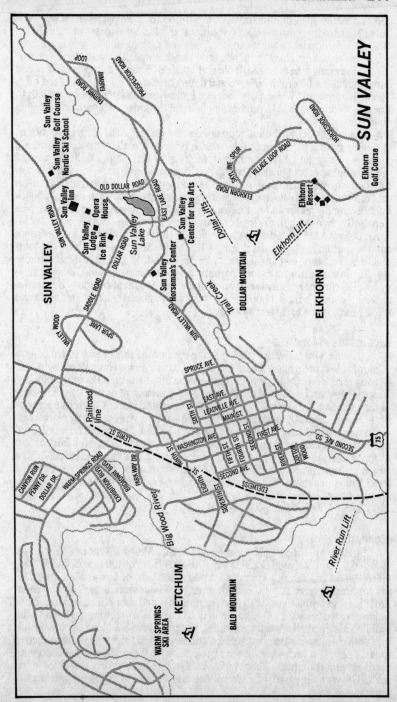

beds, attractive furnishings, and marble bathrooms. It's a place where bell service will do anything from picking you up at the Hailey Airport to canceling a plane reservation when the weather is poor and making one for you on the bus while you're out grabbing extra hours on the ski slope. The staff is very experienced in keeping guests comfortable and satisfied. There's a comfortable, quiet bar; the Duchin Room, a more casual dining area open all day; and the Lodge Dining Room with "white glove" service for guests. (Just send the bored kids to a nearby cafeteria, then to the bowling alley in the lodge basement for the evening.)

The inn, built in 1937 and renovated a few years ago, has attractive rooms, also with marble bathrooms and oversize tubs, and similar service. There is a Mexican restaurant and a continental cafeteria for fast dining. Both the inn and the lodge have large, heated, round outdoor swimming pools completely surrounded with high glass walls to keep the wind out. The lodge and the inn are on the Sun Valley Mall, close to restaurants and shops. There are several condominium complexes spread out beyond the mall, but shuttlebuses tour the area frequently. In winter, rates for hotel and inn rooms range from $95 for a standard room to $135 for a deluxe room and $210 for a parlor suite. One-bedroom condos start at $190, and the price is $315 for a four-bedroom. There are four-night and seven-night packages with lodging and lifts. Children 11 and under stay free in the same unit as their parents. Anyone staying in Sun Valley Company lodging can charge meals and other amenities bought at company properties to their rooms. There is a booth in the mall where guests can buy lift tickets and make reservations for ski-school classes.

Expensive to Moderate

Anyone who insists on staying at the base of the lifts checks into a condominium at Warm Springs. There are several condominium complexes here, and lodging arrangements for any of them can be made through the Warm Springs Resort. Most of the newer buildings have very attractive units; however, some of the units in the older buildings are more plain and worn. (There is a renovation project currently under way.) Question where you are being placed and make sure it has the amenities (pool, Jacuzzi) desired. Dining out here is limited mainly to Creekside and Barsotti & Benz, so expect to travel to Ketchum or Sun Valley some evenings. There is a small grocery store. Prices range from $75 for a studio to approximately $375 for a four-bedroom condo. There are seven-night lodging/lifts packages. For information and reservations in the Warm Springs area, contact **Warm Springs Resort,** P.O. Box 228, Sun Valley, ID 83353 (tel. 208/726-8274, or toll free 800/635-4404).

Moderate

In Elkhorn Village, **Elkhorn Resort at Sun Valley,** Elkhorn Road (P.O. Box 1067), Sun Valley, ID 83353 (tel. 208/622-4511, or toll free 800/635-9356, 800/632-4101 in Idaho), a complex located at the base of Dollar Mountain, skiers can stay in basic hotel rooms or a range of condominiums. The 150-room hotel is set in a small mall with a few restaurants and shops. The condominium buildings are spread out around the mall. As with Warm Springs, ask about the building assigned and nearby amenities, because there is a blend of older buildings with plain, sometimes worn units, and newer buildings with more attractive units. There is a restaurant in the hotel, a few in the mall, and a saloon with après-ski entertainment. There is day-care service for toddlers and older in the mall. The complimentary shuttle service takes skiers to Baldy, approximately ten minutes away.

The **Tamarack Lodge,** P.O. Box 2000, Sun Valley, ID 83353 (tel. 208/726-3344), on Sun Valley Road just a few blocks from the center of Ketchum, has pleasant, basic hotel rooms, some with fireplaces and refrigerators. The rooms on the top floor are the same price but have high ceilings. Ask for one facing the mountain. There is a small indoor pool and an outdoor Jacuzzi. Prices begin at $68.

The **Christiana Lodge,** 651 Sun Valley Rd., Ketchum, ID 83340 (tel. toll free 800/535-3241, 800/225-9804 in Idaho), a Best Western motel, offers the basic hospitality one expects from that chain. The rooms are comfortable, a few have fireplaces and kitchen facilities, and all guests have the use of an outdoor Jacuzzi. The motel is just a few blocks from the center of Ketchum and within walking distance of a variety of restaurants and shops. Rooms run from $74 to $86. During low season room prices drop dramatically.

Less Expensive

Check with the lodges mentioned above. In some units, the per-person price for a group in a unit is equal to the cost of staying in a less fancy place.

WHERE TO EAT: As one might expect in a resort that has been frequented by skiers since the 1930s, the competition between restaurants is strong. The result is a large number of good eateries.

Expensive

Old-world elegance describes the atmosphere in the **Lodge Dining Room** at Sun Valley Lodge (tel. 622-4111, ext. 2150). Attentive waiters, soft background music from a group near the dance floor, luxurious chairs, and candlelight reflecting off the crystal chandeliers are all part of the experience. Dinner hours are 6:30 to 10 p.m. Sunday brunch is memorable! Dinner entrees range from $14.50 to $22.

Diners relax in upholstered couches set against a rock wall at the **Christiana Restaurant,** 209 Walnut (tel. 726-3388), where the two-story-high ceiling is supported by massive wood beams. Leisurely continental meals are enjoyed here. Entrees range from $11 to $17. Reservations are recommended.

Freddy's **Taverne d'Alsace** at 520 East Ave. (tel. 726-4660) offers country French cuisine in a house with white walls and dark wood beams. Entrees range from $5 for crêpes to $12 for more elaborate dishes. Dinner is served from 5:30 p.m. daily.

Moderate

One of the most imaginative restaurants in town, the **River Street Retreat,** 12 River St. (tel. 726-9502), is off the regularly tracked tourist path. Guests are seated in the intimate, rustic dining room. Those who request wine are taken through a narrow, underground passage to the nearby hops shed-turned-wine cellar to pick out their own bottles. Entrees, including steak, shrimp Dijon, and brandy pork, go from $6 to $12.75. Reservations are suggested because this restaurant fills up during prime dinner hours. Hours are 6:30 to 9:30 p.m. daily.

A sleigh ride is the prelude to dinner at the rustic **Trail Creek Cabin.** The fare is American and the meals are hearty. Entrees range from $11.50 to $22 (a few dishes are available in children's portions) so meals here run the gamut from moderate to expensive. Dinner sleighs leave at 6, 7, 8, and 9 p.m. The lunch sleigh leaves at 11:30 a.m. Reservations are required and must be made through the Sun Valley Lodge (tel. 622-4111, ext. 2435.)

Warm Springs, Warm Springs Road (tel. 726-8238), like its sister restaurant, the Pine Tree Tavern in Bend, offers trout, ribs, steaks, and more for dinner, all served with sourdough scones and honey butter. Entrees range from $7 to $15. Lunch is from noon to 2:45 p.m. Monday through Friday, and dinner hours are 6 to 10 p.m. daily.

The Austrian atmosphere at the **Ram** (tel. 622-4111, ext. 2225) on the mall draws a large après-ski crowd and many stay for dinner. Entrees here include cheese fondue. Prices range from $10 to $15. Hours are 5:30 to 10:30 p.m.

The **Yacht Club,** at 205 Main (tel. 726-5233), has an open, warm-looking dining room on the top floor. The bar on the main floor is a gathering spot for skiers who like to party. Seafood and steak entrees range from $6 to $19. Hours are from 6 p.m. daily. Lounge hours are from 4:30 p.m. to 1 a.m.

What may be the best prime rib in the West is spread over diners' plates at the **Pioneer Saloon,** 320 N. Main St. (tel. 726-3139). Don't be intimidated by the rough-looking atmosphere in the big, noisy front-room bar. The rustic dining room in the back and the newer downstairs room are filled with families and other diners sampling the prime rib, shrimp, lobster, or sandwiches. Meals range from $4 to $16. They offer a petit cut of prime rib. This local landmark won't take reservations, so come early or be prepared to have a drink while you wait. Hours are 5:30 to 11 p.m. daily.

Jessie's, in Elkhorn Village, on the backside of Dollar Mountain (tel. 622-4534), is decorated in big-city fern-bar style and has a good salad bar to go with the steak and seafood. Ranging from $10.75 to $20. Dinner is served from 5:30 p.m. daily.

Louie's, 331 N. Leadville (tel. 726-8325), set in what was once Ketchum's first church, is touted as producing some of the most filling meals in town. Pizza and a variety of Italian dishes, priced from $4 to $9, are available in this family restaurant. Hours are noon to 11:30 p.m. daily.

There's a typical, comfortably casual **Ore House** in the Sun Valley Mall (tel. 622-4363) that offers steak, seafood, and a salad bar. Entrees range from $4 to $17. Hours are 5:30 to 11 p.m.

Barsotti's Mountain Café, located at the base of Baldy near the Warm Springs lift (tel. 726-3838), is a casual, open dining room. It's a popular lunch spot on a cold day. No reservations at dinnertime.

Less Expensive

Slavey's, Main Street and Sun Valley Road (tel. 726-5083), with its central rectangular bar and booths topped with fringed, fabric shaded lamps, is one of the hot spots in Ketchum. Slavey's boasts a variety of hamburgers, sandwiches, and salads with fries. Plates run from $4 to $6.

According to the locals, **Andy's Cabin,** 320 N. East Ave. (tel. 726-3629), serves the best breakfast for the buck in town. Belgium waffles, pancakes, omelets, and more are available from around $3 and up. Lunch and dinner are also served in this log cabin, which was once someone's home. Hours are 7 a.m. to 9 p.m. daily.

The **Konditorei,** in the Sun Valley Mall (tel. 622-4111, ext. 2235), is a top-of-the-line coffeeshop with terrific pastries. Austrian-style sandwiches, quiche, salads, and ice-cream creations range from $5 to $7. Breakfast, lunch, and dinner are served. Hours are 7 a.m. to 10 p.m.

Barsotti & Benz (tel. 726-9845) is a little snack at the base of the Warm Springs lift where skiers grab sandwiches at lunchtime and a beer après-ski.

ENTERTAINMENT: **Creekside** (tel. 726-8200), a block from the base of the Warm Springs lifts, is the liveliest spot in the late afternoon. There is usually a humorous entertainer and country/rock music at the **Ram** bar (tel. 622-4111, ext. 2225) on weekends. The **Elkhorn Saloon** (tel. 622-4511) also has live entertainment après-ski and dancing in the evening. The **Duchin Room** (tel. 622-4111, ext. 2144) at the Sun Valley Lodge often has a jazz group or a trio playing. During the evening, the crowd drifts to Main Street in Ketchum and into the bar with sounds that appeal. **Slavey's** (tel. 726-5083) moves the tables off the dance floor, and bands produce rock-and-roll sounds nightly during the season. Skiers and locals unwind in the country-western atmosphere of **Whiskey Jacques** (tel. 726-5297).

There are two local theater groups; check the papers to see what's playing. There are two theaters in Ketchum and another at Sun Valley that runs two different movies each night.

SHOPPING: Unusual shops and galleries are located throughout the main streets of Ketchum. Once an Idaho backwater town, in recent years many local merchants have geared their merchandise and decor to free-spending skiers. **Vargold Lane** and **Giacobbi Square,** both at Leadville and Fourth have interesting shops. Stop by the chamber of commerce office at Main Street and Fourth for a guide to the local art galleries. Many artists show their work by appointment only. Visit the **Hissing Goose,** which specializes in Americana; **Images,** which features contemporary art; and the **Kneeland Gallery,** which displays classic and western art. The **Sun Valley Center** displays arts and crafts by local, regional, and national artists.

NON-SKIER ACTIVITIES: Soaring over Baldy Mountain to watch the skiers from above appeals to some. For information and reservations, contact **Sun Valley Soaring** (tel. 788-3054). The company offers glider rides and glider instruction. There are two **ice skating rinks** at Sun Valley. They are free to visitors staying at Sun Valley properties, but anyone can use them for a fee. For sleigh rides into the wilderness, contact **Sawtooth Sleighs** (tel. 726-4024). **Indoor tennis courts** are available, for a fee, at Woodside, 11 miles south of Ketchum. For information call 788-3475. Pick up a gallery guide and explore the many art galleries in town. (There are maps in each of the participating galleries. See the Shopping section, above.)

MOVING AROUND: KART operates no-fare public buses between Warm Springs, Sun Valley, and Ketchum, so skiers can get around the region without their own cars, although they must expect to spend time waiting for buses. KART hours are from 7:30 a.m. to 10:30 p.m. (Call 726-7140 for the routes.)

Although the Sun Valley Company offers transportation for its guests to and from the ski slopes, the buses and even the lodge courtesy vans will not stop in or go to Ketchum. The courtesy transportation at Elkhorn has a similar policy. This can make it difficult for visitors who want to spend an evening away from their main base. There are several cab companies, and rides are priced according to zones and the number of passengers. The price may vary from company to company. **Sun Valley Taxi Limo** (tel. 726-3260) offers local service and pickups at Hailey Airport.

GETTING THERE: Sun Valley is located on Idaho 75, off I-84, about three driving hours from Boise and five from Salt Lake City. Sun Valley has several gateway cities: Salt Lake City, Boise, and Idaho Falls, plus Twin Falls on Saturday during the winter. **Horizon Air** runs flights from Salt Lake and Boise to **Hailey Airport,** 20 minutes from the resort. Sun Valley provides ground transportation for its guests. The **Sun Valley Limousine** meets flights at Hailey. Call 208/726-3260 for reservations.

Sun Valley Stages (tel. 208/622-4200, or 383-3085 in Boise, or toll free 800/821-9064 outside Idaho) provides daily scheduled bus service from the Boise airport to the resort. The trips are timed to leave after major flights arrive. They also meet some flights arriving at Twin Falls.

Many major rental car companies offices are located at the Boise Airport and **Hertz** and **National Car Rental** have offices in Sun Valley.

TOURIST INFORMATION: For general information about the area, contact the **Sun Valley-Ketchum Chamber of Commerce**, P.O. Box 2420, Sun Valley, ID 83353 (tel. 208/726-3423). For information about Sun Valley, contact the **Sun Valley Company**, Sun Valley, ID 83353 (tel. toll free 800/635-8261, 800/632-4104 in Idaho). There are several numbers for lodging information and reservations (see Where to Stay). The visitors information center is open daily at the corner of Main Street and Fourth. At the resort, find one of the free copies of the *Sun Valley Escort* or *Steppin' Out,* both free guides to activities and services in the area.

The **emergency number** is 911.

2. Ski Schweitzer

THE RESORT: Ski Schweitzer, with a 2,000-foot-vertical, is a textbook version of a good family ski area with its variety of terrain for every skill level, including experts, a friendly lodge, and a good ski school. The land around the base of the ski runs is dotted with condominiums, and there is a lodge with bare-bones rooms, good food, and a friendly bartender. The town of Sandpoint, 20 minutes down the mountain road, is a summer resort at the edge of Lake Pend Oreille with several good restaurants and motels in the moderate and inexpensive price ranges. The clientele here come from the Pacific Northwest and from Canada, which is just 60 miles north. On a "getting a good experience for your dollar" scale, Ski Schweitzer would be on or near the top. It's not a glamour resort—but it's an excellent way station between the beginner ski factories (to quote this area's ski school director) and the glamour resorts.

THE SKIING: Schweitzer's open bowls and 39 runs are spread over the Schweitzer and Colburn basins. The 2,000 vertical feet of rise is serviced by seven double-chair lifts and a T-bar. The runs spill into two basins (the Schweitzer and the Colburn). In the Schweitzer area, beginners have their own runs off chair 2 as well as cat tracks, which start at the top of chair 1 and the top of chair 4, and meander downhill across more difficult runs. They also have a few long runs on the Colburn side that end by the bases of chairs 5 and 6 near the Outback Inn, a small day lodge for skiers who want to warm up before heading back to the main base area.

On the front side, the Ridge, a wide, open swath skirting the basin, is one of the most popular blue runs. The Colburn basin is really an intermediate's playground. (Visually this side is a treat because there's nothing in sight except other mountainsides.) There's more trail skiing here than on the front side, but the runs are wide enough for competent intermediates. Off chair 5, Zip Down is a long cruising run and Timber Cruiser lives up to its name. Everything off chair 6 is blue.

Advanced skiers have a few shorter runs on the back side but the most interesting turf is the open section called the South Bowl on the front side. Depending on your line, it goes from steep to very steep, and trees can create a natural slalom course. For a warmup, however, try Quicksilver and some of the other runs off chair 4.

On a powder day there's an endless amount of terrain at this ski area, especially above the tree line. Skiers willing to hike can head to the north bowl (with the ski patrol's permission), an open area on the Colburn side where a future lift is planned.

Mountain Facilities

There's a cafeteria and a bar in the base lodge. The ski school is in a nearby building. The Outback Inn is a small lodge in the Colburn basin. There is a retail and rental shop with a repair department.

Snow Coverage

The average annual snowfall is 180 inches at Schweitzer, which is usually open from late November to mid-April. There is no snowmaking. Grooming is as needed.

Ski School

In addition to the regular group and private lessons, Schweitzer's ski school has several programs including women's ski seminars, intermediate skiers packages, and advanced skiers seminars. There's a childcare/snow-play program for the younger children, and the older ones go into the Mogul Mice program.

Childcare

Youngsters from infants to age 8 can go into the Kinderbin, a childcare facility in the same building as the Alpine ski shop. All-day sitting is available, and half-day snow play to teach basic skiing skills with instructors is an option.

Rental Equipment

Regular rental and high-performance equipment is available in the Alpine ski shop at the base area.

Cross-Country Skiing

The Nordic ski school offers both set tracking and telemarking lessons. There is eight kilometers (five miles) of groomed terrain and logging trails nearby.

WHERE TO STAY: There's one lodge and several condo complexes on the mountain. In the town of Sandpoint, 11 miles down the mountain, there are many motels. When compared to the prices at most major destination resorts, nothing here ranks as truly expensive. Even the lodging on the mountain ranges from moderate to less expensive when two persons are placed in each bedroom. Many, if not all, of the following accommodations can be booked through **Schweitzer Central Reservations,** Schweitzer Ski Area, P.O. Box 815, Sandpoint, ID 83864 (tel. 208/265-4576).

The renovated **Overniter Lodge,** with ski access via the T-bar (primarily used by guests to get to the base lodge and ski lifts accessing the mountain runs), has bare-bones rooms with showers (no tubs) which sleep four. There is a Jacuzzi and a sauna in the building and the St. Bernard Keg restaurant is next door. Room rate per night ranges from $36 to $53.

There are several condo complexes around the base area with accommodations ranging from minuscule efficiency units in the **Blue Beetle** to plush, nice-size rooms in the Wild Flower. The **Wild Flower** units are particularly attractive and every four units share a private outside Jacuzzi. They are a ten-minute walk from the T-bar, so many guests staying here drive their own cars up to the base area. The **Crystal Run** condos are nice looking and they are located by chair 2, so they have ski-in/ski-out access. There are no telephones in the condo units and few televisions. Nightly per-unit prices range from $70 to $130. Meal packages at the St. Bernard Keg Restaurant are available with any lodging on the mountain. There are multiday lift/lodging and meal packages available. For on-mountain accommodations, call 208/265-4576.

Connie's Motor Inn, 323 Cedar St. (P.O. Box 126), Sandpoint, ID 83864 (tel. 208/263-9581), has rooms of the expected Best Western quality. King-size beds and waterbeds are available. There is a Jacuzzi and an outdoor pool. Located in the middle of Sandpoint, Connie's has a restaurant and an attractive fireplace lounge which is a popular après-ski spot. Room rates are about $42 per person double occupancy, and waterbeds are a few dollars more. Children under 12 stay free in the same room as their parents.

The **Quality Lodge,** 805 N. Fifth Ave. (P.O. Box 187), Sandpoint, ID 83864 (tel. 208/263-2111), has standard motel rooms wrapped around an indoor swimming pool in the new wing. Located in the central part of town, the Quality Inn rooms cost between $35 and $44 a night.

The comfortable rooms at the **Edgewater Lodge,** 56 Bridge St., Sandpoint, ID 83864 (tel. 208/263-3194 in Idaho and Canada, or toll free 800/635-2534 elsewhere in the U.S.), overlook Lake Pend Oreille, and there is an attractive Jacuzzi and sauna area for guests. The Beach House Restaurant on the premises serves three meals daily. The rooms cost between $44 and $58 per day.

Rooms at the **Lakeside Motel,** 106 Bridge St., Sandpoint, ID 83864 (tel. 208/263-3717), may be one of the best buys in town. Many of these basic motel rooms, which sleep four, have kitchenettes. There is a Jacuzzi and a sauna for guests. Room rates range from $35 to $56.

WHERE TO EAT: There's only one place for dinner up at the ski area, the St. Bernard. However, as in any resort town, there are many restaurants down in Sandpoint battling for skier's dollars.

Expensive to Moderate

In the **Garden Restaurant,** 15 East Lake (tel. 263-5187), guests seated in the various attractive greenhouse rooms have a choice of beef, seafood or international cuisine. Entrees range from $6.50 to $25. No reservations. Children's portions are available. Dinner is served from 5 to 10 p.m. daily. Sunday brunch is from 10:30 a.m. to 2:30 p.m.

Guests sit in highback, carved wooden chairs in the blue-and-white dining rooms at **Ivano's,** at Second and Lake (tel. 263-0211), a "ristorante Italiano" located in a former home. Pasta starts at $8. Chicken, veal, and other main dishes run $10 to $16.50. Dinner hours are 5 to 10 p.m. Tuesday through Saturday. Lunch hours are 11 a.m. to 2 p.m. Tuesday through Friday.

Moderate

The **St. Bernard Keg** (tel. 263-9564) is the only restaurant on the mountain (other than the cafeteria in the base lodge). A rustic place, the dining room is on the main floor and the bar is on the balcony of this high-raftered room. There is a tasty skier's buffet most mornings to ensure a speedy breakfast hour. Beef and seafood dinners include a trip to the extensive salad bar. Meals range from $8 to $15.

The **Beach House Restaurant** (tel. 263-3194) at the Edgewater Lodge serves three meals a day, but the breakfasts are a particularly tasty buy for the money. Prices go from $6 to $15. Hours are 6:30 a.m. to 10 p.m.

The **Hydra,** 115 Lake (tel. 263-7123), is a casual, trendy restaurant offering prime rib, fresh fish, and steaks. Entrees go from $8 to $15. You can make a meal on 50¢ tacos or $2 spaghetti in the bar area during happy hours on certain nights. Call the Hydra for specific days.

Less Expensive

Papandrea's, 215 S. Second Ave. (tel. 263-9321), produces the best pizza in town, according to many locals. It's available in the informal restaurant located in an old building, and it can be ordered to go. Pizzas start at $5. Calzone and sandwiches run $2 to $4. Hours are 4 to 10 p.m. on Monday, 11 a.m. to 10 p.m. Tuesday through Thursday, to 11 p.m. on Friday and Saturday, and noon to 10 p.m. on Sunday.

Connie's, located in Connie's Motor Inn at 323 Cedar St. (tel. 263-9581), is the coffeeshop of choice for many Sandpoint residents. Skiers mix with the business clientele during breakfast and dinner hours. There is a small, pleasant dining room in the back for more relaxed dining. Burgers and sandwiches start at $3. Dinners start at $7. There is a children's menu. Hours are 5 a.m. to 11 p.m. Sunday through Thursday and until midnight on Friday and Saturday.

The **Cupboard,** at 300 N. First Ave. (tel. 263-9012), only has a few stools at the counter but most skiers order take-out food to eat at the slopes or stop by for a piece of pastry après-ski. Freshly ground coffee and pastries are available from 6:30 a.m. to 5:30 p.m. Call to order lunches. The selection includes quiche, hot steak and potato pasties, sandwiches, and salads. Sandwiches average $2.75.

SHOPPING: **Cedar Street Bridge** is an enclosed public market that you might expect to see in a cosmopolitan city rather than in a town in Idaho. Utilizing the existing bridge right-of-way over a creek, the two-story structure (bright with both light and warmth coming from a passive solar design) houses many galleries displaying the works of Idaho craftspeople and other artists ranging from the expected paintings to a chess set with dried apple faces and handmade costumes, and scrimshaw. Other storefronts house specialty shops and boutiques and vendors' carts fill one section. A continental café has indoor tables usually filled with people-watchers.

The **Smoke House** proprietors make a variety of incredibly tasty smoked fishes, cheeses, beef jerky, turkey, duck, and even pheasant. Everything is prepared in-house, with 100% natural smoking techniques. Definitely worth a stop to sample the smoked salmon, the Smoke House (tel. 263-6312) is located at the south end of Long Bridge on U.S. 95 at Lakeshore Drive. Delicacies can be packed for travel or mailing. Hours are 9 a.m. to 6 p.m. daily.

Antique and Country Shops, 504 Oak St. (tel. 263-5911), now houses a variety of stores, a small restaurant offering hearty sandwiches and freshly ground coffee, a bookstore, and 19 antique dealers and 15 country craftfolks. Hours are 9:30 a.m. to 5 p.m. Monday through Saturday.

NON-SKIER ACTIVITIES: Non-skier activities are all in the Sandpoint area. Wandering through the Cedar Street Bridge is usually good for a leisurely hour of people-watching and gallery hopping. **Pucci,** northern Idaho's award-winning winery, is located in Sandpoint and there are occasional winter tours. Call 208/263-5807 for information. There's a good collection of antique cars, horse-drawn vehicles, and more in the **Vintage Wheel Museum.** Located in the back of the Company Store at 218 Cedar St., it's open from 9:30 a.m. to 5:30 p.m. daily. Call 208/263-7173 for more information.

GETTING THERE: Delta, Northwest Orient, United, P.S.A., Horizon, and other airlines fly into **Spokane International Airport,** 75 miles from the ski area.

Transfers are available to Schweitzer Ski Area if arrangements are made with Central Reservations in advance. Many rental-car companies have booths at the Spokane airport. Sandpoint has an airport for private aircraft. **Amtrak** (tel. toll free 800/USA-RAIL) stops in Sandpoint. Arrangements for a ride to the mountain may be made in advance with Schweitzer Central Reservations.

Once in Sandpoint, skiers can use rental cars or taxi service—**A-1 Taxi** (tel. 263-1557) or **Sandpoint City Taxi** (tel. 263-9330)—to get to the ski area. **K & K Transit** (tel. 263-2161) has daily bus service between the ski area and Sandpoint.

MOVING AROUND: Skiers staying at the lodging on the mountain close to the T-bar or the chairs could get by without a car. However, for freedom of movement and a choice of après-ski activities, a car is a must.

TOURIST INFORMATION: For more information, contact **Schweitzer Ski Area**, P.O. Box 815, Sandpoint, ID 83864 (tel. 208/265-4576 for central reservations, 208/263-9555 for information). The **Spokane snow report** number is 509/328-5632. For general information about the region, contact the **Sandpoint Chamber of Commerce**, P.O. Box 928, Sandpoint, ID 83864 (tel. 208/263-2161).

3. Bogus Basin

THE RESORT: Bogus Basin isn't really a resort. It's a very good day area with as much interesting skiable terrain as many destination areas, but less vertical than many, and enough ski-in/ski-out condos to house approximately 240 persons. The resort is some 108 turns up a winding road from (and 3,000 feet higher than) Boise, Idaho. In distance that's 16 miles; in time it means between 40 minutes to an hour depending on road conditions. Although it is considered a locals' area, management tries to fill the 72 slopeside condominium rooms with vacationing skiers during the week. Families, especially those with novice and intermediate skiers, could spend several enjoyable days skiing here, as long as they are comfortable living in close quarters and are self-sufficient for entertainment.

THE SKIING: Six chair lifts and two rope tows service 2,000 skiable acres. The vertical is 1,800 feet. (To put those figures in perspective, Sun Valley's Bald Mountain has less terrain but the vertical is almost double.) There are 45 listed runs and lots of off-trail terrain for skiers on several peaks. The rating is 20% easiest, 44% more difficult, and 36% most difficult.

There is night skiing off the Deer Point, Showcase, Superior and Morning Star chairs, all grouped around the original day lodge. The Morning Star chair is for beginners, and the slopes around the Deer Point and Showcase chairs are comfortable intermediate terrain. There is a mile-long advanced run off the Superior chair lift for night skiing. To reach the majority of the area's runs, take the Morning Star chair up to the Pioneer Lodge, a mid-mountain day lodge offering three meals a day and a lounge frequented by overnight guests in the nearby condos. The runs around the Bitterroot chair, set off by itself, are usually less crowded than the other beginner and intermediate runs. This is the area where intermediates practice their powder turns when conditions are right. From mid-mountain, advanced skiers take War Eagle while the others take Smugglers down to the base of the Superior chair, which tops on Shafer Butte, the highest peak (elevation 7,590 feet) at the ski area. Superior, underneath the chair, is the locals' bump run. Because there is so much terrain here and so few skiers on this mountain there's always untracked powder, especially in the lightly treed terrain between the formal trails. On a powder day, head off the backside of Shafer Butte for a powder run between the trees. Then take the cat track to the Pine

Creek chair and test Paradise (the blue ego run) or Wildcat (the black ego run). When the snow is deep, good skiers may want to explore the tree-skiing terrain between Upper Nugget and Wildcat.

Insider's Tips

It's possible to ski in the sun here most of the day. To follow the sun, start on the Pine Creek chair lift and work south toward the Deep Point chair, or ski the runs under the Superior chair that have the same exposure.

Because there is so much off-trail terrain, one local suggested "there is nothing wrong with [better skiers] tailing a local" to explore some uncharted terrain. The "south side," which can be reached from the top of the Superior chair, offers open, advanced powder skiing when the snow is good.

The Pioneer Lodge is another two miles up the winding road from the base lodge, but it's a good place for skiers who want to park and end the day with dinner and après-ski entertainment on weekends before heading back down the mountain.

Mountain Facilities

There is a base lodge with a cafeteria, lockers, and the day-care center. The Pioneer Lodge also has a cafeteria, a lounge, and a ski shop.

Snow Coverage

The average snow depth is 100 inches at Bogus, where the normal operating season is from December to mid-April. There is no snowmaking. Grooming is as needed.

Ski School

Bogus has a large ski school for an area its size. The school specializes in innovative programs for preschoolers and children. (For instance, youngsters follow Snoopy, who skis in a wedge.) Lessons for all skill levels are offered during the day and in the evening. Reduced rates on rental equipment and lift tickets are available to ski-school students.

Childcare

There is childcare for walking toddlers through 7-year-olds in the Mogul Mouse Day Care Center, a set of large rooms in the Bogus Creek Lodge. Reservations are required for toddlers and the fee is slightly higher per hour. Children 3 to 5 years old can go into the Mogul Mouse Ski School, a special program for that age group. Parents in group of full-day private lessons receive free day care for their children.

Rental Equipment

Regular rental and demo equipment is available at McU Sports, next to the Bogus Basin Lodge. The price varies according to the number of hours rented.

Cross-Country Skiing

Bogus Basin has 17 km (10½ miles) of groomed trails. Equipment is available at the trailhead, approximately half a mile past the first lodge.

WHERE TO STAY: The **Pioneer Inn** is actually 72 condominium rooms in several small buildings, and a large lodge with a restaurant and bar which also serves as the mid-mountain day facility. There are small one-bedroom suites in which the main room has a fireplace, kitchen, sofa bed, bunks, television, and a bathroom. The lock-off bedroom has a private bath and technically sleeps four. The efficiency units are tiny one-room apartments that sleep up to six in a sofa bed, a murphy bed, and double bunks, and has one bath. The units are adequately furnished and all have ski-in/ski-out access. Meals are eaten in the condo or at the Pioneer Lodge. There are two outdoor whirlpools and a sauna for the complex. Prices range from $55 for a lock-off bedroom to $135 for a one-bedroom suite.

Some of the Boise hotels have ski packages. Currently skiers need their own transportation to the ski area.

WHERE TO EAT: The **Pioneer Lodge** is a multilevel building, just a few hundred yards from the condos, that houses a fast-food cafeteria on one floor and the **Firewater Saloon and Restaurant** on the top floor. Hearty skiers' breakfasts are available in the morning, and burgers, soup and salad, and sandwiches are offered at lunchtime in the large, open Firewater Saloon. Dinners, served after 6 p.m., come off a limited menu that includes chicken and steak. Breakfasts are $3.50 to $5; lunches are $4 to $6; dinners are $7 to $12. There is live entertainment on weekends and sometimes during the week.

The Pioneer Lodge also runs a free **grocery service** for condo guests six days a week. Guests leave a list in the morning and the groceries are delivered later in the day.

GETTING THERE: Bogus Basin is located on Bogus Basin Road, 16 miles from Boise. There is a bus service to the ski area on weekends and some weekdays. Continental, Alaskan Airlines, United and Horizon fly into Boise. The city is served by the Amtrak "Pioneer" line. Several major car-rental agencies have booths at the Boise airport. The Bogus Basin Limo will pick up skiers at the airport.

TOURIST INFORMATION: For information and lodging reservations, contact **Bogus Basin,** 2405 Bogus Basin Rd., Boise, ID 83702-0994 (tel. 208/336-4500, or toll free 800/367-4397 outside Idaho). The **snow report number** is 208/342-2100.

4. More Idaho Ski Areas

BRUNDAGE MOUNTAIN: Located seven miles north of McCall and 100 miles north of Boise, this area receives some of the deepest powder in the Northwest. Slopes range from steep bowls to wide, gentle trails. The 1,600 feet of vertical is serviced by two chairs and a poma. There is a free rope tow on the novice slope. There's a day lodge with a beer and wine bar. Day care is available for youngsters from 6 weeks to 8 years of age. Lodging is in nearby McCall. For information, contact Brundage Mountain, P.O. Box 1062, McCall, ID 83638 (tel. 208/634-4151). The snow phone is 208/634-5650.

PEBBLE CREEK: Pebble Creek, in southeast Idaho, has 2,000 feet of vertical climbing up the side of Mount Bonneville. A triple and two double chairs open up 24 runs. Contact the Pebble Creek Land Company, P.O. Box 1056, Pocatello, ID 83201 (tel. 208/775-4451).

LOST TRAIL: Lost Trail sits just on the Idaho-Montana border on 93, 42 miles north of Salmon. It has a 1,200-foot vertical drop, with ten runs, two double chairs, and two rope tows. There is a day lodge at the base with a snackbar and rental shop, and lodging can be obtained in Salmon, Idaho, and Darby, Montana. For information, contact Lost Trail, P.O. Box 191, Darby, MT 59829 (tel. 406/821-3211).

MORE IDAHO SKI AREAS

MAGIC MOUNTAIN: Magic Mountain, with a vertical rise of 800 feet, is 35 miles southeast of Twin Falls. The area has 11 major slopes, and the longest run is 1½ miles. There is a cafeteria and day lodge at the base and lodging is available in Twin Falls. For information, contact P.O. Box 158, Albion, ID 83311 (tel. 208/638-5555).

POMERELLE: Pomerelle, in the Sawtooth National Forest near Albion, has a 1,000-foot vertical drop. The terrain is 30% beginner, 50% intermediate, and 20% advanced. It is open six days and five nights a week. Children age 6 and under ski free with a parent. There is cross-country skiing terrain and snowmobiling nearby. For information, contact Pomerelle, P.O. Box 158, Albion, ID 83311 (tel. 208/638-5599).

SILVERHORN: Ten feet of powder falls annually on Silverhorn in the Bitterroot Mountains in the northern part of the state, seven miles south of Kellogg. This area's vertical drop is 1,900 feet and there are 14 runs on 600 acres. It is serviced by two chairs and a rope tow. For more information, contact Silverhorn, P.O. Box 417, Kellogg, ID 83837 (tel. 208/786-9521). The snow phone is 209/786-7661.

SOLDIER MOUNTAIN: Soldier Mountain is located 60 miles southwest of Sun Valley and 12 miles north of Fairfield on 20. There are 36 runs on the mountain with a vertical drop of 1,400 feet. It is served by two double chairs. There is a day lodge and cafeteria at the base. Contact P.O. Box 337, Fairfield, ID 83327 (tel. 208/764-2300).

BALD MOUNTAIN: Located 42 miles east of Orofino and six miles north of Pierce, Bald Mountain has a vertical drop of 975 feet and the runs are served by five lifts. There is a day lodge at the base. For details, contact P.O. Box 1126, Orofino, ID 83544 (tel. 208/464-2311).

COTTONWOOD BUTTE: Five miles west of Cottonwood, the mountain has a 845-foot vertical rise and the runs are served by a T-bar and a rope tow. There is a day lodge and lodging can be found in Cottonwood, Grangeville, and Craigmont. Contact P.O. Box 38, Cottonwood, ID 83522 (tel. 208/962-3831).

KELLY CANYON: The ski area is 25 miles northeast of Idaho Falls on 26. The vertical rise is 870 feet with seven runs and three trails spread over 300 acres. There are three double chairs. Call or write 2767 Surrey, Idaho Falls, ID 83401 (tel. 208/538-6261).

LOOKOUT PASS: Lookout Pass is on 90, 12 miles east of Wallace. Its 850-foot vertical has ten runs, the longest run one mile. It is served by a double chair and a rope tow. There is a day lodge with a cafeteria at the base. For information, contact P.O. Box 983, Wallace, ID 83873 (tel. 208/744-1301).

Chapter XII

WYOMING

1. Jackson Hole Ski Area
2. Grand Targhee
3. Snow King Area
4. Lodging and Dining
5. Daytime and Evening Entertainment
6. Non-Skier Activities
7. Practical Matters
8. Other Wyoming Ski Areas

THERE ARE A DOZEN SKI AREAS scattered around the state of Wyoming, but the majority are tiny "local" areas in the most accepted use of that word. The ski resort of record here is Jackson Hole, set in that particularly scenic northwest corner of the state. Visitors will discover that the landscape is of poster pinup quality, the skiing is exciting on the intermediate to expert levels, and there's a wealth of outdoor activities even for the sedentary. The people "scene," so important to some skiers, is noncompetitive here. Dress is more three-year-old ski parkas than $500 one-piece suits, and après-ski is more country music and T-shirts than jazz and fur coats. Keep that in mind when booking a Wyoming resort!

THE RESORT: "It's the best backyard I've ever found," said a local resident racking cross-country skis next to my downhill ones. His words are the most accurate description of Jackson Hole I've found. The problem in this hole (named Jackson Hole by trapper Davey Jackson in the early 1800s) is deciding how much skiing and which other activities can be fitted into a vacation—and how much sleep one can safely do without. There's downhill skiing at Jackson Hole Ski Area, at that powderhound's mecca Grand Targhee on the back side of the Tetons, and even at Snow King in the town of Jackson. There's cross-country skiing all over the region, sleigh rides in the National Elk Refuge, and snowmobiling in Yellowstone National Park. This is one of the nation's busiest resorts during the summer, but there are far fewer visitors wandering around during the wintertime, so the cowboy bars may be the most crowded spots. Jackson Hole is not for vacationers who want glittery nightlife and ski slopes carpeted with high-fashion outfits. It's for visitors who want first-class outdoor activities to keep themselves entertained—and are satisfied with a limited amount of après-ski entertainment and dining.

THE SKI AREAS: Skiers have their choice of three areas: Jackson Hole Ski

Area, Grand Targhee, and Snow King. Jackson Hole has the reputation for steeps—and greatly underrated intermediate terrain. Grand Targhee is primarily wide-open intermediate terrain and famous for incredible powder days. Snow King is a ski area set at the edge of the town of Jackson, with a base lodge that doubles as the Americana Snow King Hotel's atrium lobby.

1. Jackson Hole Ski Area

THE SKIING: Reams have been written about the experts' terrain on this 4,139-foot-vertical ski mountain, which has—undeniably—an abundance of challenging and "sheer terror" slopes. What's often skimmed over, however, is the variety of intermediate terrain—covering more acreage than exists in many eastern ski areas. The range for intermediates goes from gentle to ultra-challenging, making this a mountain for the intermediate who is interested in improving skills and learning to ski more challenging ski runs. Terrain for novices is limited. When they progress from the beginner's lifts, they make a big jump in terrain tilt.

There are four square miles of terrain at Jackson Hole accessed by six chairs and a tram. The terrain is divided into five difficulty levels. This ski area uses a five-color rating: the traditional green and blue, red rectangles, black and yellow triangles. The green- and blue-rated runs are on a par with those at most areas. Skiers who schuss down the black runs at small "local" ski areas should test these red runs before trying any black slopes. The red runs here are for better than average but not truly advanced skiers—and they would be rated black at many smaller areas. There are several degrees of black here. The red-lined yellow triangles indicate chutes and ultra-steep slopes. If you're hesitant about jumping in—don't!

The novice trails are off the Eagle's Rest and Teewinot chair lifts. They are nicely pitched and wide enough for skiers practicing the basics. (This is a good area for learning the basics, because there are so few beginning skiers here that the classes are relatively small.) The crunch comes when it's time to move over to the blue runs, so pick carefully. Try the South Pass Traverse, a long cat track that crosses other trails back down to the green runs.

The management here understands there's an image problem that is scaring off intermediate skiers, so they've increased grooming efforts to include the smoothing of some 22 miles of trails. The intermediate runs off Casper Bowl and Après Vous chairs receive top priority. The blue runs off both chairs are popular because they are open and usually groomed. Moran and Werner are long runs pitched well for practicing beginning parallel turns. Sundance Gully, a lower mountain trail reached by runs off the Casper Bowl chair, is a fun intermediate cruising run because of the steady pitch and easy curves. Once comfortable on the Casper Bowl area runs, which range from easy to advanced intermediate terrain, take the Ampitheatre Traverse over to the Thunder double chair, the highest of the chairs. Don't let the runs under the lift jolt you: the blue portions of Gros Ventre from the top of this chair all the way to the bottom of the ski area provide 3,000-plus vertical feet of comfortably pitched terrain for cruising or practicing parallel turns.

Intermediates who want to move on to tougher slopes should try some of the red terrain off in the Casper Bowl and Après Vous areas. Most of these runs are groomed and wide enough for some traversing but have a steeper pitch than the blue runs. (In fact, skiers moving up to a Rocky Mountain resort for the first time may find that these runs equate in steepness to the black ones at their smaller "local" areas.) St. Johns, off the Après Vous chair, is a particularly enjoyable red run because of its varying pitches.

Advanced and expert skiers revere this mountain. There are black runs for the barely advanced and others to keep fast-turning skiers grinning while negotiating chest-high bumps or too-steep-to-side-slip chutes. At Jackson, skiers buy a chair-lift ticket, then pay for each tram ride separately. There are several black runs off the chairs, however, most are shorter than the black runs from the top. The real murky terrain is off the tram. The starting point for that "first black run" can be Rendezvous Bowl—despite its reputation and the incredible visual impact from the top. Since the grooming crew began smoothing some parts of Rendezvous Bowl, many barely advanced skiers have worked their way down it. (It's so wide there is plenty of room for long traverses and wide turns.) Once down the uppermost stretch, skiers can find red and blue terrain for the rest of the way.

From the top of the tram, advanced skiers can take black runs from top to bottom, or they can cut down on cat tracks part of the way to ease their legs. Although some Jackson regulars may disagree, an informal survey places the following runs on a scale of light to pitch black. (Factors considered were steepness of terrain and the trail width. The lightest blacks have plenty of room to bail out of fall-line skiing.) Rendezvous Bowl was listed first, then Cheyenne and Laramie Bowls. The High Traverse to Cirque and Pepi's Run came next, followed by Bivouac and the murky Bivouac Woods, all on the upper half of the mountain. South Colter Ridge, Lower Sublett Ridge, and the other long, often bumped and steadily steeply pitched runs on the lower half of the mountain were all rated as solid blacks. When word is passed that the Hobacks are open, knowledgeable skiers head directly to the cutoff, off the Rendezvous Trail, for a special treat. This never-groomed area delivers more than 3,000 feet of memorable steep to steeper (depending on your line) fall-line skiing for experts. (Maintaining good quality snow on the Hobacks dictates when this area opens. It is usually closed by midafternoon, before the sun softens the snow enough for skiers to track up the terrain too much.) The Alta and Expert chutes, labeled with yellow triangles, are among the steepest formal runs in the country. Those with the necessary skills to ski these runs safely will find them on the trail map.

INSIDER'S TIPS: Getting across the skiable mountain (which is 2½ miles wide at the base) is easy if you are aware there are upper and lower long traverses going both ways that bisect most of the trails.

Ask about the host program. At regular intervals, hosts or hostesses wait by the map at the top of the tram to answer skiers' questions about the terrain, then lead a guided tour back down to the bottom.

Temperature inversions aren't uncommon in this valley during midwinter. It can be below freezing at the base area and hot at the top of the mountain. Layer clothes to cope with bitter cold temperatures near the bottom of the mountain (unfortunately where the beginner's runs are set) and the much hotter temperatures at the top.

Pick up a scorecard when you arrive and record the vertical feet you ski each day. Special pins come with records of 100,000 and 150,000 vertical feet, but the owners of the hardiest bodies can earn a bronze buckle for 300,000 feet, a silver buckle for 500,000 feet, and a gold one for a million feet.

MOUNTAIN FACILITIES: There is a cafeteria in the tram building and several other restaurants in neighboring buildings and hotels. Lunch and snack items are available at the mid-mountain restaurant at the base of the Casper Bowl chair lift, and at the Summit cafeteria at the top of the tram. Rental and retail ski shops and the ski school are located in the village center.

JACKSON HOLE / GRAND TARGHEE

SNOW COVERAGE: The average annual snowfall is 33 feet at this area, which is usually open from mid-December to early April. There is snowmaking. As part of this area's effort to attract more intermediates, there is a strong emphasis on grooming approximately 22 miles of primarily beginner and intermediate runs.

SKI SCHOOL: Regular half- and full-day group and private lessons are available as well as other special programs. Because there is so much upper intermediate and advanced terrain here, classes in the upper level skills are popular. The "small class" option is a two-hour class limited to four students per instructor. Children can join the SKIwee ski school. There is a combination childcare/ski-school option. Students in the Mountain Experience class head for less-known runs and secret powder spots with the instructor. (All runs in this "for advanced skiers or better" class are off the tram, and this class must be formed a day in advance. Certain ski instructors can also be hired as alpine guides to lead skiers beyond the area's boundaries. Race clinics are offered.

CHILDCARE: There is a new center, the Kindi School (tel. 733-2292) housing day care and children's ski school at the base of the mountain. Call for details.

RENTAL EQUIPMENT: Both alpine and cross-country rental equipment is available in the ski shops at the base of the ski area.

CROSS-COUNTRY SKIING: There are several cross-country operations in Jackson Hole and an endless choice of untracked terrain in the Grand Teton and Yellowstone National Parks as well as other national forest areas. The **Jackson Hole Cross Country Center,** (tel. 733-2292), headquartered at Teton Village, has a network of double-tracked cross-country trails that link up with the Grand Teton National Park. Contact the center for details about lessons, telemark clinics, ski packages, and backcountry tours. There are several other touring centers, including **Spring Creek Ranch** (tel. 307/733-8833); **Togwotee Mountain Lodge / Rossignol Touring Center** (tel. 307/543-2847), 45 miles north of Jackson; and **Teton Mountain Touring** (tel. 208/354-2768), at Grand Targhee Ski area, which operates a hut system.

HELICOPTER SKIING: High Mountains Helicopter Skiing brings skiers to the peaks in nearby mountain ranges for unforgettable days of skiing untracked snow. For more information, read the section on helicopter skiing in Chapter XVIII, or contact **High Mountains Helicopter Skiing,** Dusty Acres, Jackson, WY 83001 (tel. 307/733-3274).

2. Grand Targhee

THE SKIING: On a powder day Grand Targhee is the place to cruise! The slopes are open and primarily of intermediate grade, so the trip downhill, even in two feet of light white, shouldn't terrify skiers new to powder. The float downhill in fresh light stuff is a real buzz for advanced skiers. Lift lines are rare here, in part because Grand Targhee is so far from major cities. A busy day would be considered far too slow at many other areas Grand Targhee's size.

Three chairs and a tow open up the 2,200-vertical-foot mountain located on the flip side of the Grand Tetons from Jackson Hole. The ski area is technically in Wyoming but only reachable through Driggs, Idaho. It is about a 1½-hour drive from Jackson. The terrain is rated 10% beginner, 70% intermediate, and

20% advanced. Most of the skiable terrain is wide, open slope of gentle or middling steep grade, or lightly gladed terrain (although there is one very steep, treed area for advanced skiers). The trail map lists only the major runs on the 1,500 skiable acres, but the open terrain makes the number of ways down almost unlimited. Intermediates, in particular, will enjoy this mountain. The more they explore the open slopes (snow conditions permitting) off the obvious trails, the more fun they'll have.

Beginners have their own flat section with a few short, wide trails off the Shoshone chair. Intermediates have the majority of the mountain, from the wide-open front faces accessible from the Bannock chair to the gladed area on the far side of the Blackfoot chair. The wide-open, long Crazy Horse Ridge is a popular cruising run, as is Sitting Bull Ridge. The Blackfoot Bowl off the Blackfoot chair is another well-pitched blue slope. The gladed section to the left of the bowl is gently pitched, and in many areas the trees are rooted far enough apart for competent intermediates to enjoy this easy version of tree skiing. Advanced skiers have the Headwall, an open face from the top of the mountain, and neighboring Good Medicine. Bad Medicine, a steep descent through the trees, may be the most difficult terrain on the mountain and is just for expert skiers.

INSIDER'S TIPS: For the most spectacular view of the Grand Tetons (from either Jackson Hole or here), ride up the Bannock chair and follow the Teton Valley traverse along the ski area's edge toward the Fourth of July Bowl, way around the backside of the mountain almost as far as you can go, staying within the boundaries.

The reasonably priced Grand Targhee Express brings skiers staying in Jackson Hole to this mountain for the day. For the days and time schedules, contact the Grand Targhee Resort.

MOUNTAIN FACILITIES: The base area lodge has a cafeteria, a sit-down restaurant, and a ski shop. There are condominiums and hotel rooms at the base (see the Less Expensive section in Section 4 of this chapter for details).

SNOW COVERAGE: The average snowfall is 504 inches a year at Grand Targhee, which is normally open from mid-November to late April. There is no snowmaking. There has been a stronger emphasis on grooming in recent years as management has recognized how much intermediates prefer groomed slopes.

SKI SCHOOL: In addition to the regular group and private lessons, there are powder lessons—on the right days—that are particularly popular with intermediates. On a fresh powder day, early-bird private lessons are available in which skiers beat the lifts. The "experience" classes are for advanced skiers who want 80% skiing in off-trail areas and 20% instruction to cope with the experience. The Small Fry ski school is for children 4 to 7 years of age. There is a ski school/nursery/lunch package.

CHILDCARE: Reservations are required for youngsters in the nursery at the base area. (No diapers allowed.) There is a ski school/nursery option.

RENTAL EQUIPMENT: Rental equipment is available in the base area.

CROSS-COUNTRY SKIING: Set track and telemark lessons are available at the ski school. Ask about day or overnight tours. Teton Mountain Touring has a wide range of options from basic lessons for the inexperienced cross-country skier (and day care for the youngsters) to backcountry touring between huts and custom tours for the more experienced. For information, contact **Teton Mountain Touring**, P.O. Box 514, Driggs, ID 83422 (tel. 208/354-2768).

3. Snow King Ski Area

THE SKIING: The slopes at Snow King Ski Area, which utilizes the dramatic Snow King hotel's atrium lobby as its base lodge, are mostly peopled by locals, hotel guests, and other visitors to Jackson who are taking ski lessons or want a change from the bigger mountain. Two chairs and a tow open up the 1,571 vertical feet of mountainside at this oldest of Wyoming's ski resorts. There is night skiing Wednesday through Saturday at this area, which opened in 1939.

The beginner's area is minuscule, 100 vertical feet accessed by a rope tow. Novices and lower intermediates slide down Cat's Meow, the popular Kelly's Alley and Turnpike off the Rafferty chair. Advanced intermediates and beginning advanced skiers tackle Elk and Grizzly, relatively steep runs off the Snow King chair. Ask a local for the way into Cougar. Advanced and expert skiers steer to Exhibition, then to Belly Roll and Liftline with some terrain too steep to groom.

INSIDER'S TIPS: Locals say this area can be very cold until Valentine's Day because it has a northern exposure, but that also helps make the spring skiing terrific.

MOUNTAIN FACILITIES: The ski shelter at the base has a warming area and a snackbar. The ski-school desk is near the beginner's rope tow. The main base lodge is the Snow King Hotel.

SNOW COVERAGE: There is no snowmaking at this area, which is open from mid-December to mid-April. The lower mountain is groomed regularly, and the upper mountain is done occasionally.

SKI SCHOOL: The ski school director, Bill Briggs, offers a "money-back guarantee." If skiers aren't satisfied with their lessons, they get a second one free. If they still aren't happy, they can have their money back. (The area manager claims that few skiers have asked for refunds.) In addition to the conventional teaching approach, this school promotes an approach called the "Certainty Training Method," an elaborate teaching program available to skiers from 15 years old and up. (For information, contact Snow King.) Ask about the downhill and cross-country touring adventures.

CHILDCARE: There are childcare facilities in the town of Jackson that accept vacationing children.

RENTAL EQUIPMENT: Rental equipment is available.

4. Lodging and Dining

WHERE TO STAY: Skiers who want to walk to the slopes or be within a three-minute shuttlebus ride should stay in Teton Village set at the base of the tram. Other lodging is strung alongside the route into Jackson, 20 minutes away. The lodging in the town of Jackson is generally less expensive, and there is a public bus service to the big ski area. The Snow King Ski Area is located at the edge of town. There is a **central reservations service for Jackson Hole** for information about lodging and reservations (tel. 307/733-4005, or toll free 800/443-6931 outside Wyoming).

There is also lodging at the base of Grand Targhee Ski Area (tel. toll free 800/443-8146), located on the other side of the Tetons.

Ask about the ski combo packages that include a few days at each area.

Most Expensive

The **Spring Creek Ranch,** P.O. Box 3154, Jackson Hole, WY 83001 (tel. 307/733-8833, or toll free 800/443-6139), provides comfortably luxurious accommodations in an isolated setting with a spectacular view of the Tetons. There are hotel rooms as well as condos with two queen-size beds or a king-size bed, rustic rock fireplaces, executive refrigerators, and remote-control TV. Shuttle service to the mountain, several miles away, is available. Rates range from $65 in the single rooms to $155 for a two-bedroom loft for three to four persons.

The **Sojourner Inn,** P.O. Box 348, Teton Village, WY 83025 (tel. 307/733-3657 or 307/733-3657), in Teton Village, has ski-in/ski-out access. The Sojourner provides a basic comfortable motel situation, and has convention facilities for up to 200 people. With 97 rooms, it is the largest and most complete facility in the village, with an outdoor pool, sauna, Jacuzzi, restaurant, and lounge. The Stockman's Restaurant features hearty western fare at reasonable prices, and the Sojourner Lounge has live entertainment frequently. Room rates start at $60.

The **Inn at Jackson Hole** (tel. toll free 800/842-7666) is located at the other end of the base. There is an outdoor pool and a whirlpool, a restaurant, and a lounge on the premises. The rooms are comfortable. Room rates start at $80 for a standard, and mini-suites with a loft area and a kitchenette are available.

The **Jackson Hole Racquet Club Resort** (for information, contact central reservations), with deluxe condominiums, a health club, shops, and restaurants, is located four miles from the ski area. The fully equipped units range from studios to three-bedrooms, and there are private homes for rent in the complex. All guests can use the athletic center's racquetball courts, indoor tennis courts, lap pool, and gym. Room rates begin at $90 a night.

The **Alpenhof Lodge,** P.O. Box 288, Teton Village, WY 83025 (tel. 307/733-3242), with its Bavarian decor, is at the lifts and is rated four diamonds by AAA for service. The rooms are comfortable. The attic rooms with vaulted ceilings and quilts are particularly attractive, but you must walk up from the second floor. The dining room features American and continental cuisine. Economy rooms for two start at $90 and go up to $275 for a two-bedroom suite for four.

Moderate

The **Jackson Hole Realty Company,** P.O. Box 568, Teton Village, WY 83025 (tel. 307/733-7945, or toll free 800/443-8613), manages units in several condominium complexes that range from basic to plush. All units have complete kitchens, and some have fireplaces, washer-dryers, separate dining and living rooms, heated garages, and other amenities. The Sleeping Indian has studios at $216 per person for three nights' lodging and lifts, or you can stay for three nights at the Timber Ridge in a four-bedroom/three-bath with a loft. Group rates are also available in many ranges. There is no communal swimming pool although some complexes do have Jacuzzis. The condos are within sight of the slopes (and many are within walking distance), but there is shuttle service to the slopes.

The **Snow King** (contact central reservations for information) is a hotel/convention center, five blocks from Jackson's main square, with a 1,571-vertical-foot ski area just outside the back door. The rooms are comfortable, and there's a dramatic atrium lobby where guests can watch skiers on the slopes, two restaurants and a lounge, a hot tub, and a heated outdoor pool. Rooms start around $65 a night.

The **Wort Hotel and Convention Center,** P.O. Box 69, Jackson, WY 83001 (tel. toll free 800/322-2727), located in downtown Jackson, is a classic old city hotel with pleasant rooms and two attractive dining rooms and a coffee shop that cater to families and feature western food. Rates vary slightly with the seasons, but average $65 per night for attractive single rooms up to $300 for the Governor's Suite, which includes two bedrooms and a sitting room. There's a bus stop for skiers just outside the hotel.

Less Expensive

The **Hostel,** Teton Village, WY 83025 (tel. 307/733-3415), at the base of the ski area, is inexpensive and good for families. Each room has two twin beds and a double bunk. The Buffalo Pit lounge has a large stone crackling fire where you can grill your own steaks, and after dinner you can enjoy skiing and mountain-climbing movies. A room for one or two persons is $33, and for three of four, $44. They also run Pooh Corner, the only childcare center on the mountain, which is open during the hours the tram is in operation.

The **Virginian Lodge,** P.O. Box 1062, Jackson, WY 83001 (tel. 307/733-2792), has a range of accommodations, including some configurations especially good for a family. Located at the joining of U.S. 26, 89, and 187, one mile west of the center of Jackson, this motel has 150 rooms. The restaurant features home-style cooking and is open for breakfast, lunch, and dinner. The lodge has neither pool nor Jacuzzi, but will arrange transportation to three ski areas. The rates range from $31 for one person in a room to $53 for a two-room suite (with a $4 charge for extra persons).

There is a variety of basic motel-style rooms and condominiums in the Teewinot Lodge, Targhee Lodge, and Sioux Lodge Apartments at the base of Grand Targhee ski area. Contact **Grand Targhee** (tel. toll free, 800/443-8146, 800/433-0637 in Wyoming) for prices and details. Amenities include the restaurant at the ski lodge, a hot tub, and a heated swimming pool. With certain packages, children 12 and under can stay free, ski free, have free lessons and nursery care, and free rentals. Lift/lodging packages are available.

A Unique Place to Stay

The reasonably priced **Teton Teepee Ski Lodge,** Alta, Wyoming, via Driggs, ID 83422 (tel. 307/353-8176), on the road to Grand Targhee, is an incredibly large wooden teepee-like structure with a massive public eating and game room area in the center surrounded by small, attractive bedrooms with private baths. There are double doors between the bedrooms and the communal area for sound privacy. The lower floor of the lodge is divided into pleasant dorms (with quilts on the bunk beds) used by children whose parents are staying in the private bedrooms. There's even a hot tub. The meals are family style and the après-ski noshers can just take hot chocolate, coffee, or beer—all part of the package price. Transportation to and from either Grand Targhee or Jackson Hole ski areas is available. With advance arrangements, there is also transportation to and from the Jackson Hole and Idaho Falls airports to the lodge, which is 15 minutes from Grand Targhee. Call for package prices.

WHERE TO EAT: Because the restaurants are shared by ranchers, cowboys, skiers, and other vacationers, there's an eclectic group of menus here. Everything from honest-to-goodness sourdough pancakes to fine French cuisine can be sampled in this valley.

Expensive

The **Alpenhof Lodge** dining room, in Teton Village (tel. 733-3462), with its old-world atmosphere, is a four-star restaurant open for breakfast from 7:30 to 10:30 a.m., for lunch from 11:30 a.m. to 2 p.m., and for dinner from 6 to 10 p.m. The continental cuisine includes bratwurst and sandwiches for lunch, ranging from $4 to $5.50. Dinner entrees include venison, elk, and other unusual wild game dishes, plus veal and steak. Entrees range from $10 to $17. Meals for two —chateaubriand, rack of lamb, and others—run $39 to $45. Reservations are not required, but are recommended.

The **Granary** at the Spring Creek Ranch (tel. 733-8833), one in the string of posh Colony Resorts, offers gourmet meals in the understated dining room with a high soaring ceiling and spectacular views of the Snake River through the glass window wall. There are fixed-price dinners (in the mid-$20s) for a set five-course meal (the menu changes daily), or you can order off the à la carte menu. Dinner is from 6 to 10 p.m. The Granary is in the main building at Spring Creek Ranch, up a side road partway between the ski area and Jackson Hole.

Reserve your evening at **Lost Horizons** (tel. 307/353-8226) well in advance, because seating is limited in this unique restaurant. Shoes are left at the door and drinks are served in the lower lounge. Only diners are allowed up the spiral staircase to the second-floor dining room, with its cathedral ceiling, Oriental accents, and glass window wall filled with the nearby Tetons. The owners spend the day preparing a fixed-price, ten-course gourmet meal, a blend of Japanese and Chinese tastes, which takes diners about three hours to enjoy. Lost Horizons is located on the access road to Grand Targhee. This restaurant's uniqueness makes it worth the drive from Jackson. Consider skiing Grand Targhee during the day and stopping at Lost Horizons on the way home. Be sure to reach the restaurant in time for drinks so you can unwind while watching the Tetons bathed in the alpenglo.

A sleigh ride to a heated cabin for a steak dinner is one way to spend an evening. For information or reservations for this experience, stop by the **Hideout Restaurant** at the Casper chair lift or call 733-6657. The price for an adult for the sleigh ride and meal is in the mid-$20s; children's meals are considerably less.

Moderate to Expensive

Dietrich's Bar and Bistro, the upper-level lounge in the Alpenhof Lodge (tel. 733-3242), is only open for lunch from 11:30 a.m. to 2:30 p.m., but does a thriving après-ski business, and there is live entertainment most nights. The limited menu has sandwiches, pizza, salads, and soup. Ski movies and sporting events are shown on a giant-screen TV.

Stieglers, in the Jackson Hole Racquet Club (tel. 733-1071), is a warm, quietly elegant Austrian restaurant open for lunch and dinner. Lunch features interesting sandwiches, bratwurst, and linguine, from $4 to $6. Dinners are primarily Austrian, ranging from wienerschnitzel to tournedos Kaiser Franz, and entrees run $8 to $16. Call for reservations. Lunch hours are noon to 2 p.m. Tuesday through Friday and dinner hours are 6 to 10 p.m. Tuesday through Sunday.

The **Cadillac Grill,** 56 N. Cache (tel. 733-3279), on the square in Jackson Hole, has an art deco feel with its white tablecloths and burgundy booths, and pictures of Cadillacs adorning the walls. Open for lunch and dinner, it features various ethnic dishes, pasta, plus steaks and burgers. The restaurant transports people from Teton Village to the square via their double-decker bus, leaving Monday through Saturday at 7 p.m. The Cadillac Grill also has a lounge area.

The **Blue Lion,** at 160 N. Millward (tel. 733-3912), features creative cuisine. This small, attractive restaurant is open for lunch Monday through Friday from 11:30 a.m. to 2 p.m. and for dinner from 6 to 10 p.m. Entrees run $10 to $14. On Sunday the restaurant is open from 10:30 a.m. to 2 p.m. for champagne brunch. Pastries are baked on the premises. Reservations accepted.

The most popular restaurant at the base of the ski area is the **Mangy Moose** (tel. 733-4913). The lively bar is usually full of diners waiting for their turn to head to the dining room and enjoy barbecued ribs, steak, or chicken. The decor is rustic, the atmosphere is casual, and the prevailing mood is laid-back, although the conversations about which ski runs were best that day can get pretty heavy. Hours are 5:30 to 10 p.m.

Less Expensive

Nellie's, at 802 W. Broadway in Jackson Hole (tel. 733-7999), is a family restaurant with that first-class coffeeshop look associated with many of the more popular restaurant chains. Breakfast features Nellie's cakes and waffles, most in the $3 to $4 range; the luncheon menu contains sandwiches disguised under unusual names, from $3 to $5; and dinners, including country chicken and a 16-ounce prime rib, go from $7 to $16. Juniors and seniors menus are available for light eaters. Hours are 7 a.m. to 10 p.m. Nellie's also has a lounge.

The **Sweetwater Restaurant,** a local's favorite, is set in a rustic log cabin at the corner of King and Pearl (tel. 733-3553). At lunch, served from 11:30 a.m. to 2:30 p.m., soups and sandwiches are specialties. Dinners, from 5:30 to 9:30 p.m., feature lamb, seafood, and Greek specialties. Meals run $6 to $12.

Jedediah's Original House of Sourdough, one block east of the town square in Jackson at 135 E. Broadway (tel. 733-5671), is housed in a historic log cabin and features authentic sourdough cooking. It's popular for breakfast, from 7 a.m., lunch is from 11 a.m., and dinner is available from 5:30 p.m. Tuesday through Saturday.

5. Daytime and Evening Entertainment

SHOPPING: Lots of interesting shops are tucked in side streets around Jackson Square, the town's focal point, with its walk-through arches made of antlers. There is everything from rock and T-shirt shops to a taxidermy museum and art galleries.

ENTERTAINMENT: The **Million Dollar Cowboy Bar** on Jackson Square (tel. 733-2207) is a popularized barn of a place with lots of action swirling around the pool tables, on the dance floor, and in between drinkers sitting on the saddles lining the long bars. Another popular spot where cowboys and tourists coexist is the **Wort Silver Dollar Bar,** in the Wort Hotel (tel. 733-2190). Here skiers set their drinks on the 2,032 silver dollars embedded in the famous Silver Dollar Bar. Over the bar is a burnt-leather mural depicting the history of the area. The **Mangy Moose Saloon** in Teton Village (tel. 733-4193) is usually busy at night. Check the local guides to see where the live entertainment is that evening.

6. Non-Skier Activities

Choices range from sleigh rides through the elk herds to a snowcoach ride through Yellowstone National Park to Old Faithful. There are lots of outdoor activities here for the sedentary person.

The 45-minute **sleigh or wagon rides** through the elk herd wintering in the refuge just outside of town are very popular. Leave your car in the visitor center or take a van from town (check locally for the schedule), then join one of the tours that leave several times each day. Dress warmly.

The south gate of **Yellowstone National Park** is just 55 miles away. The park isn't open to cars, but you can go snowmobiling or take a snow-coach tour to see **Old Faithful.** Stop by the **Jackson Hole Chamber of Commerce Information Center,** 532 N. Cache (tel. 733-3316), for more information about the park. For reservations on the snow coaches or lodging reservations in the park, contact **TWS services** (tel. 344-7311). For information about snowmobile rentals (it's a 1½-hour ride into Old Faithful), contact **Flagg Ranch** (tel. 733-8761, or toll free 800/443-2311).

Ranger-led snowshoe hikes, cross-country skiing, and limited snowmobiling are options in **Grand Teton National Park.** For information, contact Grand Teton National Park, P.O. Drawer 170, Moose, WY 83012 (tel. 307/733-2880). The Moose Visitor Center, 12 miles north of Jackson, is open every day except Christmas from 8 a.m. to 4:30 p.m. There is a **Fur Trade Era museum** at the Moose Visitors Center.

The **Wildlife Taxidermy Museum** is located in a working taxidermy shop in the Grand Teton Plaza on West Broadway (tel. 733-4909).

For information about **ice skating** in the town rink, call 733-3316. Rentals are available.

To warm up, try the **Teton Hot Pots** (tel. 733-7831) at 365 N. Cache or the **Granite Hot Springs,** which can be reached by driving 23 miles south, then snowmobiling or cross-country skiing in ten miles. (Contact the chamber of commerce for more specific directions.)

7. Practical Matters

GETTING THERE: Air service to Jackson has an erratic history since jets were first allowed to land in this national park area just a few years ago. Last year, American flew direct from Chicago, Continental came from Denver, and another airline had flights through Salt Lake City. The list is constantly changing and more airlines are flying direct from major cities. Call central reservations for the most current list of scheduled and chartered flights.

Avis, National, Budget, and Hertz **rental cars** are available in the region.

Jackson Hole is located in northwestern Wyoming just south of Yellowstone. By **auto** it can be reached via all-weather highways that connect with I-90 on the north, I-25 to the east, I-80 to the south, and I-15 to the west. This valley is 265 miles from Salt Lake City.

Grand Targhee is located nine miles east of Driggs, Idaho, just inside the Wyoming border on the western side of the Tetons. The ski area is 42 miles west of Jackson Hole via a mountain pass, and 87 miles northeast of Idaho Falls. Airline gateways include Idaho Falls and Jackson Hole. With advance notice, a resort shuttlebus will meet incoming flights.

MOVING AROUND: A car isn't a necessity here but it makes moving around a lot easier if you're not staying in Teton Village or at the base of Grand Targhee. The **START bus service** has scheduled runs between Jackson, Teton Village, and the Jackson Hole Racquet Club from 7 a.m. to midnight.

The **Caribou Cab Company** (tel. 733-2888) has 24-hour service.

TOURIST INFORMATION: For lodging reservations or more information about the Jackson Hole area, contact **Jackson Hole Central Reservations,** P.O. Box 510, Teton Village, WY 83025 (tel. 307/733-4005, or toll free 800/443-6931 outside Wyoming). For information or reservations at Grand Targhee, contact **Grand Targhee Ski Area,** Driggs, ID 83422 (tel. 307/353-2304, or toll free 800/443-8146, 800/443-0637 in Wyoming).

For **emergencies** in Jackson Hole, call 911. The local **hospital** is St. John's (tel. 733-3636).

8. Other Wyoming Ski Areas

SNOWY RANGE: Three chairs and a T-bar open up the 900 feet of vertical at this ski area in Medicine Bow National Forest. It is open from mid-November to late April. There are cross-country trails threading Medicine Bow National Forest. Lodging is in nearby Centennial and Laramie. For more information, contact the Snowy Range Ski Area, Centennial, WY 82055 (tel. 307/745-5750).

Chapter XIII

NEW MEXICO AND ARIZONA

1. Taos
2. Ski Apache
3. Red River
4. Angel Fire
5. Sandia Peak
6. Other New Mexico Ski Areas
7. Fairfield Snowbowl
8. Apache Sunrise
9. Other Arizona Ski Areas
10. Arizona Cross-Country Skiing

MOST TRAVELERS HEAD TO Arizona or New Mexico for warm weather vacations: floating on Lake Powell, golfing in Scottsdale, looking over the rim of the Grand Canyon, or exploring art galleries in Santa Fe or Taos. The reality is that in both states you can mix and contrast ski days with golfing, exploring Indian reservations and art galleries, or playing tennis. New Mexico boasts Taos, Ski Apache, and several other areas. Arizona has two ski areas, one just a short drive from the Grand Canyon, and the other on the eastern side of the state.

Skiers choosing the Rocky Mountain Powder in New Mexico get a bonus. Although most of the ski areas are up above the 9,000-foot level, skiers can combine a cold-weather vacation with some warm-weather sightseeing in historic and culturally rich towns, such as Taos, which are thousands of feet lower and usually many degrees warmer. The only full-fledged resort in New Mexico is Taos, but Ski Apache is right up there in the number of skier visits. Smaller ski areas with good bed bases, such as Angel Fire and Red River, which markets heavily for the family crowd, are also popular with skiers from such states as Oklahoma and Texas.

For a ski report about any ski area in this state, call the **Ski New Mexico snow phone:** 509/984-0606. It runs from November to Easter.

1. Taos

THE RESORT: Taos is unique. The European charm here lures skiers into re-

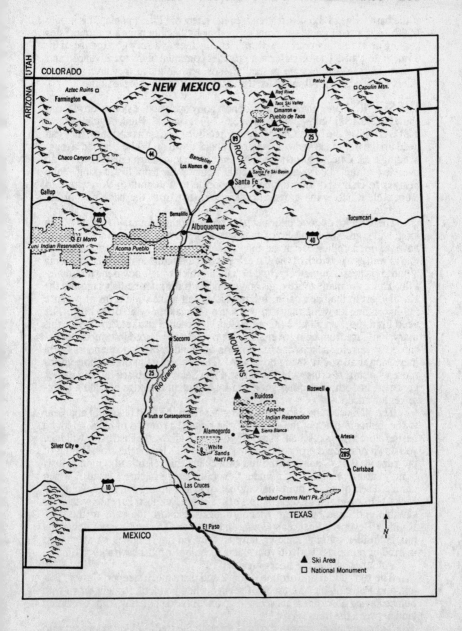

turning year after year after year. Visitors either love it because of the closeness —the valley is tiny; most guests eat meals where they are staying and spend the week in ski school with the same group—or they leave because there's little glitter amid the substantial quality. The village consists of a handful of condominiums and inns perched in the small (but not flat) floor of this box canyon. The sign at the base lodge of the ski area reads to the effect of "Don't panic. This is only 1/30th of the mountain"—a point gasped at by beginners and intermediates looking up at the infamous Al's Run. Actually there's a very good range of intermediate trails. The black terrain provides continual highs for advanced and expert skiers. Ski weeks are pushed at Taos, and although they aren't cheap, skiers know what they'll spend for the vacation before they leave home.

THE SKIING: Seven chairs, a poma, and a pony open up the slopes, bowls, and chutes at Taos Ski Valley, which has a 2,612-foot vertical. Rank beginners have a little ski hill at the base. Once they can handle wedge turns and stop, they can head up the front face and work their way back down on White Feather, a long, winding trail. Once comfortable, adventuresome low intermediates can get an overview of the 1,000 skiable acres by heading up the front lifts, taking White Feather to chair six, then taking Honeysuckle to Totemoff to Winkelreid to Rubezahl, which is the green-rated long run-out from the back side of the mountain.

There's a lot of good intermediate terrain on this mountain, ranging from long, wide, groomed trails to open slopes with varying pitches. Intermediates have the open, rolling Porcupine and Powderhorn on the front side of the mountain as well as a network of wide, nicely pitched interconnecting trails, including Sinuoso, Lower Stauffenberg, and Firlefanz, which wiggle down the mountainside. There are many more trails and open bowls for intermediates around the Kachina lift in the back basin. Intermediates can make wide turns or practice fall-line skiing knowing they can bail out on Shalako, a wide-open bowl. The need for a short uphill hike (about 30 feet) to reach Hunziker Bowl keeps this marvelous face from being overskied. It's more for advanced intermediates because the terrain suckers one in. It starts out mildly, but the steepness keeps increasing until you're flying downward. There's a plateau on the bottom for those who start to cruise a little too fast. Papa Bear, rated black but sometimes groomed smooth, is another good run for skiers on the edge of calling themselves advanced.

The advanced and expert terrain ranges from the light black of Papa Bear to the midnight black of the chutes off the ridge. The depths of black might be best explored in a ski-school class. (If your skills allow, the instructor will take you down runs you'd probably never ski alone.) Al's Run is the most famous of the runs at Taos. Skiers get the fun of tackling this relentlessly, monstrously bumpy surface, running right under the entire length of chairs 1 and 5, which parallel each other. (Count the number of skiers opting for the bailout catwalks.) However, Al's Run is more work than fun for most. For runs with more variable and large but more friendly moguls, explore the runs to the side: Rhoda's Revenge, Spencer's Bowl, and Inferno. They all weave down the mountainside, offering quieter havens with varying degrees of steepness, marred by bumps to work on your skiing technique or just have a good time.

And these aren't the steepest runs. . . .

The runs under and around chairs 2 and 6 are much steeper. Castor, Pollux, and Reforma blend a touch of vertigo when you look straight down with bumps having downsides that seem to go on forever set on tiny strips of cleared land between the trees.

There are black runs that weave through the trees, taking skiers out into quieter parts of the mountain away from all sounds and other people. The Walkyries, which drifts through open woods, is the easiest of these trails. El Funko, where one steep face is followed by a moguled catwalk sidling sideways in the woods to another steep face, is another such run. Then there is the tree skiing!

The description of expert terrain could go on indefinitely because there is so much of it here. (And that's why there are so many good skiers in ski-school classes here. The combination of a "tune-up" to eliminate bad habits and the opportunity to ski some of these runs lure them to Taos.)

Skiing off the ridge (for experts only) is allowed at times. Skiers must sign out with the ski patrol at the top of chair 6 and must ski with at least one other person. Maps outlining the ridge runs are located at the top of chair 2.

Insider's Tips

If you'll be at Taos for several days you should consider signing up for classes even if you think you're "past ski school." They'll show you places on the mountain you'd never find yourself, and possibly, you'd never ski, in addition to improving or refining your skills.

Look for the martini trees. They grow best toward the end of the week.

Mountain Facilities

There's a base lodge with a snackbar, ski-school office, ski shop, rentals, and ticket windows. The Phoenix, at the base of the Kachina lift, has a restaurant. There's lunch in the St. Bernard Rathskeller and on the inn's Hondo deck, where the specialties are fajitas and stuffed potatoes. La Croissanterie, by the beginners area, is a pleasant spot for lunch, and the "Out of Bounds" Food Emporium has sandwiches.

Snow Coverage

Snowfall here averages 315 inches annually at this area normally open from mid-November to mid-April. There is snowmaking on 25% of the mountain. Green and blue trails are groomed regularly.

Ski School

At Taos, week-long visitors are encouraged to go into a ski-school class every morning. The group, especially at the upper levels, often evolves into a sort of "rat pack" that skis together, has a good time, and—by the way—learns a lot. Because of the terrain here, many advanced and expert skiers take classes. Even youngsters vocally anti–ski school enjoy it here. Teenagers are grouped together (and often decide to ski together in the afternoon). Children between the ages of 7 and 12 go into Junior Elite, which includes ski school in the morning and supervised skiing in the afternoon. Youngsters between the ages of 3 and 6 can be placed in the Kinderkaefig, a combination skiing/snow-play/nursery-school program.

There are three- and four-day ski weeks available in conjunction with three- and four-day packages. Lessons can be either in the morning or the afternoon.

In addition to the ski-week classes (which stay as a unit all week), there are daily group and private lessons. Beginners can get a Yellow Bird ticket that includes lessons.

Childcare

Youngsters ages 3 to 6 can join the Kinderkaefig.

Rental Equipment

Rental equipment is available at the shop in the Ski Center at the base. Shops in the town of Taos also rent equipment.

Cross-Country Skiing

There's terrain in the canyon for cross-country skiers to explore, and telemarkers use the mountain.

WHERE TO STAY: Skiers who want to immerse themselves in the "Taos experience" take the week-long packages, which include staying at a lodge in the ski valley, skiing, meals, lift, and lessons. (Even experts come to Taos for a week-long refresher course from the super-experts who teach here.) Generally the rooms in the lodges are small but comfortable. The push here is to keep visitors on the slope or busy elsewhere so they'll only use the rooms for sleeping. There are several condominium complexes, but guests who want to eat meals out will have a problem. There's one public restaurant in the evening; the lodges open their restaurants to the public only if their guests haven't filled up the space. However, there are many excellent places for dinner on the road down to and in the town of Taos. Many of the valley guests drive down to explore the town of Taos at least once during their stay. Visitors who want a selection of restaurants, plus the option to stroll through art galleries and the town's historic plaza every day, should stay in the town of Taos. There are several good hotels. Most of the lodges in the ski valley want ski packages, but some, especially the condo complexes, will "fill in" with shorter days.

For detailed information on packages and current prices, get this year's brochure from the **Taos Valley Resort Association,** Taos Ski Valley, NM 87571 (tel. 505/776-2233, or toll free 800/992-7669). The prices are too varied to summarize accurately here. Package prices vary greatly according to the lodge and the type of rooming configuration desired. However, when broken down and compared to stays at other resorts, Taos packages are skewed toward the upper middle range. They are not inexpensive, but they are not the highest-priced trips. In terms of value for your money, a vacation here should be placed on or near the top of the scale.

The **Hotel St. Bernard,** Taos Ski Valley, NM 87571 (tel. 505/776-2251), has such a following that returning guests are allowed to make reservations starting June 1, newcomers can make reservations starting July 1, and by fall most of the rooms are gone. The rooms in the main hotel are small but attractively decorated, with quilts on the beds. The rooms in the chalet next door are a little bigger. Meals include a lavish breakfast buffet, a hot lunch, and leisurely gourmet dinner by a chef whose recipes have appeared in national food magazines. There's a rathskeller with nightly entertainment and a spa.

The **Hotel Edelweiss,** Taos Ski Valley, NM 87571 (tel. 505/776-2301), is a charming European-style inn. When on a package ski week, guests stay in comfortable rooms, have breakfast in the inn's restaurant, the Croissanterie, and go to the St. Bernard for dinner. There's an attractive spa room and a sauna.

Ski packages at the **Thunderbird Lodge** place guests in small but comfortable rooms in the main lodge or in larger rooms in the chalet. Breakfast and lunch are usually buffet style and the dinners are gourmet. There are saunas and a whirlpool, and nightly entertainment in the bar.

Condos range from the modern, luxurious ambience of the **St. Bernard Condominiums** to the more rustic, older units at the **Kandahar** and the **Rio Hondo.** (The latter two are located across the beginner's hill, away from the main village.) Room configurations vary greatly. The St. Bernard Condominiums offer a package option to dine at the hotel. The other condo complexes offer just the unit or the unit and skiing. (Skiers must get groceries in the town of Taos.) Contact central reservations for detailed information about the various complexes.

The **Austing Haus Hotel,** P.O. Box 8, Taos Ski Valley, NM 87571 (tel. 505/

776-2649), a few miles down the road from the ski valley, has quiet and spacious but spartan rooms. There's a hot-tub room and a restaurant offering tasty food in large portions. Room rates range from $52 to $88 per night depending on the number of persons.

The condos at the **Quail Ridge Inn** (tel. 505/776-2211, or toll free 800/624-4448), 12 miles down the road from the ski valley, are small but very attractive with their adobe walls, fireplaces, and modern kitchens. Amenities include a swimming pool, indoor tennis courts, hot tub, sauna, and a restaurant.

The rooms at the historic **Taos Inn** (tel. 505/758-2233, or toll free 800/TAOS-INN) in the town of Taos have a cool elegance with their adobe walls, hand-woven Zapotec bedspreads, and tiling. Most rooms have fireplaces. Packages include lodging and lift tickets. There's a Jacuzzi room, lobby lounge, and a good restaurant in this very charming inn. Single nights are available here. Room rates run $50 to $85 double.

WHERE TO EAT: Guests staying at the Hotel St. Bernard, the Hotel Edelweiss, the Thunderbird Lodge, and the Innsbruck Hotel have meals included in their packages.

More Expensive

Guests in condos can make reservations at the **Hotel St. Bernard** (tel. 776-2251) or the **Thunderbird Lodge** (tel. 776-2280) and can dine there when space is available. The food is French gourmet at the St. Bernard and continental cuisine at the Thunderbird. Prices usually run in the low or mid-$20s.

La Croissanterie (tel. 776-2301) in the Hotel Edelweiss is open for gourmet breakfasts and lunches featuring croissant sandwiches, salads, and quiche. Lunch runs between $7 and $10. Espresso and pastries are available during the early après-ski hours.

Dining in the elegant **Casa Cordova** (tel. 776-2200), once a hacienda, is a pleasant experience. Relax with a drink in the wing chairs before the fireplace in the lounge, then dine leisurely surrounded by works from local artists. The menu is a combination of Italian and European dining. Entrees range from $9 to $20. Casa Cordova is located eight miles up the road toward the ski valley. Dinner starts at 6 p.m. Monday through Saturday.

The dining is leisurely at the **Brett House Restaurant** (tel. 776-8545) in the historic Dorothy Brett House on the Taos Ski Valley Road. The specials are written on the chalkboard every night, but the emphasis is on international cuisine and there is an extensive wine list. Dinners are from 6 p.m. Tuesday through Saturday. Call for the evening menu and reservations. Entrees range from $13.50 to $18.

Moderate to More Expensive

The restaurant at the **Hondo Lodge** (tel. 776-2277) is the only public restaurant in the valley that is open in the evenings. The menu in this rustic, casual restaurant stretches from a good salad bar to steaks, seafood, veal, and ribs. Most meals cost between $13.50 and $22.50. Open nightly.

New Mexican cuisine and continental fare can be chosen by diners relaxing in the southwestern atmosphere at **Doc Martin's** (tel. 758-2233) in the historic Taos Inn. Dinners run $6 to $15. Reservations are recommended. Open nightly.

The **Apple Tree,** located in an old adobe house at 26 Bent (tel. 758-1900), in Taos, specializes in serving very fresh foods in creative international styles. Entrees range from $7 to $14. Hours are from 11:30 a.m. to 9:30 p.m. daily.

The **Glass Dining Room** at the Austing Haus (tel. 776-2649) serves steaks and creatively prepared seafood, veal, and more in hearty portions. The chef promises that if diners don't like what's on the menu, he'll make any dish they want, if he has the ingredients. This is the closest public restaurant to the ski valley. Dinner is from 6 to 9 p.m. nightly.

Less Expensive

Dolomite Pizza (tel. 776-8153) delivers within the ski valley.

There will be far more locals than skiers in the clean, casual **Comidas del Mantes** (tel. 758-9317) on South Sante Fe Road, but this is the place for great New Mexican cooking. The chef promises "good home-cooking" in large portions. Both Mexican and American food, including steak and trout, are on the menu. Ranging from $2 to $6. Hours are 5 to 9 p.m.

ENTERTAINMENT: The emphasis here is really on conversation with interesting old (and new) friends. The Thunderbird, the Hotel St. Bernard, and Hotel Edelweiss have entertainment most nights. It varies from guitar players to talent shows. There are movies many nights at the Hondo Lodge. Down in town, there is often entertainment at the **Ski Valley Junction** (tel. 776-2265), a casual, open place where skiers can also get burgers and steaks, the **Kachina Lodge** (tel. 758-2275), the **Sagebrush Inn** (tel. 758-2254), and the **Taos Inn** (tel. 758-2233).

SHOPPING: Ski shops and a few galleries are about the extent of what's available in the ski valley. Stop by the **Twining Weavers** and the gallery in Arroyo Seco on the road down to town. Taos is renowned for its art galleries, many specializing in Indian and southwestern art, and boutiques. Start at the historic plaza in the center of town and just keep strolling. Visit the **Grycner Gallery,** a mile north on N.M. 3 from the Ski Valley junction, the **Stables Art Center,** on one side of the Taos Inn, and **Martha of Taos,** on the other side of the Taos Inn, for women's southwestern clothing.

NON-SKIER ACTIVITIES: Most visitors take at least a day off to explore the town of Taos. The **Taos Pueblo** is the oldest continuously occupied adobe "condominium" in the country. Still home for many Indians, the pueblo, which is open daily, welcomes visitors. Explore the shops and galleries stretching out from the historic Taos Plaza. The **Millicent Rogers Memorial Museum** (tel. 758-2462) has one of the most outstanding collections of Indian and Spanish-Colonial arts and crafts in the southwest. It is located on Museum Road, a half mile south of the junction of N.M. 3 and U.S. 64 to the ski valley. The **Kit Carson Home and Museum** is located on Old Kit Carson Road, a few blocks from the plaza. The restored **Martinez Hacienda,** located two miles west of the plaza, is open to the public. The **Ernest Blumenschein home,** three blocks west of the plaza, is open to the public. (He was co-founder of the Taos Society of Artists.) For information about these three historic sites, call 758-0505. Ask locally for a guide map and more information detailing the galleries and the many places to explore in this region.

GETTING THERE: Taos is in a box canyon at the end of U.S. 64, approximately 20 miles from the center of the town of Taos. It is a 2½-hour drive from Albuquerque International Airport. Many major airlines land at Albuquerque, and many car-rental companies have counters at the airport. **Mesa Airlines** (tel. toll free 800/545-5119, 800/432-5267 in New Mexico) has three round-trip flights between Taos and Albuquerque on Saturday. **Faust Transportation** (tel. 505/758-3410 or 505/758-1443) has shuttle service to the ski valley and offers charter and taxi service.

MOVING AROUND: Once in the ski valley, skiers don't need a car. However, anyone wanting to move between the valley and the town frequently should have private transportation. There's a free shopper's shuttle from the ski valley to the town of Taos on Tuesday and Thursday.

TOURIST INFORMATION: For more information about Taos, contact the **Taos Valley Resort Association,** Taos Ski Valley, NM 87571 (tel. 505/776-2233, or toll free 800/992-7669). Also contact the **Taos Chamber of Commerce** (tel. toll free 800/732-TAOS). For emergencies in the ski valley, call 776-8118 for **fire** and 758-1911 for an **ambulance.**

2. Ski Apache

THE RESORT: The skiing at this area, owned by the Mescalero Apache Indian tribe, is at the top of the tallest mountain in the region. Lodging is in the Ruidoso area, 16 miles below via a curvy road which descends more than 2,000 feet. Ski Apache vies with Taos for the top number of skier visits in the state. It's popular with Texans because El Paso is just 135 miles away. Many Mexicans ski here too.

THE SKIING: A gondola, seven chairs, and a tow open up the terrain at this 1,800-vertical-foot ski area in southern New Mexico where the weather is usually warmer than one would expect at a ski resort. The terrain is rated 40% beginner, 40% intermediate, and 20% advanced. There's a short beginners' chair at the base, then skiers can move onto Snow Park off the midway unloading platform on the Lincoln chair. They can also use chair 7. However, the green runs off chair 7 are also the run-out for many of the advanced trails. Smokey Bear is for lower intermediates. Intermediates can explore the open Capitan area; one side is usually left moguled.

The gondola climbs up the ridge, and there's skiing on both sides (ensuring that some trail will be in the sun). The open, treeless Apache Bowl is rated by regulars as the most entertaining place on the mountain and this "giant funnel," as one skier describes it, pulls you into Upper then Lower Deep Freeze. The rest of the ride down is "like a toboggan run" that skier added, because you don't know what's around the next corner.

On the other side of the ridge, intermediate runs—including the blue cruiser called The Meadows—come off the top. Heading down the ridgeline, expert trails spill off. There's a catwalk (listed as green but really for competent beginners) that runs across many of the black trails so skiers can bail out at certain points. Try Incredible and Lower Peebles first, then move onto runs like The Terrible and Geronimo, which are relatively narrow and usually heavily moguled.

Mountain Facilities

There's a main day lodge with food facilities, a bar, and a sport shop. The Gazebo Snack Bar and the Lookout Snack Bar are both located near the top of the mountain.

Snow Coverage

There's an average snowfall of 180 inches each year at this area, which is usually open from Thanksgiving to Easter. There's snowmaking in the beginner areas and partway up the mountain.

Ski School
The ski school offers group lessons twice a day and private lessons.

Childcare
There is no nursery at the mountain. Children 6 and older can go into class lessons. Younger children who take a private lesson will get a free lift ticket.

Rental Equipment
There's a rental shop at the base.

Cross-Country Skiing
There are no cross-country facilities in the area.

WHERE TO STAY: There is no lodging on the mountain. Skiers must stay in the Ruidoso area. The luxurious **Mountain of the Gods Inn** (tel. 505/257-5141, or toll free 800/545-9011), also owned by the Mescalero Apache Tribe, is the place everyone talks about in this region. Located four miles from Ruidoso and 20 miles from the ski area, this mountain-contemporary building with a soaring copper fireplace in the center of the lobby has comfortable rooms with private balconies, dining facilities, including a fine dining room, and lounges. There is live entertainment many evenings. The inn runs a shuttlebus to the ski area. Prices go from approximately $68 for a double on weekend nights to $80 for a suite. Packages are available.

There are many other lodging places in the area. For a listing, contact the **Ruidoso Chamber of Commerce**, P.O. Box 698, Ruidoso, NM 88345 (tel. 505/257-7359). **AAA Reservations**, P.O. Box 873, Ruidoso, NM 88345 (tel. 505/257-2557, or toll free 800/345-4848 outside New Mexico), can provide all types of lodging, airport transportation, and more.

WHERE TO EAT: There are many restaurants and bars in the town of Ruidoso. There's a fine dining room at the **Inn of the Mountain Gods**.

The **Inncredible** (tel. 336-4312), a restaurant/saloon in Alto, serves steaks, seafood, and prime rib.

The popular **Cattle Baron**, 657 Sudderth Dr. (tel. 257-9355), has steaks, seafood, and a salad bar.

ENTERTAINMENT: The **Inncredible** (tel. 336-4312) and **The Bull Ring** (tel. 258-3555) are popular drinking spots.

GETTING THERE: The closest large airport is in El Paso, Texas, 135 miles from Ruidoso (Ruidoso has a small airport). Several major airlines fly to El Paso, and rental cars are available at the airport. The ski area is off N.M. 37, 16 miles from Ruidoso up a very curvy road that ascends more than 2,000 vertical feet.

TOURIST INFORMATION: For information about skiing, contact **Ski Apache**, P.O. Box 220, Ruidoso, NM 88345 (tel. 505/336-4356). The snow phone is 505/257-9001). Contact the police for **emergencies** at 257-7365.

3. Red River

THE RESORT: Red River is a party town that caters to families. There's even a place for youngsters to play in the evening! The skiing is geared toward intermediates on the slopes, which rise directly from town.

THE SKIING: Four chairs and two pony lifts open up the 1,524-foot vertical at Red River. Terrain is rated 40% beginner, 45% intermediate, and 15% advanced. The Lil Blue lift may have the distinction of being the lowest, slowest chair in the Rockies, a bonus for teaching never-evers and young children. It's near the Yellow chair on an open beginner's slope. Beginners can graduate to the top of the mountain quickly here. They head to Dipsy Doodle, a gentle road that winds down the mountain. The Gold chair at the top opens up blue terrain. Kit Carson down to Broadway to Big Vanilla is a popular intermediate's route down. Advanced skiers could start on Ute Chute or Chicken Drop. Then they might move to the more narrow Mine Shaft, Airplane Hill, and Landing Strip—New England–style runs that have sharp pitches, level off, then drop sharply again. Trails have been cut in the West Basin and a chair lift is planned within the next year or two.

Many skiers here for a week choose to spend a day or two at other nearby ski areas. Taos ski area is approximately 50 minutes away, Angel Fire is approximately 40 minutes away, and Rio Costilla is approximately 45 minutes away.

Mountain Facilities

The base lodge has a cafeteria, rentals, a retail shop, and ski school. The Lifthouse, at the bottom of the main chair, has a lounge and restaurant serving sit-down lunches and dinners. The Ski Tip Restaurant is at the top of the mountain.

Snow Coverage

During a normal year the area receives approximately 165 inches of snow and is open from Thanksgiving to late March. Snowmaking covers 75% of the mountain.

Ski School

The ski school offers group and private lessons. Children ages 4 to 12 can go into Kinderski, a program with morning and afternoon lessons and lunch. Parents can take part or all of the program.

Childcare

Children 4 to 12 can go into Kinderski. There are nurseries in town (contact the chamber of commerce for numbers).

Cross-Country

For information about cross-country skiing in Red River, contact **Enchanted Forest Cross Country Ski Area** (tel. 754-2374).

WHERE TO STAY: The **Red River Chamber of Commerce** (tel. 505/754-2366, or toll free 800/348-6444) can answer questions about lodging and handle reservations. A sampling includes:

The **Lifts West Condominium Hotel** (tel. 505/754-2778 or 505/754-6185, or toll free 800/221-1859) has comfortable units. These condos have fireplaces, microwave ovens, and balconies. The ones on the upper floor have high ceilings and lofts. There's a massive stone fireplace in the atrium lobby and an indoor Jacuzzi.

Sit on the balcony of one of the **Woodland Condominiums** (tel. 505/754-2303, or toll free 800/762-6469 outside New Mexico) and listen to the nearby rushing river. Units have fireplaces. There's a free shuttlebus to town.

Locals claim **True's Bed and Breakfast**, P.O. Box 588, Red River, NM 87558 (tel. 505/754-2224), serves "the best cooking in the West." True's takes individuals and small groups in the five bedrooms and three baths. They also handle a six-bedroom house with a wood-burning stove in town.

WHERE TO EAT: **Texas Red's Steakhouse** on Main Street (tel. 754-2964) is the restaurant name most visitors pass on. Steaks are the main fare served in the Old West atmosphere here. Entrees range from $6 to $20. Hours are 5 to 9 p.m. seven days a week during the winter.

Locals swear that **True's Family Restaurant**, 558 High St. (tel. 754-2286), behind City Hall, has the best cooking in the West. The menu at this moderately priced restaurant includes American and Mexican fare.

ENTERTAINMENT: There are several swinging bars in this town, so ask a local which ones are in fashion. Check out the action at **Texas Red's** (tel. 754-2964), the **Motherload** (tel. 754-2213), and **Kate and Gary's** (tel. 754-2593).

NON-SKIER ACTIVITIES: Snowmobiling is popular in this area. Contact the local chamber of commerce for names of companies that rent machines and lead tours.

The town of Taos, with its historic plaza, dozens of art galleries, and the Taos Pueblo, is approximately a one-hour drive from Red River.

GETTING THERE: Red River is located 12 miles east of Questa, which is on N.M. 3. The closest airport is in Albuquerque, 165 miles away. Many major car-rental booths are located at the Albuquerque International Airport. Continental Trailways has daily transportation for Sante Fe, Taos, and Questa. Skiers can make arrangements with **Faust Transportation** (tel. 505/758-3410) for a shuttle to the ski area. There is a landing field for private planes at Angel Fire, 30 minutes away.

MOVING AROUND: Most skiers have a car. Depending upon one's choice of lodging, skiing, restaurants, and shops can all be within walking distance.

TOURIST INFORMATION: For information about the **Red River Ski Area,** contact the ski area at P.O. Box 900, Red River, NM 87558 (tel. 505/754-2223). Contact the **Red River Chamber of Commerce** (tel. 505/754-2366, or toll free 800/348-6444 outside New Mexico) for information about lodging in town or about the ski area.

4. Angel Fire

THE RESORT: Angel Fire is a major grouping of condominiums set at the base of a ski area designed mainly for intermediates. The condos are set on an open, wide floor of the Moreno Valley in the Sangre de Cristo Mountains. It's part of a triangle—Taos, Red River, and Angel Fire—in northeast New Mexico. Skiers at one resort for a week often take a day or two to sample the others. Angel Fire is popular with Texans and Oklahomans because it's about a five-hour drive from the Amarillo area.

RED RIVER / ANGEL FIRE

THE SKIING: Six chairs open up this ski area with runs over two sides of a mountain. Terrain at the 2,180-vertical-foot area is rated 35% beginner, 47% intermediate, and 18% advanced. The ski area has 30 miles of runs. Beginners can move over much of this mountain. Headin' Home, a 3½-mile-long green run that meanders down the mountainside, is the most popular beginners' run. Hallelujah, on the back side, is another favorite. Most of the blue runs on the mountain are wide and have steady pitches. Hully Gully, which offers varying pitches and some bumps, is one of the most challenging intermediate runs. The black runs aren't real long, but they can challenge advanced skiers. Bumps build on Minder-Binder, site of the USSA/FIS finals in 1983, and Nice Day. There are plans to expand this area considerably; meanwhile lift lines are rare.

Mountain Facilities

There are eating places plus a rental and a retail shop at the base. Food is also available in the Back Basin. There's a warming hut at the top of the mountain.

Snow Coverage

Angel Fire receives an average of 135 inches each year, and there is snowmaking on 60% of the mountains. The area is usually open from mid-November to early April. Grooming is treated seriously here.

Ski School

The ski school offers both group and private lessons. Children from the ages of 5 to 11 can enter the Junior Mountain Masters, a full-day program geared for each specific age group. SKIwee is for ages 2 to 11.

Childcare

The **Little Angels Learning Center** (tel. 377-2301) will take toilet-trained children from 6 weeks to 11 years old. They have a babysitting referral service for infants.

Rental Equipment

Rentals are available at the base and at other ski shops in the area.

Cross-Country Skiing

The **Angel Fire Nordic Center** (tel. 377-2301) is headquartered at the Angel Fire Country Club. Cross-country trails are maintained. Lessons and equipment rentals are available. The center runs moonlight tours.

WHERE TO STAY: Angel Fire offers very reasonable midweek packages. Most of the more than 600 condominium units in Angel Fire Village range from one to three-bedrooms. Condos range from spartan rooms to plush units with private Jacuzzis (at the Gold Dust). Condo prices range from $130 a night for a one-bedroom to $226 for a three-bedroom/three-bath. For lodging reservations, contact the **Angel Fire Resort Chamber of Commerce** (tel. toll free 800/545-4022) or **Angel Fire Resort** (tel. toll free 800/633-7463).

WHERE TO EAT: The **Angel Fire Country Club** (tel. 377-2301), where guests are treated to spectacular mountain views, is open to the public and offers lunch and continental dinners. Entrees go from $8 up.

Aldo's Lift Restaurant (tel. 377-6681) is right at the base. This casual spot is open for lunch, which averages $5, and dinner, averaging $12.

NON-SKIER ACTIVITIES: The Moreno Valley Recreation Area, north of the Valley Market, offers snowmobile rentals. Taos, with its art galleries and the Taos Pueblo, is just 26 miles away.

GETTING THERE: Angel Fire is located 26 miles east of Taos via 64 to N.M. 38. The resort is a three-hour drive from Albuquerque and most skiers arrive in private cars. Mesa Airlines flies from Albuquerque to the ski resort twice a day.

MOVING AROUND: Most skiers arrive in cars. However, there is a shuttlebus that tours the village and moves skiers to and from the far parking lots.

TOURIST INFORMATION: For more information, contact **Angel Fire Resort**, Drawer B, Angel Fire, NM 87710 (tel. 505/377-2301, or toll free 800/633-7463).

The emergency numbers are 377-2308 for **ambulance** and **fires.** The **sheriff's number** is 377-6565.

5. Sandia Peak

When skiers and sightseers (heading up for the spectacular view) step into the Sandia Peak Tram, they don't see any ski runs. The runs are on the back side of the mountain. (Those who don't want to ride the tram can drive 16 miles from the city to the day lodge at the base of the wooded ski area.) Sandia Peak is popular with Albuquerque residents, who often zip the six miles from the city line to the tram for a half day on the slopes. The 25 runs is primarily beginner and intermediate terrain on the 1,700-vertical-foot mountain. The terrain is rated 35% beginner, 55% intermediate, and 10% advanced at this area serviced by three chairs and two pomas. Cross-country ski trails start near the top of the tram.

For more information, contact **Sandia Peak Ski Area,** 10 Tramway Loop NE, Albuquerque, NM 87122 (tel. 505/242-9052 for the ski area or 505/296-9585 for the main office).

6. Other New Mexico Ski Areas

SANTA FE: Although the Santa Fe ski area is primarily a day area for locals from the town of Santa Fe 16 miles away, some visitors sneak in a few days of skiing in between exploring the mouthwatering dining, the many galleries, and the historic aspects of this town.

The 1,600-vertical-foot ski area has 32 runs with terrain rated 20% beginner, 40% intermediate, and 40% advanced. A triple chair, two double chairs, three pomas, and two Mitey Mites service terrain with a combination of open bowl and trail skiing.

For more information about the ski area and packages with lodging in town and skiing, contact **Santa Fe Central Reservations** (tel. 505/983-8200, or toll free 800/982-SNOW in New Mexico) or write Santa Fe Ski Area, 1210 Luisa St. No 10, Santa Fe, NM 87501.

PAJARITO: Located seven miles west of Los Alamos, Pajarito tends to be a community ski area. However, many skiers are discovering that it has some very challenging terrain. On its 1,200 vertical feet, the terrain is 25% beginner, 25% intermediate, and 50% advanced, spread over 30 runs. The area is open on Wednesday, weekends, and federal holidays (except Christmas Day), usually from mid-December to April. Los Alamos can house a limited number of skiers.

For information, contact the **Los Alamos / White Rock Chamber of Com-**

merce, P.O. Box 888, Los Alamos, NM 87544 (tel. 505/662-8105). For snow reports, call 505/662-7669.

RIO COSTILLA SKI AREA AND SUMMER RESORT: Set in the Costilla Valley, two triple chairs, a double chair, and a pony tow open up 2,150 vertical feet of mountainside, including a large snowbowl. The terrain is rated 20% beginner, 55% intermediate, and 25% advanced. Lodging for 432 people is available on the mountain.

For information, contact **Rio Costilla Ski Area and Summer Resort**, P.O. Box 59, Costilla, New Mexico 87524 (tel. 505/758-1800).

SIPAPU: Sipapu is a 900-vertical-foot area in the Carson National Forest in the mid-northern part of the state. It appeals to the advanced intermediate and beginner alike, as the terrain on its 18 runs is rated 20% beginner, 50% intermediate, and 30% advanced. Two pomas and a chair provide uphill transportation. Contact **Sipapu**, Route Box 29, Vadito, NM 87579 (tel. 505/587-2240).

SUGARITE: Sugarite, 12 miles from Raton, has an 825-foot vertical. The terrain on the 17 runs is rated 29% beginner, 42% intermediate, and 29% advanced. Being in high mesa country, the area offers spectacular scenery and a wide variety of skiing conditions on their yearly 120 average inches of snow. Lodging for 1,300 skiers is in nearby Raton.

For information, contact **Sugarite**, P.O. Box 1043, Raton, NM 87740 (tel. 505/445-5000).

CLOUDCROFT: Cloudcroft is a small but good family area, due to its variety of terrain off five lifts. On its 750-foot vertical, there is 45% beginning terrain, 25% intermediate, and 30% advanced. There are wide, open spaces for cross-country. Nearby lodging can accommodate 750 people about 2½ miles from Cloudcroft in the southern part of the state.

For information, contact **Cloudcroft Visitors Bureau**, P.O. Box 125, Cloudcroft, NM 88317 (tel. 505/682-2733).

ARIZONA

Arizona is considered desert country—except, of course, for the Grand Canyon areas—but there are actually five downhill ski areas, one with a 1,700-foot vertical and another with a 2,300-foot vertical! Most of the skiers here are Arizonans, but southern visitors with ski bags have reportedly been seen coming into the state—not heading away from it. This is a state where you can have a hot/cold-weather vacation. Consider spending half the week golfing in the Phoenix/Scottsdale area, then head for ski country. Or how about combining a trip to Lake Powell or a visit to the Grand Canyon, a short drive from Flagstaff, with a few days on the slopes? It works in this state!

There are several sources for information about arranging a hot/cold-weather vacation in Arizona. Contact the **Arizona Office of Tourism**, 1480 E. Bethany Home #180, Phoenix, AZ 85014 (tel. 602/255-3618), for information about the ski resorts and touring the state. Also the **Phoenix and Valley of the Sun Convention & Visitors Bureau**, 505 N. 2nd St., Suite 300, Phoenix, AZ 85004 (tel. 602/254-6500). They also have a visitors' hotline (tel. 602/254-6500). For **hotel reservations** in Phoenix, Scottsdale, and even Sedonia and at the Grand Canyon National Park Lodges, call 602/257-4111, or toll free 800/528-0483 outside Arizona. Ask for a copy of the Visitors Guide. See Tourist Information under the ski areas for specific information about Apache Sunrise and Fairfield Snowbowl.

7. Fairfield Snowbowl

THE SKIING: This ski area in the San Francisco Peaks, towering above the rugged Coconino National Forest, has terrain rated 30% beginner, 40% intermediate, and 30% advanced on its 2,300 vertical feet of mountainside, the highest in the state. Four chairs open up the 32 trails and some open slopes. Regulars say it's a good area for both beginners and advanced skiers. Beginners have their own section around the Aspen and Hart Prairie chairs. Then they move to the runs around the Sunset chair or unload midway on the longest chair. Advanced skiers can start on Casino or Tiger, then move onto the often-moguled White Lightning. The better skiers hike over to the Upper Bowl area when it's open. Tree skiing is popular at this area.

Mountain Facilities

There are lodges, with cafeterias and ski-accessory shops, a ski school, and a nursery for children ages 5 months to 5 years.

Snow Coverage

Fairfield Snowbowl receives an average of 250 inches of snow yearly, and is usually open from Thanksgiving to Easter.

WHERE TO STAY: There are some condos at the base and many hotels and motels in nearby Flagstaff. For information, contact the **Fairfield Flagstaff Resort**, P.O. Box 128, Flagstaff, AZ 86002 (tel. 602/526-3232). For a luxurious vacation, check into one of the resorts in Sedonia so you can golf one day and drive 40 minutes to the ski slopes the next. (See the above addresses for the Phoenix and Valley of the Sun Convention & Visitors Bureau, or the State of Arizona, for where to write about lodging in Sedonia.)

GETTING THERE: Fairfield Snowbowl is located off I80, seven miles outside of Flagstaff. There is a shuttlebus from Flagstaff, a convenience when the roads are bad.

TOURIST INFORMATION: For information about the ski area, contact **Fairfield Snowbowl**, P.O. Box 1208, Flagstaff, AZ 86002 (tel. 602/779-6127, or toll free 800/352-3524). For the snow report, call 602/779-4577.

8. Apache Sunrise

THE RESORT: Apache Sunrise, on the Fort Apache Indian Reservation in the White Mountains, is busy on weekends, but practically empty during the week. It's a four-hour drive from Phoenix, Albuquerque, or Tucson.

THE SKIING: Seven chairs and three surface lifts open up some 41 trails on three interconnected mountains at Arizona's largest ski area. The 1,700-foot vertical has terrain rated 30% beginner, 40% intermediate, and 30% advanced. Beginners have the entire bottom of the mountain here. (And there is a guaranteed "learn to ski" program here for first-timers.) Sunrise boasts the best intermediate cruising in the Southwest, according to the San Antonio (Texas) Ski Club. The intermediate runs are "a football field" wide in places. Advanced skiers start on Superstition and Lupe's Rainbow, then head toward Cyclone Circle, where the runs are short but challenging. There is night skiing on Friday and Saturday.

Mountain Facilities

There is a base lodge with a cafeteria, bar, and ski rental and sport shop. The mountaintop lodge has a restaurant.

Snow Coverage

This area receives an average of 250 inches of snow annually and is usually open from mid-November to late April.

WHERE TO STAY: There is no lodging at the base. Skiers stay in the Sunrise Lodge, with its indoor pool and restaurant, three miles away, or in other condos or lodges on the road or in Pine Top or Lakeside, 30 miles away. Call **Sunrise Central Reservations** (tel. toll free 800/55-HOTEL or 800/882-SNOW) for information about ski/lodging packages and reservations for lodging.

GETTING THERE: From Phoenix, take Ariz. 87 to Payson. Take 260 to Show Low and continue to Sunrise. There is a private airport in Springerville, 16 miles away. Car rentals are available.

TOURIST INFORMATION: Contact **Sunrise Ski Resort**, P.O. Box 217, McNary, AZ 85930 (tel. 602/735-7676, or toll free 800/722-SNOW or 800/882-SNOW).

9. Other Arizona Ski Areas

MOUNT LEMMON SKI VALLEY: This is a day area for Tucson residents, 35 miles away. A chair and two surface lifts open up the 900-foot vertical ski area. There is a rental shop, ski school, and snackbar. Ski season runs from late December through early April.

For information, contact **Mount Lemmon Ski Valley**, P.O. Box 612, Mount Lemmon, AZ 85619 (tel. 602/576-1321). The snow phone is 602/576-1400.

10. Arizona Cross-Country Skiing

There's a surprising number of cross-country operations in this state. Contact each company for complete details.

Alpine Ski Tours (tel. 602/339-4574, 602/339-4470, or 602/339-4434), located in Alpine near the New Mexico border, offers cross-country skiers 40 miles of trails. Rentals and instruction are available.

The **Forest Lakes Touring Center** (tel. 602/535-4047), located at Forest Lakes, 36 miles northeast of Payson, boasts the General Crook Trail, apparently the longest cross-country trail in the state. Lessons, rentals, tours, and cabins are available.

Greer Ski Area (tel. 602/735-7560), located in Greer in the White Mountains, has 25 miles of trails. Rentals, lessons, and tours are available.

Hannagan Meadows Lodge (tel. 602/399-4370), 22 miles south of Alpine, has 25 miles of trails. Lodging is available.

The Montezuma Nordic & Mormon Lake Ski Touring Centers are 25 and 28 miles southeast of Flagstaff. The **Mormon Lake Ski Touring Center** (tel. 602/354-2221) has a groomed 19-mile trail system and the **Montezuma Nordic Center** (tel. 602/354-2240) has 16 miles of groomed trails. Lessons, rentals, and tours are available. For information, contact the centers at P.O. Box 18, Mormon Lake, AZ 86038.

Chapter XIV

MONTANA

1. Big Mountain
2. Big Sky
3. Bridger Bowl
4. Red Lodge
5. Other Montana Ski Areas
6. Montana Cross-Country Skiing

MONTANA'S MOUNTAINS collect the same light powder as the other Rockies! But in this state, the light snow falls on several ski areas, including resorts and ski towns that cater to families. As one local said, "You won't find wild nightlife here—but you will get good entertainment at Big Mountain and Big Sky." Family-priced resorts, good and comparatively inexpensive food, and low skier counts (would you believe 14 cars in a parking lot) are the trademarks of Montana's ski areas.

Every winter Travel Montana, the state's tourism department, publishes a guide to Montana skiing that outlines all the possibilities, from alpine skiing at resorts to Nordic skiing in Yellowstone or to hot springs in the wilderness. For a copy of the guide (plus an accommodations guide, vacation planner, and state map), contact **Travel Montana**, Dept. of Commerce, Helena, MT 59620 (tel. 406/444-2654, or toll free 800/548-3390 outside Montana).

1. Big Mountain

THE RESORT: Big Mountain is an accurate name for this ski area. A definite surprise, tucked away in northern Montana not too far from the Canadian border, it is perhaps better known to Canadians from Alberta, who come down here on weekends, than to Americans in California or the Rockies. However, this mountain is a find! The terrain open to skiers is vast, with a variety of wide trails, open slopes, and some tree skiing. When you are skiing on the front side, the town of Whitefish and Whitefish Lake are always beneath your feet. There's a growing base of lodges and condos with enough restaurants to feed the skier population, including those up for the day from nearby Whitefish. It's a laid-back area where dress is casual, the prices are reasonable, and children carpet the slopes. The slopes are not crowded during the week, and there's an effort to bring skiers up in midweek. Ask about special breaks for bringing children.

THE SKIING: Six chairs, a T-bar, and a platter open up 2,145 feet of vertical on

Big Mountain, where the front and back sides of the mountain boast very different terrain. There's a formal list of trails, but good skiers have most of the mountain. The front side has a classic mix of trail skiing and open-bowl skiing, occasionally dodging snow ghosts (wind-blasted snow and ice-laden trees), always looking down at a valley. The back side of the mountain has a completely different feel: it's quiet, the trails are cut through trees, and the views are of other mountain peaks.

Novices start on a slope serviced by a platter lift and then move on to a triple chair. Once they can stop well enough to negotiate some blue terrain, they can head up the mountain and take Easy Street, the long beginner's trail (which has some blue at the top) that winds around one edge of the ski area. Then they can move to the back side of the mountain where there are a few green and some easy wind-sheltered blue trails.

Intermediates and better skiers who like to cruise will enjoy Toni Matt, a sort of ridge run with plenty of room for wide turns. Slalom, off the T-bar is another popular run for locals, especially during night skiing. Hogan and Hogan's East are other usually well-groomed blue runs.

Advanced skiers have several open slopes and endless variations of tree skiing, especially in the Good Medicine area. School Run to Lower Mully's is an interesting way down. Inspiration is another good choice for advanced cruising.

Insider's Tips

The fastest way up the mountain—especially if there is a weekend crowd—is to take the Great Northern and the Glacier View chairs, which are newer and faster than the Going-to-the-Sun chair.

Big Mountain runs the North American Ski/Yachting Championships every spring. Call for information about this dual-sport competition.

Mountain Facilities

There's a base lodge with a cafeteria and a convenience store, several restaurants in nearby lodges, the Big Mountain Ski Shop, a ski hut near the Great Northern chair with snacks some days, and a mountain photography and general store. The Summit House has food.

Snow Coverage

The average annual snowfall is 245 inches at the top, 131 inches at the base. There is snowmaking in some high-traffic areas. The beginning and intermediate runs are groomed regularly and others when needed. Currently the area is open from late November through April, but the exposure of the expansion terrain may allow the ski area to stay open longer.

Ski School

There are half- and full-day as well as private lessons. Mountain guides are available, for a fee, to skiers who want to learn where to ski on the mountain. Parents must deliver and pick up their children from ski-school classes; the ski school will not take youngsters to and from the childcare center.

Childcare

The Kiddie Korner is located in the Alpinsnack Day Skier Center. Advance notice is required for babies under 1 year of age.

Rental Equipment

Both regular and high-performance equipment rentals are available in the Big Mountain Ski Shop. Equipment for children 6 and under is half price.

Cross-Country Skiing

There is a cross-country touring center at the base. A three-mile cross-country trail starts from the top of the Tenderfoot chair lift and nearby forest roads can be explored. Cross-country skiers can use the chair lifts here when properly ticketed. There are lighted groomed tracks on the Whitefish Lake Golf Course in town.

WHERE TO STAY: There are a few lodges with ski-in/ski-out access and several lodges and condominiums within walking distance of the lifts. (There is only a small convenience store on the mountain, so skiers must pick up supplies for condos in the town of Whitefish.) Some skiers choose to stay at the motels or a lodge in nearby Whitefish, a popular summer resort town. A few lodges have shuttles to the mountain, but transportation is easiest with a private car. There is a **central reservation number** (tel. 406/862-3511) which you can use to make reservations for all the lodging at the base of the mountain. This service will also provide information on places to stay in Whitefish, and if you have a specific location in town, they will make the reservation. Many lodges have special children's stay-free and ski-free packages during low season and discounts at other times. Ask for details.

The **Anapurna Alpine Homes**, P.O. Box 55, Whitefish, MT (tel. 406/862-3687), at the base of the mountain, offers a wide variety of units, all within walking distance of the slopes. In some cases one can ski in and ski out. The units are privately owned homes or condominiums that are completely furnished. Sherpa has a swimming pool and whirlpool. All units are rented on a nightly basis, and prices range from $68 to $267 per unit.

The **Alpinglow Inn**, P.O. Box 1770, Whitefish, MT 59937 (tel. 406/862-6966; call collect to make reservations), at the base of the ski slopes, allows one child per adult free in a room. There is a heated outdoor pool and whirlpools, and a restaurant with tall glass windows opening on a spectacular view. Prices range from approximately $42 for one down to $17 each for six in a room. Packages with lodging, lifts, and meals are available.

The owners and other guests are friendly at the **Kandahar Lodge**, P.O. Box 1659, Whitefish, MT 59937 (tel. 406/862-6098), where skiers are encouraged to gather around the massive stone fireplace in the sunken living room of this natural cedar building with windows of etched glass depicting mountain forest scenes. There's a separate lounge room where guests without kitchens can leave drinks and snacks for après-ski. You can book a comfortable single room up to a two-bedroom suite with a kitchen. Room rates start at approximately $68 for a single. There are two whirlpools and a restaurant at the lodge, and the American plan is available. The lodge is ski-in, but a shuttlebus takes skiers to the slopes, a short walk away.

The condos at the **Edelweiss**, P.O. Box 846, Whitefish, MT 59937 (tel. 406/862-5252), with fireplaces and oak accents, are very comfortable. The studio, one- and two-bedroom units are located at the base of the slopes. There's an indoor spa and sauna room. Rentals run approximately $105 to $195.

Hibernation House (tel. 406/862-3511) is economy lodging a short hike from the slopes. This place offers bed-and-breakfast in motel-style rooms, and has a large lobby area for mingling, a hot tub, and a video game room. Call for rates. **Ptarmigan Village**, P.O. Box 458, Whitefish, MT 59937 (tel. 406/862-3594), offers complete condominium units and private homes, fully equipped including complimentary wood. If you stay there, you'll need a car, as it's a five-minute drive to the slopes. Rates run from a room for two at $60 to a unit for nine at $155. They give 20% discounts for stays of five nights or longer.

The attractive **Grouse Mountain Lodge**, 1205 U.S. 93W, Whitefish, MT

59937 (tel. 406/862-3000, or toll free 800/321-8822, 800/621-1802 in Montana), is adjacent to a 15-km (9 mile) cross-country touring center. This AAA four-diamond lodge is comfortable, with nice-looking, reasonably priced rooms and deluxe suites. There is an indoor pool, sauna, and spa. Logan's Bar and Grill, set in an attractive dining room, features continental cuisine. A shuttlebus takes skiers to the slopes at Big Mountain, eight miles away. Room rates, double occupancy, are approximately $78. (Set this lodge in a megaresort and the prices would leap.)

WHERE TO EAT: There are a half dozen restaurants on the mountain, including the ski area's cafeteria. The style of restaurants is varied, as is the type of food offered. The town of Whitefish, down the mountain, also has many restaurants.

More Expensive

Frederic's, 130 Central Ave. (tel. 862-7362), is a casual place offering nicely prepared beef, seafood, and a few unusual Oriental dishes. Entrees range from $10 to $20. Hours are 6 to 10 p.m. nightly, and reservations are suggested.

Logan's Bar and Grill, in Grouse Mountain Lodge, 1205 U.S. 93W (tel. 862-3000), offers continental fare in an attractive dining room with mountain scenes etched in glass panels. Full dinners, including chicken Cordon Bleu, campfire grouse, and duckling, range from $8.75 to $17. The lighter fare includes burgers or shrimp, and runs $5.75 to $7. Reservations are suggested. Dinners is from 6 p.m. Monday through Saturday, and from 7 p.m. on Sunday.

Moderate to Expensive

The **Snowgoose,** at the base of the mountain (tel. 862-4733), serves breakfast, lunch, and dinner, either by the scramble cafeteria system or in their dining room by a large fireplace, where an atrium offers diners a view of the mountain. Breakfasts, from $3, start at 8:30 a.m.; lunches are salads, burgers, and sandwiches in the $4 to $5 range. Dinner from 5:30 to 9 p.m. stretches from ribs and chicken to fish and pasta, priced from $8 to $14. Stop by after skiing to refuel on appetizers with a drink.

The **Hellroaring Saloon and Eatery,** also at the base of Big Mountain (tel. 862-6364), is open for lunch and dinner. Lunches feature sandwiches, a salad bar, soup, and stuffed baked potatoes. Prices are in the $3.25 to $4.25 range. They have an après-ski oyster bar, and dinners include steaks, chicken, and other specialties for very reasonable prices. Hours are 10 a.m. until 10 p.m. or later.

The **Alpinglow Inn** (tel. 862-6966) overlooks the picturesque Flathead Valley, and is located in the center of Big Mountain Village. Arched large windows around the dining room open up a gorgeous view. It is open to the public for breakfast and lunch from 7:30 a.m. to 2 p.m., and for dinner from 5:30 p.m.

Less Expensive

The **Bierstube** (tel. 862-3028) is a funky spot with entertaining adult grafitti on the walls (not a place for small children with sharp eyes, but definitely for adults with an earthy sense of humor). It was justly named "one of the great ski bars of the West" by *Ski* magazine. Burgers and chicken go for $2.50 to $7.50. Hours are 10 a.m. to 2 a.m. Monday to Thursday and 8 a.m. to 2 a.m. Friday to Sunday.

Moose's on the Mountain (tel. 862-3514) serves soup, pizza, and sandwiches from 10 a.m. to 10 p.m. and Italian dinners from 5 to 9 p.m. In warmer weather they serve tacos, burritos, and cocktails on the deck. Pizzas range from

$4 to $11, spaghetti dinners begin at $4, and sandwiches are in the $3 to $4 range. There is also Montana-style gambling on the premises.

ENTERTAINMENT: In the base area there is live entertainment at the **Snowgoose, Moose's on the Mountain,** and the **Hellroaring Saloon and Eatery.** Hours and nights vary, so check locally for entertainment schedules. There's always foot-stompin' music at the **Bierstube.**

Whitefish also has its share of lively local night spots. Just walk down the main street and step into the bars to see where the action is. The bars ranges from Old West atmosphere to the yuppy look. Stop in at **Stump-Town Station** and look at the old photographs showing the region in the pioneering days.

SHOPPING: Big Mountain Chocolates, in a little log cabin in the base area, stocks European chocolates and gourmet hard candy.

NON-SKIER ACTIVITIES: Evening sleigh rides are available several days a week. Call 862-2538 for information. There is snowmobiling in the area but not at the mountain.

GETTING THERE: Big Mountain is near the crossroads of U.S. 93 and U.S. 2, approximately nine miles up a winding but maintained road from the town of Whitefish. **Cascade** and **Delta Airlines** fly into Kalispell, approximately 30 minutes from the ski area. There is charter service to and from Calgary for weekend and week-long trips. Charters from northwestern U.S. cities were under discussion; ask for details. **Amtrak** stops daily in Whitefish.

GETTING AROUND: The mini-village at the base of the ski area is small enough that everything is within walking distance. If you're staying in town, a private car is the easiest means of transportation. There is a daily shuttlebus from Whitefish to the ski area for a minimal fare. Schedules are posted in the motels and lodges. Some accommodations in town and on the road to the mountain have shuttle service. Ask central reservations for the details. You can also use **Whitefish Sober Chaufeur Taxi** (tel. 862-7733).

TOURIST INFORMATION: For general information about the ski area, contact **Big Mountain,** P.O. 1215, Whitefish, MT 59937 (tel. 406/862-3511).

For **emergencies** occurring during ski hours, report to the lift operators at the base of each lift or directly to the ski patrol. From 4:30 to 10:30 p.m., contact the desk clerks at any hotel. After 10:30 p.m., contact the desk at Hibernation House.

2. Big Sky

THE RESORT: The slopes at this ski area are skewed toward intermediates, but there is plenty for beginners and some pleasant cruising terrain and a few good bump runs for advanced skiers. The clientele is a casual crowd on site for good skiing and friendly times rather than a hot après-ski scene. There is good lodging and dining at and very near the base of the lifts.

SKIING: Moving skiers around without a wait is a high-priority item at this ski area, which has a lot of terrain and rarely enough skiers to call the place crowded. Two gondolas, as well as three double chairs, a triple chair, and a rope tow, open up 45 miles of groomed trails on terrain rated 25% beginner, 50% intermediate, and 25% advanced.

Novices start on the Lone Wolf chair, then move up to the top of gondola 1 for views with their trip down Mr. K. Lower intermediates can then take the Lone Peak chair, above the gondola, and ski the bowl, then slide to the Big Rock Tongue area to the Bozeman trail for a long downward run.

Intermediates have a variety of interesting runs off gondola 2, the Ram's Head chair, and the Mad Wolf chair. Calamity Jane is one of the easier popular blue runs. Elk Park Ridge, with its long, steady downward pitch, is a good cruiser. Tippy's Tumble and Big Horn are also popular because they are long, wide, and well-pitched blue runs. Ambush is the intermediate bump run, short enough so the end is near but the bumps aren't allowed to build too high.

Advanced skiers could start in the Sundown section of the bowl area off Lone Peak chair. One local claims he can spend a day on the steeper South Wall taking different fall lines every time. Mad Wolf is the advanced skiers' bump run. There's a very steep face at the top, then lots of bumps through the middle section until the trail connects with Big Horn and turns into an intermediate-level run-out. Narrow and steep War Dance, with a headwall halfway down, also build good bumps.

Insider's Tips

To follow the sun, ski the Mad Wolf chair first, then head to the bowl or to the gondola 2 area. In the afternoon, ski the front side and the Ram's Head chair.

Some advanced skiers trek over to the country club for steep, open-bowl skiing or some tight tree runs. Check to see if it's open. To get there, ride the Lone Peak chair, then take the Little Rock Tongue traverse and hike uphill.

Mountain Facilities

Seven restaurants, five bars, shops, the ski school, and more are located in the two malls at the base of the lifts.

Snow Coverage

There is an average annual snowfall of more than 400 inches at Big Sky, which usually stays open from mid-November to mid-April. Modern grooming equipment is utilized primarily to keep the green and blue slopes in good condition. The black runs in the bowl area are "skier groomed."

Ski School

Regular group and private lessons are available from a staff of certified American and Austrian professionals. A modified version of GLM is offered. Children 6 and older can join the Kinderstadt ski school, which includes four hours of instruction and lunch with their class and instructor. The ski-school desk is located on the main floor of the Mountain Village Mall.

Childcare

Youngsters 1 year and older can go to the First Run Child Care Center on the lower level of the Mountain Village Mall. The activities are programmed and lunches are available. The Ski Cub program offers a full day of ski and recreational activities for children 3 to 5 years old.

Rental Equipment

Regular rental and demo equipment is available in the Ram's Head Ski Shop on the main floor of the Mountain Village Mall and in Lone Mountain Sports in Arrowhead Mall.

Cross-Country Skiing

Cross-country skiers have 45 miles of groomed trails in the area. The trails at Lone Mountain Ranch (see Where to Stay for the address and telephone number) are praised by cross-country enthusiasts.

WHERE TO STAY: There's lodging at the base, and it ranges from spartan to luxurious. There are many condos and lodges within a short driving distance. Some have transportation to and from the mountain for guests, but private cars are the easiest way to move around this region. Accommodations at the Huntley Lodge and many condominiums by the slopes and in the meadow village down the road can be reserved through **Big Sky's lodging number:** 406/995-4211, or toll free 800/548-4486 outside Montana. Other lodges must be contacted directly.

More Expensive to Moderate

The **Huntley Lodge,** P.O. Box 1, Big Sky, MT 59716 (tel. 406/955-4211, or toll free 800/548-4486 outside Montana), is a deluxe resort hotel at the base of the ski lifts. The rustic, timbered, three-story lodge has a spectacular view of the Spanish Peaks and Lone Mountain. The heated outdoor swimming pool is very popular, as is their ice skating rink. There are more than 500 studios, one-, two-, and three-bedroom units, and excellent convention facilities. Rates run $80 to $167.

Lone Mountain Ranch, P.O. Box 145, Big Sky, MT 59716 (tel. 406/995-4644), built in 1926 of native log, stone, and handmade ironwork, features deluxe separate cabins with fireplaces, electric heat, and modern conveniences. The ranch dining room serves meals that have been mentioned in many travel and food magazines. There is a cross-country skiing operation at the ranch with 45 miles of groomed tracks, and trips to Yellowstone Park, gourmet winter picnics, and sleigh rides are offered. Most visitors come for a week, but shorter stays can be arranged if there is an opening. Contact the ranch for the package (lodging, meals, and trail fees) prices, which were yet to be set at the time this was written. (Last year, a one-week package for two in a cabin was $595 per person.)

Golden Eagle Management, P.O. Box 8, Big Sky, MT 59716 (tel. 406/995-4800, or toll free 800/548-4488), offers condominiums from basic to deluxe, located in both Meadow and Mountain Villages. The deluxe condos are equipped with full kitchens and fireplaces, and most have access to a pool, Jacuzzi, or sauna. The Meadow Village condos are near the cross-country ski tracks, and some of the Mountain Village facilities are within walking distance of the slopes. Prices range from $70 for a studio (sleeping four) to three-bedroom units at $250 per night. Ski packages are available on request.

Buck's T-4 Lodge, P.O. Box 895, Big Sky, MT 59716 (tel. 406/995-4111), is a Best Western facility with a restaurant, lounge, game room, Jacuzzi, and free shuttle service to the ski slopes. Room rates vary from about $45 up, depending on the number of persons. Lodging/meal packages are available.

Less Expensive

The rustic **Corral Motel,** P.O. Box 204, Canyon Route, Gallatin Gateway, MT 59730 (tel. 406/995-4249), has lots of Montana charm, and the restaurant features family-style home-cooking. There are only seven lodging units, each accommodating four people. The quad rate is $28 per person, including lift ticket. It is located five miles south of the Big Sky entrance.

Economy is the theme at the **Mountain Lodge**, P.O. Box 56, Big Sky, MT 59716 (tel. 409/995-4560, or toll free 800/831-3509). For approximately $27 you can stay in a four-bed room with private bath—and the price includes an all-day adult lift ticket. It is located just a six-minute walk from the base of the slopes. The philosophy here is to replace the frills with comfortable beds and plenty of hot water; however, luxury rentals are also available. The restaurant serves hearty ski breakfasts and pizza in the evening. They can handle groups as large as 330, and 80% of their customers are repeaters.

The **Rainbow Ranch**, P.O. Box 202, Gallatin Gateway, MT 59730 (tel. 406/995-4132), located just south of the Big Sky entrance, has 15 comfortable units, some of which will accommodate up to six people, with prices ranging from $29 to $67 per night (slightly more during the Christmas holidays). There's a lounge, a hot spa, dining, and a recreational building at the ranch, which is five miles south of the entrance to Big Sky resort.

Triple Creek Realty Management Company, P.O. Box 219, Big Sky, MT 59716 (tel. 406/995-4847, or toll free 800/548-4632), can provide lodging from single lock-off bedrooms and studios to three- and four-bedroom condos with electric kitchens, stone fireplaces, and views. Some are close to the slopes and others are nearer to the cross-country ski center. They also have a pool, saunas, and Jacuzzis. Prices range from $80 for a studio to $300 for a three-bedroom in the Arrowhead and Beaverhead units, which are also ski-in/ski-out units.

WHERE TO EAT: There are several good restaurants, both at the base area and a short drive from the slopes. Everything from pizza to gourmet cuisine is available, most at particularly reasonable prices when compared to menus at other major resorts.

More Expensive

If you're lucky, you'll be able to get a reservation for the sleigh ride and dinner in a rustic log cabin, lit by kerosene lamps, in the backwoods of **Lone Mountain Ranch** (tel. 995-4644). The chef prepares meals on the wood-burning cook stove. The fixed-price dinner is in the upper $20s. Reservations are required for the single seating in the rustic dining room at the Lone Mountain Ranch. The menu changes nightly: the only guarantee is a high-quality and often gourmet meal served family style. (The limited table space goes first to guests staying at the ranch.) There is musical entertainment at dinner.

The **Furst Place** (tel. 995-4244) is labeled the finest dining spot in the area by many locals. Fireside dinners in this relaxing restaurant begin at 6 p.m., but the bar opens at 5 p.m. Reservations are definitely recommended. The continental menu features fresh seafood, lamb, veal, game, and steaks, ranging from $11 to $19. The restaurant is located in the Meadow Village Center, adjacent to the post office.

The elegantly rustic, open **Huntley Lodge** dining room (tel. 995-4211) features a magnificent buffet breakfast from 7 to 11 a.m. daily. It opens again for dinner at 6 p.m. with continental cuisine including such items as fettuccine, saltimbocca, and salmon en croûte, and of course, steak. Entrees range from $11.50 to $15.

Whiskey Jack's in the Mountain Mall (tel. 995-4211) offers steak, prime rib, and chicken entrees ranging from $9 to $13. There's a Sunday brunch. Music is live on Friday and Saturday.

For a different experience, try the **Fondue Stube** in the Huntley Lodge (tel. 995-4221), where there are only two nightly seatings (at 6:10 and 8:30 p.m.). Since it has a capacity of 35, reservations are recommended. Chicken, beef tenderloin, and seafood fondue are on the menu. Prices run $13 to $16.

Relax in the European atmosphere of the **Café Edelweiss,** in the Chace Montana Building, Meadow Village (tel. 995-4665), an attractive shop for an après-ski espresso and wonderful pastries. The café also serves lunch and dinner.

Moderate to Less Expensive

M. R. Hummers, in the Mountain Mall at the base of the slopes (tel. 955-4543), is usually packed—thanks to location, good prices, and great service. A huge bull moose head above the back bar oversees customers, who can enjoy snacks and sandwiches from 11 a.m. to 4 p.m., and steaks or chicken for dinner from 6 p.m. with prices ranging from $7 to $12. Happy hour is from 4 to 6 p.m. Be sure to ask for a Moose River Hummer—the drink you'll see others around you chugging!

"Good food—good spirits" is the slogan on the menu for the **Mountain Lodge,** located near Big Sky's base (tel. 995-4560), open daily from 7:30 to 10 a.m. for breakfast and from 5 to 10 p.m. weekdays, on Friday and Saturday until midnight, for dinner and snacks. The claim to fame here is pizza with dough made from scratch and multitudinous toppings. Prices range from $5 to $16 for the biggie. Inexpensive hamburgers and sandwiches are also available.

The **Snoshoe Inn,** three miles south of the Big Sky entrance on U.S. 191 (tel. 995-4565), with one of the best dining views in the area, isn't fancy but the owner/managers give every detail careful attention. Open from 7 a.m. to 9 p.m., it serves hearty breakfasts, sandwiches, and specializes in steaks for dinner. The sandwiches go from $3.50 to $5 and dinners range from $7 to $12 for a steak with all the trimmings.

Local color infuses the cozy log building of the **Corral,** on U.S. 191, five miles south of the Big Sky entrance (tel. 995-4249), where there is always a fire roaring in the fireplace. Family-style dining features everything from sandwiches to steaks, plus breakfast all day. The Corral is open from 7 a.m. to 9 p.m., and the bar stays open until 2 a.m. Lunches are extremely reasonable, in the $3 to $5 range, and dinners run from $6 to $15. There is a children's menu for those 12 and under.

Buck's T-4 Lodge, on U.S. 191 in the motel of the same name (tel. 995-4111), is a local institution with good prices, great food, and western character. Breakfasts include large omelets and homemade sweet rolls. Entrees such as chicken mireille, steak au poivre, and your basic steak range from $10 to $14. Dinners include a trip to the salad bar, a vegetable, and homemade rolls.

ENTERTAINMENT: Ask locally what's happening. Check out **Whiskey Jack's** for louder music, and the **Caboose** for a more mellow sound, both in the Mountain Village Mall.

Sissorbills, a beer and wine bar with a large champagne selection, at Buck T-4 Lodge (tel. 955-4111), is another popular spot.

NON-SKIER ACTIVITIES: For information about sleigh rides to dinner, contact the Lone Mountain Ranch (tel. 995-4644). There is daily bus service between Big Sky and West Yellowstone, called by some "the snowmobiling capital of the world." For information about **snowmobiling** and **snowcat rides** in Yellowstone National Park, contact the Huntley Lodge activities desk (tel. 995-4211). There's an ice skating rink behind Huntley Lodge.

GETTING THERE: Delta, Continental, and Northwest Airlines fly into Bozeman, 40 miles south via U.S. 191. Avis, Hertz, Budget, National, and American International rental cars are available at Bozeman.

MOVING AROUND: Skiers who plan to move around the region should have their own cars. Lone Mountain Ranch and Buck T-4 have shuttle services to the slopes for their guests. There is a shuttlebus service that runs around the Big Sky complex, between the base area, the condominium complexes, and the Meadow Village.

TOURIST INFORMATION: For more information, contact **Big Sky of Montana**, P.O. Box I, Big Sky, MT 59716 (tel. 406/995-4211, or toll free 800/548-4486). The **emergency number** for an ambulance, the sheriff, and the fire department is 585-1390.

3. Bridger Bowl

THE RESORT: Although Bridger Bowl is mainly a local's area—a popular spot with university students from the nearby University of Montana—it's considered a "find" by those few skiers who find their way into the limited lodging at the base or the motels in Bozeman.

THE SKIING: Terrain is rated 25% beginner, 45% intermediate, and 30% expert on this 2,000-vertical-foot mountain. Think of a bowl with sides that curve steeply at first but more gently as they near the bottom—then cut it in half to get Bridger Bowl's contour. Beginners and intermediates have the run of the bottom half of the mountain. There's even glade skiing for comfortable intermediates. The upper half of the mountain has trails and open-bowl skiing for all levels. The Alpine chair accesses top-to-bottom runs for beginners and intermediates.

Pierre's Knob chair—not for those with an extreme fear of heights—also opens up blue and green runs. Intermediate and advanced skiers share the open terrain on Bridger Bowl north. Bump skiers gravitate toward the short but steep runs with names like Avalanche and Devil's Dive. The ridge rats climb past the chairs up to the rim of the bowl (they must check in with ski patrol and avalanche beepers are required) to reach the upper steep terrain in the couloirs with informal names like Mad Men Only.

Mountain Facilities

There's a base lodge with a cafeteria and a deli. The Deer Park Coffee Haus, in a mid-mountain chalet, offers imaginatively prepared sandwiches, hot food, and several types of coffee.

Snow Coverage

The annual snowfall here is 400 inches, and the area is open from mid-December to mid-April.

Ski School

There are group and private lessons. The ski school also offers a guide service to take skiers to out-of-bounds powder areas, including the ridge.

Childcare
There is childcare for toddlers and older children.

Rental Equipment
Regular rental equipment is available at the base of the mountain.

Cross-Country Skiing
Crosscut Ranch nearby has 20 km (12 miles) of groomed trails with backcountry huts. Rental equipment and lessons are available.

WHERE TO STAY: There is lodging in a few condos and private homes at the base of the mountain and in motel-style accommodations at the nearby Crosscut Ranch. There is also lodging in Bozeman 16 miles away. Packages, which include lodging, lifts, and more, can be arranged through Bridger's **central reservations** office. For information call 406/587-2111 from Montana and Canada, or toll free 800/223-9609 from other states.

WHERE TO EAT: Dining is in the ski area restaurants or at the **Crosscut Ranch** (tel. 587-3122), where the dining room features "made in Montana" fare with beef, lamb, trout, and more. Prices range from $9 to $20.

There are also restaurants in Bozeman.

NON-SKIER ACTIVITIES: Yellowstone National Park is 90 miles away. Contact **TW Services, Inc.,** Attention: Sales Department, Yellowstone National Park, WY 82190, for information about the ski touring adventures, snowmobiling and other winter activities in the park.

There are **sleigh rides** at the ski area. Call the main number for information.

Snowmobiling is a popular sport in this region. For more details, contact the Bozeman Chamber of Commerce, P.O. Box B, Bozeman, MT 59715 (tel. 406/586-5421).

GETTING THERE: Bridger Bowl is located on U.S. 86, 16 miles northeast of Bozeman. Skiers can fly into Bozeman and rent a car or take a limo to the ski area. Crosscut Ranch guests are transported to the ski area via a horse-drawn sled. There is a shuttlebus from town on weekends and holidays.

MOVING AROUND: The condos and homes at the base are within walking distance of the slopes. Skiers staying in Bozeman need a private car.

TOURIST INFORMATION: For more details, contact **Bridger Bowl Ski Area,** 15795 Bridger Canyon Rd., Bozeman, MT 59715. For **lodging information,** call 406/587-2111 from Montana and Canada, or toll free 800/223-9609 from other states. For **snow conditions,** call 406/586-2389.

For information on lodging and dining in Bozeman, contact the **Bozeman Chamber of Commerce,** P.O. Box B, Bozeman, MT 59715 (tel. 406/586-5421).

4. Red Lodge

THE RESORT: Red Lodge is a down-home mid-size ski area with a friendly staff and clientele. It's up the mountain from the town of Red Lodge, where skiers stay and party. It's a fun place for long weekends or three- to four-day trips. Prices are very reasonable and the food is good!

THE SKIING: A triple chair, four double chairs, and a Mitey Mite lift open up the 2,016-vertical-foot mountain with 500 skiable acres. (Snow and weather conditions permitting, experts can also go into neighboring Coal Creek, the site of future expansion.) The terrain is rated 15% beginner, 60% intermediate, and 25% expert.

Beginners have their own area, Miami Beach, set off to the side so better skiers can't zip through the crowd of novices. They also have a few runs off the main lift. Intermediates head up the main mountain to challenge long, easy cruisers such as Lazy M and Barriers.

The formal black trails on the front face are light to medium black. However, Red Lodge's secret is the Drainage area, a large section of steep, wooded mountainside for real advanced and expert skiers. Because Widow Maker, Jones Park, and the treed areas around the Main Drainage are protected, they hold some of the best snow on the mountain. Experts who enjoy backcountry conditions will also want to try the Coal Creek area when it's open. (Ask the ski patrol and *never* go alone!) Someday the ski corporation hopes to expand the ski area into neighboring Coal Creek, opening up a concave bowl with advanced and intermediate terrain. Meanwhile, expert skiers can sample this double-black-diamond terrain by challenging some of the chutes now skied, each with approximately 900 to 1,000 vertical feet, or the treed area; then take the run-out back to the ski area.

Mountain Facilities

The base-area buildings house a cafeteria, rental shop, and ski school. There are good sandwiches at the Willow Creek Saloon, next door. Try the soup-in-a-bread-bowl at the Midway Restaurant, at the mid-mountain chalet. Some skiers take sack lunches to the Hancock Summit House.

Snow Coverage

This area receives an average snowfall of 250 inches, and snowmaking covers 40% of the mountain. Red Lodge is usually open from mid-November to April.

Ski School

There are regular and private lessons. The Children's Winter Sport Center has classes for youngsters from ages 3 to 6. Older children go into the regular ski-school classes.

Childcare

The Children's Winter Sport Center has a program combining skiing, crafts, and snow-play activities through the day, excluding lunch.

Rental Equipment

There's high-performance and regular rental equipment in the Winter Sports Complex at the base.

Cross Country Skiing

There are U.S. Forest Service trails at the base of the mountain on the West Fork.

WHERE TO STAY: There are 1,000 pillows in the town of Red Lodge, in ten lodges and motels. For lodging information and reservations, contact **Red Lodge Central Reservations,** P.O. Box 750, Red Lodge, MT 59068 (tel. 406/446-2503, or toll free 800/468-8977, 800/227-5006 in Montana).

The **LuPine Inn,** 702 Hauser, Red Lodge, MT 59068 (tel. 406/446-1321), is a Best Western property with comfortable, basic motel rooms and "no-smoking" rooms. There is an indoor heated pool and spa. Rooms go for approximately $55 a night.

The **Château Rouge,** Red Lodge, MT 59068 (tel. 406/446-1601), on the south edge of Red Lodge, has comfortable one- and two-bedroom condominiums. There is a pool and a gym. Prices range from approximately $65 for two to $120 for six people in a unit.

Families or good friends can stay in the restored two-bedroom/one-bath **Pitcher House** on the main street (tel. 406/446-2859 or 406/446-1119). The rate is approximately $55 a night, with a three-night minimum. Stay seven days and the last night is free.

WHERE TO EAT: There's a surprising variety of good restaurants in this town. Most of the restaurants are on a few-block stretch of the main street (South Broadway). You can walk down the street and choose from the menus.

More Expensive

Guests dining at **Old Piney Dell,** a rustic old lodge six miles south of Red Lodge on U.S. 212 (tel. 446-1196), choose from continental fare, butterknife filets, or fresh fish. Prices range from $9 to $21 for some very tasty food. Hours are 5 to 10 p.m. Monday through Saturday, and 8 a.m. to 1 p.m. for brunch and 3 to 9 p.m. for dinner on Sunday. Reservations are suggested.

While waiting for your meal at the **Pius' International Room,** 115 S. Broadway (tel. 446-3333), explore one of the world's largest collections of J. M. Beam bottles. Food specialties are pasta and gourmet fare. Hours are from 5:30 p.m. Monday through Thursday, 5 to 11 p.m. on Friday and Saturday, and 3:30 to 10 p.m. on Sunday.

Moderate

Bogart's, 11 S. Broadway, (tel. 446-1784), decorated as you would suspect, specializes in pizza and Mexican food. Sandwiches and dinners average $5. Pizza run $4.25 to $15.50. Hours are 11 a.m. to 9 p.m. Sunday through Thursday, to 10 p.m. on Friday and Saturday.

Sylvia's, 123 S. Broadway (tel. 446-2810), specializes in fresh ingredients and herbs in their creative sandwiches, burgers, and omelets, ranging in price from $4.50 to $6. Entrees, shrimp to steak, range from $7.75 to $16. Hours are 4 to 7 p.m. Wednesday to Saturday, noon to 7 p.m. Sunday.

Less Expensive

Coffee is 25¢ at **P. D. McKinney's,** 407 S. Broadway (tel. 446-1250). There's a full breakfast menu at this coffeeshop. Try the breakfast quiche. Small eaters will appreciate the mini-breakfasts. Hours are 6 a.m. to 2 p.m.

Cheap Eats

Coffee-and-roll breakfast eaters can grab their meal at the **bakery** located at 104 S. Broadway. The baked goods (even the bread sticks) are delicious. Hours are 8 a.m. to 6 p.m.

ENTERTAINMENT: Just walk down South Broadway and look in the bars. Some skiers move from bar to bar as the entertainers take a break. There's cowboy music for dancing, more current beats, quiet bars, bars with big-screen TVs, and more.

MOVING AROUND: Skiers need their own cars here.

GETTING THERE: Fly to Billings and take a rental car to Red Lodge, 60 miles south on U.S. 212.

TOURIST INFORMATION: For one-stop shopping from a central reservations center which emphasizes customizing trips, contact **Red Lodge Central Reservations**, P.O. Box 750, Red Lodge, MT 59068 (tel. 406/446-2503, or toll free 800/468-8977, 800/227-5006 in Montana).

5. Other Montana Ski Areas

LOST TRAIL: A ski resort in two states, Lost Trail lies 90 miles south of Missoula and 42 miles north of Salmon, Idaho. This ski area receives good early snow and usually opens Thursday through Sunday from December through early May. There are 12 trails on this 1,200 foot-vertical mountain. Four lifts service open and bowl skiing. There is a day lodge at the base, a rental shop, and lodging facilities at **Lost Trail Resort** (six miles north), P.O. Box 191, Darby, MT 59829 (tel. 406/821-3211).

MARSHALL: Marshall is located only seven miles from Missoula in the western part of Montana and receives an annual snowfall of 160 inches. Night skiing is popular here. A triple chair, a T-bar, and a rope tow service the 1,500-foot vertical with 25% beginner terrain, 60% intermediate, and 15% advanced. There are two base lodges, and overnight lodging is available in Missoula. Contact **Marshall Ski Area**, 5250 Marshall Canyon Rd., Missoula, MT 59802 (tel. 406/258-6619).

MAVERICK MOUNTAIN: Two lifts serve the 1,720 vertical feet of terrain on Maverick Mountain in the southern part of Montana, 38 miles northwest of Dillon on Mont. 278. It is open Thursday through Sunday and holidays, and has an average annual snowfall of 140 inches. The seven trails are rated 20% novice, 40% intermediate, and 40% expert terrain. The longest run is 2¼ miles. The base lodge has a cafeteria and wine room. There are two restaurants, lodging, and hot springs nearby. Contact **Maverick Mountain Resort**, 101 N. Montana St., Dillon, MT 59725 (tel. 406/683-4521 off-season or 406/834-3454 in-season).

SHOWDOWN: Some 300 inches of snow annually provide a long season for Showdown, open from mid-November through mid-April. Located in central Montana, 60 miles southeast of Great Falls, Showdown has a vertical drop of 1,400 feet with terrain rated 40% novice, 40% intermediate, and 20% expert. The longest run at this family-oriented resort is two miles, and the mountain has four lifts. Lodging is available at White Sulphur Springs and Great Falls. Ski touring is unlimited and there are some groomed telemark trails.

For information, contact **Showdown Resort**, P.O. Box 92, Neihart, MT 59465 (tel. 406/236-5522).

SNOW BOWL: Located 12 miles northwest of Missoula, Snow Bowl also boasts 300 inches of snow per year, which affords a long season and good spring skiing. Open Wednesday through Sunday and all holidays. Snow Bowl is serviced by two chairs, one T-bar, and one rope tow. Located in the Lolo National Forest adjacent to the Rattlesnake Wilderness Area, this ski area has 20% beginner terrain, 40% intermediate, and 40% advanced on a 2,600-foot-vertical mountain. There are more than 25 runs, open bowls, and trails. The steepest runs are on the bottom of the mountain at this ski areas frequented by Missoula locals and college students.

For details, contact **Snow Bowl Resort,** 1700 Snow Bowl Rd., Missoula, MT 59802 (tel. 406/549-9777).

"SKI THE GREAT DIVIDE": Also known as Belmont, this area serves Helena skiers, being only 25 miles northwest on Mont. 279. Open from mid-December through mid-April, the area is open Thursday through Sunday and all holidays during the season. The 1,500-foot-vertical mountain has four trails on two open slopes, with terrain rated 20% beginner, 55% intermediate, and 25% expert. There is a day lodge at the base and a warming hut at the top. There is ski touring in the area, but trails are not groomed.

For more information, contact **"Ski the Great Divide,"** 5120 Hidden Valley Dr., Helena, MT 59601 (tel. 406/443-9953).

TETON PASS: Located in the northwestern part of the state 30 miles northwest of Choteau, Teton Pass has a vertical drop of 1,200 feet serviced by a chair, a poma, and a Mitey Mite. It is open Friday through Sunday and holidays from Thanksgiving to Easter. Cross-country skiers have 15 miles of groomed trails for touring. Some rentals are available. There is a day lodge with food and a bar, but lodging is in Choteau or the 7-Lazy-P dude ranch.

Contact **Teton Pass Ski Area,** P.O. Box 727, Choteau, MT 59422 (tel. 406/466-2672, 406/467-2789 after October 1).

TURNER MOUNTAIN: Turner Mountain is tucked away in the far-northwest corner of Montana, 22 miles north of Libby. Open weekends only from the first part of December through mid-April, it is considered an excellent powder area with good glade skiing. Its 2,100-foot-vertical drop has six runs serviced by a T-bar. It is primarily for high intermediate and expert skiers.

Contact **Turner Mountain Ski Area,** P.O. Box 210, Libby, MT 59923 (tel. 406/293-7531).

6. Montana Cross-Country Skiing

Nordic skiing possibilities are limitless here, ranging from touring in Yellowstone or Glacier National Park to trekking toward hot springs in the wilderness. In Yellowstone National Park, there are 37 miles of groomed trails, 100 miles of tracks, and more than 1,000 miles of backcountry trails. Guide service, ski instruction, and ski rentals are all available, as is lodging within the park at the Mammoth Hot Springs Hotel. For information and/or reservations, contact Marketing & Sales, TW Services, Inc., **Yellowstone National Park,** WY 82190 (tel. toll free 800/421-3401 during the winter).

Glacier has 14 marked but ungroomed cross-country ski trails. Ski rentals are available at West Glacier. Lodging and other services are all outside the park. For information about exploring **Glacier National Park** with a guide, write the Superintendent, Glacier National Park, West Glacier, MT 59936 (tel. 406/888-5441).

There are several guest ranches in Montana that cater to cross-country skiers during the wintertime. The most notable is **Lone Mountain Ranch** at Big Sky, P.O. Box 69, Big Sky, MT 59716 (tel. 406/995-4644), 20 miles northwest of Yellowstone National Park. Guests stay in cozy log cabins, burn off calories on 45 miles of groomed trails during the day, and put those calories back on at night tackling gourmet meals served informally in the rustic dining room. Guests here can spend a day on a cross-country tour of Yellowstone guided by a naturalist, or try downhill skiing at nearby Big Sky ski area. There's free airport transportation.

There are several resorts with hot springs in Montana geared for cross-country skiers. At **Chico Hot Springs Resort,** Pray, MT 59065 (tel. 406/333-4933 or 406/331-4490), 29 miles north of Yellowstone, Nordic skiers can stay in deluxe condos or an old inn, spend the day skiing, and unwind in the mineral hot springs. Guide service and equipment rental are provided. Skiers can combine alpine and Nordic skiing when staying at the **Lost Trail Hot Springs Resort,** P.O. Box 37, Sula, MT 59871 (tel. 406/821-3574). There are miles of trails around the lodge and unlimited U.S. Forest Service lands nearby. The Lost Trail ski area isn't far from the resort, which has accommodations in lodges, cabins, and motels.

The **Izaak Walton Inn,** P.O. Box 653, Essex, MT 59916 (to phone, ask the Montana operator for Essex #1), is a historic railroad inn where guests can have a fireside chat in the lobby, then fill up on home-style food after a day of cross-country skiing on the 30 km (18 miles) of groomed trails which start near the inn's front door. There are networks of ungroomed trails in nearby Glacier National Park, the Flathead National Forest, and the Great Bear Wilderness.

Crosscut Ranch, 12065 Bridger Canyon Dr., Bozeman, MT 59715 (tel. 406/587-3122), near Bridger Bowl, has 22 miles of groomed trails which have been the site of several national and international cross-country races.

Chapter XV

OREGON

1. Mount Bachelor
2. Mount Hood Area: Mount Hood Meadows, Mirror Mountain, and Timberline
3. Other Oregon Ski Areas

SLOPES IN THE PACIFIC NORTHWEST come in all tilts, from barely angled to too-steep-to-stand. They're carved into tiny day areas exposed to the snowstorms coming directly off the ocean, and into the more easterly larger ski mountains that may have drier snow because moisture has been leached out of the storm as it flowed over these mountains. The day areas in Oregon and Washington draw skiers from the main cities along this part of the coast. The destination spots draw from as far away as Canada and northern California. Because the snow is wetter than the powder falling on the Rockies and the resorts are not as well developed as others midwestern skiers must pass by to get there, few skiers from the Rockies eastward head that far west. During the summer, however, Oregon is one of the few places where skiers can combine their sport with an afternoon of golfing, rafting, or working on a full-body suntan.

In Oregon, several ski areas crawl up the flanks of dormant volcanic cones, which punctuate the generally rounded mountains in the Cascade Range. The ski slopes on Mount Hood are considered day areas by Oregonians, although lodging is available. Mount Bachelor, approximately three driving hours southwest of Portland, is a destination resort—northwestern style. (That means the lodging is in or near a town several miles from the ski mountain.)

The main skier factory in Washington is Ski Snoqualmie, just 50 miles from the coast. Here, and at other day areas located within a 1½-hour drive from Seattle, skiers gain enough confidence and usually the desire to move on to destination resorts. Crystal Mountain, considered a day area by many because of its proximity to the coastal population, is a bare-bones destination spot with excellent terrain for advanced and expert skiers. Skiers who want to slide down the eastern flank of the mountain range head for Mission Ridge, a classic mid-size ski area with lodging in the town of Wenatchee, 13 miles away.

During the winter, the weather in these mountains can most charitably be described as changeable (although after five days of snow while touring these northwestern ski areas, the standard joke was "I'll send you a postcard of the view")—sun one day, rain the next, snow the next. A special on plastic raincoats in one ski-area retail shop—on a day when it was snowing hard—reinforces that belief. "Layer clothes" is the other most often repeated bit of advice in regard to dealing with the weather. Gortex and other waterproof fabrics are used by skiing regulars here.

However, during the spring and early summer, Oregon is the main place for skiers to play. Shorts and T-shirts are in fashion on the slopes at Mount Bachelor and at Timberline, which usually stay open through midsummer.

Both Oregon and Washington require special sno-park permits on cars parked in designated winter recreation parking areas during the winter months. (Many ski-area parking lots are in those zones.) Money from the permits is used by the state highway departments to plow parking lots and roadside parking areas used by winter sports enthusiasts. Cars without permits parked in designated areas are fined. The inexpensive daily and annual permits are sold in many retail locations, by the Office of Winter Recreation, Washington State Parks and Recreation Commission, and by the Motor Vehicles Division Field offices in Oregon. Ask locally for details.

1. Mount Bachelor

THE RESORT: Mount Bachelor is Oregon's major destination resort. At this area, draped around an extinct volcano, skiers have a 360° choice of fall lines. Although it has long attracted skiers from all parts of Oregon and Washington, since the installation of the Summit chair (which nearly doubled the vertical and extended the ski season into midsummer) Mount Bachelor is drawing more skiers from Canada, Idaho, and northern California. Because Mount Bachelor is completely on public land, which is managed by the U.S. Forest Service, there is no (and probably will never be) lodging at the base. Skiers stay in the town of Bend, where the restaurants and shops are a blend of small-town USA and tourism chic, or in the nearby resort community of Sun River.

Because Mount Bachelor is on the inland side of the Cascade Mountain range, the powder tends to be dryer than that at Mount Hood. However, the mountain rises so far above its neighbors, it can wear a mantle of fog or clouds. But the weather is usually sunny and warm during the summer season here, which starts in May and often lasts through July. Summertime packages often include skiing in the morning and golfing, fishing, or rafting during the afternoon.

THE SKIING: Two quad-, three double-, and five triple-chair lifts open up 1,600 skiable acres on a 360° sweep of Mount Bachelor. Because the lift capacity far surpasses the bed capacity in the surrounding communities, skiers can usually find lightly trafficked runs or even untracked powder on this 3,100-vertical-foot mountain.

The terrain is rated 15% novice, 25% intermediate, 35% advanced intermediate, and 25% expert. The majority of the 40 connecting trails are on the north side of the mountain. The summit area is high alpine open terrain.

Park near the base lodge at the foot of the lifts accessing the runs you want to ski the most. There are four base lodges here, and it takes a lot of time—even without lift lines—to move from one end of the skiable terrain to the other. Access to the Summit chair is via the Sunrise lift, so anyone wanting to head straight to the top should park near the Sunrise Lodge. When the chair is closed, advanced skiers might park near the Main Lodge because it's closer to the tougher runs. Families with beginning and intermediate skiers might park near the Sunrise Lodge because there is a wide range of easier runs off the Rainbow and Sunrise chairs. (There is also day care at this lodge.)

Beginners can start on the Orange and Yellow chairs by the base lodge. If

270 □ DOLLARWISE GUIDE TO SKIING USA—WEST

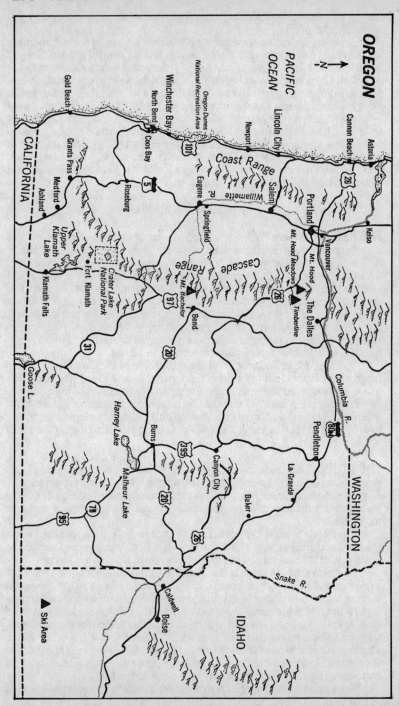

they've parked by the Sunrise Lodge, they can try the longer, wide, well-groomed runs off the Sunrise and Blue chairs.

This is a mountain for intermediates because there are so many broad, rolling, groomed trails to explore. The Rainbow chair above the Sunrise Lodge has broad, gentle runs for lower- and middle-level intermediates. There are also good intermediate cruising runs off the Blue and Green chairs. Advanced intermediates should be able to explore some of the black runs. Competent intermediates will also want to explore the groomed areas off the Summit chair.

If plans went as expected last summer, the Outback chair was replaced with a high-speed quad, the Outback Super-Express, which starts a half mile northwest and 200 feet lower than the old chair, allowing 1,800 vertical feet of skiing, the greatest amount off any chair on the mountain.

Advanced skiers steer toward the Outback chair with its network of trails cut through the trees. The black runs here offer a variety of acceptably steep pitches (the "hair-raising" rides are up at the top of the mountain). Regulars in search of untracked powder head off the formal trails for a ten-minute uphill hike to ski the Cinder Cone. (The really serious powderhounds ski the inside of this mini-volcanic cone, then have to climb out.) The best bump runs are usually around the Red and Pine Marten chairs.

Beginning tree bashers can get lots of practice on this mountain. There's an almost unlimited choice of terrain around the tree line, where the trees grow so far apart from each other that shaky tree skiers should have room to hone their turning skills.

"Coneheads" describes those skiers who climbed to the top of the mountain long before the Summit lift was installed. Now, the open upper flanks of this extinct volcano are open to any intermediate or advanced skier hitching a ride on the high-speed detachable chairs on the Summit lift. When the chair is open—most of the summer and weather permitting during the winter (which has averaged about 30% of the time)—skiers can head off the top in any direction. The skiing can be spectacular or "challenging," depending on the chosen route. A big piece of this high alpine terrain is groomed constantly for intermediate skiers. Skiing around the ungroomed parts of the peak can be an instant lesson in dealing with changing snow conditions and pitches. The snow can change from rutted, to powder, to breakable crust during the run. A "catchline" around the south face of Mount Bachelor stops skiers in time to follow a ski road back around the mountain to the main base areas on the north side.

The Pinnacles is expert's-only turf. Just think spectacular ski-magazine cover shots to get the feel.

Insider's Tips

Many regulars claim that when it's foggy and snowing around the Outback and Red chairs, they move toward the Sunrise and Rainbow chairs because there's a good chance the sun might even be shining. (It was true the day I was there. The winds seem to clear the fog away from that area of the mountain.)

Many ski-school members tout the food at the Egan Lodge, the old day lodge set on the ski slopes several hundred feet above the Main Lodge. The limited menu here is a cut above standard ski-lodge fare. The Castle Keep, a multilevel bar in the main lodge, offers several varieties of good wine by the glass to go with well-made, creative lunches. The best brunch in the region is set up here on Sunday morning during the winter.

Mountain Facilities

There are four base lodges. The biggest is the Main Lodge, with a cafeteria, the Castle Keep Lounge, and a fresh (watch them make it) doughnut counter, a day-care center, a ski school, and a retail and rental shop. The Sunrise Lodge has a cafeteria, lounge, day care, ski school, and a rental and retail shop. The Egan Lodge has a cafeteria, and the Blue Lodge has a cafeteria and a rental and ski shop. There's a separate Nordic Center near the Main Lodge.

Snow Coverage

The annual snowfall usually leaves between 150 and 200 inches at the 6,000-foot level. Mount Bachelor opens in mid-November and offers skiing through mid-July. The beginner and intermediate terrain is groomed continually.

Ski School

The ski school offers full-day class lessons and half-day afternoon lessons for never-evers. Private lessons are by appointment only and may include up to four people of the same ability level. The Children's Ski School is open to youngsters 6 to 12 years of age. The Tiny Tracks Ski School is for youngsters age 4 to 6. (This is separate from day care, although children may be enrolled in both because classes are only for 1½ hours in the morning and in the afternoon.) NASTAR is very popular here. There are recreational racing clinics twice a day, a combination of clinic and race, and a coin-op race course. Mount Bachelor runs a summer training center serviced by the Summit chair. (The U.S. Ski Team trains here in the summer.)

Childcare

Day-care facilities are located in both the Main and Sunrise Lodges. The rooms are open from 8:30 a.m. to 4:30 p.m. daily, and there are planned activities for youngsters from the ages of 6 weeks to 7 years of age. Parents must provide lunch. Full-day reservations should be made in advance to guarantee space. Payment for childcare, any lessons, and rental (if needed) should be made at least two weeks in advance. Contact **Mount Bachelor Day Care Center,** P.O. Box 1031, Bend, OR 97709 (tel. 503/282-2607), for details.

Rental Equipment

There are rental shops at the Main, Blue, and Sunrise Lodges. There are also rentals at ski shops in Bend.

Cross-Country Skiing

Free cross-country trail maps are available at all of the area lodges, outlining the 50 km (30 miles) of machine-groomed trails. There are nine loop trails for everyone from the beginner to racers. Trail tickets for maintained trails can be purchased at Mount Bachelor's Nordic Center, the log cabin next to the Main Lodge parking lot. The center has a warming area with a wood stove, a lunch room, a public waxing room, and a full-service repair shop. There is also a retail shop for Nordic equipment, a rental shop where racing demo equipment can be rented, and a cross-country ski-school desk in the two-story building. The ski school offers a range of classes from basic lessons to guided picnic tours in the Cascades to multiday technique clinics.

WHERE TO STAY: There are no accommodations at the base of this mountain, located entirely on Forest Service land. Skiers who visit here expect to travel to the mountain; the only question is how far—7 miles, 15, or more. There are a few lodges and motels on Century Drive, the main road from Bend to the mountain. There are also many motels and hotels in the town of Bend, 22 miles away, a thriving place where locals mix with skiers in the winter and vacationers during the warmer weather. Sunriver, a resort/residential community located 17 miles from Bend but just 20 minutes from the mountain, is the other main lodging spot for skiers. Mount Bachelor has a **lodging reservations and information** number (tel. 503/282-8334, or toll free 800/547-6858 outside Oregon), which covers many of the accommodations in the area. Several of the properties have toll-free "800" numbers that are listed below.

Skiers can stay at the **Sunriver Lodge and Resort** (tel. toll free 800/547-3922, 800/452-6874 in Oregon) for extremely reasonable prices (especially when matched against similar accommodations at megaresorts). The lodge condos have a mountain-style decor, with wood-paneled walls, and fireplaces, and many have sleeping lofts. Skiers can also rent many of the private homes lining the winding lanes in this 3,300-acre year-round resort residential community. Since a paved road was set in the national forest from the resort to the highway just three miles from the ski area (making the trip 18 miles long), Sunriver has become the closest community to Mount Bachelor. Sunriver has its own shopping village with a full-service gas station, a grocery store, 20 shops, an ice rink, and approximately a dozen restaurants. Sunriver Lodge has two restaurants: The Provision Co., a family dining room open for three meals daily; and The Meadows, a formal dining room open for dinner and Sunday brunch. There's dancing to live music in the Owl's Nest Lounge. There is an outdoor pool and two Jacuzzis near the main lodge, and many condos include free access to the Racquet Club. Daily shuttle service to the mountain is available, as are ground transfers to Redmond Airport. Skiers who come during the winter can take snowmobile tours and horse-drawn sleigh rides. Skiers who come in April, May, or June can ski in the morning, then go rafting or play tennis or golf in the afternoon. Sunriver Lodge offers a variety of lift/lodging packages. Winter per-unit rates range from $59 for a lodge bedroom to $105 for a suite. Private homes and condominiums range from $99 for a standard unit to $160 for a VIP unit.

Mount Bachelor Village (tel. toll free 800/547-5204, 800/452-9846 in Oregon) may be the closest lodging to the area. However, guests need cars to get to the mountain (although they can walk across the highway and get a bus) and to any restaurants. The condos (all with rooms of normal height) are nicely decorated and many have fireplaces. The pool is only open during peak seasons, but the Jacuzzi is open daily. Mount Bachelor Village has lift/lodging package rates. There are no studio rooms, only one- and two-bedroom condos. Nightly per-unit rates range from $65 for a one-bedroom to $115 for a two-bedroom that sleeps six.

Inn of the Seventh Mountain (tel. 503/382-8711, or toll free 800/547-5668 in the western states, 800/452-6810 in Oregon), just 14 miles from the mountain, offers everything from lodge rooms to family suites. Question what you are getting. The most basic rooms, now listed as economy lodging, are dark and tiny, but the studios are very attractive and the two-bedrooms on the top floor have plenty of light. Daily maid service is provided. Amenities include a pool, whirlpool, saunas, ice rink, and restaurants. There is bus service to the mountain from the inn. Nightly rates range from $60 for a standard lodge room to $206 for a two-bedroom/two-bath family suite.

The **Riverhouse Motor Inn**, at 3075 N. U.S. 97, Bend, OR 97702 (tel. 503/389-3111), is in Bend, where most of the skiers' nightlife is located. It has pleasant, basic hotel rooms with everything from queen-size to waterbeds. There are also family units and rooms with spas. Some rooms with fireplaces and river views are $4 more. Prices range from $40 for two people in a room with one queen-size bed to $95 per night for the spa units. Amenities include an indoor pool, spa, saunas, cable TV, and restaurants.

WHERE TO EAT: Because Bend is a major year-round tourist area as well as a thriving city, there is an unusually wide range of restaurants. Even the guests staying in lodges outside town head for Bend's restaurants several nights during their stay. Prices are generally reasonable because the restaurants need local support as well as the tourists.

Expensive

Le Bistro, 1203 N.E. Third (tel. 389-7274) is set in a redecorated small old church. French gourmet fare is served from 5:30 p.m. on every Tuesday through Saturday. Prices range from $8.25 to $16.50.

The Sunday brunch at Mount Bachelor is touted by both locals and visitors as the best brunch in the region. Reservations are suggested for this elaborate feast, which runs from 8 to 11 a.m. in the **Castle Keep,** a sit-down restaurant/bar in the Main Lodge.

The formal **Meadows Dining Room** at Sunriver Lodge in the Sunriver Resort (tel. 593-1221), 17 miles south of Bend, has an elaborate menu backed with fancy service. The creative offerings range from fresh fish to aged beef, with tableside preparation of Caesar salad and flaming desserts. Entrees range from $13 to $19. Dinner is from 6:30 to 9:30 p.m. Reservations are requested.

Moderate

Reservations are suggested for the **Pine Tavern Restaurant,** 967 N.W. Brooks Ave. (tel. 382-5581), because the waiting times lengthen as the evening progresses at this popular restaurant. Diners are finishing well-prepared basic fare ranging from prime rib to Rocky Mountain trout here, at tables set around the bases of two massive, old trees which, of course, poke out through the roof. Every meal starts with sourdough scones and honey butter, the main draw for many repeat diners. Petite dinners, including leg of lamb, and children's meals are available. Entrees range from $6.50 to $15. Daily hours are 11:30 a.m. to 2:30 p.m. for lunch Monday through Saturday, 5:30 to 9:30 p.m. daily for dinner, and 10:30 a.m. to 1:30 p.m. for Sunday brunch.

Cyrano's Restaurant, 119 N.W. Minnesota St. (tel. 389-6276), offers creative regional and nouvelle fare three meals a day. Breakfast, from 7 to 11 a.m. (basic eggs, smoked trout, omelet, coulibec, and more), averages $8; and lunch runs $3.50 to $5. Dinner, from 5 to 9 p.m. Tuesday through Thursday, to 10 p.m. on Friday and Saturday, includes entrees such as chicken paillards Sante Fe, two-cheese strata, and steak au poivre. Entrees range from $8 to $13. Reservations are needed for the fixed-price, multicourse dinners held during some holiday and weekend evenings. Call for details.

The **Black Forest Restaurant,** 25 S.W. 14th St. (tel. 389-3138), specializes in such Bavarian specialties as Black Forest mushrooms and wienerschnitzel as well as American and Italian fare. Examine the Bavarian memorabilia while waiting for your meal. Entrees range from $7 to $15. The restaurant opens at 5 p.m. daily.

Relax amid the plants, rock walls, and natural-oak fixtures decorating **Kayo's Dinner House and Lounge,** on South U.S. 97 (tel. 389-1400). Steaks, seafood, and the chef's and Italian specialties on the menu range in price from $7.50 to $17. Dinner is served from 5:30 to 10 p.m. Monday through Saturday, but only until 9 p.m. on Sunday. Reservations are suggested.

El Crab Catcher, at the Inn of the Seventh Mountain (tel. 382-8711), located seven miles west of Bend on Century Drive, specializes in seafood but steaks are on the menu too. Entrees range from $8 for light suppers to $20. Dinner from 5:30 to 10 p.m.

Less Expensive

The airy greenhouse atmosphere in the **Poppy Seed Café,** at the Inn of the Seventh Mountain (tel. 382-8711), is the place for very reasonably priced complete meals, such as fish and chips, chicken, or beef, averaging $9. Sandwiches cost less. The Poppy Seed Café hours are 7 a.m. to 7 p.m. daily.

Sample burritos, enchiladas, and more, washed down with margaritas served by the pitcherful, at **Mexicali Rose,** 301 N.E. Franklin (tel. 389-0149). Prices range from $3.25 to $7.50. Lunch hours are 11:30 a.m. to 2:30 p.m. weekdays, and dinner is from 4:30 to 10 p.m. daily.

ENTERTAINMENT: There are several lounges and restaurants in the region that offer entertainment in the evening. Check for hours and nights because the activity gets more frenetic as the slopes get more crowded—and slows down as the crowds thin out.

Player's Grill, 61 N.W. Oregon (tel. 382-5859), and the **Pine Tavern,** 967 N.W. Brooks (tel. 382-5581), are usually packed during the après-ski hours, often with skiers waiting for dinner.

Brandy's, 197 N.E. 3rd St. (tel. 382-2687), has live entertainment in the lounge Tuesday through Sunday. The sounds tend to draw the younger crowd.

El Crab Catcher, a trendily decorated restaurant/bar at the Inn of the Seventh Mountain (tel. 382-8711), also has live entertainment several nights a week. This is a popular spot, especially with the many skiers staying in the inn's condos.

SHOPPING: There are three good ski shops at the edge of town on Century Drive, the main road heading from the mountain into town. Locals frequent the specialty shops on Brooks, Bond, and Wall Streets in the downtown area. There are many shops in the Sunriver Mall ranging from the **Cookie Corner to the Wooden Duck,** an unusual toy store.

NON-SKIER ACTIVITIES: There are **ice-skating rinks** at Sunriver and at the Inn of the Seventh Mountain. There are **snowmobiling** trails in the region for those who bring their machines. **Wildcat Packers and Outfitters** (tel. 389-9458) runs short **sleigh rides** in the countryside and dinner rides. There are indoor **tennis and racquetball courts** at Sunriver.

GETTING THERE: Mount Bachelor is 150 miles from Portland and 22 miles from Bend, the nearest town. Skiers can take most major airlines to Portland and a connecting flight via Horizon Air to Redmond, 17 miles north of Bend. PSA flies to Redmond from Los Angeles and San Francisco. Airline limousine service is available from Redmond to Bend after incoming flights. Many major car-rental agencies are located at Portland's airport, and some at Redmond's. Check for skier's rates and rent cars with snow tires and chains. The **Central Oregon Shuttle** (tel. 503/382-9371) runs from Portland airport to Bend. **Pacific Trailways** has daily bus service from Portland to Bend. **Amtrak** stops in Chemult, an hour from Bend. **Resort Bus Lines** (tel. 503/389-7755) will meet skiers if arrangements are made in advance. Resort Bus Lines has daily service from Bend to the mountain.

MOVING AROUND: The easiest way to get around is via your own car. The Resort Bus Lines service operates daily between the mountain and Bend. Sunriver, the Inn at the Seventh Mountain, and other properties offer service to the mountain in the morning and from the mountain to the lodge in the afternoon. During the evening, skiers must find their own transportation or stay near their lodges.

Call-A-Cab (tel. 382-1687) and **Transcentral** (tel. 382-0800) service the Sunriver/Bend/Redmond area.

TOURIST INFORMATION: For reservations and information about the skiing and skiing/lodging packages, contact **Mount Bachelor Ski and Summer Resort**, P.O. Box 1031, Bend, OR 97709 (tel. 503/382-8334, or toll free 800/547-6858 in Oregon). Many of the lodges in the area (see Where to Stay) have toll-free "800" numbers. The **snow report** number is 503/382-7888.

2. Mount Hood Area: Mount Hood Meadows, Mirror Mountain, and Timberline

THE RESORT: Mount Hood, an 11,245-vertical-foot extinct volcano, dominates Portlanders' eastern panoramic view. When the snowy cone is clear, they rush up to one of the ski areas set on its treed flanks: Mount Hood Meadows and Timberline. Oregonians consider Mount Hood Meadows and Timberline, approximately 65 miles from Portland, as day areas, but there is limited lodging at the unique, historic Timberline Lodge and in a few tiny towns along the road heading up the mountain. City folk may start out in the sun or rain at Portland, but as they drive up I-84N, then on U.S. 26, they'll begin climbing. When the rain changes to snow and the snowbanks on the side of the roads are piled high enough to block the view, they know they're nearing ski country.

THE SKI AREAS: Between the three areas—Timberline, Mount Hood Meadows, and Mirror Mountain—day skiers can find an incredible range of learn-to-ski programs and slopes to practice or play on. Mirror Mountain is the smallest and closest to Portland. Timberline's well-pitched beginner and intermediate terrain is filled with clothed skiers during the winter, but during the summer ski season the recreational skiers and racers practicing on the upper slopes are often considerably less dressed in response to the warm weather. Mount Hood Meadows has the most variable terrain, with good slopes for all skill levels.

MOUNT HOOD MEADOWS SKIING: Located on the east side of Mount Hood, the 2,777 vertical feet of terrain encompasses more than 40 trails and slopes with an honest mix of beginner, intermediate, and some very steep—but short—pitches of advanced terrain. The statistics read: 30% beginner, 40% intermediate, 20% advanced, and 10% expert. Seven double chairs and a triple chair access the 2,000 skiable acres, which includes terrain lit for night skiing.

Facing Mount Hood's rocky pinnacle, beginners have the terrain on the left around the Red, Buttercup, and Daisy chairs, where there are well-packed, wide, short runs. They also have one top-to-bottom run stretching down the area's perimeter, accessible when the Texas chair is open. The Texas chair, the only one that pokes above timberline and is very exposed, opens if weather conditions permit. It holds approximately one-third of the ski area's vertical.

Intermediates have the long, smoothly groomed runs off the Hood Run Meadows chair, on the opposite end of the mountain. On rough-weather days, skiers may find these protected runs more fun to ski. However, because these runs start so much lower than most of the trails (the chair starts more than 1,000 feet lower than the base lodge), the snow may be icier than at the top some days. Intermediates also have a network of trails heading off the top of the Texas chair as well as a network of trails belling off the right side of the Blue chair, with good cruising runs such as Middle Fork.

Advanced and expert skiers cruise down Ridge Run to challenge the bowl area, a piece of mountainside to the left of the Blue chair with a grade ranging from steep to ultra-steep. The advanced skiers may test out the Four Bowl section to build up their courage and skills. Experts head straight down (almost literally) One Bowl. The most talked-about run (which is only reachable from the top of the Texas chair) is Heather's Canyon, a three-mile-long outback trail for experts.

When the Express lift was installed a few years ago, it doubled uphill capacity from the base area and eliminated lines. However, skiers must still walk uphill several hundred feet to get to the lifts.

There is night skiing off five chairs on the front of the mountain. Runs for all skill levels are illuminated.

Mountain Facilities

Mount Hood Meadows has a two base lodges and a mini-lodge located below the Hood River Meadows chair (intermediates who use this chair can park here and avoid the more crowded base area). There are several bars, a deli, a snack shack, a bakery (with fresh chocolate-chip cookies), and a pizza-by-the-slice and salad bar area in the two lodges. There is often live entertainment during late afternoon and evening hours.

The north lodge has a large rental department and both lodges have changing areas with lockers for skiers. For a minimal fee skis can be checked in and out all day or for the night.

At the main lifts, there is a large building housing a "try before you buy" demo center. Any skier can test top-of-the-line equipment prior to purchase. (Skiers can try two pairs of skis or boots for their rental price.) At the end of the day, the skier receives a card with pertinent data about the equipment they tested and a list of shops in the metro area where the equipment is for sale.

Snow Coverage

There is no snowmaking. The average yearly accumulated level of snow is 190 inches at this area, where the skiing season is from mid-November to mid-May.

Ski School

The in-house ski school has a variety of programs for skiers from never-evers to racers. In addition to regular privates, there are super privates with video analysis. This ski area also runs a "Kids Over 50" program on weekends in which groups of adults of similar age are placed with special instructors who are trained in techniques for skiing all terrains under all conditions. Mount Hood Meadows also offers a Kidski first-timer program for ages 4 to 7 with supervision throughout the day and a weekend program for youngsters ages 6 to 11. There is a mini-mite program offering three days of lessons, snow play, rental, and transportation for parents who can ski midweek. The area promotes midweek, and

Sundowner programs offering lessons and après-ski activities to skiers who can travel from the metro area on regularly scheduled buses.

Childcare
Children can be placed in a variety of ski-school programs.

Rental Equipment
Rentals are available in the main lodge. High-performance demos can be rented in the large building above the lodges.

Cross-Country Skiing
The Nordic Center is located at Hood River Meadows, by the lower parking lot. There is a nominal fee for track skiing on the 26-km (15½-mile) trail system. Telemarking lessons are available.

Getting There
From Portland most skiers take I-84 N, U.S. 26, and Ore. 35. To make a scenic loop, return home via Ore. 35 and I-84, which borders the Columbia River. (This will avoid the traffic jams created by skiers from all Mount Hood areas heading home.) There is bus transportation (tel. 503/297-8801) from the Portland area.

MOUNT HOOD MEADOWS TOURIST INFORMATION: Contact **Mount Hood Meadows**, P.O. Box 470, Mount Hood, OR 97041 (tel. 503/297-8802 or 503/337-2222). For **weather** and **snow conditions** call: 503/227-SNOW. Lift-ticket prices vary according to the block of time skiing and there are imaginative multiticket programs. Call for details.

MIRROR MOUNTAIN SKIING: Formerly called Multipour Ski Bowl, Mirror Mountain is the oldest ski area on Mount Hood. Four double chairs and rope tows access the fully lighted slopes at this 1,400-vertical-foot area, the smallest in the region.

Mountain Facilities
There are two day lodges with cafeterias; the West Lodge has a fully licensed Stube. Because it is adjacent to Government Camp, the local ski village, there are ski shops and restaurants and some lodging within walking distance.

Ski School
Regular and private alpine and cross-country lessons are available.

Getting There
Mirror Mountain is 53 miles east of Portland on U.S. 26, next to the ski village of Government Camp.

MIRROR MOUNTAIN TOURIST INFORMATION: Because Mirror Mountain was up for sale at the time this was written, contact the **Mount Hood Recreation Association**, P.O. Box 342, Welches, OR 97067 (tel. 503/224-7158), for the status of this ski area.

TIMBERLINE SKIING: There are two styles of vacation at Timberline, site of the unique Timberline Lodge. During the winter it's a conventional ski trip to a pleasant, mid-size area. In the summer it's a blend of cruising down smooth, primarily intermediate terrain in the mornings, followed by afternoons of golfing at Rippling River, rafting the swift water of the Deschutes River, windsurfing at Columbia Gorge or just sitting poolside. The combination of skiing in a T-shirt all morning, followed by hot-weather activities in the afternoon creates the unmistakable aura of decadence!

At Timberline the number of skiable vertical feet depends on the time of year. During the winter it's 2,000 vertical feet. During the summer the number jumps to 2,500, but the skiing starts a thousand feet higher, up at 6,000 feet above sea level (near the day lodge) and climbs to 8,500, which means glacier skiing on the treeless section of Mount Hood.

This area is terrific for beginners and intermediates during the winter months because there are so many gentle trails. The lower runs here, especially off the Victoria Station chair (which often has the shortest lift line), are set between thickly wooded sections of trees, so protected during poor weather. The upper runs off the Magic Mile double chair are more open, so when the wind sweeps through, it's not the place to be. The biggest network of beginner runs is off the Pucci chair, while intermediates can find many cruising runs off the Blossom chair.

The runs off the Pucci chair and some of the runs off the Victoria Station chair are lit for night skiing.

When the towers for the Palmer Lift are uncovered, this lift opens for the summer. Usually this means glacier skiing from late May until September 4. Although the weather can range from blizzards to swimsuit temperatures, the snow usually softens by midday, so the lifts open early in the morning and close early in the afternoon. (Check locally for hours.) Although there are many recreational skiers on the slopes, this is the main summer racing camp site in North America. It's most usual to see more than a dozen race clinics working in well-defined lanes stretching across the mountain. (Olympic team members racing through gates to keep their legs in shape is a common sight here.)

Mountain Facilities

The Wy'East day lodge has stores, lift-ticket windows, and the ski-school desk on the lowest level. The Wy'East Kitchen, which serves three meals a day, is on the second level, as is the skiers' bar. (As you move around here, notice some of the artworks, from the enameled metal frieze to the kinetic work, set throughout the building.) The Blue Ox Bar, the Ram's Head Bar, and the Cascade Dining Room are located in the spectacular Timberline Lodge, a short walk uphill from the day lodge. (Under continual renovation by the Friends of Timberline, this historic lodge, built during the Depression's Works Progress Administration, is a usable museum of craftsmanship during the '30s. There are 57 guest rooms in this unique building. See Where to Stay for additional information.)

Snow Coverage

An average of 21 feet of snow falls on this ski area, which is open in the late fall and often stays open through early September. Slopes are groomed as needed.

Ski School

The runs here are filled with ski classes brought out by schools based in Portland and with those from the in-house ski school. Timberline's ski school offers regular group lessons, and both midweek and weekend multiple-lesson packages. The SKIWEE program is available here. The resident ski-school counter is in the Wy'East day lodge.

Childcare

Children can be put in the SKIWEE program.

Rental Equipment

Both alpine and cross-country skis for adults and children are available in the day lodge.

Cross-Country Skiing

Timberline Nordic, Inc., offers both classes and private lessons in set-track skiing at the White River Nordic Center and cross-country downhill lessons on the ski slopes. Both day and overnight guided ski tours are available. Tours with a gourmet meal in the wilderness, midway through a guided tour/lesson, are available for groups of six or more.

TIMBERLINE TOURIST INFORMATION: Contact the **Timberline Ski Area Lodge**, Timberline, OR 97028 (tel. 503/272-3311, 226-7979 in Portland; or toll free 800/547-1406 in Washington, Idaho, Utah, Nevada, and northern California; 800/452-1335 in Oregon).

WHERE TO STAY: Most skiers drive up to one of these ski areas just for the day, but some choose to stay at the unique Timberline Ski Area Lodge (see Tourist Information above for address and phones). A stone/and/wood castle constructed during the '30s under the Works Progress Administration, it was outfitted and furnished by hand-craftsmanship. It takes more than one tour of the building's public areas to notice such details as the hand-carved animals decorating the tops of the posts on the stair railings, the wrought-iron hinges, full doors and ornaments throughout the building, the hexagonal man-thick columns that support the lobby lounge, and the hexagonal stone chimney with three walk-in fireplaces which is the focal point of the two-story lobby. There are two lounge areas, one set around the base of the stone chimney and the other on the balcony, as well as a dining room with an elaborate continental menu. Ask for one of the renovated guest rooms; most of the 59 rustic rooms have been restored in keeping with the original handmade furnishings. Lodging options range from bunk rooms (without a private bath) in the chalet to a large bedroom with a fireplace and a sitting area. Prices range from $39 for two people in the chalet to $105 for two in the best of the fireplace rooms. (Ask for the one with Roosevelt's chair.) Timberline Ski Area Lodge is isolated, so skiers must create most of their own evening entertainment.

There are other accommodations in Government Camp, the few-block ski town on the highway near the access road to Mount Hood Meadows and Timberline and in other small towns on the way down the mountain. **Rippling River** at Mount Hood, 68010 E. Fairway Ave., Welches, OR 97067 (tel. 503/622-3101, or toll free 800/452-4612 in Oregon, 800/547-8054 in other western states), has reasonably priced skier packages which include lifts and lodging in a condo complex with a heated pool, Jacuzzi, and sauna. However, lodging quality varies widely here from luxurious and renovated to older units, so question what you're getting. Skiing golfers might want to stay here during spring or early summer because there are 27 holes of golf to test when skiing is over by midday.

ENTERTAINMENT: The **Blue Ox** and the **Ram's Bar** in the Timberline Ski

Area Lodge are relaxing après-ski spots for skiers at Timberline. Regulars at Mount Hood's ski resorts stop for a drink and a hamburger or a grill-your-own-steak at **Charlie's Mountain View Restaurant** in Government Camp. Although the place is short on "atmosphere," it is a popular spot that has been put on the locals' map by woodcarvings of the Mahre brothers, Debbi Armstrong, and Bill Johnson, which decorate one wall. Created by John Zipprich, each has been signed by the racer depicted. Sandwiches start at $3, and steaks go up to approximately $8.

TOURIST INFORMATION: For additional information about the Mount Hood ski areas, contact the individual ski areas or **Mount Hood Recreation Association,** P.O. Box 342, Welches, OR 97067.

3. Other Oregon Ski Areas

MOUNT ASHLAND: Two chairs and three surface lifts open up the slopes and bowl skiing at Mount Ashland Ski Area during the day and on Thursday, Friday, and Saturday evenings. The terrain on the 1,150-vertical-foot mountain is rated 10% beginner, 25% intermediate, and 65% advanced. For information, contact **Ski Ashland, Inc.,** P.O. Box 220, Ashland, OR 97520 (tel. 503/482-2897).

MOUNT BAILEY: Powderhounds should check into the operation at Mount Bailey, where snowcats take skiers up the mountainside for runs of more than 2,800 vertical feet. For more information, contact **Mount Bailey,** Diamond Lake Resort, Diamond Lake, OR 97731 (tel. 503/793-3333).

HOODOO SKI BOWL: Hoodoo Ski Bowl, 86 miles northwest of Eugene, has exceptionally low rates for skiers using the three chairs and rope tow which service the 16 runs on the 1,000-vertical-foot ski area. For information about hours, lift-ticket prices, and ski-school classes, contact **Hoodoo Ski Bowl,** U.S. 20 (P.O. Box 200), Sisters, OR 97759 (tel. 503/342-5540).

Chapter XVI

WASHINGTON

1. Crystal Mountain Resort
2. Mission Ridge
3. Ski "The Big 3"
4. Other Washington Ski Areas

SKIING CONDITIONS IN WASHINGTON, like those in Oregon, are subject to the very changeable winter weather. For an overview of the areas in both states of the Pacific Northwest, see the introduction to Chapter XV.

1. Crystal Mountain Resort

THE RESORT: A bare-bones resort, the few lodges, restaurants, and amenities —two communal pools and a whirlpool—are clustered around the base of Crystal Mountain. (The ski runs reach upward framed by neighboring 14,410-foot Mount Rainier.) But before comparing this to megaresorts, remember that it's the only ski complex in the Northwest with all the amenities at the base of the ski runs versus those whose amenities are miles away in a town. The slopes are peopled with a blend of day skiers from the coast (Seattle is 76 miles away) and visitors who want a relaxed ski vacation. They can beat their bodies on the ski runs during the day, but the après-ski life is so limited it would be hard to do the same at night. This is a place for skiers who come with friends and/or for better northwestern skiers who want to test their skills against some very challenging slopes.

THE SKIING: This is one of the few areas where there are more trails and skiable slopes in the unmarked areas of the map than outlined on the map. The 3,102-vertical-foot mountain is accessed by six double- and three triple-chair lifts. The terrain is rated 20% beginner, 37% intermediate, and 43% advanced and expert. The front side, which holds the groomed green, blue, and black runs, encompasses approximately 600 acres. The experts-only northern backcountry has about 1,400 acres, and the south backcountry encompasses 300 acres.

Considered a day area by Seattle residents, it should be considered a destination area for advanced skiers located anywhere in the Northwest. Much of the terrain here resembles the more famous steeps at Snowbird and Jackson Hole. Unfortunately, skiers must deal with the usually much heavier northwestern snow.

The beginner terrain is limited here; it encompasses about 10% of the mountain. It is beginner, as compared to the rest of the mountain, but there are pitches that would be in the intermediate category at many other slopes (although the trails are wide enough for big wedge turns). Queens, the top-to-bottom beginner run off the 20-minute chair 5, rolls down the mountainside. There are several other easy runs off chair 4.

The intermediate terrain stretches from the classical blue runs, such as Mr. Magoo and Boon Doggle, to the Snorting Elk, a powder bowl that can be an easy blue for skiers taking wide traverses or a borderline run if they head straight downward. There's enough intermediate terrain to keep skiers occupied for the weekend, and management continues to develop more slopes for both intermediates and beginners.

The skiers who spend time at this resort become very good—rapidly—if they venture onto the black terrain regularly. Intermediates following the cat-track trails (they aren't wide enough for beginners) through the expert areas will see ski tracks plunging off perpendicular mountainside between the trees—in places considered unskiable by all but the very good. For the merely advanced skiers, there are many sections where there is good bowl skiing, intermixed with areas where the trees are spaced apart just enough to allow for a few mistakes. Many of the popular routes down the mountain aren't on the map; just watch while riding up the lift to see where locals are making tracks. Exterminator is a particularly popular run; it's long with lots of steeps and often bumps. The popular, locally named Orgasm Meadows has steep sides funneling into a wide gulley. Bull Run is the local "show-off" slope for hot shots.

The backcountry sections are for expert skiers. They are never groomed, but there are several trails cut in the 1,400-acre north backcountry and open powder bowls in the south backcountry. The ski patrol requests that skiers at least have a companion, if not in a gaggle of skiers. The entrance to the north backcountry is off lift 3. The ski patrol encourages first-timers to the backcountry to stop and ask what the conditions are and which runs might be best that day. Although there are a few ways down that end up back at the area, many of the runs (which are several miles long) end on a road, and skiers must wait for the shuttlebus that runs approximately every 20 minutes.

Crystal Mountain Resort, considered a day area by residents of Seattle, has night skiing around three chairs. Check locally for hours and days.

Mountain Facilities

There's a day lodge with a cafeteria and a beer stube, and a summit house. The Rafters, an attractive dining area in the day lodge, has sit-down breakfasts and lunches, and live entertainment on the weekends. The ski shop is located at the base, and the rental shop is on the lower level of the tower-topped building. There's a small grocery shop.

Snow Coverage

There is no snowmaking at Crystal, which receives an average of 17 feet of snow each winter. The ski area is usually open from mid-November to the end of April. The green runs are groomed regularly and many blue runs are groomed as needed.

Ski School

Both morning and afternoon group lessons are available, as are private lessons. Ask about the beginner's special and the backcountry tours.

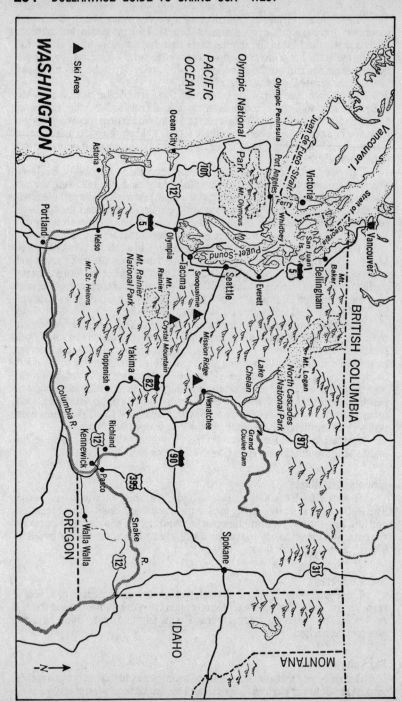

Childcare

The **Crystal Mountain Childcare Center** (tel. 663-2300) is located in the poolside building next to the Crystal Inn. Activities are organized, and there is supervised outdoor play. Children can be left by the hour, or half or full day. Reservations are recommended.

Rental Equipment

Rental equipment is available in the Crystal Mountain Ski and Rental Shop located on the lower level of the tower-topped building.

Cross-Country Skiing

Cross-country lessons are available through the ski school.

WHERE TO STAY: Skiers choose between the handful of lodges set around the edges of the main parking lot at the base of the ski area. The lodging is moderate to expensive by most ski-area standards. Information about nightly rates, lodging/lift and lodging/lift and meal packages, as well as **reservations at most of these lodges,** can be arranged by calling 206/663-2558).

The rustic condominiums at the **Silver Skis Chalet** sleep from four to eight people. They are geared for families or groups, with one or two bedrooms and a kitchen-living area, many with fireplaces. A standard apartment, sleeping four, is in the $84 range; add a fireplace and the price jumps approximately $8. There is a heated outdoor pool in the central courtyard.

The **Crystal House** has comfortable rooms with queen-size beds. Some units have added a loft with twin beds, which is ideal for families. During non-holiday midweeks, food packages are available. Nightly rates for one or two people to a unit is $63; nightly rates for the rooms with sleeping lofts average $75.

The **Village Inn,** next door, features custom furniture and stenciled wallpaper in the compact rooms. The rooms are designed for two people with either a queen-size bed or two twins. They will provide champagne and flowers for special occasions. Food packages are available during midweek non-holiday seasons. Rooms for one or two start at $66, and midweek rates are less.

The **Alpine Inn,** Crystal Mountain, WA 98022 (tel. 206/663-2262), is basic lodging at the base of the ski area. You can share bathrooms for lesser rates, but a double with a private bath is $55 for two. Midweek vacation packages with breakfast, dinner, and lift tickets are also available at reasonable rates.

WHERE TO EAT: Dining choices here are limited. The **Crystal Inn and Saloon** (tel. 663-2526) has prime rib, seafood, and Cajun dishes. Entrees range from $7 to $16.

There are chef's buffets at **The Rafters,** in the base lodge (tel. 663-2526), on Friday, Saturday, and Sunday nights.

The **Alpine Inn Restaurant** (tel. 663-2262) serves three meals daily. Breakfasts are in the $3 to $4 range; lunches sell for $5 to $6; and dinners, ranging from weinerschnitzel and pork paprika to game hen and seafood Créole, run $7 to $15.

The **Snorting Elk Deli** in the Alpine Inn is open from 11 a.m. to 8 p.m. serving homemade meat and vegetarian pies, deli sandwiches, soups, pastries, and more. Espresso, beer, and liquor are available.

There are hearty skier breakfasts in the ski area's base cafeteria.

If you're driving to Crystal Mountain for the day, pick up a brown-bag lunch from **Baumgartner's** in Enumclaw (tel. 825-1067), with atmosphere reminiscent of a country store. It's open from 10 a.m. to 6 p.m. daily, and the sandwich list includes excellent deli meats, salads, and bagels. You can call ahead to order sandwiches to take to the mountains. Prices range from $2 to $5.

GETTING THERE: Crystal is located in the Snoqualmie National Forest on the northeast boundary of Mount Rainier National Park. From Seattle (76 miles away), skiers come in private and rental cars by driving south on I-5 (take exit 142A, Wash. 18) to Auburn, then Wash. 164 to Enumclaw. Drive through Enumclaw and follow Wash. 410 for 33 miles to the Crystal Mountain turnoff. There is bus service from Enumclaw during the winter.

MOVING AROUND: Everything is within walking distance of the lodges.

TOURIST INFORMATION: For more information, contact **Crystal Mountain Resort**, P.O. Box 1, Crystal Mountain, WA 98022 (tel. 206/663-2265). The **snow phone** is 206/634-3771.

2. Mission Ridge

THE RESORT: Mission Ridge, a classic mid-size ski area, is carved out of a mountainside on the eastern side of the Cascades. The snow might be a little drier here, especially when the storms come from the northwest and sweep over the Cascades before dumping on this ski resort. All the beds, the nightlife, and restaurants are located in the town of Wenatchee, set in the valley 13 miles below. Keep in mind that Wenatchee is a town fueled by interests other than skiing—so skiers blend into the general picture rather than dominating the scene.

THE SKIING: Mission Ridge has ego-building terrain for intermediates on the 33 major runs off the four chair lifts opening up the 2,140-vertical-foot mountain. The mountain stair-steps: steep at the top, flat, then steep, then flat again. The terrain is rated 10% beginner, 70% intermediate, and 20% advanced. The longest run, Wayhut, is the top-to-bottom 4½-mile beginner run that winds its way down the mountainside. In many places it crosses more difficult runs, so beginners can see what they'll ski at a later date. Mimi is a smooth, graded-to-make-beginners-feel-good run.

Intermediates can roam over 70% of the mountain down runs that appear to wander through the woods. (If you look upward, you can see that the trails at Mission Ridge wander down the mountainside without the sharply defined edges that create the "freeway" effect so common at ski areas. This gives skiers more of that feeling of drifting through the woods.) Runs such as Tumwater, with its consistent grade and fall line, and Kiwa are good ego-building intermediate runs. Outback, wide-open terrain with lots of rolls, is a popular area. Chak Chak and Bombers Bowl are for more advanced intermediates.

Most of the advanced terrain is light to medium black. Skiers can explore Upper Toketie, Lip Lip, and Tillikum for starters. The locals say there is good expert terrain on this mountain—if you know where to go. They say to ask how to find Nertz, Chute 1, or Snake Pit. (Taking an advanced ski-school class is another option.)

There is night skiing several times each week around chair 4 and the beginner rope tow. Check for hours and days.

Mountain Facilities
There's a day lodge with a cafeteria, ski rental and repair, lockers, and a ski check. The Snak-Shack is midway up the mountain.

Snow Coverage
There is snowmaking on some of the lower runs at this area, which normally receives 70 inches of snow each year. Mission Ridge is usually open from December to April. The runs are groomed as needed, especially the blue and green trails.

Ski School
The ski school offers group and private lessons as well as a variety of special programs ranging from specially priced noon "clinics" to "little people" packages for children from 4 to 8 years old.

The Mission Ridge Ski Training Academy is a full-time racing program that attracts aspiring ski racers. (Three students, including Bill Johnson, made the U.S. Ski Team.) Recreational racing and the Buddy Werner junior racing program are both very popular here.

Childcare
There is no childcare facility on the mountain. Call 509/663-5395 for daycare referrals in Wenatchee.

Rental Equipment
The **Arlberg Ski Shop** has regular and high-performance rentals. The main shop is located at 25 N. Wenatchee Ave., but there is a satellite shop in the lower floor of the ski lodge at Mission Ridge.

Cross-Country Skiing
There are 42 km (25½ miles) of cross-country trails. Cross-country skiers taking the trails starting at the top of the ski lifts (which go around, not just straight down) can buy a one-ride lift ticket.

WHERE TO STAY: There are lots of motels in this mid-size town halfway between Seattle and Spokane. Two of the most comfortable motels are the Chieftain and the Thunderbird. The **Chieftain Motel**, 1005 N. Wenatchee Ave., Wenatchee, WA 98801 (tel. 509/663-8141, or toll free 800/572-4456 in Washington), has surprisingly large, comfortable rooms with queen-size beds. Some suites are available at this motel located in the center of Wenatchee near downtown stores, theaters, and a shopping center. Packages of a double room with lift tickets go for approximately $41 per night, and there is a dining room on the premises.

There are 150 comfortable rooms with queen-size beds in the **Thunderbird Motor Inn**, 1225 N. Wenatchee Ave., Wenatchee, WA 98801 (tel. 509/663-0711, or toll free 800/547-8010). Amenities include a coffeeshop and a plush dining room. Rates are reasonable, going from approximately $80 for a room and lift tickets for two persons.

WHERE TO EAT: In this Middle America town, the food choices range from gourmet to Mexican or burgers. Although there are some expensive restaurants, there are several moderate and inexpensive choices frequented by locals that welcome skiers.

More Expensive
In the **Chieftain Motel,** 1005 N. Wenatchee Ave. (tel. 663-7188), there's a comfortable restaurant with American cuisine in the $3 to $7 range for the light dinners, or $7 to $13 for more complete meals. It is open weekdays from 6 a.m. to 10 p.m., and on Friday, Saturday, and Sunday from 7 a.m. to 10 p.m. The nearby **Pow Wow Lounge** provides live entertainment regularly.

David Brown's **Second Story,** at 23 S. Wenatchee Ave. (tel. 662-1508), is a pleasant restaurant with exposed brick walls and rich blue carpeting. It is open from Monday to Sunday at 11:30 a.m. for lunch with prices in the $4 to $12 range, and for dinner from 4:30 to 10 p.m., with the continental cuisine priced from $5 to $18.

J.P. Beans, 29 N. Columbia (tel. 662-2582), has novel decor and is a popular casual spot. Sandwiches are in the $3 to $8 range. It is open Monday through Saturday from 11:30 a.m. to 2 a.m., on Sunday from 11:30 a.m. to 10 p.m.

Less Expensive Restaurants
Burgerbeers, at 821 N. Wenatchee Ave. (tel. 662-8208), has an entertaining variety of inexpensive burgers and other sandwiches in the $3 to $5 range. They are also open for breakfast and prices average $3 to $4. Dinners are available from chicken at $4 to steaks at $8.

Serving food from 10 a.m. to 10 p.m., the **Orondo,** at 111 Orondo St. (tel. 663-1018), is a favorite with the locals. The back area houses pool tables, and ball team pennants decorate the walls. Lunches and dinners are light, from salad to steak, for $3.50 to $10.

NON-SKIER ACTIVITIES: The **North Central Washington Museum,** 127 S. Mission (tel. 622-4728), has two floors of exhibits about local history and a fine arts gallery. Check locally for hours. The **Rocky Reach Dam,** on U.S. 97 north of town, has a museum within the dam's main structure which includes a sampling of local geology and a gallery of electricity. Check locally for hours. Visit the Bavarian town of **Leavenworth,** for the Christmas lighting ceremony if the timing is right.

GETTING THERE: Mission Ridge is located 13 miles from Wenatchee, approximately 150 miles from Seattle and 165 from Spokane. **Horizon Airways** has daily service to Wenatchee from Seattle, Spokane, Tri-Cities, and Portland. Many major airlines serve Seattle. Both east- and westbound **Amtrak** trains stop in Wenatchee daily. **Greyhound** has daily service from Seattle, Spokane, and other major cities. **Budget** and **Hertz** have car-rental offices in town.

MOVING AROUND: Most skiers drive to the area.

TOURIST INFORMATION: For more information about this area, contact **Mission Ridge,** 212 S. Mission St. (P.O. Box 1765), Wenatchee, WA 98801 (tel. 509/633-7631). The **snow report** and **mountain office** number is 509/663-7631. For **ski packages,** call **Arlberg Sport Tours** at 509/663-7401.

3. Ski "The Big 3"

THE RESORT: Ski "The Big 3" is the skier factory of the Northwest. Actually three separate day ski areas under one management, Ski Acres, Snoqualmie, and Alpental are strung alongside I-90, less than 50 miles from downtown Seattle. All three are available on one lift ticket, and a shuttlebus system takes skiers on the frontage road between the resorts. The hours vary but at least two of the three areas are open daily, and there is night skiing for those who rush up after work. (There's daily and nightly bus service.)

THE SKIING: Snoqualmie, with a 900-foot vertical, is a learn-to-ski mountain with eight chairs and five beginner rope tows to move skiers up the open slopes. The neighboring 1,050-foot vertical Ski Acres has a lot of beginner terrain off the seven chairs and six beginner rope tows. There are several short, steep pitches off the top. Alpental has a blend of beginner, intermediate, and some very challenging advanced terrain on the 2,200-foot vertical serviced by four chairs, a platter pull, and four beginner rope tows. (PSIA examiners training other instructors have commented on the skill needed to control skis on some black-rated steep sections here when the snow is icy.) When the backcountry is open, the size of the skiable area just about doubles.

Mountain Facilities

There are lodges with food service at the base of each ski area. There is sit-down dining in the Restaurant Continental and cocktails in the Winestube at Snoqualmie. Petter's Place is the lounge at Ski Acres. There's often live entertainment and dancing at Alpental and Snoqualmie.

Snow Coverage

Because these ski areas are so close to the ocean, the snow is wet and can compact quickly into an icy surface. There's a strong emphasis on grooming at this complex, which usually stays open from mid-November through April.

Ski School

Each area has its own resident ski school offering a wide range of programs from single morning, afternoon, and evening group lessons to multilesson packages. Contact Ski "The Big 3" for a complete list. In the Northwest, other ski schools are allowed to teach on the slopes. Ask locally (at the ski area or in ski shops) for a list of which schools are offering classes where.

Childcare

The day-care center is located in the main lodge of Ski Acres. For information and reservations, call the **Mercer Island office** (tel. 206/232-8182 before the area opens, 206/434-6400 during the season). There are ski-school programs for children age 3 and up.

Rental Equipment

Rental equipment is available at all three base areas.

Cross-Country Skiing

The **Ski Acres Cross Country Center** has a groomed track. Set track and telemark lessons, special clinics, and avalanche and backcountry seminars are all available. Contact the Seattle office (tel. 206/946-0443) or the mountain office (tel. 206/434-6646) for more information.

TOURIST INFORMATION: For information about the current season, contact **Ski "The Big 3"**, 3010 77th Ave. SE, Suite 201, Mercer Island, WA 98040. Call the **Ski "The Big 3" Snow-line** (tel. 206/236-1600) for ski reports, updates, and special events.

4. Other Washington Ski Areas

WHITE PASS: White Pass has made the news because it is the home of Olympic and World Champion skiing twins Steve and Phil Mahre. It is the most southerly area in Washington, with a vertical rise of 1,500 feet and an average snowfall of 100 to 150 inches. It has 20% beginner terrain, 60% intermediate, and 20% advanced. There is night skiing on Thursday, Friday, Saturday, and during school vacations. There is limited (300 pillows) lodging nearby.

For more information, contact **White Pass**, P.O. Box 354, Yakima, WA 98907 (tel. 509/453-8731).

STEVEN'S PASS: Steven's Pass, 78 miles east of Seattle on U.S. 2, is a popular area with skiers who live on the coast. The average annual snowfall of 120 inches guarantees dependable snow from mid-November to mid-April. The 1,800-foot vertical drop accessed by eight chairs includes 20% beginner, 55% intermediate, and 25% advanced slopes. There is night skiing every evening. Childcare is available several days a week.

For more information, contact **Steven's Pass**, P.O. Box 98, Leavenworth, WA 98826 (tel. 206/973-2441).

MOUNT BAKER: Mount Baker is a favorite of Canadian skiers because it is located near their border a 2½-hour drive from Seattle. Three tows and six chairs open up the 1,500-foot vertical ski area with open slopes and bowl skiing. It has the longest season in the state, usually running into mid-May.

For more information, contact **Mount Baker**, 2014 Moore St., Bellingham, WA 98225 (tel. 206/734-6771).

MOUNT SPOKANE: Mount Spokane sits in the western part of the state, 30 miles northeast of the city of Spokane. The mountain's 1,514-foot vertical has 23 runs and open slopes accessed by five chairs and two tows. There is limited lodging at the base.

For more information, contact **Mount Spokane**, P.O. Box 159, Mead, WA 99021 (tel. 509/238-6281).

49° NORTH: Located near Chewelah, the ski area is about an hour's drive north of Spokane. Its 1,850-foot vertical covers 30% beginner, 40% intermediate, and 30% advanced terrain. Out of the total 700 acres serviced by four chairs, this ski area has set aside 80 for the powderhounds, and there is night skiing. There is very limited lodging nearby.

For information, contact **49° North**, P.O. Box 166, Chewelah, WA 99109 (tel. 509/935-6649).

Chapter XVII

SKIING IN WESTERN CANADA

1. Whistler and Blackcomb
2. Banff National Park: Lake Louise, Sunshine Village, and Mount Norquay
3. Nakiska at Mount Allan
4. Heli-Skiing and Snowcat Skiing
5. Information Sources

ALTHOUGH THE NAME OF THIS BOOK is *Dollarwise Guide to Skiing USA—West,* it would be wrong to ignore skiing in western Canada. Long familiar to many U.S. skiers as that place where experts go to heli-ski, in reality the extended mountain ranges in western Canada are dotted with ski resorts that Canadians have enjoyed for years. Because the dollar is worth considerably more in this neighboring country, and the ambience at the Canadian resorts is so different, many U.S. residents are heading up to try the slopes. Calgary is the site of the 1988 Winter Olympics, so scenic Banff National Park, with three ski areas will be a popular vacation spot this winter.

The spine of the Canadian Rockies, the Continental Divide, stretches close to the imaginary line dividing the provinces of Alberta and British Columbia (B.C.). There are several major ski resorts in the scenic Banff and Jasper National Parks on the Alberta side. On the flip side of the Continental Divide, Panorama offers 3,200 vertical feet of skiing to challenge all skill levels and there are "beginner" helicopter-skiing programs here. Farther west, skiers can try the mid-size areas such as Big White and Apex Alpine. The ski areas with the largest lift-accessed vertical in North America—Blackcomb and Whistler—are located closer to the Pacific coast.

1. Whistler and Blackcomb

Whistler and Blackcomb, rising out of the same base village set in the coastal mountain range just two driving hours from Vancouver, boast some of the longest verticals on this continent. Blackcomb Mountain has the longest serviced vertical in North America since the addition of its high-alpine T-bar. The Mile High Mountain (5,280 vertical feet) has two temperate zones, so it's not uncommon for the lower slopes to be in clouds and the top 2,000 feet to be clear. Conditions are often similar on Whistler Mountain, which stretches 5,006 vertical feet.

The runs on Whistler Mountain can be attacked via the gondola from the original base or from a chair starting at the edge of the village. Both access long, rolling runs for beginners, an exciting variety of intermediate terrain, and five bowls, including Harmony Bowl with its powder chutes and never-groomed bump fields. There are free, on-mountain guided tours for those who want to quickly find comfortable terrain off one of the area's 15 lifts.

A triple chair lifts skiers out of the village, across a road and pastures to Blackcomb. A nouveau hi-tech ski area, Blackcomb delivers continually manicured runs and possibly the longest (up to seven miles) relaxed fall-line skiing on the continent. In fact the majority of the area's 48 runs set skiers up for ego-building experiences—however Seventh Heaven has some very challenging expert terrain.

The base village, Whistler, has a blend of accommodations ranging from basic to luxurious, where the equivalent at a trendy Stateside resort would cost considerably more. Après-ski amenities range from good, quiet restaurants to noisy discos in this fast-growing town.

Although staying in the resort town of Whistler is a real getaway, many day skiers use the express buses that run regularly to and from Vancouver. For additional information, contact the **Whistler Resort Association,** P.O. Box 1400, Whistler, British Columbia, Canada V0N 1B0 (tel. 604/932-4222, or toll free 800/663-8668 in Washington, Oregon, Montana, and Utah).

2. Banff National Park: Lake Louise, Sunshine Village, and Mount Norquay

THE RESORT: Driving to Banff, a roadside elk herd is framed by the triangular peaks and a wetsuited windsurfer skims by on a lake still fringed with ice. The road winds toward a small vacation town where the massive Banff Springs Hotel, a castle with a resident ghost, is the focal point. A resort town since the 1880s when a Canadian Pacific Railroad official decided that the confluence of the Bow and Spray Rivers was a perfect tourist site, Banff has remained a hot-springs anchor for a cinematic, 360° view of mountain wilderness. Its surrounding peaks lend a stark European feel and an awe-inspiring environment that has withstood the onslaught of visitors. There's plenty of lodging in Banff National Park, from the venerable Banff Springs Hotel and the Château Lake Louise to small motels in the town of Banff. The region boasts some 40 restaurants, shopping, and of course, the hot springs, for soaking after a rough day on the slopes. Most of the lodging and après-ski life is centered around the town of Banff, with the exception of the cluster of lodging near Lake Louise.

THE SKI AREAS: There are three ski areas in the park: Lake Louise, Sunshine Village, and Mount Norquay. Lake Louise is very large; skiers have several peaks to explore. Sunshine Village, perched on the Continental Divide, has a lot of open-bowl skiing. Mount Norquay, on the edge of the town of Banff, is most famous for North American, a steep run which experts discuss with great respect.

LAKE LOUISE SKIING: Lake Louise, which stretches over two mountains, is the largest ski area in the Canadian Rockies. Two triple and four double chairs, a T-bar, and a kid's tow open up 43 named runs (up to five miles long), bowls, mogul fields, and gladed timberline skiing. Terrain, rated 24% novice, 45% intermediate, and 30% expert, is spread more than 11 square miles! The vertical is 3,250 feet.

Look at the notes on the trail map outlining the best routes for novice and low intermediate skiers. Basically, start on the Sunny T-bar, then move on to the longer green runs which allow you to visually explore most of the ski area while you are moving around.

Intermediates will find good skiing in the Larch area. Larch is a local's favorite cruising run and Wolverine is narrower but of a nice length. There are two intermediate runs (reached by skiing Bobcat), with varying pitches, which are often less crowded. Skyline, off the Summit T-bar, is another popular run.

Advanced skiers can warm up on Boomerang to Brown Shirt, or Ptarmigan and Lynx if they like bumps. Then move on to Paradise Bowl, an open expanse with steeps and bumps. Some of the more radical terrain is in the Ptarmigan Glades, off the back side of the T-bar (in bounds), and around Tower 12, under the Larch chair (trees, powder/crud, and trees).

Insider's Tips

Locals say: "Never come over a rise without caution." (The snow cover apparently can vary in these spots.)

"Ski friends," volunteer hosts and hostesses, give free guided tours of the ski area daily at 10 a.m. and 1 p.m. Meet at the north end of the Whiskeyjack Lodge.

The Paradise chair is rarely crowded.

Try the granola breakfast or the buffet lunch at the Northface.

Mountain Facilities

The day lodge has a restaurant, a cafeteria, bar, ski and rental shop, and ski school. There is a cafeteria at the mid-mountain Whitehorn Lodge, and a cafeteria, the cozier Bear's Den and Sawyer's Nook, at Temple Lodge. There is a barbecue and "free hamburgers in the spring" at Temple.

Snow Coverage

The average annual snowfall is 140 inches and there is snowmaking on 125 acres on the south face and 20 acres on the back side and Larch. Lake Louise is usually open from early November to May.

Ski School

There are regular group and private lessons and many special theme days (bumps, powder, etc.) for better skiers. Look for the mobile Training Stations on the slopes. (You pay a flat fee for an instructional run with a ski instructor.) Ask about the action ski week, which includes social activities, instruction, and guiding.

Childcare

The nursery takes youngsters under age 2. Reservations are required for newborns to 18-month-olds. There is day care for ages 2 to 6 and kinder-ski (ski school and indoor play) for children age 3 to 7. Kids-Ski is for ages 8 to 12. Children under 8 ski free.

Rental Equipment

The ski shop has regular and high-performance rental equipment.

Tourist Information

Contact **Skiing Louise Ltd.**, 1550 8th St. SW, Suite 408, Calgary, Alberta, Canada T2R 1K1 (tel. 403/2-LOUISE, or toll free 800/661-1158 in western Canada and northwest U.S., 800/332-8307 in Alberta).

SUNSHINE VILLAGE SKIING: Skiers at Sunshine Village, perched on the Continental Divide, can explore the 3,514-foot-vertical mountainside via a gondola, a triple and five double chairs, three T-bars, and a beginner's tow. (That figure includes the trails leading down to the base of the gondola. The areas accessed by chairs has a shorter vertical.) Skiers travel the last three miles into the ski area by a gondola built several years ago to replace a twisting road. That road is now a ski run back to the gondola base. Skiers here can explore the wide, open bowl area: some sections have been turned into bump fields while other areas are groomed.

Skiers can pick their lines according to their personal skiing skills. Because the terrain is so open, even low intermediates will be comfortable in the bowl. There are runs cut between the trees in a separate area below the open bowl. There are runs with some cliff-steep sections next to the Tee Pee Town chair. Advanced skiers heading to the parking lot at the end of the day often take the Canyon trail, a narrow scenic gulley paralleling the road.

Insider's Tips

Avoid the Angel chair around lunchtime. Ski the lower lifts in the trees when the light is bad.

Free mountain tours leave from the mountain map in front of the Sunshine day lodge at 10:30 a.m. daily, and at 1 p.m. Monday through Friday.

Mountain Facilities

There is a cafeteria, a lounge with burgers and salads, a deli, and a western-style saloon in the Sunshine day lodge. There is sit-down dining, and the Chimney Corner Lounge, which has light meals, in the Sunshine Inn, a 90-room hotel at the top of the gondola which features ski weeks (see Where to Stay). There's a rental shop by the parking lot and a ski shop in the day lodge.

Snow Coverage

There is an average annual snowfall of almost 30 feet. Snowmaking isn't needed at this area, which is usually open from early November to early June.

Ski School

There are regular class and private lessons. There is a special program for never-evers.

Childcare

Kid's Kampus offers classes for children. Kindercare is for children from 19 months to 6 years old. Kinderday is a childcare/ski-instruction program for youngsters age 3 to 6. Kid's Day has lessons, both half and full day, for children age 6 to 12.

Rental Equipment

The Spoke 'N Edge Rental Shop, in the parking lot of the gondola terminal, has both Nordic and alpine equipment.

Tourist Information

Contact **Sunshine Village**, P.O. Box 1510, Banff, Alberta, Canada T0L 0C0 (tel. 403/762-6500, or toll free 800/661-1363, 800/372-9583 in Alberta).

MOUNT NORQUAY SKIING: The mogul fields and steep sections at Mount Norquay, considered a "locals" area because it's just five miles from town, challenge any expert. The 14 runs are accessed by three chairs, two T-bars, and a tow. The 1,300-foot-vertical rise includes some very tough black runs. Skiers getting off the main chair must take a long catwalk (which cuts back and forth across the top of the hill—it's not for people with a fear of heights) before reaching the skiable slope. Although there are some easier trails, vacationing beginners and intermediates might better enjoy exploring the shop windows in town.

Mountain Facilities

There's a cafeteria at the day lodge and the "Cliffhouse" restaurant at the top. Ski and adult clothing rentals are available. There's a ski school and childcare for children 2 years of age and older.

Tourist Information

Contact **Banff Lifts Ltd.**, P.O. Box 1258, Banff, Alberta, T0L 0C0, Canada (tel. 403/762-4421). The Calgary **snow phone** is 403/253-3383.

CROSS-COUNTRY SKIING: The Canmore Nordic Centre, designed for the 1988 Nordic Olympic events, has 56 km (34 miles) of trails for both relaxing skiing and Olympic-level competition. For information on the Canmore Nordic Centre and other Kananaskis cross-country ski facilities, contact the **Kananaskis Country Office,** Alberta Recreation and Parks, 1011 Glenmore Trail SW, Suite 412, Calgary, Alberta, Canada T2V 4Y8 (tel. 403/297-3362).

Nakiska has 40 km (25 miles) of double-track set trails from the base to Kananaskis Country ski trails. Sunshine Village has 20 km (12 miles) of track and unlimited off-track touring. The Nordic Centre offers information and equipment rentals. There are also cross-country trails around Château Lake Louise, and many people trek around the lake. There's a trail to Skoki Lodge (open during the winter for cross-country skiers). For more information or reservations at the lodge, contact **Skiing Louise Ltd.**, P.O. Box 5, Lake Louise, Alberta, Canada T0L 1E0 (tel. 403/522-3555). Ask locally for directions.

WHERE TO STAY: The Banff/Lake Louise area offers a wide range of accommodations to fit every pocketbook. Call for lodging prices—they vary during any ski season, and are expected to do so even more this year because the 1988 Alpine and Nordic Winter Olympic Games are nearby. For lodging information, contact one of the following places, your travel agent, or Banff Club Ski or write for the *Alberta Winter Activities Guide* for a more complete list of accommodations (see Tourist Information).

A stay at either the Banff Springs Hotel or the Château Lake Louise sets you in a different era. The baronial-style castle called the **Banff Springs Hotel,** Banff, Alberta, Canada T0L 0C0 (tel. 403/762-2211, or toll free 800/828-7447 in the U.S., 800/268-9411 in Canada, 800/268-9420 in Ontario and Québec), overlooks a valley and two rivers. It was founded in 1888 and its public rooms, from the massive meeting halls to the indoor health club, are all reminiscent of an opulent era when guests brought families to the mountains for weeks at a time. The more than 500 bedrooms are decorated in a variety of styles, with armoires or other antiques. The rooms range from very tiny to two-bedroom suites with parlors and entry halls housing guest bathrooms. The hotel is adding 250 more moderately priced rooms in another building, scheduled to be completed in time for the 1988 Olympics. There is an Olympic-size indoor pool and a Jacuzzi tucked in a rock grotto, as well as a heated outdoor pool. A small private (reserve early) hot-tub deck overlooks the winding river. There are several restaurants for dining, ranging from gourmet to sweets, and a glittery disco.

Looking out from the summit of the Lake Louise ski area, one can see the

Château Lake Louise, Lake Louise, Alberta, Canada T0L 1E0 (tel. 403/522-3511, or toll free 800/828-7447 in the U.S., 800/268-9411 in Canada, 800/268-9420 in Ontario and Québec), mirrored in its namesake lake. Guests are lodged in 380 rooms (and the lodge was being renovated and a 125-guest wing was scheduled to be finished before the Olympics), some of them overlooking the lake. Meals here are served in high rooms whose decor preserves a strong sense of history. As a more modern touch, the indoor pool and Jacuzzi provide a nice après-ski break before dining and visiting one of the nightspots in the hotel.

The **Inns of Banff Park,** P.O. Box 1077, Banff, Alberta, Canada T0L 0C0 (tel. 403/762-4581, or toll free 800/661-1272), offers basic, comfortable hotel rooms. There is an indoor pool, squash court, whirlpool and sauna, a restaurant, and a lounge.

Lake Louise Inn, P.O. Box 209, Lake Louise, Alberta, Canada T0L 1E0 (tel. 403/522-3791), offers basic hotel rooms, economy units, and condos. There is a restaurant, pub, and an indoor pool, sauna, and whirlpool.

The older section of log, brick, and stone **Deer Lodge,** P.O. Box 100, Lake Louise, Alberta, Canada T0L 1E0 (tel. 403/522-3747), has some quaint rooms. There is a dining room and a lounge in the lodge, just a few minutes' driving time from Lake Louise, and an outdoor rooftop hot tub.

WHERE TO EAT: There are more than 40 restaurants in this region. Choices range from elegant gourmet meals to fast food.

More Expensive

The French cuisine and tableside service at **Le Beaujolais,** on the corner of Banff Avenue and Buffalo (tel. 762-2712 or 762-5365), is highly rated by regulars. Dinner for two with wine can run between $50 and $60. Dinner hours are from 5 to 11 p.m. Call for reservations.

There are several restaurants at the **Banff Springs Hotel** (tel. 762-2211) offering everything from sushi to continental fare. Make reservations for the main dining room.

La Casa, upstairs at Giorgio's 219 Bauff Ave. (tel. 762-5116), has a few intimate dining rooms where guests can unwind over a leisurely meal. The full Italian menu features northern Italian cuisine at prices ranging from $13.50 to $16.50 for entrees. Dinner is from 5:30 p.m. Reservations are suggested.

Ticino's Restaurant, at 205 Wolf St. (tel. 762-3848), features Swiss cuisine with an Italian influence. Veau zurichoise (veal with mushrooms, cream, and white sauce) is one of the house specialties, and beef and fish dishes are available in this restaurant with a classic Swiss-style decor. Entrees go from $10 to $17. Try the soufflé glâcé Grand Marnier for dessert. Reservations are recommended at this restaurant which is open from 5 to 10 p.m. daily.

Moderate

Guido's, upstairs at 116 Banff Ave. (tel. 762-4002), is a casual Italian restaurant where couples and families can enjoy fresh pasta. The menu includes spaghetti and a variety of fettuccine and veal dishes. Dinners at this restaurant, which opens at 4:30 p.m. daily, range from $8 to $15.

Bumpers, 603 Banff Ave. (tel. 762-2622), offers inexpensive basic fare in hefty portions. You have your choice of the number of ribs, both prime and barbecued, as well as Canadian mountain stew and the chicken cafoosalum (chicken breasts basted in maple sugar–lime sauce), and other entrees ranging in price from $7 to $15. Dinner is from 4:30 to 10 p.m. daily; the upstairs lounge is open from 4:30 p.m. to midnight Sunday through Thursday and until 1 a.m. on Friday and Saturday.

Giorgio's, 219 Banff Ave. (tel. 762-5114), has two restaurants. La Pasta, the downstairs restaurant, is a very popular pasta and pizza stop where casually dressed skiers can replenish the calories burned during the day on fresh fettuccine, spaghetti, a variety of antipasto, and veal, chicken, or seafood entrees. Prices range from $7 to $13 at La Pasta, which opens at 4:30 p.m.

Less Expensive

Smitty's, 227 Banff Ave. (tel. 726-2533), is a family restaurant serving three meals a day. Waffles, burgers, steaks, chicken, and more are on the menu at this restaurant open from 6:30 a.m. to 9 p.m. during the winter.

The **Paris** restaurant, 114 Banff Ave. (tel. 726-3554), offers family dining in the moderate price range. There are croissant sandwiches and gourmet burgers, wienerschnitzel, veal paprika, and more. Lunches begin about $4, and dinners start at $7.50.

ENTERTAINMENT: Check out the action at the locals' favorite haunt—the **King Edward Hotel**—or **Silver City**, both on the main street. The more upscale-looking **Works**, a disco at the Banff Springs Hotel, is also crowded most nights.

NON-SKIER ACTIVITIES: Non-skiers can spend days exploring this resort town. The streets are lined with interesting **shops and galleries**. Shops in the Banff Springs Hotel are stocked with well-made apparel ranging from handmade sweaters to furs. Concerts are scheduled through the winter at the **Banff Centre**. A dip in the mineral waters filling the **Upper Hot Springs** pool soothes sore muscles. Massages here at the hot springs cost significantly less than in the United States, thanks to the monetary exchange rate.

GETTING THERE: **Calgary airport,** 83 miles from Banff and 122 from Lake Louise, is serviced by many major airlines. Regularly scheduled **buses** travel between the airport and Banff. Many major **car-rental companies** also operate out of this airport.

By car, take the **TransCanada Hwy.** (Hwy. 1) from Calgary and follow the signs to Banff. Banff is on the **Canadian Pacific Railway** main-line route.

MOVING AROUND: Many skiers have their own cars because it increases mobility, especially at night. However, daily buses offer transport from resort hotels to the ski areas. In Banff, there is an evening "Happy Bus" shuttling between resort hotels and popular restaurants.

TOURIST INFORMATION: For information about ski vacations in Banff, contact **Ski Banff/Lake Louise (Banff Club Ski)**, P.O. Box 1085, Banff, Alberta, Canada T0L 0C0 (tel. 403/762-4561). Also write for the *Alberta Winter Activities Guide* published by **Travel Alberta**, P.O. Box 2500, Edmonton, Alberta, Canada T5J 2Z4 (tel. 403/427-4321, or toll free 800/661-8888, 800/222-6501 in Alberta).

3. Nakiska at Mount Allan

THE RESORT: Nakiska, created to showcase the alpine skiing events during the 1988 Winter Olympics, will remain as a ski area for Calgaryites and visitors who check into the hotels near the base built for downhill watchers. Approximately an hour's drive from Calgary via a superhighway and a good secondary road with a dose of spectacular views of the craggy Canadian Rocky peaks, Nakiska has terrain skewed for intermediates.

THE SKIING: The terrain on this mountain, rated 16% novice, 70% intermediate, and 14% expert, is serviced by three chairs. The vertical is 3,012 feet, including the Olympic Men's Downhill run; recreational skiers have 2,700 feet of vertical from the top of the Gold chair. The Bronze chair, set below the main mountain so that novices won't have to contend with hotshots skimming past, opens up easy beginner terrain. The Silver chair, one of the first high-speed quads in Canada, opens up the majority of the mountain, including the runs designed for the Olympics. Most of the intermediate runs are open and nicely pitched, reminiscent of Keystone's runs in the U.S. Eye Opener, Blue Maverick, and Mighty Peace are comfortably pitched runs for ego-building skiing. Most of the advanced skiing is off the Gold chair. The black runs here are in the light- to middle-black range; however, it's easy to build speed, especially on those runs comprising part of the Olympic downhills. Bull's Head and Red Crow have good terrain variation. Eagle Tail, part of the Olympic Men's Downhill run, is very steep in parts and changes in pitch.

Mountain Facilities

There is a cafeteria and an upstairs lounge serving lunch in the day lodge at the base, and a cafeteria in the mid-mountain lodge. There are day lockers, a ski rental shop, and a retail boutique.

Snow Coverage

Nakiska boasts the most advanced computerized snowmaking facility on the continent. It was created for the Olympics, and is capable of covering 80% of the mountain. The average annual snowfall is 200 to 250 cm (80 to 100 inches) at this area which is usually open from mid-November to the end of April.

Ski School

There are regular group and private lessons, achiever workshops, special clinics, and a variety of special programs.

Childcare

There is day care for children aged from 19 months to 6 years.

WHERE TO STAY: This is basically a day area at this time. Many skiers stay in Calgary and drive up for the day. Others drive from Banff, less than an hour away.

The **Lodge at Kananaskis** is by the base of the ski area. An elegant small lodge built by Canadian Pacific Hotels which owns the Banff Springs Hotel, it was scheduled to open before the Olympics. There are 225 spacious guest rooms and suites, gourmet dining, plus a disco and nightclub. Plans include an indoor/outdoor swimming pool and health-club facilities. For more information and reservations contact the Lodge at Kananaskis, 133 Ninth Ave. SW, Calgary, Alberta, Canada T2P 2M3 (tel. 403/234-7877 or 234-7876). For CP Hotels reservations, call toll free 800/828-7447 in the U.S., 800/268-9411 in Canada, 800/268-9420 in Ontario and Québec.

Calgary is a major western Canadian city and there are thousands of pillows in everything from Westin and Delta Bow hotels to motels and bed-and-breakfast facilities. The **Calgary Tourist & Convention Bureau,** Dept. C, 237 Eighth Ave. SE, Calgary, Alberta, Canada TG2 0K8 (tel. 403/263-8510), created a special department to handle requests for lodging and information about the 1988 Olympics. Theoretically, the rooms in this section of the country will all have been taken by the time you read this book, but try anyway! The special department will remain in operation after the Olympics, so anyone wanting more information about Calgary or help with lodging should still contact the Tourist & Convention Bureau.

For **lodging in Banff,** see Where to Stay in Section 2.

WHERE TO EAT: As in any big city, there are dozens of good restaurants. Here are a few "locals" favorites. Pick up an *International Guide to Calgary* or a *Key to Calgary* guide for a more complete listing.

The French cuisine at **La Chaumière** (tel. 228-5690) is a six-time winner of the *Travel/Holiday* magazine award. The **Owl's Nest** at the Westin (tel. 266-1611) has a menu for sophisticated palates. **La Caille** at the Delta Bow (tel. 262-5554) offers a traditional dining experience in one of several attractive dining rooms.

Popular restaurants in the more moderate range include the airy **Green Street Café** (tel. 266-1551), with its creative continental fare, and **4th St. Rose** (tel. 228-5377), with its imaginative, tasty dishes. Also try **J. R. Houston's** (tel. 252-2260), where the lengthy, eclectic menu includes everything from sandwiches and ribs to steak and fish.

For less expensive food, try the Italian dishes at **Claudio's** (tel. 262-5335), the pasta at **Pasta Frenzy** (tel. 245-1888), or the corned beef or blintzes at **Sam's Original Deli** (tel. 228-6696).

ENTERTAINMENT: The **Ranchman's** (tel. 253-1100) is the place to dance and drink to country-western music. Notice the memorabilia and photographs around the walls of this large western saloon. Most items were given by rodeo cowboys. (There is a dinner menu.) For quieter conversations, try the bar at **J. R. Houston's** (tel. 252-2260).

Wander along Electric Avenue (so named because of the neon signs over the nightspots) and check out which lounge has the most action. **Bandito's, Claudio's, The Rave,** and others are strung along 11th Avenue from 4th to 6th Streets.

GETTING THERE: Nakiska at Mount Allan is located in Alberta's Kananaskis Country. From Calgary take the TransCanada Hwy. (Hwy. 1) and turn off at Hwy. 40, following the Nakiska signs. It's 90 km (55 miles) southwest of Calgary and 83 km (50 miles) from Banff.

MOVING AROUND: Nakiska is primarily a day area and skiers stay in Calgary or Banff, so most have a private car.

TOURIST INFORMATION: For information, contact **Nakiska at Mount Allan,** P.O. Box 1718, Canmore, Alberta, Canada T0L 0M0 (tel. 403/591-7777).

4. Heli-Skiing and Snowcat Skiing

The major heli-skiing operations utilize the smaller mountain ranges in British Columbia that parallel the Rockies. The goal of many powderhounds is to systematically conquer them all: the Bugaboos, the Cariboos, the Monashees, the Selkirks, and the Bobbie Burns. So they return year after year to chase the ultimate powder slopes for week-long stretches. Accommodations for these trips range from motels with swimming pools near towns to lodges that can be reached only by helicopter. Skiers in Banff or B.C. resorts for a holiday can take day trips. According to local guides, the best terrain is a two- to three-hour drive from Banff to the takeoff points. However, there is skiing on the eastern side of the Divide.

Although the Canadian heli-skiing guides might tell you that an intermediate skier can spend a week heli-skiing, realize that his definition of an "intermediate" is someone "comfortable on black runs." Mark Kingsbury, of **CMH Heli-Skiing,** P.O. Box 1660, Banff, Alberta, Canada T0L 0C0 (tel. 403/762-4531), suggests that people who want to try heli-skiing should be strong skiers who are able to get down black runs *safely*—style isn't important. They also need a sense of adventure and a willingness to challenge. CMH Heli-Skiing runs programs for strong intermediates with no experience in deep snow. The guides keep these skiers in a separate group and work with them at a slower pace.

When you go heli-skiing, you are literally putting your life in the guide's hands. So check the heli-skiing company and its guides' qualifications before signing up. Kingsbury suggests verifying that the guides are licensed by the Association of Canadian Mountain Guides or the International Association of Mountain Guides. Ask them how much experience they have had guiding. Then look at accommodations, food, and the ambience. Finally, break down what you are really getting for your money. It can turn out to be different from company to company.

Snowcat Skiing also opens up thousands of untracked vertical feet of backcountry powder to both alpine and Nordic skiers seated in the heated cats crawling up the mountainsides. (You have more time to rest in a snowcat than in a helicopter, and anyone uncomfortable with flying in a helicopter will find the scenery the same but the snowcat ride less stressful.) There are several companies in B.C. offering two- to seven-day all-inclusive packages for skiers who want to remove themselves from the crowds.

See the Alberta winter activities guide for a list.

5. Information Sources

For more information about skiing in British Columbia, contact **Tourism British Columbia,** 100 Bush St., Suite 400, San Francisco, CA 94104 (tel. 415/981-4780). For a current *Alberta Winter Activities Guide,* contact **Travel Alberta,** P.O. Box 2500, Edmonton, Alberta, Canada T5J 2Z4 (tel. 403/427-4321, or toll free 800/661-8888 in the U.S., 800/222-6501 in Alberta). Also contact the specific ski areas listed in other sections of this chapter.

Chapter XVIII

BEYOND LIFTS

1. Heli-Skiing
2. Snowcat Skiing
3. Cross-Country Skiing
4. Snowboarding
5. A Ski Cruise

SKIERS BORED WITH WAITING in lift lines are moving into the wilderness via cross-country skies, helicopters, and snowcats. Downhill experiences via snowcat and helicopters are open to intermediate and advanced alpine skiers. Combining a day or two of helicopter skiing with a skiing vacation is an option at several major resorts. Heading uphill on remote mountainous terrain via snowcats is another, less expensive, option. Cross-country skiing on set tracks is for anyone who wants to be placed inside a picture-postcard setting. Instruction and rentals are provided at all the major resorts today, either through the ski area, at private cross-country complexes, or at guest ranches that run cross-country operations during the winter. Guided cross-country tours are open to any skier with a basic understanding of cross-country skills. The type of tour is usually geared to the experience level of the skiers. Day-long and overnight treks into the wilderness are popular with experienced cross-country skiers. Arrangements can be made for guided trips through many cross-country operations in ski country.

1. Heli-Skiing

The guide beckons, pantomining "heads down" to the skiers huddled nearby. They scuttle over to the helicopter and climb in. The doors are locked and the machine shoots up—straight up—but gently. The riders stare at the ground rushing past, beneath the Plexiglass floor, as the machine whirs over a lake and upward over steep, wooded terrain. It floats over a ridge—in this case the Continental Divide—and enters a different world, landscaped with broad bowls, far-off clumps of trees, and a panorama of mountaintops. The helicopter touches the tundra gently and settles so the riders can step into the whiteout created by the whirling blades. The guide unlashes the skis and the poles, and the helicopter leaves to ferry another group.

Instant isolation! Just you, the other skiers, and the wilderness.

Almost every skier, whether Nordic or alpine, who has used a helicopter shuttle to a distant mountaintop relates a similar story. Only the gut reaction is phrased differently:

"If heaven isn't like this, I don't want to go!" shouts one enthusiast to the world falling away at his feet.

Both heli-skiing (downhilling in alpine equipment) and heli-touring (using cross-country gear) offer skiers the chance to carve first tracks down a mountainside, then fly to another mountain summit for a repeat performance. However, heli-skiing is primarily for advanced or expert downhillers in good physical condition. Heli-touring is open to desk-bound executives, car-pooling spouses, retirees, and anyone else who enjoys spending time in fresh air. (Although preconditioning to tone up the muscles always helps.)

Hard-core powderhounds have been lauding heli-skiing in northwest Canada for years (see Section 4 in Chapter XVII), but the U.S. version is gaining in popularity. In Wyoming, California, Utah, or Colorado, a heli-skiing experience can be tucked into a vacation, along with time on conventional ski slopes, gourmet dining, browsing through boutiques and galleries, and nightclubbing. It costs a lot, an average of $250 a day, but the price is still less than the tab for a week in the Monashees. And if the snow is unstable and the pilots won't fly, you can still visit Yellowstone National Park if you are in Jackson Hole, head up the tram at Snowbird, or test your skills on the slopes at Mammoth, depending on where you've unpacked for the nights.

Takeoffs range from the one-time introductory ride for "never-evers" to the all-day backcountry high for experienced powderhounds. Before deciding how much of a vacation you want to set aside for heli-skiing, assess—honestly—your physical condition. A single run may be enough for the skier whose exercise consists of dashing from one business meeting to another. However, a marathon runner could probably roam the backcountry for days. Heli-skiers out for a full day must be in good shape, stress the guides, if they plan on skiing the hoped-for minimum of 10,000 vertical feet. There are no warm lodges nearby for midday breaks.

A TYPICAL DAY HELI-SKIING: A day of heli-skiing begins with safety drills. Snow avalanches are a fact of life in the backcountry, so skiers are trained in the use of electronic devices designed to lead searchers to buried skiers quickly—just in case. But the guides leading these groups are skilled in avalanche forecasting and control, as well as in first aid and rescue techniques. The operating company has checked weather conditions and snow stability before deciding to go ahead with the day's tours. If there's a serious question about weather or snow conditions—the day is cancelled. (But there are always those ski-area lifts running nearby.)

The skiers are split into groups according to ability. Be honest when discussing your skill level with the guides: They'll know if you've exaggerated by your third turn down the mountainside. The expert skiers may tackle steep terrain and heavy powder from the first run, but guides take the newcomers to gentler, smoother slopes for a first-time backcountry powder-skiing experience. Most companies will take strong advanced intermediates. The guides for High Mountain Helicopter Skiing in Jackson Hole, for instance, claim that they can teach most skiers with strong advanced intermediate skills the art of powder skiing within three or four runs.

HELI-TOURING: Heli-touring is a different type of wilderness experience. Because the mountainsides toured usually aren't in avalanche-prone territory, the day is more laid-back and tension-free. Many of the Norpine (a word blending Nordic and alpine coined to describe cross-country skiing primarily downhill) adventures open to heli-tourers require little uphill climbing. At the Golconda resort in Lake City, Colorado, a helicopter lifts cross-country skiers uphill daily during the winter. Other helicopter operations will drop cross-country skiers with a guide in the backcountry so they can work their way back to civilization.

Generally, heli-touring is less expensive than heli-skiing, because less flight time is involved. Even city folk who've only tried a flat track or two can go heli-touring with some operations, because the terrain is chosen to fit the skiers' skill levels and physical condition.

EQUIPMENT/CLOTHING: Whichever type of skiing you choose, arrive at the scene with appropriate gear—and enough of it. It can make the difference between a memorable experience and memories of a frozen, uncomfortable day. When you make reservations (and that should be done well in advance), ask the company for a list of recommended clothing and gear. If you're downhilling, bring extra gloves, sweaters, and hat in case they get soaked and you want a midday change. A powder outfit is great, but just be sure not to bring any outfit that "grabs" snow (such as corduroy). However, what's perfect for heli-skiing may be downright uncomfortable for heli-touring. Wear loose long pants, or knickers, and knee-length wool socks with a pair of light wool or cotton socks underneath. Gaiters are a must to keep snow out of your boots. Of course, sunscreen and sunglasses are vital at the higher altitudes, even if the sun is behind a cloud.

CHOOSING THE TRIP: The number of helicopter skiing operations in the United States is growing. So how do you choose? Dave Miller, president of High Mountain Helicopter Skiing in Jackson Hole, notes: "Go with established operators who have good track records." He suggests that before signing up for a trip, skiers ask certain basic questions. What are the guides' minimum qualifications? Are they well trained in advanced first aid and CPR? How much training have they had in avalanche control? How well do the guides know the terrain to be skied on? (Have they apprenticed with the company for a few seasons so they've spent a lot of time exploring the terrain you're going to ski on?) What kind of helicopter is used, and is it appropriate for flying in the mountains at the altitudes reached by that particular heli-skiing operation?

The following are companies that have been in operation for a while and have good reputations:

High Mountain Helicopter Skiing, P.O. Box 2217, Jackson, WY 83001 (tel. 801/733-3274), opens up a 25-mile-long range of mountain surrounding Jackson Hole, including the Snake River Range and the Palisades. The day trips include a minimum of six runs, depending on the area skied. The runs range between 2,000 and 3,200 vertical feet, many starting on open slopes above the timberline and descending through the trees to the valley floor. The choice of slopes is geared to the groups, which range from hard-driving experienced heli-skiers to intermediates who can learn the fundamentals of powder skiing from the friendly guides in a run or two. This company also offers heli-touring, cross-country tours in Yellowstone or Teton National Park, and overnight treks.

Ruby Mountain Heli-Ski, P.O. Box 1192, Lamoille, NV 89828 (tel. 702/588-2228), has multiday packages for intermediate and expert skiers in the Ruby Mountains near Elko, Nevada. Days are for skiing and nights can be for casinos and cabaret shows.

Nordic Mountain on the Continental Divide is reserved for cross-country skiers, who stay at the **Golconda**, P.O. Box 95, Lake City, CO 81235 (tel. 303/944-2256). Owner Ron Jackson takes Nordic skiers on more than 50 miles of trails in this remote wilderness area in southwestern Colorado. The helicopter handles most of the uphill here, but cross-country skiers must handle the gentle downhills that run up to 3,000 vertical feet. There are five-night/two-day heli-touring packages (which include a day of ski school and a day of local touring) and two-night/one-day heli-touring packages. Skiers are divided into ability-level groups. Experts can ski top to bottom or sidetrack up pinnacles and off ski jumps; less experienced skiers wander around the gentle slopes above the timberline. Skiers average two runs a day. There's also a special telemarking tour strictly for experienced backcountry skiers. If plans go as scheduled, Golconda Resort will be adding alpine skiing with runs up to 3,000 vertical feet on nearby mountains. The week-long heli-skiing packages will include three days of helicopter skiing and three days of skiing at Crested Butte, approximately 1½ hours away by a "party" bus. Call for details.

The scenic Wasatch and Uinta National Forests provide endless first tracks for heli-skiing enthusiasts with the **Wasatch Powderbird Guides,** P.O. Box 57, Snowbird, UT 84092 (tel. 801/742-2800). Trips are available both for heli-skiing regulars as well as the more cautious tourist wanting to add another dimension to a skiing vacation. The majority of the powder-skiing terrain contains ski runs averaging 2,000 feet of vertical descent and some sections are closer to 3,000 feet. The terrain used in springtime generally has ski runs of 3,000 feet of vertical descent, and some sections average closer to 4,000. During the ski season there are reservation desks located both in Snowbird and in Deer Valley.

Intermediates and experts can sign up for half- or full-day trips into the mountain ranges surrounding Sun Valley. For additional information, contact the **Sun Valley Helicopter Ski Guides,** P.O. Box 978, Sun Valley, ID 83353 (tel. 208/622-3108). There are also overnight trips into the Pioneer Mountains with lodging in yurts for cross-country and mountaineering skiers.

Mammoth Heli-Ski, P.O. Box 600, Mammoth Lakes, CA 93546 (tel. 619/934-4494), takes skiers along the ridge lines surrounding Mammoth Mountain ski area in the High Sierra. Most days skiers will get in five runs totaling between 12,000 and 15,000 vertical feet. Ask about the two-run specials scheduled throughout the year and the one-run specials during the spring. Multiday packages, which include skiing and lodging at Mammoth Mountain, are available.

Colorado Heli-Ski, P.O. Box 64, Frisco, CO 80443 (tel. 303/668-5600), offers single runs and full-day packages for skiers on intermediate and expert terrain.

Telluride Helitrax, P.O. Box 1560, Telluride, CO 81435 (tel. 303/728-4904), offers day heli-skiing excursions to intermediate through expert terrain in the San Juan Mountains in southwestern Colorado.

2. Snowcat Skiing

Snowcat skiing is a popular alternative for those who can't or won't spring for the high cost of heli-skiing. For anywhere from approximately $40 to $120 a day, skiers can head up untouched mountainsides in snowcats to make first tracks. Companies are springing up to meet this growing demand, so ask locally if snowcat skiing is available. A partial list includes:

Backcountry excursions into the Bridger Range around Bridger Bowl are offered by **Montana Powder Guides,** 15792 Bridger Canyon Rd., Bozeman, MT 59715 (tel. 406/587-3096).

Wolf Creek Ski Adventures, 5489 Cyclamen Cove, West Jordan, UT 84084 (tel. 801/649-2200, or toll free 800/262-6319), takes skiers to several locations in the Uintas, 40 miles from Salt Lake City.

Steamboat Powder Cats, P.O. Box 2468, Steamboat Springs, CO 80477 (tel. 303/879-5188 or 303/879-0576), takes skiers up to the Continental Divide for powder skiing. Groups are split according to ability.

In a day of snowcat skiing on Mount Bailey, **Diamond Lake Resort,** Diamond Lake, OR 97731 (tel. 503/793-3333), skiers log approximately 15,000 vertical feet of skiing in bowls, chutes, and glades. Lodging is at Diamond Lake Resort.

Guests come by snowmobile to the rustic **Irwin Lodge**, P.O. Box 457, Crested Butte, CO 81224 (tel. 303/349-5140), set on a remote ridge in southern Colorado. Snowcats take alpine skiers up to nearby ridges for two-mile runs down to Irwin Lake.

Weather permitting, snowcats take skiers up to Parsennes Bowl at Winter Park in Colorado. The bowl is part of the Vasquez, a new ski area on the drawing board.

3. Cross-Country Skiing

Not so long ago, skiers were either downhillers or "those baggy-suited characters who trekked through the backcountry on skinny skis and ate granola for lunch." But today there is no longer an either/or, and in fact, many vacationers have equipment and clothing in their airplane bags for challenging both disciplines of this sport called skiing. Others who only carry Nordic equipment enjoy setting themselves inside picture-postcard views and would never dream of taking an uphill lift.

Today many ski areas offer cross-country lessons and groomed trails, and all the resort towns have businesses or lodges that maintain groomed cross-country trails or offer guides who lead treks through the wilderness, so vacationers can experience the Rockies away from crowds. Vacationers bent on really getting away from civilization can head to one of the guest ranches tucked away in remote mountain locales.

The knowledge that this sport can be inexpensive—as compared to downhill skiing—is a deciding factor for many. For example, adult cross-country ski rentals at one major resort run $9, and the track fee to use the resort's groomed cross-country trails is only $4. Nordic lessons cost less than downhill ones and only one or two are needed, while alpine lessons can go on for years. Even basic, but good quality, cross-country equipment costs less than downhill gear. However, as in the alpine end of skiing, skiers tend to buy fancier clothing and more expensive equipment as they become more involved.

EQUIPMENT: The increasing interest in cross-country skiing has brought a rush of new cross-country skis, boots, and bindings to the ski stores. Regarding choosing equipment, the manager of one Colorado shop selling cross-country equipment was very explicit:

"Basically you want to know what type of skiing you are going to be doing. If you are just beginning, you don't need any of the hot skis—like the metal-edged skis. You have two types: the track skis and the out-of-track skis. For the most part a beginner will go with the track-type ski. These are generally narrower and lighter than the out-of-track ski and they have no metal edge. You can get those in two different styles—the waxable type and the nonwaxable type with the fish-scale bottom. A lot of beginning skiers are going with the no-wax skis these days. There is no muss or fuss with them. You don't need to learn about the waxes. The only problem with these skis is that they don't glide as well because of the bottom. They glide, but don't slide backward, because the fish scale catches them. Of course, owners of skis that must be waxed must learn about that end of the sport rapidly. Those who have been on skinny skis a couple of years often decide to step out of the tracks and into the backcountry. Their best bet is to go with a metal edge or wider ski. These are heavier and more expensive."

Prices vary widely, and buying the top-of-the-line equipment is not the best deal for everyone. Packages (which include skis, boots, and bindings) can range from $99 to $160 for track skis. If there are no packages available, expect to spend more for items purchased individually. Many beginning cross-country skiers opt for boots and the standard 75-millimeter bindings versus the more expensive boot/binding combinations (a narrower 50 millimeters), which may cost more but are very popular with experienced cross-country skiers. Backcountry skis and mountaineering boots cost more. But one shop manager suggests that skiers moving in backcountry equipment for the first time not be gulled into buying top-of-the-line skis because there are some "very fine skis" at the lower end. (Although, he added, skiers should buy the best boot they can afford.) Anyone who has been into this sport for a while will know what he or she wants. Chat with salespeople before actually buying what they recommend to determine if they really know the equipment and the sport or are just spouting words from the printed descriptions that come with the equipment.

HOW TO DRESS: Dressing properly can make the difference between having a wonderful outing or a perfectly miserable day. The key—in a word—is "layering." Many novices overdress because the day is cool, but once they start working they discover they are too hot. However, when they stop the chill comes back quickly, and that is why layering is so important. Start with thermal underwear. Although cotton underwear is still the bestseller, the hottest item is polypropylene underwear, which keeps a skier dry by wicking the perspiration away from the body. (After skiing hard, soggy cotton chills the body.)

Top the long underwear with several layers that can be easily taken off and stuffed in a backpack. The image of the skier wearing a warm shirt and heavy wool sweaters over knickers has changed, of course, but that style of clothing is still available and still offers tremendous warmth. However, today many cross-country skiers put on a turtleneck and a sweater, then cover them with one of the cross-country pullover or zip-front light jackets that are also used for everything from biking to hiking or running to the neighborhood grocery store in cool weather. (Those made with Gore-Tex are very popular; however, some Nordic skiers prefer fabrics that breathe more.) Wind pants are also increasing in popularity. The most fashion-conscious cross-country skiers, as well as the racers, are wearing one-piece suits that hug the body. In addition to the long underwear underneath, many cross-country skiers top these outfits with a vest for additional warmth. Whatever style is picked, the clothes should never bind or hamper arm and leg movements. (This means that those tight stretch pants fashionable on downhill slopes can be very uncomfortable when cross-country skiing.) Warm jackets or vests should be added when touring in the backcountry. Slip a water-proof shell in the backpack if going any distance from the touring center or car. When skiing off groomed trails, gaiters and clothes that fit snugly around the neck, wrists, and waist are essential. When in doubt, ask someone at the touring center, the cross-country instructor, or your guide for help in choosing appropriate clothing.

GETTING STARTED: Once equipped and ready for action, many first-timers head for the hills and step into their skis, expecting to glide gracefully away. Usually they're in for a shock.

"The guy who said 'If you can walk, you can ski'" is correct. But if you remember, we all crawled before we could walk. In a 1½-hour lesson you can go through the crawl stage and up to a walk. "You get all the basics you need for life," pointed out one long-time instructor.

The cross-country skiing experiences open to skiers at the resorts are listed under The Skiing in the section on each resort. Many of the cross-country operations have banded together in regional organizations. For more information about what is available in specific regions, contact:

Cross Country Ski Areas of America, RD 2, Bolton Road, Winchester, NH 03451 (tel. 603/239-6387); send $2 for postage and handling.

Colorado Cross Country Ski Association, P.O. Box 378, Granby, CO 80446.

For a cross-country skiing guide to the Jackson Hole area, write **Jackson National Nordic Consultants,** P.O. Box 3483, Jackson Hole, WY 83001.

Ski Montana, a publication available from **Travel Montana,** Department of Commerce, Helena, MT 59620 (tel. 406/444-2654, or toll free 800/548-3390), lists cross-country opportunities.

Sun Valley Cross Country Ski Association, P.O. Box 1806, Ketchum, ID 83340 (tel. 208/726-3266).

4. Snowboarding

The heads turn as the eyes follow the graceful skier, blonde hair streaming over a Hawaiian shirt, sliding down the slope on a snowboard. She looks like a surfer with her low-down stance, but the wiggling motion to keep the board going is a little different. Eyes swivel as she drops into a bump run, literally hovering on the downside of a Volkswagon-size mogul, glued to the snow by a mere five or six inches of steel-edged board. They follow her into trees so tight that the best tree skier would simply cruise on by. The rider, balancing sideways on the board, simply wiggles through. Swishing back onto a gentler slope, she heads for the side of the trail, zooms up the bank, takes air to make a 180° turn, lands, and slides back down on the run.

She's one of a new breed: snowboarders. Five years ago they weren't allowed on the ski slopes. However, the modernization of equipment (putting steel edges on the boards) and the increase in proper instruction are letting these snow surfers loose on more than 100 ski areas in the country.

The number of snowboarders is a matter of speculation; board manufacturers claim more than 100,000, based on the number of boards that have been sold. Most of the snowboarders tend to be younger—teens through the early 30s—but even that is changing as more ski areas add snowboard instructors. Because the safety of this sport is still controversial (many ski areas feel that out-of-control snowboarders are more dangerous than out-of-control skiers, while others suggest that beginning snowboarders fall down sooner), better equipment and proper instruction are the key factors in its acceptance by ski areas. Anyone starting this sport should take a lesson from a qualified instructor! Breckenridge Ski Area in Colorado is one hot spot of snowboarders where instructors are teaching dozens of students each week. Stratton Mountain in Vermont is another key place for instruction; more than 100 students go through the program there weekly.

EQUIPMENT: Recreational snowboards range in price from approximately $150 to $320, bindings included. (Most bindings are polyurethane straps which are tightened over boots and fastened with a ratchet buckle.) Snowboarding boots can run approximately $100; however, many riders use hiking boots. Riders don't use poles. An increasing number of sport and ski shops are carrying this equipment.

WHERE TO GO: More than 100 ski areas now allow snowboarders alongside skiers and the list is lengthening rapidly. Call an area before going and ask about the rules for snowboarders. Some ski areas require certification, others require instruction, and still others limit the days or the slopes.

Currently, the list appears heavier with the smaller areas, while the many of the major resorts with large numbers of skiers still have a "wait-and-see" attitude. As of last winter, some of the western areas which allowed snowboarders on the slopes (some on a test basis), are: Araphahoe Basin, Aspen Highlands, Breckenridge Ski Area, Buttermilk Mountain, Copper Mountain, Purgatory, Telluride, and many smaller areas in Colorado; ParkWest, Powder Mountain, and Brighton in Utah; Squaw Valley, Mountain High Ski Area, Boreal Ridge, and Mount Baldy in California; Bogus Basin and Ski Schweitzer in Idaho; and Red Lodge in Montana.

5. A Ski Cruise

A ski cruise sounds like a contradiction in terms—but for ski nuts it combines pieces from the best of both worlds. After a day of snorkeling at Cozumel, skiers in bathing suits race down a World Cup course through the eye of a camera held by former Olympian and AT&T Skiing Award winner Billy Kidd. After watching Hank Kashiwa, co-host of ESPN's "Skiing Magazine," show skiers how to stretch muscles for skiing, they slather suntan lotion on the aching muscles and loosen them poolside. The ready access to other ski enthusiasts eager to schmooze about the sport, and the accessibility to vacationing ski celebrities are the big drawing cards for this annual cruise. While the ship sails between ports of call, celebrities run workshops, give lectures, and chat with vacationers.

The fall 1987 cruise on the M/S *Skyward* leaves Miami on November 8 and is scheduled to stop at Barbados, Martinique, St. Maarten, Antigua, St. Thomas, and San Juan. Prices for the week-long cruise range from $895 to $1,970, depending on the choice of room. For information about the 1987 or 1988 cruises, contact Tour Development, Sport Stalker, P.O. Box 775128, Steamboat Springs, CO 80477 (tel. 303/879-4536, or toll free 800/525-5520, 800/332-5530 in Colorado).

Appendix

RATING THE SKI AREAS

SKI AREA FACTS

Ski Area	Statistics			Pricing						Additional Features					
	Vertical Drop	Skiable Acreage/ Runs	Number of Lifts**	1-Day Adults Lift Pass	1-Day Junior Lift Pass	6 Days Adult	Single Class Lesson	1-Day Lesson	Rentals (skis, boots, poles)	High Performance/ Demo Rental	Night Skiing	Cross-country***	Snowboards****	Ski-In/Ski-out	Walk to Lifts	Childcare
CALIFORNIA																
Alpine Meadows	1,797	2,000/100	13	$27*	$11*		$16	$22	$16	$25	N	N	N	N	N	snow school
Goldmine	1,800	28 R	8	$25	$10		$13	$19	$12		N	Y	N	N	Y	N
Heavenly	3,600	20 sq mi	26 incl 1 tram	$29	$15	$150	$23	$18	$14	$17	N	Y	N	Y	Y	Y (nearby)
June Mountain	2,562	30 R	7 incl 1 tram	$25	$13		$16	$22	$12	$21	N	Y	Y	N	Y	Y
Kirkwood	2,000	2,000/68	11	$27	$10		$15	$22	$14	$20	N	Y	N	N	N	Y
Mammoth	3,100	3,000 SA	31 incl 2 gond	$25 credit card	$13 credit card		$16	$22	$12	$21	N	Y	Y	Y	Y	Y
Mtn. High	1,600	200 SA	10	$27	$13		$15		$14		Y	N	Y	N	N	N
Northstar-at-Tahoe	2,200	1,700/48	9 incl 1 gond	$27	$14	$124*	$16*	$22*	$15	Y	N	Y	Y	Y	Y	Y
Sierra Ski Ranch	2,212	34 R	10	$21*	$12*		$15*		Y		N	N	N	N	N	N

Snow Summit	1,200	190 SA	9	$23.50*			$20*		Y		Y	Y	N	N	N	
Snow Valley	1,141	230 SA	13	$25*	$15*		$14*		$12*		Y	Y	Y	N	N	snow school
Squaw Valley	2,700	6,000 SA	27 incl cable car & gond	$29	$5	$135	$21	$27	$15	$25	Y	Y	Y	Y	Y	
Sugar Bowl	1,502	33 R	8	$28*	$12*		$14*	Y	$12.50*	Y	N	Y	N	N	N	

COLORADO

Arapahoe Basin	1,670	350 SA	5	$30	$12	$156	$25	$50	$15	$25	N	Y	N	N	N	Y
Aspen Highlands	3,800	515 SA	11	$30	$16	Y	$23	$32	$12		N	Y	Y	Y	Y	snow school
Aspen Mountain	3,267	625/75	8	$35	$16	$180		$35	$13	$25	N	Y	N	Y	N	
Buttermilk Mountain	2,030	452/47	6	$32	$16	$180	$35		$14	$25	N	Y	Y	Y	N	snow school
Beaver Creek	3,340	796 SA	9	$30*	$20	$108	$35		$10	Y	N	Y	N	Y	Y	

Notes: 6 days refers to pass; rental price quote is average cost for one-day; ski in/ski out means ski slope is next to the lodge; walk-to means you have a 5- to 10-minute walk to the slopes.

*86/87 prices used when more current prices not available at time of printing
**rope tows not included
***cross-country equipment with safety straps allowed on lifts
****check for regulations

SKI AREA FACTS

Ski Area	Statistics			Pricing						Additional Features					
	Vertical Drop	Skiable Acreage/ Runs	Number of Lifts**	1-Day Adults Lift Pass	1-Day Junior Lift Pass	6 Days Adult	Single Class Lesson	1-Day Lesson	Rentals (skis, boots, poles)	High Performance/ Demo Rental	Night Skiing	Cross-country***	Snowboards****	Ski-in/Ski-out	Walk to Lifts	Childcare
Breckenridge	2,613	1,480 SA	15	$30	$13	$126	$23	$30	$ 8	$15	N	Y	Y	Y	Y	Y
Copper Mountain	2,760	1,180 SA 76 trails and bowls	20	$27*	$12*	$126	$22	$30	$12	$20	N	Y	Y	Y	Y	Y
Crested Butte	2,300	805 SA	11	$28	$16	$150	$20	$40	$10.50	$20	N	Y	Y	Y	Y	Y
Cuchara Valley Resort	1,562	135/20	4	$18	$ 8		$12*	$18*	$12*		N	Y	N	Y	N	N
Keystone Mountain, North Peak	2,340 1,620	680 SA	13 & 1 gond	$30	$12	$156	$25	$50	$15	$25	Y	Y	N	Y	Y	Y
Monarch	1,000	750 SA	4	$18	$ 9	$ 90	$12	$18	$9	$14	N	Y	N	N	N	Y
Purgatory	2,022	630 SA	9	$27	$12	$150	$22	$29	$13	$23	N	Y	Y	Y	Y	Y
Silvercreek	982	208 SA	5	$18	$ 9		$16	$22	$10	$14	N	Y	Y	Y	Y	Y

Snowmass	3,615	1,560/84 SA	17	$32	$16	$180	$35	$14	$18	N	Y	N	Y Y
Steamboat	3,600	2,500 SA	20 incl 1 gondola	$29	$18	$165	$32	$11	$20	N	Y	Y	Y Y
Telluride	3,155	735 SA	10	$28	$13	$144	$32	$12	$25	N	Y	Y	Y Y
Vail	3,100	1,800 SA	19 incl 1 gond	$30*	$20*	$108	$39	$9	Y	N	Y	N	Y Y
Winter Park/ Mary Jane	2,220	1,105	19	$26	$12	$144	$26	$12	Y	N	Y	Y	Y Y
IDAHO													
Bogus Basin	1,800	2,000/45	6	$19	$15	$91	$15	$12*	Y	Y	Y	Y	Y Y
Ski Schweitzer	2,400	39 R plus bowls	8	$20	$16		$11	$22	$13	Y	N	Y	Y	Y Y
Sun Valley	3,400	1,275	16	$29	$19	Y	$38	$13	$20	N	Y	N	Y Y
MONTANA													
Big Mountain	2,170	45 R plus bowls	7	$19.50	$11*	$12*	$23*	$12.50*	$20*	Y	Y	N	Y Y
Big Sky	2,800	46 R plus bowls	6 incl 2 gond	$23	$15	$138	$15	$30	$15	$20	N	Y	Y	Y Y

Notes: 6 days refers to pass; rental price quote is average cost for one-day; ski in/ski out means ski slope is next to the lodge; walk-to means you have a 5- to 10-minute walk to the slopes.

*86/87 prices used when more current prices not available at time of printing
**rope tows not included
***cross-country equipment with safety straps allowed on lifts
****check for regulations

SKI AREA FACTS

Ski Area	Statistics			Pricing							Additional Features					
	Vertical Drop	Skiable Acreage/ Runs	Number of Lifts**	1-Day Adult Lift Pass	1-Day Junior Lift Pass	6 Days Adult	Single Class Lesson	1-Day Lesson	Rentals (skis, boots, poles)	High Performance/ Demo Rental	Night Skiing	Cross-country***	Snowboards****	Ski-in/Ski-out	Walk to Lifts	Childcare
Bridger Bowl	2,000	40 R plus bowls	5	$17	$8		$12	$24	$11	Y	N	Y	N	Y	Y	N
Red Lodge	2,016	30 R	5	$17	$8	$88	$11		$11.50	$15.50	N	Y	Y	N	N	Y
NEVADA																
Mt. Rose	1,440	20 R	4	$20*	$10*		$14*	Y	Y	Y	N	N	N	N	N	ski/snow school 3-7
Ski Incline	1,840	600 SA	7	$24	$14		$14	$22	$14	$20	N	Y	N	N	N	Y
NEW MEXICO																
Angel Fire	2,180	46 R	6	$24	$15		$15	$21	$14	Y	N	Y	N	Y	Y	Y
Red River	1,600	135 SA	6	$23	$13		$15		$10		N	Y	N	N	Y	ski/snow school
Taos	2,612	1,000 SA	9	$27	$15	Y	$19		$12	$16	N	Y	N	N	Y	ski/snow school 3-6
OREGON																
Mt. Bachelor	3,100	1,600 SA	10	$23	$14	$119	$17	$20	$13	$19	N	Y	Y	N	N	Y
Mt. Hood Meadows	2,777	40+R	8	$20*	$13*		Y	Y	Y	Y	Y	Y	Y	N	N	N

Resort	Vertical	Acres	Lifts	Rental	6 days	All-day	Half-day	Child		ski-in/ski-out	walk-to	rope tows	snow making	ski school
Timberline	2,500	1,000 SA	6	$16*	$10.50*	Y	Y	$12*	$14*	Y	Y	Y	N	N
UTAH														
Alta	2,000	1,700+SA trails and open slopes	8	$16	$16	$15	$30	Y	Y	N	Y	N	Y	Y
Brianhead	1,350	40 R	7	$21	$13	$16	$26	$12	$25	N	Y	N	Y	Y
Brighton	1,445	43 R	5	$10/$14	$10	$14		$7	$11	Y	Y	Y	N	N
Deer Valley	2,200	42 R	8	$33/$36	$19 $22	$35*	$45*	$22*	$30*	N	Y	N	Y	Y
Snowbird	3,100	1,900 SA	7 chairs 1 tram	$24 chairs $30 all lifts	$18	$20	$30	$12	$24	N	N	N	Y	Y only for lodge guest
Snowbasin	2,400	1,800 SA	5	$19	$14	$12*		Y		N	N	N	N	N
Solitude	2,000	1,000 SA	5	$10/$14	$10	$10		$12	$15	N	Y	N	N	N
Sundance	2,150	34 R	4	$20	$13	$15		$10	$18	N	N	N	Y	Y
Park City	3,100	82 R plus bowls	13 chairs 1 gondola	$30	$13	$158	$22	$27	from $11	$15	Y	Y	Y	Y	Y
ParkWest	2,200	50 R	7	$24	$ 8	$102	$16	$21	$12	Y	N	Y	N	Y	ski/snow school

Notes: 6 days refers to pass; rental price quote is average cost for one-day; ski in/ski out means ski slope is next to the lodge; walk-to means you have a 5- to 10-minute walk to the slopes.

*86/87 prices used when more current prices not available at time of printing
**rope tows not included
***cross-country equipment with safety straps allowed on lifts
****check for regulations

SKI AREA FACTS

Ski Area	Statistics			Pricing							Additional Features					
	Vertical Drop	Skiable Acreage/Runs	Number of Lifts**	1-Day Adults Lift Pass	1-Day Junior Lift Pass	6 Days Adult	Single Class Lesson	1-Day Lesson	Rentals (skis, boots, poles)	High Performance/Demo Rental	Night Skiing	Cross-country***	Snowboards****	Ski-in/Ski-out	Walk to Lifts	Childcare
WASHINGTON																
Crystal Mountain	3,102	2,250/36	9	$21	$14		$12		$18	$30	Y	Y	Y	Y	Y	Y
Mission Ridge	2,140	33 R	4	$18	$13		$10*	$20*	$13	$20	Y	Y	N	N	N	N
WYOMING																
Grand Targhee	2,200	1,500 SA	3	$20	$11		$14	$28	$12.50	$20	N	N	Y	Y	Y	Y
Jackson Hole	4,139	2,500 SA	9 incl tram	$27	$14	5 of 7 $130	$18	$30	Y	Y	N	Y	Y	Y	Y	Y
CANADA (Canadian dollars)																
Nakiska	3,012	30 R	4	$25			$15	Y	$15	Y	N	Y	N	N	N	Y
Lake Louise	3,250	43 R plus bowls	9	$26*	$6*	Y	$14	Y	$15*	$25*	N	Y	N	N	N	Y
Sunshine Village	3,514	75 R	10 incl 1 gond	$26*	$21/$10		$14		$13*	$18*	N	Y	Y	Y	N	Y

Notes: 6 days refers to pass; rental price quote is average cost for one-day; ski in/ski out means ski slope is next to the lodge; walk-to means you have a 5- to 10-minute walk to the slopes.

*86/87 prices used when more current prices not available at time of printing
**rope tows not included
***cross-country equipment with safety straps allowed on lifts

QUALITY CHART FOR 31 SELECTED RESORTS

Resorts	Terrain			Facilities				Resort		Pricing	Overall
	Beginner	Intermediate	Advanced/Expert	Ski School	Snowmaking	Grooming	Handicapped Programs	Lodging	Packages	Ease/Efficiency of Booking a Trip	Restaurants	Après-Ski		Clientele
Aspen (Buttermilk, Aspen Mtn & Highlands)	3	3	3	3	2	2.5	2	3	2	2.5	3	3	$$-$$$$$	E
Beaver Creek	2.5	3	2	3	2.5	2.5	1	2	2	2.5	1.5	1.5	$$$$-$$$$$	A
Breckenridge	2.5	3	2.5	2.5	2.5	2.5	2.5	3	2.5	2.5	3	2.5	$-$$$$	E
Copper Mountain	3	3	2.5	3	2.5	3	2	2.5	2.5	2.5	2	2	$$-$$$$	E
Crested Butte	2	2.5	2.5	2	2	2	1	2.5	2	2.5	2.5	2	$-$$$$	F/S/B

1 = Below average, 2 = Average, 3 = Excellent; In pricing column $-$$$$$ = inexpensive to luxury; In clientele column A = Affluent, F = Families, S = Singles, B = Budget-Conscious Skiers, E = Every Skier Budget to Affluent

CRITERIA: Snowmaking (enough to cover sufficient terrain when too little snow and to cover problem areas?); Ski School (Variety of programs? Well-trained instructors?); Handicapped programs (1 = few or no specifically trained personnel 2 = programs for some handicaps 3 = extensive program)

Lodging, Packages, Restaurants, Après-Ski (variety and broad price range?); Reservations (Does Central Reservations Service merely refer you to lodge or can they reserve everything from nursery to transportation?)

QUALITY CHART FOR 31 SELECTED RESORTS

Resorts	Terrain			Facilities				Resort				Overall
	Beginner	Intermediate	Advanced/Expert	Ski School	Snowmaking	Grooming	Handicapped Programs	Lodging	Packages	Ease/Efficiency of Booking a Trip	Restaurants	Aprés-Ski	Pricing	Clientele
Keystone (Keystone, No. Peak Arapahoe)	3	3	3/3	3	2	3	1	2.5	3	2.5	2	2	$$$-$$$$	F/A
Purgatory	2	2.5	2.5/2	2	2	2	2	2.5	2.5	3	2.5	2	$-$$$$	E
Snowmass	2.5	3	2/2	3	2.5	3	2.5	3	2	2.5	2	1.5	$$-$$$$$	E
Steamboat	2.5	3	2.5/2	2.5	2	2.5	2	3	3	3	3	2.5	$-$$$$	E
Telluride	2	2.5	3/3	2	2	2	1	2.5	2.5	2.5	2.5	2	$-$$$$	F/S/B
Vail	2.5	3	3/2.5	3	2	2.5	2	3	2	2.5	3	3	$$-$$$$$	E
Winter Park/Mary Jane	2	3	3/2.5	2.5	2	2.5	3	2	2	2	2	1.5	$-$$$$	E
Mammoth	2	3	3/3	2	2	2.5	2	3	2	2	2.5	2	$-$$$$	E
South Lake Tahoe (Heavenly Valley, Kirkwood & Sierra Ranch)	2.5	3	2.5/2.5	2	2	2	2.5	3	2	2.5	3	3	$-$$$$$	E

Resort	Snowmaking (terrain)	Snowmaking (problem areas)	Handicapped Programs	Ski School	Lodging	Packages	Restaurants	Après-Ski (variety)	Après-Ski (price)	Reservations	Pricing	Clientele
North Lake Tahoe (Alpine Meadows, Squaw Valley, Northstar-at-Tahoe)	2.5	3	3	2	2	2	3	3	2	2.5	3	3	$–$$$$$	E
Ski Schweitzer	2	2.5	2	2.5	2	2	1	1.5	2	2	2	1.5	$–$$$	F/B
Sun Valley and Dollar Mtn.	2.5	2	3	2	2	2	1	3	2	2	3	2.5	$$–$$$$$	E
Big Mountain	2	2.5	2	2	2	2	1	2	2	2	2	1.5	$–$$$	F/S/B
Big Sky	2	2.5	1.5	1	2	2	1	2	2	2	2	1.5	$–$$$$	F/S/B
Taos	1.5	2	3	3	3	2	2	2	3	3	2	1	$$$–$$$$$	F/S/A
Red Lodge	2	2	2.5	3	2	2	1	2	2.5	3	2.5	2.5	$–$$$	F/S/B
Red River	2	1.5	1	2	2.5	2	2	1.5	2	2	2	2	$–$$$	F/S/B
Mt. Bachelor	2	3	2.5	2	2	2	1.5	2	2	2	2.5	2	$$–$$$$	E
Brianhead	2.5	2.5	1	1	2	1	2	1	2	2	1.5	1	$$–$$$$	F/B
Deer Valley	2.5	3	2.5	1.5	2.5	3	3	1	2	2	3	3	$$$$$	A

1 = Below average, 2 = Average, 3 = Excellent; In pricing column $-$$$$$ = inexpensive to luxury; In clientele column A = Affluent, F = Families, S = Singles, B = Budget-Conscious Skiers, E = Every Skier Budget to Affluent

CRITERIA: Snowmaking (enough to cover sufficient terrain when too little snow and to cover problem areas); Ski School (Variety of programs? Well-trained instructors?); Handicapped programs (1 = few or no specifically trained personnel 2 = programs for some handicaps 3 = extensive program)

Lodging, Packages, Restaurants, Après-Ski (variety and broad price range?); Reservations (Does Central Reservations Service merely refer you to lodge or can they reserve everything from nursery to transportation?)

QUALITY CHART FOR 31 SELECTED RESORTS

Resorts	Terrain — Beginner	Intermediate	Advanced Expert	Facilities — Ski School	Snowmaking	Grooming	Handicapped Programs	Lodging	Packages	Ease/Efficiency of Booking a Trip	Resort — Restaurants	Après-Ski	Pricing	Overall Clientele
Snowbird	2	2	3	2	2	2	2.5	2	2.5	2.5	2	1.5	$$$-$$$$	F/S/A
Park City and Parkwest	2.5	3	2.5	2	2	2	2.5	3	2.5	2.5	3	3	$-$$$$	E
Crystal Mountain	1	2	3	2	1	1.5	1	1	2	2	1	1	$$-$$$	F/B
Mission Ridge	2	2	2	2.5	1.5	2	1	1	2	2	2	1	$$$	F/S/B
Jackson Hole, Grand Targhee, Snow King	1	2.5	3	2	1	2	2	2	2	2	2.5	2	$$-$$$$	E
Banff (Mt. Norquay, Lake Louise, Sunshine Village, Nakiska)	2	3	2.5	2	2	1.5	2	3	2	3	3	3	$-$$$$$	E

1 = Below average, 2 = Average, 3 = Excellent; In pricing column $-$$$$$ = inexpensive to luxury; In clientele column A = Affluent, F = Families, S = Singles, B = Budget-Conscious Skiers, E = Every Skier Budget to Affluent

CRITERIA: Snowmaking (enough to cover sufficient terrain when too little snow and to cover problem areas?); Ski School (Variety of programs? Well-trained instructors?); Handicapped programs (1 = few or no specifically trained personnel 2 = programs for some handicaps 3 = extensive program)

Lodging, Packages, Restaurants, Après-Ski (variety and broad price range?); Reservations (Does Central Reservations Service merely refer you to lodge or can they reserve everything from nursery to transportation?)

NOTES

NOW, SAVE MONEY ON ALL YOUR TRAVELS!
Join Arthur Frommer's $35-A-Day Travel Club™

Saving money while traveling is never a simple matter, which is why, over 26 years ago, the **$35-A-Day Travel Club** was formed. Actually, the idea came from readers of the Arthur Frommer Publications who felt that such an organization could bring financial benefits, continuing travel information, and a sense of community to economy-minded travelers all over the world.

In keeping with the money-saving concept, the annual membership fee is low—$18 (U.S. residents) or $20 U.S. (Canadian, Mexican, and foreign residents)—and is immediately exceeded by the value of your benefits which include:

(1) The latest edition of any TWO of the books listed on the following pages.

(2) An annual subscription to an 8-page quarterly newspaper *The Wonderful World of Budget Travel* which keeps you up-to-date on fastbreaking developments in low-cost travel in all parts of the world—bringing you the kind of information you'd have to pay over $35 a year to obtain elsewhere. This consumer-conscious publication also includes the following columns:

Hospitality Exchange—members all over the world who are willing to provide hospitality to other members as they pass through their home cities.

Share-a-Trip—requests from members for travel companions who can share costs and help avoid the burdensome single supplement.

Readers Ask . . . Readers Reply—travel questions from members to which other members reply with authentic firsthand information.

(3) A copy of *Arthur Frommer's Guide to New York*.

(4) Your personal membership card which entitles you to purchase through the Club all Arthur Frommer Publications for a third to a half off their regular retail prices during the term of your membership.

So why not join this hardy band of international budgeteers NOW and participate in its exchange of information and hospitality? Simply send $18 (U.S. residents) or $20 U.S. (Canadian, Mexican, and other foreign residents) along with your name and address to: $35-A-Day Travel Club, Inc., Gulf + Western Building, One Gulf + Western Plaza, New York, NY 10023. Remember to specify which *two* of the books in section (1) above you wish to receive in your initial package of member's benefits. Or tear out the next page, check off any two of the books listed on either side, and send it to us with your membership fee.

Date_____

**FROMMER BOOKS
PRENTICE HALL PRESS
ONE GULF + WESTERN PLAZA
NEW YORK, NY 10023**

Friends:

Please send me the books checked below:

FROMMER'S $-A-DAY GUIDES™
(In-depth guides to sightseeing and low-cost tourist accommodations and facilities.)

☐ Europe on $30 a Day $13.95	☐ New Zealand on $40 a Day $10.95
☐ Australia on $25 a Day $10.95	☐ New York on $50 a Day.............. $10.95
☐ Eastern Europe on $25 a Day $10.95	☐ Scandinavia on $50 a Day........... $10.95
☐ England on $40 a Day............... $11.95	☐ Scotland and Wales on $40 a Day..... $11.95
☐ Greece on $30 a Day................ $11.95	☐ South America on $30 a Day $10.95
☐ Hawaii on $50 a Day................ $11.95	☐ Spain and Morocco (plus the Canary Is.) on $40 a Day $10.95
☐ India on $15 & $25 a Day........... $10.95	☐ Turkey on $25 a Day $10.95
☐ Ireland on $30 a Day................ $10.95	☐ Washington, D.C., & Historic Va. on $40 a Day $11.95
☐ Israel on $30 & $35 a Day $11.95	
☐ Mexico on $20 a Day $10.95	

FROMMER'S DOLLARWISE GUIDES™
(Guides to sightseeing and tourist accommodations and facilities from budget to deluxe, with emphasis on the medium-priced.)

☐ Alaska $12.95	☐ Cruises (incl. Alaska, Carib, Mex, Hawaii, Panama, Canada, & US) $12.95
☐ Austria & Hungary $11.95	☐ California & Las Vegas $11.95
☐ Belgium, Holland, Luxembourg $11.95	☐ Florida............................ $11.95
☐ Egypt............................. $11.95	☐ Mid-Atlantic States $12.95
☐ England & Scotland $11.95	☐ New England...................... $12.95
☐ France............................ $11.95	☐ New York State $12.95
☐ Germany.......................... $12.95	☐ Northwest $11.95
☐ Italy............................... $11.95	☐ Skiing in Europe $12.95
☐ Japan & Hong Kong $12.95	☐ Skiing USA—East $11.95
☐ Portugal (incl. Madeira & the Azores) . $12.95	☐ Skiing USA—West $11.95
☐ South Pacific...................... $12.95	☐ Southeast & New Orleans........... $11.95
☐ Switzerland & Liechtenstein $12.95	☐ Southwest........................ $11.95
☐ Bermuda & The Bahamas........... $11.95	☐ Texas............................. $11.95
☐ Canada $12.95	
☐ Caribbean $13.95	

TURN PAGE FOR ADDITIONAL BOOKS AND ORDER FORM.

THE ARTHUR FROMMER GUIDES™

(Pocket-size guides to sightseeing and tourist accommodations and facilities in all price ranges.)

☐ Amsterdam/Holland	$5.95	☐ Mexico City/Acapulco	$5.95
☐ Athens	$5.95	☐ Minneapolis/St. Paul	$5.95
☐ Atlantic City/Cape May	$5.95	☐ Montreal/Quebec City	$5.95
☐ Boston	$5.95	☐ New Orleans	$5.95
☐ Cancún/Cozumel/Yucatán	$5.95	☐ New York	$5.95
☐ Dublin/Ireland	$5.95	☐ Orlando/Disney World/EPCOT	$5.95
☐ Hawaii	$5.95	☐ Paris	$5.95
☐ Las Vegas	$5.95	☐ Philadelphia	$5.95
☐ Lisbon/Madrid/Costa del Sol	$5.95	☐ Rome	$5.95
☐ London	$5.95	☐ San Francisco	$5.95
☐ Los Angeles	$5.95	☐ Washington, D.C.	$5.95

FROMMER'S TOURING GUIDES™

(Color illustrated guides that include walking tours, cultural & historic sites, and other vital travel information.)

☐ Egypt	$8.95	☐ Paris	$8.95
☐ Florence	$8.95	☐ Venice	$8.95
☐ London	$8.95		

SPECIAL EDITIONS

☐ A Shopper's Guide to the Best Buys in England, Scotland, & Wales	$10.95	☐ Marilyn Wood's Wonderful Weekends (NY, Conn, Mass, RI, Vt, NH, NJ, Del, Pa)	$11.95
☐ A Shopper's Guide to the Caribbean	$12.95	☐ Motorist's Phrase Book (Fr/Ger/Sp)	$4.95
☐ Bed & Breakfast—N. America	$8.95	☐ Swap and Go (Home Exchanging)	$10.95
☐ Fast 'n' Easy Phrase Book (Fr/Ger/Ital/Sp in *one* vol.)	$6.95	☐ The Candy Apple (NY for Kids)	$11.95
☐ Guide to Honeymoons (US, Canada, Mexico, & Carib)	$12.95	☐ Travel Diary and Record Book	$5.95
☐ How to Beat the High Cost of Travel	$4.95	☐ Where to Stay USA (Lodging from $3 to $30 a night)	$9.95

ORDER NOW!

In U.S. include $1.50 shipping UPS for 1st book; 50¢ ea. add'l book. Outside U.S. $2 and 50¢, respectively.

Enclosed is my check or money order for $_____

NAME _____

ADDRESS _____

CITY _____ STATE _____ ZIP _____

It's 2 am.
It's far from home.
It's more than
a tummyache.

American Express Cardmembers can get emergency medical and legal referrals, worldwide. Simply by calling Global Assist.℠

What if it really is more than a tummyache? What if your back goes out? What if you get into a legal fix?

Call Global Assist – a new emergency referral service for the exclusive use of American Express Cardmembers. Just call. Toll-free. 24 hours a day. Every day. Virtually anywhere in the world.

Your call helps find a doctor, lawyer, dentist, optician, chiropractor, nurse, pharmacist, or an interpreter.

All this costs nothing, except for the medical and legal bills you would normally expect to pay.

Global Assist. One more reason to have the American Express® Card. Or, to get one.

For an application, call 1-800-THE-CARD.

Don't leave home without it.®

© 1986 American Express Travel Related Services Company, Inc.

If you lose cash on vacation, don't count on a Boy Scout finding it.

Honestly.

How many people can you trust to give back hundreds of dollars in cash? Not too many.

That's why it's so important to help protect your vacation with American Express® Travelers Cheques.

If they're lost, you can get them back from over 100,000 refund locations throughout the world. Or you can hope a Boy Scout finds it.

Protect your vacation.